MICKEY

MICKEY

Short Stories and Anecdotes

Neurosis Can be a Good Thing after All

A Memoir

Written by Ray "Mickey" E. McCoy

Compiled by Thelma M. McCoy

iUniverse, Inc.

New York Lincoln Shanghai

Mickey
Short Stories and Anecdotes
Neurosis Can be a Good Thing after All

iUniverse, Inc.

For information address:
iUniverse, Inc.
2021 Pine Lake Road, Suite 100
Lincoln, NE 68512
www.iuniverse.com

ISBN: 0-595-30744-2 (pbk)
ISBN: 0-595-66197-1 (cloth)

Printed in the United States of America

—to my children

*I have had a great life in large part because of my neuro-
ses—and some good luck. My life never seemed dull or unfulfilled. I always enjoyed my work because my jobs were chosen
to complement my obsessions. To all my family and descendants, I sincerely hope your life will be as interesting and satisfying for you as mine has been for me.*

—Mickey McCoy
April 2001

Contents

Part I   STORIES OF SELF-DISCOVERY

Part II   STORIES OF WORLD WAR II

Part III   STORIES OF CIVILIAN LIFE

Part IV STORIES OF THE SPACE PROGRAM YEARS

List of Illustrations

ACKNOWLEDGEMENTS

As I compiled the stories that my husband Ray (nicknamed "Mickey") had written, I received a great deal of assistance, for which I am extremely grateful.

I am especially grateful to his son and daughter-in-law, Craig and Vana McCoy, for their help and support. They gathered photographs for the book, copied them into a publishable format, and spent many hours carefully reading the manuscript and clarifying points of chronology and narrative.

Additionally, I would like to thank his daughters, Audrey Chamness and Barbara Lawson, and his sister, Shirley Barris, for their contributions to the book. Audrey, Barbara, Craig, and Shirley each provided narratives of their memories of Mickey in the foreword, as well as sharing their personal collection of photographs.

I would like to express my appreciation to Beatrice McCoy for contributing pictures of Mickey taken during his years in Japan, and family photographs taken during the early years of their marriage.

I could not have compiled these stories into a book without the help I received from my son, John Haigerty. He kept my personal computer running, upgraded the software, and helped me debug error messages when they occurred. His technical expertise in the areas of computer software, hardware, and networking was a most valuable and readily available resource. Additionally, he provided much needed encouragement, and performed the final proofing of the text. I appreciate his help and encouragement very much.

Finally, I would like to thank the editors and assistants at iUniverse Publishing Services for their advice and assistance in putting the book into its final published form.

Thelma McCoy

ABOUT THE BOOK

Ray (also known as "Mickey") wrote this book during the last two years of his life. He died May 31, 2001 at age 75 in Pasadena, Texas, which is an outlying city adjacent to Houston. He had planned the book to be a compilation of short stories that described his life from childhood until his retirement. The stories are all true and are written from his memory. He had almost finished the book at the time of his death.

I knew him only by his given name, Ray, which he began to use when he was drafted into the service. His family and childhood friends still refer to him as "Mickey." Therefore, the pictures in this book will sometimes be captioned as "Mickey" and sometimes as "Ray," depending on his age at the time the picture was taken and the contributor of the picture.

Ray was born and raised in Los Angeles, California. He was passionate about his hobbies as a child, and passionate about his work as an adult. I met him in 1967 when we both worked at Kennedy Space Center in Florida. We were married in 1982.

Ray worked at Kennedy Space Center from the inception of the space program in 1957 until after the completion of the Apollo Program. He transferred to the Johnson Space Center in Houston in 1973 and worked on the Space Shuttle Program until his retirement in 1987.

His extensive experiments with electricity, chemistry, and explosives as a child became the basis for his expertise in these fields as an adult. The stories alluding to his obsessive/compulsive behavior regarding these scientific activities reflect, in a humorous way, an intentional theme declaring that neurosis can be a good thing. He points out that the neurotic behavior reflected in his childhood activities, hobbies, and educational pursuits provided the foundation of knowledge *that led to his career in the Space Program and some of his greatest satisfactions. These are the stories that describe his life.*

Thelma McCoy

FOREWORD

—contributed by Craig McCoy

I always knew I had a special father. This was the case, despite the fact that my father lived three thousand miles away and I only saw him every third summer. Fortunately, my parents' divorce was amiable and my mother rarely spoke ill of my father (actually, she seemed to still admire him). Additionally, all the adults that knew him, particularly those on my mother's side of the family, continued to think the world of him. For me, three things made my dad truly special.

1. Craig McCoy and Ray—ca. 1993

First, my dad worked in the space program. In the 1960's, the race to the moon was in full swing. The nation was captivated by the exploits of the rocketeers. Having a father who was associated with all of that was a big deal. My dad sent us many space mementos and souvenirs. I'd take these items to school for show-and-tell, impressing not only the other kids, but the teachers as well. This made me—a shy and awkward kid—feel important and seemed to help compensate for not having my father around.

The second reason was because he was extremely intelligent and could build anything. I always looked forward to the summers I spent with my dad. Sure, the vacations he took me on were fun and exciting. However, it was the projects we built together that made my time with him magical. He taught me about photography, electronics, chemistry, astronomy and mathematics. He showed me how to solder, develop film, make circuit boards, shoot movies, program a calculator, do time-lapsed photography, and write computer applications. We built model train layouts, model rockets and launch systems, model RC boats, metal detectors, electronic dice, digital alarm clocks, lie detectors, dark rooms, computers and much more. It was a thrill to bring these projects back home and show off my accomplishments to my friends and family. Having these experiences gave me a self-assuredness that I was able to carry into my adult life.

Lastly, my dad was special because he had extraordinary experiences, and being a master storyteller, he could bring his adventures and escapades to vivid life. We are very fortunate that my dad was able to write down and record a little over half of his life's unique journey. His memoirs are a treasure I will cherish for the rest of my life. Additionally, I believe they will be a special gift to many generations that follow.

—contributed by Audrey

I was proud of Dad and his accomplishments. I thought no one could spin a yarn better. If ever the Irish came out in him, it was through his story telling. He could captivate an audience of my friends better than any of my teachers could. He could even captivate an audience of adult friends and family better than anyone I had ever met. I believe that is why my mother's family thought so highly of him…and he was not even Catholic. Being Catholic was a big deal to them.

2. Audrey and Ray—ca. 1971

When I was 16, I went to live with my dad in Florida. By then, he had participated for several years in a therapy group. He taught me a lot about myself, although at 16 and 17, I was not yet ready to hear about my faults and hang-ups. Nevertheless, I sat and listened like a good student, because after all, Dad was the person talking to me and I selfishly wanted him to favor me over my siblings. Mom not only had kicked me out; she seemed to find nothing wrong with my brother and sister, so I was seeking my own favoritism. Through all his talks with me, things began to make more sense, and with the psychological tools he gave me, I began to learn how to analyze the motivations of other people, the situations I found myself in, and most importantly to more easily recognize my own motivations. I respected his judgment and will always cherish his memory.

—contributed by Barbara

3. Barbara and Ray—ca. 1982

I loved my dad, and although I miss him tremendously, I cherish all my memories of him. Through his memoirs, others can take a peek into his life and enjoy his humor, his adventurous spirit, his intellect, and even his mischievious side.

—contributed by Shirley

"Mickey"
My brother
My friend
My mentor
My hero
"Shirley"

4. Ray and Shirley—ca. 2001

PREFACE

The main body of this book consists of my memoirs, mostly in short story form. I have grouped these by categories of similar or associated experiences, presented more or less in chronological order. I hope my extant family and future descendants will be able to smile instead of shudder at some of the odd activities that gave color to my life.

My motivation for writing this autobiography, in addition to providing my descendants some knowledge of my life, is to present my belief that neurotic individuals, such as I, may experience more interesting and rewarding lives than do many normal people.

Emotions have a strong influence on our thought processes and behavior, and when neuroses are involved they can totally dominate areas of the mental process in which they operate.

My neuroses interfered with doing well in certain subjects in school, such as history, English, foreign language and art, because I was generally distracted, dwelling on some current obsessive interest. As a result, I was an erratic student, getting A's in math and science, B's in gym and art, and C's or worse in the rest. Although I often blamed economic reasons for my lack of a scholastic degree, the truth was that attending college required a measure of discipline that competed with my neurotic, compulsive needs. This is not a lament—just an analysis. On reflection, I would not wish to have traded my neurotic life for a normal one.

My neuroses enabled me to enter two professional fields: chemistry and electrical engineering, without any degrees, simply because my obsessions resulted in learning the material needed to perform those functions.

I have had a great life, in large part because of my neuroses—and some good luck. My life never seemed dull or unfulfilled. I always enjoyed my work because I unconsciously chose my jobs to complement my obsessions.

A secondary motive for writing this book is to provide some tangible material for any descendants who take an interest in our family history. For this purpose, I have included a chronology of the whereabouts, travels, and activities of our family, a few family stories, and in the addendum, a genealogical descendant lineage.

A final note: if you live as long as I have, you are likely to bump into a famous person or two along the way. You may view anecdotes about such encounters as "name dropping." Well, of course they are, but to minimize any seeming attempt at self-aggrandizement, I have provided a facetious note: "[Caution: Name drop ahead.]" So consider yourself fairly warned.

To all my family and descendants, I sincerely hope your life will be as interesting and satisfying for you as mine has been for me.

Mickey McCoy
April 2001

_____INTRODUCTION TO THE FAMILY

❖

Dad
Mom
Me
Sis
Our Old Maid
Grandma Lewis' Last Days
[Suffering like Jesus]
Psycho-sciolistic Digression

DAD

Dad was born in Ohio. He was the second of four children. According to his birth record, he was born in West Township, Columbiana Co., June 12, 1894. Oddly, he always said he was born in Lynchburg, Pennsylvania. Perhaps his parents had lived there.

The record gives his name as "Ernest Ray McCoy," his father's name as "Emmet Forest McCoy," and his mother's as "Emma Martin." It says they resided in Greenhill, Ohio. At some time, the family moved to Cleveland where my father attended school until the 8th grade…considered a basic education in those days. He did well with only a grammar school education. He was a good reader, had a good vocabulary, and kept up with current events and politics. Mom had much more education than Dad did, but when she had trouble with the spelling of a word, she would turn to him, since he was the better speller. Most people regarded him as quite smart.

When Dad was young, his right leg became crippled. Even Mom never knew for sure what happened. According to one story, he won an ice-skating event, after which a bunch of enthusiastic kids piled on top of him, leaving his leg paralyzed. Another story says the impairment resulted from spinal meningitis. Since handicaps were viewed as a weakness in those days, I suspect the ice-skating story was used because it sounded more commendable. All his life, he had to bind his lame leg in bandages in order to walk.

Although he was the right age for WWI, his crippled leg made him ineligible for the service. For a while he worked as a sign painter, and eventually became a chauffeur for a wealthy Cleveland family. While working for this Cleveland family, he became acquainted with their maid, Gertrude Peters. She was the daughter of German immigrants—a widow the same age as Dad—and she had a young son named Mark. She and Mark lived with her parents. She was looking for a new husband, and Dad was looking for some love life, so they were married (in 1917) and Dad moved in. Not long after, this whole family group (Dad, Gertrude, her parents, and Mark) moved to California.

Gertrude's parents bought a house in Inglewood, a suburb in southwest Los Angeles, where they all took up residence. Gertrude came down with pneumonia and died in 1920. Antibiotics were still some 20 years in the future.

Dad decided to move out, and he left Mark to be raised by his grandparents. Dad moved to Seligman, Arizona, and then to Mojave, California, where he found work in a drug store, filling prescriptions. He met my mother in Mojave.

Dad died of a heart attack November 16, 1946 in Los Angeles, California, and he was buried at Rose Hills Cemetery, Whittier, California. He was 52 years old.

MOM

Mom was born in Wisconsin, April 18, 1900, at the family farm near Bloomington. She was the sixth of seven children. They never gave her a name; just called her "Baby," naively thinking she would be the last. When it was time for her to begin school, they realized she would need a proper name. Her mother asked her what she would like to be called. Mom knew a girl on a nearby farm named Lenys, and said she liked that, so she became Lenys Emma. Emma was her mom's name. Not many people have the opportunity to name themselves.

Mom's birth record says her father was William Garside Lewis. He was born in western Iowa. His life is rather well-covered in his memoirs. Her mother was Emma Jane Brookens from Beetown, Wisconsin. The children were raised on a farm near Bloomington, Wisconsin, but when Mom was a teenager, the family moved to Platteville. The oldest son, Raymond, remained on the farm. Mom attended the Normal (a college for training teachers) in Platteville, and taught elementary grades for a while. Teaching didn't suit her, and eventually she, along with her girlfriend Ruth Hall, moved to the big city of Milwaukee for a more exciting life. They had no problem getting dates. Many sailors were on leave from the Great Lakes Naval Station near by at Green Bay. To hear Mom tell it, face slapping, followed by walking home, occurred more often than having fun. She, especially, was very uptight from her religious upbringing and complained that her dates were always trying to steal a kiss. Eventually, she decided to move on. She heard that young women who were willing to move "Out West" were being hired as waitresses for Santa Fe railroad stations. Mom thought this sounded exciting. She contacted her sister, Mina—everybody pronounced it "Miney"—about the idea, and they headed together for Chicago to join the Fred Harvey organization.

Back in the 1870's and 80's, when the Santa Fe railroad was forging its way west along the old Santa Fe Trail, Fred Harvey collaborated with the railway company to provide the railroad with first-class restaurants along its routes. He hired hundreds of young women to be waitresses. For young eastern girls, it was an exciting opportunity. In those days, it was considered very adventuresome. They were known everywhere as "Harvey Girls" and the restaurants as "Harvey Houses." Years later a book was written, *The Harvey Girls*, and a movie made, *Harvey Girls*, about them. Mom and Mina were assigned to the Harvey House in Mojave, California—a bleak desert town.

Dad had moved to Mojave. He ate his meals at the Harvey House and met Mom there. They dated a while and decided to marry. They married October 23, 1922 in Los Angeles and set up housekeeping in a small duplex on 61st Street.

Dad got a job as an electroplater. He worked for Gaffler & Sattler, a manufacturer of cook-stoves. Aunt Mina quit Fred Harvey, got a job as a waitress in a cafe nearby on Broadway, and moved in with my parents. I'm sure it helped pay the rent.

In 1931 the family moved to 6150 Northside Drive in East Los Angeles. Dad died there in 1946. Mom continued to live there until about 1965. She died in 1986 in Banning, California.

ME

I was born in the Methodist Hospital in South Central Los Angeles on May 29, 1926, and was named "Ray Ernest McCoy, Jr." The birth certificate gives my father's name as "Ray Ernest McCoy, 31, occupation: electrical platting [sic]" and my mother as "Lenys Emma Lewis, 26, occupation: housewife." However, my dad's birth record states his name as "Ernest Ray McCoy," so perhaps I am not technically a Jr.

SIS

My sister, Shirley Edna McCoy, was born September 1, 1934, at the same hospital where I had been born. Dad was 40 at the time and Mom was 34.

OUR OLD MAID

Aunt Mina—everyone called her Miney—was the one Lewis girl who was not married. She had received a heavy dose of Lewis homeliness, and to boot had a scar on her face from an auto accident. It looked like a dueling scar. When I was little, I remember her lamenting about not being married yet. However, she did have one romance with a man named Rollie. It didn't work out, even though she desperately tried to use her life savings as a lure. She shed a lot of tears over him.

Aunt Mina never earned much money. She always worked as a waitress, but she saved every penny she got from tips. She saved them in Mason jars, and when she had filled one or two she would haul them to the bank and deposit the money in her savings account. She was a true miser and never pampered herself with much of anything except cigarettes. I was her favorite nephew and may have been her only other extravagance.

When Mom was in her late teens, she and Aunt Miney had left Wisconsin together to move "Out West" and work as waitresses for the Santa Fe railroad station in Mojave, California. Aunt Miney lived with us in the duplex on 61st Street in Los Angeles from the time I was born until I was about five years old. During that time she worked at a café on Broadway. In 1931 she got a job at a restaurant in the Union Pacific station in Las Vegas, Nevada, and in about 1941 she moved to Yermo, California and worked in the restaurant of the railroad depot. There she met and married a man named George Sicks. After he died in 1950, Aunt Miney came and lived with us again until she died a few years later.

One fond memory I have of my very early childhood was that when I was about four years old, every morning when Aunt Miney would leave for work I would insist she "Fiss a Mickey frew da cat hole." The "cat hole" was a hole near the bottom of the front screen door that the cat had enlarged to get in and out of the house. The edges were lined with cat hair. Aunt Miney, who *really* hated cats, would obligingly kneel down and kiss me through this hairy hole. She was a warm, loving person who added the greatest measure of love and stability to my life.

GRANDMA LEWIS' LAST DAYS—1931

Mom got word that her mother was very sick. "Very sick" in those days translated to "dying," so she and I boarded a train and headed east to Wisconsin.

Grandma and Grandpa Lewis lived in Platteville near the Normal where Grandpa worked as the maintenance engineer. A "Normal" is a college for training teachers. Grandma was bedridden. She had a bad heart and her circulation was very poor, especially in her lower extremities. Mom and my aunts took turns massaging her feet and legs to provide some relief.

One day Grandpa took me for a walk downtown. It was a very typical mid-western town with large old trees lining the streets. The sidewalks were all cracked and broken from roots. We stopped at a fruit vendor and Grandpa bought me an orange. I remember he paid a nickel for it. In Wisconsin, this was a big treat, but where I had been raised, oranges were so common and cheap that they were dumped by the truckloads just to keep prices up. However, I recognized that he was trying to do something nice for me.

In the center of town was a large, round, gazebo-like bandstand. I had never seen anything like it, and asked Grandpa what it was. He tried to explain, but I was too little to understand. Later in the summer, some of the family went into town to listen to a band (probably from the Normal) play there. Man, I thought those tuba's were something!

[SUFFERING LIKE JESUS—1931]

I was old enough that they let me play in the Normal's schoolyard. There were swings, rings, slides, and other neat stuff. Also, there was a place at the back of the property where they burned their trash. One day I found this heap of ashes and charred wood. In the process of climbing around in it, I stepped on a piece of board with a rusty nailed protruding. I was barefoot, and the nail went completely through my foot. I managed to hobble back toward Grandpa's place with board and nail still impaled, yelling all the way. Someone finally heard the racket and rescued me. They called the doctor—Dr. Cunningham, I still remember—who without mercy pulled out the nail. People were terrified of tetanus in those days, so this sadist dipped a Q-tip-like thing into some tincture of iodine and scrubbed out the length of the wound—like cleaning a pistol. It took the whole family to hold me down.

As the end of summer approached, Grandma was still hanging on. Mom decided she would have to leave in order to enroll me in school, so back to California we headed.

I survived my crucified foot, but Grandma didn't. She died in September that year.

PSYCHO-SCIOLISTIC DIGRESSION

Dad was a very quiet person. He never told stories about his childhood or past. For years, I didn't know he had a previous marriage. Occasionally, at the dinner table, he would tell something interesting that happened at work. He rarely spoke to me except to convey a command. Although he never spanked or hit me, I was always afraid of him. I guess it was mostly a fear of the unknown. I think he preferred it that way.

He seemed to me to be defensive and withdrawn. Still, on occasion a "pseudo-father" would show through this facade. Once, after he heard I had been in a schoolyard scuffle (and got the worst of it), he brought home a pair of boxing gloves; he gave me one lesson.

Mom, on the other hand, was very talkative. She would tell stories about her life. I loved to listen to them. Only minimal communications existed between Mom and Dad—very little conversation for pleasure—just those discussions necessary to effect the business of marriage.

In my view, Mom was neurotic—mostly obsessive-compulsive and with some paranoia directed at the social system. It seemed to her that in this world, men were privileged and got to do *everything*. She believed that society considered women to be of lesser value than men except in the role of taking care of a man's needs and having kids. Her resentment of this role became so strong that she developed a near-hatred for men.

Mom was exceptionally skilled at manipulating the men about her. In such endeavors, she could be surprisingly devious while exercising her need for control. She would fabricate stories to get men to cooperate in her schemes. Her memory was good enough that she could successfully support these stories with a string of lies for as long as necessary, and she could turn on the tears, when necessary, to get her way.

When I came along, she found a new *male* subject on which to exercise her obsessive need for control. I'm sure Mom saw me as a live doll—something to show off to her friends. She spent a lot of time dressing me up and having me photographed. She created a baby book that could be used as a text for Abnormal Psychology. It contained hair from my first haircut, nail clippings from my first manicure, and a bloodstained bandage from my first cut. All in all, I was a great possession, rather than a young child to be nurtured and raised.

In the beginning, Mom seemed to compete with Dad to raise me her way. After a year or so he apparently just gave up, rejecting me as a "mama's boy." Early photos show Dad holding me in his arms with a smile of pride on his face. Later on, such poses no longer appeared.

After Dad's acquiescence, Mom began a careful program of behavior control. She wanted a well-behaved kid to show off to her friends. When she told me to be quiet, I was quiet; when she told me to sit, I sat. She was very strict and whacked me whenever I didn't obey. She was very liberal with her hands. She achieved her goal.

Probably the only genuine love I received during the first few years of my life was from Aunt Mina. In those early years she lived with us. She became a surrogate mother to me in many ways. Years later, when I was in therapy after my divorce, the psychiatrist opined that had it not been for my aunt during those formative years, I would probably have become a real nut case.

Mom's neuroses encompassed several characteristics. These included not only obsession, compulsion, and paranoia. Additionally, she had an extreme phobia of germs. She overcooked everything. Vegetables became mush. Meats were tough like jerky (sometimes overcooked even to the point of being shatterable). Eggs were always scorched, and oatmeal was lumpy with a skin on top. However, Dad was a good cook, and thankfully he did the cooking on weekends and holidays.

Mom loved to dance. Dad couldn't because of his lame leg. As soon as Dad died, when Mom was 46, she began going to dances. She kept this up well into her 60's. She never actually dated anyone—just went to the dances and then came straight home.

Mom was extremely vicarious about celebrities' lives. She read every movie magazine she could get her hands on. She had an excellent memory, accumulating unbelievable quantities of gossip about these people's lives and their romances. She was a walking encyclopedia of such nonsense, and was acknowledged as an expert on such matters by her friends. Mom was highly sought after by most of the women she knew. She could entertain them for hours.

As I grew up, Mom fed me a steady diet of propaganda about how mean her father had been to her mother, the kids, and even the farm animals. She also filled my head with many stories about Dad's wrongdoings. Over the years, she developed me into being her confidante. She divulged many secrets to me that I was expected to keep from Dad.

By the time I was seven or eight, I was thoroughly brainwashed to believe that men were pretty undesirable people. Naturally, I didn't want to be like "them," and thus I was indoctrinated almost entirely from a female point of view—a neurotic one at that. I can remember sitting around the house listening to Mom, a neighbor lady, and sometimes Aunt Mina, gossiping. I was very much a fly on the wall. No one ever asked me to leave. I never opened my mouth—just listened. I built up a repertory of these women's concerns, viewpoints, and many of their irrational conclusions. In later life I frequently found myself being selected as a confidant to female relatives and acquaintances.

Yet this didn't help me at all when I began to take an interest in girls. At that age, girls didn't find me the least bit attractive. I lacked the looks and self-confidence most young girls were looking for. My unique understanding of (older) women certainly didn't apply here. Schoolgirls were a total enigma to me. In this new game, I felt I was a complete outsider. I avoided school social events. They seemed like frightening affairs that would only expose my inadequacies and embarrass me. As a result, I never learned the usual social graces such as dancing, dating, and making small talk. I rapidly sought refuge in science, and I became a geek.

5. Infant Mickey and Dad—ca. 1926

6. Baby Mickey—ca. 1926–27

Mickey was born May 29, 1926. His mother was 26 years old. His dad was 32.

7. Baby Shirley, Mickey, and Dad—ca. 1934

Shirley was born in 1934. Mickey was eight years old. He quickly
became the primary caretaker of Shirley, even changing her diapers and
feeding her.
They remained best friends all of their lives.

8. Mickey, Dad, and Shirley on Back Bumper of Car—ca. 1934
Mickey is holding the cat.

9. Mickey, Mom, and Grandfather—ca. 1931

Mickey and his mother visiting
Grampa Lewis in Wisconsin, 1931
Mickey was five years old.

CHRONOLOGY OF WHEREABOUTS AND TRAVELS

A Chronology of Whereabouts and Travels

When I was born, my family lived at 238 West 61st street between Main and Broadway, about five miles south of the center of Los Angeles. This was in a quiet suburb, consisting mostly of small frame houses. Our house, however, was a small stuccoed duplex. The end-of-the-line for the "S" streetcar from downtown was directly in front of our house.

By 1928, times were beginning to get tough, and Dad was laid off. Mom's sister, Aunt Mina, kept things afloat. She lived with us, paid the rent, brought home leftovers from the restaurant where she worked and staples from the grocery. Dad's brother Wayne was a manager at a Ford dealership in Cleveland, Ohio, and he offered Dad a job as a used-car salesman. With little other choice, Dad, Mom, and I headed for Cleveland, leaving Aunt Mina at the duplex. After a week-and-a-half of traveling across the country by automobile, we arrived in Cleveland. Grandma McCoy (she hated being called "Grandma" and insisted we call her "Nana") lived in an old three-story house. She was a widow. Grandpa had died about ten years previously. We lived in the third story of that house.

While we lived there, Mom and I met the rest of Dad's family: Uncle Wayne, Aunt Pearl and their two daughters, June and Betty, Aunt Vesta (Dad's sister), her husband Sid (Smith) and their daughter, Nancy (a little older than I), and on one occasion, Uncle Ross (Dad's older brother) and his wife Eleanor. I don't know where they lived, but as I recall it was an all-day trip to visit them.

Uncle Ross had been in the Army—as a major, I think. He was good-looking and was considered quite dashing. At a party he had met Eleanor, who was about 10 years older than he was and excessively homely to boot; however, she had inherited a lot of money. That convinced Uncle Ross she was attractive enough, so at the end of the war they were married. Her father had become wealthy from manufacturing little kids' sunsuits, and when he died, Eleanor and her sister (who was even older, and according to Mom even uglier) had inherited some millions. A million in those days was big money. Eleanor's sister never married, and when she died her money went to Eleanor—and Ross, as well.

Uncle Ross never had to work again. He and Eleanor traveled endlessly around the world. He became interested in the McCoy family history, and during their travels in Europe, gathered much ancestral information. I don't know what ever happened to his findings. I would give plenty to have them now.

I don't know how long Dad worked in Cleveland. It was a bad time for both him and Mom. Dad, being introverted, was not cut out to deal with the public—especially not to be a salesman. As a result, he was unsuccessful and miserable.

Mom got on well with Aunt Pearl and Aunt Vesta, but she soon concluded her mother-in-law was insufferable. Nana made it clear that Mom wasn't good enough for her son. According to Mom, she constantly compared her unfavorably with Dad's first wife, Gertrude. Mom became so miserable she took me and went to Wisconsin to stay with her family. I think she and Dad almost broke up. Eventually, Dad threw in the towel. He packed up, swung by Wisconsin to pick up Mom and me, and we all headed back to California. The main thing Dad got out of this trip was a better car. It was a Pierce Arrow—a very fine, if old and well used, automobile. Since Aunt Mina was living in the duplex on 61st Street, we had a place to go.

I'm not sure where Dad finally found work, but I think it was at O'Keefe & Merritt, another stove manufacturer. (He worked for Gaffler & Sattler, a manufacturer of cook-stoves, when he and Mom were first married.) We lived in the duplex until about 1931. Aunt Mina quit the cafe on Broadway and got a job at a restaurant in the Union Pacific station in Las Vegas, Nevada. It was a good deal for her, since they provided free room and board.

In the summer of 1931, Mom got word that her mother was very ill with a heart problem. Mom adored her mother and often referred to her as a saint. She felt she had to go to Wisconsin to be with her, so Mom and I took a train to Platteville, Wisconsin.

When summer was over, Grandma was still hanging on. Mom wanted to stay with Grandma till the end, but felt she needed to get back to California and enroll me in school. Dad sent some money for a ticket and we headed back. Grandma died that September.

During our absence, Dad moved from 61st Street. Now, with a secure job, he had decided to look for a better location near shopping and a school. He settled on a new and attractive subdivision called Montebello Park, consisting of modest stucco homes in the far eastern part of Los Angeles County. New subdivisions in those days were considered complete when they had only streets, sidewalks, and empty lots with utility services. Houses were built after the lots were sold. This subdivision was only a few years old and about half of the lots had houses. Dad rented a nice two-bedroom stucco house at 6150 Northside Drive just in time for me to start kindergarten at Montebello Park Grammar School. It was only two blocks away.

In those days, grammar school was first through eighth grade, and high school was ninth through twelfth. However, times were changing, and they built a new junior high school in the area. It was named Eastmont Junior High. Because the high school in the city of Montebello was becoming overcrowded, the new junior high had grades seven through ten. When the new school opened, I was starting seventh grade, so I attended it from the beginning of its operation. Four years later I graduated to the two-year high school in Montebello.

My working career began when I was twelve and in the seventh grade. It consisted of odd jobs and some babysitting. I continued working at these types of jobs through the eighth grade. That summer—1939—I got occasional jobs helping a gardener cut down trees and helping a refrigerator repairman. The following summer—1940—when I was 15, Dad got a job for me where he worked. I became their spray-booth operator. It paid $10.00/week, minus 8 cents for Social Security.

The next summer—1941—when I was 16, I got a job at California Flaxseed Co. as a lab assistant in their research lab. The following summer I found a job at Sherwin-Williams Paint Co., also in their lab. They were pressed for help because it was wartime, and they allowed me to do chemist's tasks and even to sign affidavits verifying product specifications. The arrangement was for me to come in after school whenever I could. They would leave a list of analyses and tests for me to perform. Usually I would "punch out" (record my departure time) about 9:00 to 9:30 p.m. I continued this until after I graduated in 1944.

WWII was going on and the Navy was in desperate need of electronic technicians. Therefore, they had devised a test known as the "Eddy test" to locate high school boys with such aptitude. Students who passed were assured of acceptance into a Navy electronics school where they would be taught radio, radar, and navigation. I took the test and passed easily.

After graduation I tried to enlist in the Navy with Eddy test results in hand, but the Navy bureaucrats had closed enlistments for that month. Next thing I knew,

I got my "Greetings" from the President. I had been drafted—an irreversible thing. After my physical, I was sent to Fort MacArthur in San Pedro, CA.

Since I had passed the Eddy Test, I contacted my congressman (via his son, Bud Lane, my childhood friend) and asked for assistance. He made a phone call, and I was quickly transferred to the Navy. They sent me to Great Lakes Naval Training Station at Green Bay, Wisconsin for boot training. In addition to its own activities, this naval station was used extensively as a training center associated with the main Great Lakes Naval Station that is a few miles north of Chicago.

After a compressed boot camp of eight weeks (the usual at the time was 16 weeks), I was sent to Chicago in January 1945, where I attended a one-month course in basic math. This course was designed to filter out those who probably couldn't make it through the Navy electronics schools; about 60% were eliminated.

Then, in February 1945, I was sent to Tacoma Park, Maryland where the Navy had taken over the Bliss Electrical School. Although the course was only three months long, I learned a great deal from their excellent teaching staff.

After completion of the curriculum at Bliss, I was transferred to Corpus Christi, Texas—actually to a small island south of Corpus named Ward Island. The Navy had set up a super-secret radar school there. I completed my training in December 1945. By then the war was over and I served out my time in roles that did not relate to my training. However, later in life, this training was invaluable to me, and in large part, my career was based upon it.

I spent a couple of months in Alameda Naval Air Station near Oakland, California. Then I was sent to Breezy Point Naval Air Station near Norfolk, Virginia. At Breeze Point, I performed maintenance and repair tasks on the radars of PBY and PBM flying boats. (Both the PBM and the PBY were "flying boats," used very successfully in the Pacific during WWII. Later on in the production runs, both aircrafts were converted to amphibians. Beaching gear could be attached to either, but normally they "lived" in the water. The "P" stood for Patrol and the "B" for Bomber. The last letter was the manufacturer: "M" for Martin Aircraft, and "Y" for Consolidated Aircraft Corp., known later as Convair).

Finally, in July 1946, I had accrued enough points to be discharged. I was discharged at Fort MacArthur, California—the same place where I had entered the service two years earlier.

I moved back in with my family and got a job with W. P. Fuller Paint Co., working in their laboratory. My father died of sudden heart failure in November that same year. I continued to live with my mother until 1951.

In 1951 I got a job with Philco Corporation. Philco had a contract with the Air Force to maintain their radar sites. As a part of this work force, I went to Philadelphia for training in the latest radar and navigation equipment. Later that year they sent me on an assignment to Japan. It was a military contract, and I was stationed at Johnson Air Force Base, northeast of Tokyo.

Later that same year I became engaged to Beatrice [Bebe] Marie Waring of Bell Gardens, California, whom I had been dating since 1948. She accepted a job with Civil Service and she was assigned to the Far East Air Materiel Command (FEAMCOM) at Tachikawa, about 20 miles from Johnson AFB in Japan.

We returned to the States in late 1953, were married January 24, 1954, and both started classes at Los Angeles City College. We took an apartment over a garage near the college. During the first semester, Bebe became pregnant, so I decided not to return to school the next semester, and instead got a job as an electronic technician at Firestone Tire & Rubber Co. They had a contract with the Army to build artillery missiles (Corporals) capable of carrying an atomic warhead.

Later in 1954 we moved to Southgate, California where the Firestone plant was located. The next year, on February 11, Audrey Theresa was born. After a year in Southgate, I found a better job with Convair in San Diego as an electronics instructor. They had a contract with the Air Force to develop an intercontinental ballistic missile (ICBM). It was named the Atlas.

We lived in Point Loma, near San Diego, and Barbara Marie was born there on February 12, 1956. After a few months, we bought a house in La Mesa, California (East San Diego). We lived there until 1957, when an opportunity arose for me to obtain a promotion to Test Engineer. This required relocating to Florida.

We moved to Cocoa Beach, Florida—a location near the missile launch sites at Cape Canaveral. On November 9 of 1958, Craig Graham was born. After the launch of John Glenn into earth orbit in February 1960, I began working on the Apollo moon-landing program. NASA had awarded this contract to North American Aviation in Downey, California.

Later that year we moved back to California (Buena Park), which was within commuting distance of the North American plant. Soon Bebe and I began to have marriage problems that ended in our divorce in 1962–63.

In 1962 I moved from Buena Park to Satellite Beach, Florida, alone, to work on Apollo launch operations. Living in Satellite Beach necessitated a long drive to work, so after several months I moved into an apartment on Merritt Island, considerably closer to the Cape.

After several years I decided to move to the mainland town of Cocoa. I had learned that nuisances such as bugs and rust were not nearly as bad on the mainland.

Around 1972, the Apollo program began to phase down and a layoff of the large work force was underway. In November of 1973, in order to stay with the company (Rockwell International), I agreed to be transferred to the NASA (Johnson) Space Center near Houston, Texas. [1] I bought a town home in Pasadena, Texas in 1974 and continued to live there.

In July 1977 my friend, Thelma Haigerty from Florida, and I agreed to live together. She sold her home in Merritt Island, came to Houston, and moved in with me. We were married December 22, 1984. I retired from Rockwell International in June 1987 at age 61, after 25 years of service. Thelma worked at the NASA Space Center as a database administrator for Ford Aerospace and subsequently for Rockwell International. The Rockwell contract was then awarded to Boeing Aircraft Company. That division was formed into a separate company: United Space Alliance. Thelma retired from this company in October 2000.

---

1.   Ray lived at this location until his death on May 31, 2001.

PART I
STORIES OF SELF-DISCOVERY

_____CHILDHOOD
TECHNICAL TRIUMPHS

❖

A Propensity Found—1937
Samuel Morse Revived
Alexander Bell Reborn
The Ford Coil—1937
Marconi Resurrected
The Tree House—1938
Marconi Revisited
Paranoia
Making Old Ladies Jump
Gang Wars—ca. 1935–36
Willie the Wizard—ca. 1937–38

A Propensity Found—1937

I was 11 years old and in the sixth grade when Dad gave me his old flashlight. The switch was broken. I couldn't fix it, but I took it all apart, and after much mind-scratching I finally figured out how it was *supposed* to work. I connected the cells and bulb with some pieces of baling wire making a temporary circuit. The light lit!

It's hard to describe the euphoria I felt. I hadn't just figured out how a simple electrical circuit worked; I had discovered an unknown propensity in myself. Here was something I could do that others wouldn't know how to do. Certainly none of the other kids understood anything about electricity, and maybe I could use this unique knowledge to gain much needed self-esteem. Of course I didn't understand this in such psychological terms, but I do remember the strong feelings of discovery and self-discovery. Unbeknownst, an obsession was taking root.

During this period, our sixth grade teacher was taking us on field trips to the local public library. It was a mile-and-a-half walk each way. On the next trip I asked the librarian where I could find books about electricity. She pointed to the children's non-fiction section, and there I found a kid's book on electricity experiments. It showed how to hook up cells in series and parallel to form batteries, how to make your own cells, and how to connect other devices such as buzzers and bells. It even showed how to construct meters and measure voltage and current. I nearly wore out that book. Every two weeks I would take it back to the library and get it renewed for another two weeks. I was hooked on electricity!

Samuel Morse Revived

Almost immediately I became fascinated by the concept of the telegraph. I frequently visited the East Los Angeles Union Pacific Depot to watch the telegrapher do his thing. Although I had no ability to construct an electromagnet sounder, I reasoned that my light bulb (from the flashlight) could be used as a signaler. I made a crude telegraph key from some sheet metal cut from a tin can. Then I mounted the key, bulb, and battery on a piece of wood, wired them together, and began learning the Morse code.

My invention was fine for practicing code, but soon I wanted to communicate with another station. It wasn't easy to find someone who lived close enough to run a wire between our houses, but eventually I talked Wendall Dane into giving it a try. He lived across the street and down a couple of houses.

But where could I find enough wire to reach? Well, by this age I had become a first-rate scrounger. I spent a lot of time sorting through trash heaps behind various factories along the railroad tracks. One turned out to be a gold mine for wire. It was Sterling Motors. Any length of wire too short to wind an armature or field for their motors was piled behind their lot for pick up by a scrap-metal salvager. They didn't seem to mind if I helped myself. These short pieces were about 50 or 60 feet long and had enamel insulation.

In no time, I had spliced enough lengths together for a single line between my bedroom and Wendall's. We strung the wire from my bedroom window to the poplar tree in front of the house, then from one tree to the next, crossing the street in the middle of the block, and ending up at Wendall's house. I used the city's water pipes as a ground return. It worked fine.

Wendall and I both had recently joined the Boy Scouts. In the Scouts, signaling was an important skill for which a kid could earn a merit badge. This was a source of motivation for Wendall, and we spent many hours sending silly messages back and forth. We both became good telegraphers and the scoutmaster appointed me as Signal Master of our troop.

ALEXANDER BELL REBORN

The size of my world had expanded since I had been given a bike the previous Christmas. During summer school vacation, I happened upon a Salvation Army store a few miles away, in Belvedere Gardens, where I came across a book titled *Telephony*. It was a big book, approximately three inches thick and way over my head. In fact, I didn't even know how to pronounce "Telephony," but they were only asking 15 cents for it and I had to have it. I didn't have the money, of course, but had an idea on how I might get it.

On the next trash pick-up day, I took my wagon (it was red, naturally) and started around the neighborhood looking for discarded one-gallon jugs or cans. These would bring 3 to 5 cents each at local paint stores. The stores used them as containers when selling paint thinner from a 55-gallon stock drum. I managed to earn 13 cents that day. I got on my bike and raced to the Salvation Army store.

After I showed them my 13 cents and blurted out my story of scavenging for containers, they felt sorry for me and let me have the book for a dime. I was ecstatic.

The book was old, probably written about 1900. It was a reference book for telephone engineers to use while designing new telephone exchanges and systems. The first chapter was basic, and I was able to glean some ideas about ringing methods, ground return circuits, and battery hookups from it. However, most of the book was written about equipment I could never hope to acquire. Even so, I *had* to build my own telephone.

My first problem was equipment. I needed four basic items: a microphone, an earphone, a battery, and some wire. The library book about electrical experiments I had been renewing repeatedly showed how to make a microphone. It used two squares of thin sheet metal, separated by a cardboard spacer with a hole in the center. I elected to use a felt corn plaster for the spacer. The space in the center of the hole was to be filled with carbon granules. I crushed up the carbon rod from a dead flashlight cell for the granules. It worked, but the sound from it was crackly.

I lucked out on the earphone. In the early days of radio, people listened with headsets. I knew a kid whose dad had a headset that was stored in a shed, just corroding away. I traded my treasured pocketknife for it. The earphones needed a *lot* of cleaning up. The two diaphragms were very rusty, but eventually I got them both working.

Batteries were no longer a problem. Someone told me the police put new cells in their flashlights every couple of weeks and threw out the old ones; some still had life left in them. Therefore, digging through the trash at the local police station became a regular routine, providing me with an endless source of cells for batteries, and having learned about Sterling Motors, I never had a shortage of common wire.

A rudimentary telephone uses the same hookup as a telegraph, with the key replaced by a microphone and the sounder—light in my case—replaced with an earphone. With this knowledge, in a few days I was able to upgrade Wendall's and my telegraph into a private telephone.

However, it had a serious problem. The long line between our houses acted like a radio aerial and the batteries were acting like detectors (diodes). As a result, KFI, the local 50 KW station, was coming in as loud as our voices. Although a fix would have been easy, I didn't know enough about radio yet to implement one. So we just put up with KFI news, ads, and music and talked very loudly.

THE FORD COIL—1937

In my last year at Montebello Park Grammar, I met a kid who introduced me to a new fascination. He had a Ford coil. These devices had been used in the old Model T Fords to produce high voltage necessary for the spark plugs. The Model T had four cylinders and used one coil for each spark plug. Each Ford coil consisted of a wooden box into which an induction coil and a condenser were placed, then the box was filled with pitch to provide insulation and protection from moisture. The electrical connections were attached from inside the box to three metal buttons on the sides of the box.

Model T's were almost obsolete, so auto junkyards had plenty of these coils. They sold them for 10 to 25 cents, depending on their condition. I soon got one.

Ford coils were designed to operate from a six-volt car battery, the standard voltage for cars in those days. I persuaded a gas station to give me an old, weak battery, and I lugged it home. It didn't have enough power to start a car, but it did just fine with my Ford coil.

The neat thing about these coils was that applying six volts to them would generate a continuous stream of high voltage pulses: over 20,000 volts. Sparks could be made up to about one inch long.

A kid could do a lot of fun things with a coil like this. The high voltage they produced could make partially evacuated vessels, such as an old light bulb, glow an eerie blue. You could electrocute ants and flies. You could shock unsuspecting people. Although the high voltage it produced could kick like a mule, it was harmless. Later on, I learned that the spark could be used to ignite gunpowder, although we found better ways to do that.

MARCONI RESURRECTED

The very best use for Ford coils was high-tech. They could be used as a wireless transmitter. In the early days of radio, high voltage induction coils—similar to a

Ford coil—were used to transmit Morse code. These coils were equipped with a spark gap that generated radio frequencies. This gave radio operators the nickname "Sparky."

However, these early spark gap transmitters had one serious drawback. They created unlimited frequencies that flooded the entire radio spectrum. This prevented more than one transmitter from operating at the same time in a given area. Early designers attempted to correct this problem by adding resonant circuits that favored one frequency and attenuated the others. Although far from a totally satisfactory solution, it did make it possible for several transmitters to operate simultaneously. The final solution came with the development of vacuum tubes. Vacuum tubes made it possible to produce narrow-band signals, so hundreds, even thousands, of transmitters could operate without mutual interference. Also, they could transmit voice and music, whereas spark gap systems could not. As a result, spark gap transmitters soon became outlawed. I was, of course, ignorant about such laws, and just wanted to communicate with my friends.

Radio was still viewed as nearly magical by adults of those days. They all agreed that radio was a wonderful thing, but its workings were beyond anything they understood. Younger generations rarely have such limitations. Kids frequently astonish their elders when they comprehend the newest technologies. Well, I reckoned that I knew enough about electricity and telegraphs that I could at least try to transmit a wireless signal.

Back to the library I went. There I found another treasure: *Boy Mechanic: 700 Things for a Boy to Make*. It was written about 1913, during the heyday of spark-gap communication, and had many plans for making wireless transmitters, using high-voltage induction coils, of which my Ford coil was an example.

The transmitter circuits were simple to construct. They depended on the use of a spark gap that was easy to make. I was using an old car battery to power my Ford coil, and my parents wouldn't let me have "that damned leaky thing" in the house. So, with a little innovation, I dug a hole in the flower garden outside my bedroom window, placed a box containing the battery and Ford coil in the hole, covered the box with some boards, and ran some inconspicuous wires up to my window.

I mounted my homemade telegraph key on the windowsill and the spark gap on the outside window frame. Then I ran a wire up to the roof where I had a short aerial. For a ground, I connected the wire to a water faucet near the window, just as I had done with the telegraph and telephone.

However, the receivers described in the book were totally obsolete and quite difficult to make. The best receivers by this time were regular radios, which nearly everyone had. I set a book on the key to keep it closed, verified the sound of the sparking outside, then went into the living room and turned on our family radio. Wow! It didn't matter where I tuned, I could hear the raspy sound of the spark gap everywhere. Of course it wasn't much of a test, as the transmitter and receiver were so close to each other, but I was plenty excited. I was transmitting!

I ran over to Charley Heckman's place—a schoolmate who lived about two blocks away—and explained what I had done. We decided to see if he could pick up the signal from his house. He turned on his radio and I ran back to my place and began keying nonsense code. Charley didn't know Morse code anyway. After about ten minutes, Charley showed up outside my window, yelling that he had heard the signals fine.

Since Charley didn't have a Ford coil, we couldn't establish two-way communications, and our project sat dormant until the following weekend.

I had another "sometimes" friend. His name was Dale Firestone. His family was the very definition of the phrase "work ethic." The father worked as a grinder in a factory—a hard, dirty job. Dale, his mother, and his sister Lois, were expected to spend their free time making things the family could sell. A typical item was a string holder that hung on the wall. Theirs was a piece of wood cut out to form a head and painted as a black girl with a hole drilled at her mouth for the string to be pulled through. Her dress was formed into a bag that held the ball of string.

After they made a dozen or two of these things, Dale and his sister were sent out into the neighborhood to sell them door-to-door for about a dollar apiece. Additionally, Dale spent his summer vacations peddling ice cream bars from a homemade box that he strapped to the back of his bike. Every morning he would go to a local ice cream factory and load up with dry ice and a variety of bars. Then he would pedal about 15 miles to an industrial area and sell them for ten cents each to the workers. His profit would be about $2.00 to $3.00 a day. Dale and his sister turned all of the revenue they made over to their dad. His schedule allowed him to be only a "sometimes" friend.

However, once in a great while their family would go to the beach for an outing. On one such Sunday afternoon I was messing with my new transmitting apparatus when Dale showed up on his bike. He asked if I wanted to go to the beach with his family. I said "Sure," put on my trunks, grabbed a towel and jumped on the rack on the back of his bike.

I had opened my bedroom window to allow operation of the telegraph key on the sill. This was summer, when it hardly ever rains in Southern California. So I had left things: battery, Ford coil, key, spark gap, antenna and ground all connected ready to operate.

Well, while I was at the beach, a light shower came through. Mom went through the house, closing the open windows. When she closed my bedroom window, she crunched the homemade key closed. The Ford coil fired up, the spark gap crackled, and the neighborhood airwaves for miles around became saturated with a loud, continuous "zzzzzzzzzzzzzzzzzzz." Since I had no tuning circuits, this racket appeared on every frequency (radio station) of every band.

People in those days listened to their radios a lot. Within an hour or so the stations were receiving calls from listeners, complaining that they couldn't hear their programs. The stations, knowing the problem wasn't with their signals, called the Federal Communications Commission (FCC). In short order, the FCC dispatched a radio direction-finding truck to the neighborhood, and after making a couple of cross-bearings zeroed in on our house.

By the time I got home, the FCC had left. They had told my dad that what I had done was highly illegal and punishable by a fine. However, they told him they wouldn't write it up, since it was a first offense. You'd think my dad would have come down hard on me, but he didn't say a word. I got the whole story from my mom. All Dad did was dig up my box containing the battery and Ford coil and put them in the garage. It was clear to me that using the bedroom for my experiments was out.

THE TREE HOUSE—1938

Having received no real trauma from the previous episode, I was still obsessed with communicating with wireless signals. Charley and I discussed the dilemma, and after a brief moment Charley came up with the appealing idea of building a tree house for a transmission location.

My fantasy was to build such a treehouse somewhere on Dennison Street because it had pepper trees with nice broad branches, ideal for a tree house. The trees along my street were tall, skinny poplar trees, which I thought were not suitable for such a project. While I was visualizing what the treehouse would look like, Charley decided, "We'll build it in your tree," he said. I voiced no argument. Charley had been born with a leadership gene. I was stuck with the followership kind, so off we headed to my house to survey the proposed construction site.

Immediately, Charley got my dad's handsaw from the garage, climbed the tree directly in front of the house, and began sawing our branches. Since it was impossible to build a "house" in a poplar tree, we decided to settle for a platform. We still called it a treehouse. Charley was cutting out a cluster of the tree's vertical limbs, all at the same height, on which to lay boards for a floor.

I was busy on the ground, dragging away the cut branches to a vacant lot across the street. Occasionally I would point out a branch that I thought should go. In a flash it would be laying on the ground ready for me to haul off. Sawing green wood is hard work, and eventually Charley got pooped, but not before he made sure there was no turning back, then he climbed down and turned the job over to me. I finished cutting out branches to make room for the platform, but always leaving sufficient foliage at the outer edge to provide a layer of camouflage. We stopped for the day. I was starting to get nervous about what my dad would say when he got home. However, even though Dad was an unusually observant person, on this occasion he didn't seem to spot our handiwork. At least he didn't say anything.

Next, we needed lumber for the project. We didn't have any, but a new house was being built over on the next street. We hopped on our bikes and began circling the block every hour or so, like buzzards casing the site, until the workmen left for the day. Then, being obsessed kids whose subconscious motivations made such decisions, we just helped ourselves to some lumber and nails. It was getting late in the day. We stashed our loot under the dying branches in the vacant lot across the street.

Bright and early the next morning, the sounds of sawing and pounding could be heard. By noon we had completed the platform. It was about 15 feet off the ground. Climbing up into the tree was a bit hard, so we installed a rope to aid in pulling ourselves up.

MARCONI REVISITED

Finally, the tree house was ready for our wireless transmitter. We hoisted the car battery, Ford coil, telegraph key and some wire up to the platform. In a short while we had it operating, but we needed an aerial if we were going to communicate any distance, so we headed for J. J. Newberry's dime store. In those days, dime stores served as neighborhood hardware stores.

We picked up some glass insulators and aerial wire. Mistakenly, we thought we needed a special wire made for aerials rather than using regular wire. This was an example of baseless lore that floated about in the early days of radio. By mid-afternoon we had strung an aerial from our tree to the next one down the street—about 50 feet.

Our next hurdle was the receiver. My parents had a small 5-tube table radio in the kitchen, to which no one ever listened, but it ran off AC power and wouldn't have worked from the car battery. We decided to use a crystal set. However, neither of us had one, so our program suffered a delay of about two weeks before we got one.

I got busy leafing through my Johnson Smith catalog, thinking I had seen the makings of crystal sets in it. Sure enough, I found crystals ($0.10), cat whiskers ($0.05), and crystal/cat whisker holders ($0.15). I hurriedly scribbled an order for one of each, wrapped the order around sufficient change (God knows where I found it), stuffed it into an envelope, and pedaled off to the nearest mailbox.

Meanwhile, Charley headed for an auto junkyard to get a Ford coil for his transmitter. He would use his AC operated radio as he had done in our first transmission test. His equipment hadn't been barred from the house, as mine had, and probably never would be. He also made a copy of my telegraph key from tin-can sheet metal.

Now the agonizing waiting began. Every day I would anxiously await the mailman. In fact, after a couple of days of disappointment, my obsession drove me to intercept him two or three blocks back up in his route. It was a bother for him to sift through hundreds of letters looking for mine, but he was good-natured about it.

Finally, after about ten days, the package arrived. Sure enough, it had everything I needed. So, out came the trusty "how to" book from the library. It showed several hook-ups for crystal sets. All included a coil of some sort. Thinking this was an essential element, I set about making one, per the instructions in the books.

As a form for the coil, one plan used an oatmeal box. In those days, one could be found in nearly any household. Fortunately, our oatmeal box was almost empty and Mom obligingly emptied it into some other container for me. Next I needed about 50 feet of fine wire. Charley had an old burned-out radio transformer that we dissected for the wire. Winding the wire around the oatmeal box turned out to be a real challenge. After wrapping a bunch of turns, the box or wire would slip out of my grip, the wrapped wires would loosen, and the coil would become a mess, then I would have to start all over. Finally, I wised up and used model airplane cement to tack down the wire about every 10 turns to keep it in place.

After winding the wire successfully, I hastily put the components together according to the plan in the book. The only thing yet needed was a way to tune it. The book showed a couple of ways: a sliding contact along the edge of the coil, and a variable capacitor. Both seemed too difficult, so in my impatience I ignored the tuning. Unbeknownst to me, the coil was self-tuned to some place in the broadcast band. When I hooked it up to the aerial and my earphones, I could hear several of the stronger local AM stations, all at once!

Back at Charley's place, things were not idle. Charley had his Ford coil operating, using his electric train transformer for power and had strung an aerial out his bedroom window. With his table model radio, he was ready for a test.

After meeting to decide who would transmit first, and when, we separated to man our stations. Since I had previously been able to transmit from my bedroom to his place, we agreed I would transmit first. Assuming we would succeed, our next plan was to switch our aerials—in his case from the radio to the Ford coil, and in my case from the Ford coil to my crystal set.

After performing my transmission, I listened and listened, but no rasping code was being returned. I readjusted the cat-whisker to find a more sensitive spot on the crystal, but still no luck. After a while I gave up and pedaled over to Charley's place. I could hear the buzzing of dots and dashes from outside his room. It was unintelligible gibberish, since he still hadn't learned code. I called to him and he let me in.

We discussed our problem and finally decided the crystal set probably wasn't the way to go. We needed to get a radio into the tree house. After a bit, it occurred to me to use the porch light connection outside the front door. It was only about 25 feet from the tree. Charley's dad had a long, black ugly extension cord coiled up and hanging on a nail in his garage. In a flash it disappeared from the garage and showed up between my front porch and the tree house. I commandeered the little 5-tube radio from our kitchen, and in no time had it operating in the tree house. Charley ran back home and we tried our communication experiment again.

Eureka! We had two-way communications at last, but Charley didn't know code. His transmissions were terribly slow as he looked up the code for each letter, and when I transmitted it was even worse, because I had to wait about 10 seconds between each letter to give him enough time to look it up. With practice, things got a little better, but never to the point where it was much fun. After a few weeks the whole operation died for lack of interest.

It wasn't long before the car battery had become so weak that it would hardly run the Ford coil. I didn't have any way to charge it except to lug it back to the gas station and pay them to do it. I was always short of money; we had to look elsewhere for a solution.

In those days, every house had a doorbell. These were powered by small devices called "doorbell transformers" that transformed the 110 volts house power to 6 volts that doorbells used. The 6 volts they provided was AC. Ford coils were designed for DC, but I hoped it might work. They were inexpensive, about a dollar, but I still couldn't afford one.

Luckily, one day I happened across an old house that was being demolished. There, in the heap of rubble, was the doorbell transformer for the taking. I took. I hooked it up to my precious Ford coil, and with considerable trepidation, turned on the power. It worked fine and didn't seem to harm my coil. With power from the porch light to the tree already available, my power problems were solved.

PARANOIA

With all this *valuable* equipment in the tree house, we became concerned about other kids finding our stuff and making off with it. Charley, as usual, came up with an idea. We could thread a fine wire into the strands of our climbing rope. Then hook the upper end to the Ford coil. We could then shock the crap out of anybody caught climbing into our tree. What a delicious idea!

We found some fine wire in one of the windings of Charley's scavenged transformer. Soon the rope was prepared from top to bottom, and we connected the top end of the wire to the Ford coil. The wire, being so fine, was invisible to anyone who didn't know it was there. Since I had figured out how to power the Ford coil from a doorbell transformer, we took down the car battery. With 120 Volt AC power to the tree, we could power not only the radio, but also the Ford coil, and even a light (and eventually, a more diabolical use).

We knew we couldn't let the Ford coil run continuously—a point the FCC had made clear. The obvious answer was to turn on the Ford coil from inside the house, using the porch light switch if we saw anyone trying to climb into the tree.

It was summertime—vacation time; lots of kids were loose in the neighborhood. I spent most of my free time either in the tree house or in the garage, messing around with some geeky project or other. From the garage, I could see any kids walking along the sidewalk. If they seemed to be taking an interest in the rope dangling from the tree, I would go in through the back door of the house and watch them through a small window in our front door.

It was inevitable. In less than a week, a couple of boys—about 10 or 11 years old—spotted the rope, and I spotted them. I rushed to the front door, peered out and saw them standing beneath the tree, looking up at the platform. They eyed the rope up and down and made furtive glances at the house, then up and down the street. Their curiosity was increasing by the second. I felt like a spider, waiting for a fly to land on my web.

Then one of them grabbed the rope and started to climb. I let him get about 6 or 7 feet off the ground before flipping on the porch light switch. For a fraction of a second, I could here the characteristic buzz, but in an instant it was drowned out by an indescribable scream. The kid went flying backwards about five feet (honest injun!) and he landed on his back. He scrambled to his feet, and both disappeared down the street. Word among kids travels fast; we never saw anyone try to climb into the tree again.

MAKING OLD LADIES JUMP

Soon it was the Fourth of July. Our anticipation and excitement was equivalent to Christmas. We scraped together as much money as we could and headed for the nearest fireworks stand. No expensive fancy stuff like roman candles, fountains, skyrockets, etc. We just loaded up on Panther brand firecrackers. We remembered previous years, when our supply had run out, and we had learned to plan ahead.

With our new cache of firecrackers, we couldn't help but cast about for new uses for having fun with them. Naturally, the tree house with its new electrification (powered from the porch light) offered new ideas.

The first was to rig up the Ford coil in such a way that if we caught a kid climbing into the tree, we not only could give him a sound shock, but we could further unnerve him with a loud bang. To accomplish this, we ran a wire from the high voltage terminal on the Ford coil to where we had placed the firecracker, twisted the end of the wire around the fuse, wrapped a second wire around the fuse about a quarter inch away, and ran it to a ground. The ground was just a nail pounded into the tree. Now, when the Ford coil was turned on from the porch light, a spark would jump between the two wrapped wires on the fuse, igniting it. Neat, huh?

But no kids attempted to climb the tree again, so the idea of unnerving kids with the firecracker never panned out. However, in testing the set-up we noticed as soon as the fuse began to burn, the firecracker would fall loose and a few seconds later would explode. This led to a new idea.

We strung our wires (that ran to the firecracker's fuse) out to a branch above the sidewalk. Now, if we saw a kid walking down the sidewalk we could set off the firecracker from inside the house using the porch light switch, and with careful timing we could cause it to drop and explode right behind him, giving him a good startle.

We did this six or eight times on various kids. They all jumped gratifyingly. But one day when we were set up to play our trick again, this old lady—in her

60's—came shuffling down the walk. Should we? No. Why not? Let's do it. Setting all reasoning aside, at the precise moment when she was directly below the rigged branch, I flipped the switch. As she took a step or two further along, the firecracker lit and fell on the sidewalk behind her. BANG! Her legs flew in all directions, and she landed on her rump. While still sitting there, she looked all around, but never up at the wire from the house to the tree. Finally, she erected herself and scurried on down the street.

I've always felt badly about having played the prank on an old woman. No justification can be made for such a prank, except that it takes time for kids to grow into socially acceptable adults. I hadn't yet gotten there.

GANG WARS—CA. 1937–38

Our neighborhood had two gangs of kids. Every so often we would declare war on each other. Charley was the head honcho of the enemy gang. I was one of the grunts on our side.

Ammunition varied, but it was agreed upon by the gang leaders when a war was declared. During the rainy season (winter months), it was produced by pulling up handfuls of wild grass with mud clinging to the roots. We'd pack the mud into a ball. To propel these missiles, we would grab the shank of grass and sling it at an opponent. They would travel surprisingly far, and with practice were quite accurate.

During the summer, we often held our battles in a nearby plowed field, using dirt clods for ammunition. These were the most dangerous, and occasionally someone would get hurt. Even if one didn't get hurt, the dirt clods usually stung, and this brought up feelings of anger and desire for revenge. This emotional upwelling added intensity to the fray and these wars often ended ugly. By mutual agreement, we eventually discontinued them.

Rubber-guns were by far the most fun. They could be used in any season, required some ingenuity in their construction, and the battles using them were accompanied with the most complete rules of engagement.

The standard ammunition for rubber-guns was rubber bands, cut from automobile tire inner tubes. They were cut about 1/2" wide. We tied a knot in the center to make it fly farther.

The usual weapon was made from a piece of wood cut in the approximate profile of a pistol. A spring-type clothespin was mounted on the rear of the handle. Layers of rubber bands—wrapped around the clothespin and the handle—augmented its grip. This was the standard single-shot. A few kids had fashioned pistols with clothespins on the top and the two sides, making a 3-shot weapon. Although these had a firepower advantage, this was often compromised because the bands had to be fired in a specific order. In the heat of battle, the sequence was often screwed up and the gun would jam.

Charley, always innovative, developed a machine gun. It had a crank that wound up a length of fabric tape. This tape lay along the top of a rifle-like gun which had notches carved along its top. Rubber bands were loaded from each notch to the front of the barrel. When the crank was turned, the cloth tape would pull out one rubber band at a time and release it. His was a 10-shooter. Its psychological effect was numbing. Many on our side would throw down their guns and surrender when he would appear with it.

The *BIG Mother* of all was a cannon one of my gang buddies and I developed. It had a barrel made from a two-by-four board about five feet long, and was mounted on a crude tripod. For propelling ammunition, it used an *entire* inner tube from a bicycle tire. It wasn't very portable and was hard to aim and fire, so it was mainly used to defend a position. That it did exceedingly well, as no one would get within 50 feet of wherever it was pointing.

The rules of battle evolved over time, but one of the most basic was no aiming at the face. Other rules had to do with surrendering and the treatment of captives. Mild torture was allowed, such as pinching and pulling hair off arms. It was on one occasion after being captured that I had met Charley. Being the leader, he had decided to torture me for information about our cannon.

He ordered me to lie down on the ground face up. Then he straddled me and sat on my chest. If I didn't answer his question (which I never did), he gave me a knuckle jab in the ribs. After having no success, he let me up and tied my hands behind my back and to a supporting column in his garage. Charley was very good with knots. In the Boy Scouts, he would win the knot tying competition every year.

On the other hand, I was a good escape artist. They had left me alone in order to rejoin the battle. In a short while I had freed myself. It had cost me some skin from my hands, but soon I was also back in the fray.

I think Charley formed some admiration for me from that episode, because within a short time we became good friends. Besides, we were getting too old for gang wars.

[Caution—Name drop ahead]

WILLIE THE WIZARD—CA. 1937–38

As young kids, our perimeter of wanderings slowly expanded until it included the Golden Gate Theater. This theater had been built in the grand style, with sculptured walls, an enormous chandelier, a balcony, a stage, and a pipe organ. It was in Belvedere Gardens, about a mile and a half east of our neighborhood. If we could scrape up a dime, we'd head for their Saturday matinee. They always showed two features plus a cartoon. The feature films would be either a serial or vaudeville. In all, we got about four hours of entertainment for our dime.

One day, after the matinee, we went exploring about the area and came upon a bowling alley. None of us could bowl. We were just curious and attracted by the clamor. As we were nosing about, we came upon a group of bowlers who were talking to a short, odd-looking person. His clothing was rumpled and unkempt, and his face indicated he was retarded. The group addressed him as "Willie."

Between their turns to bowl, the players would ask him questions, such as, "My birthday was November 23, 1916. What day of the week was that on?" Willie would roll his eyes back and then shut them. After a few seconds, he'd open his eyes and announce, "Thursday, it wuz Thursday." The questioner would say, "Hey, that's right!" and give him a nickel.

Another favorite was for someone to write down two long (usually 5-digit) numbers, multiply them out by longhand, and then ask Willie to multiply them in his head. In less than 10 seconds, Willie would read off a string of numbers. The odd thing was the answer was read right-to-left. I watched this being done several times on various occasions, and Willie's answers frequently differed from what the person submitting the problem had expected. Willie would always insist his was correct, and when the person recalculated, he would find his mistake(s), and Willie *would* be right.

I was better-than-the-average-bear at arithmetic, but this was something else. I took Willie aside, thinking I could learn a great secret, and asked, "How do you do it, Willie?" He looked at me with eyes that were windows to a vacuous mind and said, "I dunno—I jes put da numers in, an in lil while, they cum out." He'd answered that question a thousand times before. This is how Willie made his living. He hung around that bowling alley for a couple of years, amazing people with various mathematical tricks.

Occasionally the Golden Gate would include a live vaudeville performance in the Saturday matinee. It was the thirties, and vaudeville hadn't quite died. One Saturday, instead of a serial, they featured Willie. This is where I learned Willie had been immortalized as "Willie the Wizard" by Robert Ripley's *Believe It Or Not*. During this performance, they took a dollar bill from a volunteer and folded it in half. Then, while holding it about a foot in front of Willie's face, they popped it open for a second and then yanked it away. They asked him what the serial number (8 digits) was, and he repeated it back perfectly.

Then they repeated this with a dollar bill from a different volunteer. Same result. Then he was asked to multiply the two numbers in his head. His eyes rolled back, and then shut. It took a bit longer than his other tricks—maybe 15 seconds. He opened his eyes and read off the answer (right-to-left, of course).

No calculators were around in those days to verify his answer, and it would have taken too long to calculate the number on stage, so the announcer challenged anyone in the audience to multiply out the numbers and give their answers to him before the next show. He would compare their answers to Willie's. As usual, every answer was wrong until recalculated and corrected. Then finally, all agreed with Willie's figures.

_____FAMILY MATTERS

✦

Mom's Obsession
Husband & Father
No Longer an Only Child—1934
Official Cinematographer
Follow the Red Brick Wall—ca. 1940
Dad's Old Obligation
No Smoking
Yermo Visit—ca. 1942
Calico Trek
Uncle George

MOM'S OBSESSION

Mom, driven by a need for financial security, became addicted to playing the stock market. She could not depend on Dad. He had absolutely no talent for handling money. Every week he put the cash from his pay envelope into his pocket. He considered that after all, it was his money because he earned it. He stopped at the store each night on his way home from work and brought home one day's worth of groceries, and once a month he doled out four or five dollars for Mom to pay the utility bills. She walked a mile or two to the utility offices in Belvedere Gardens just to save the nickel bus fare each way, then she pocketed any change left over. That's about all of Dad's money she ever got her hands on. Dad never had a savings or checking account; he banked from his pocket. He never had insurance of any kind. To him, insurance was just a racket.

When Mom's father retired, he sold his house in Platteville and split his money between his kids. They, in return, were to pay him an annuity for the rest of his days. Since he wasn't at all wealthy and had seven kids, none of them received much. Granddad lived with one of the kids, Aunt Bess, so she didn't have to make payments. Mom got three or four thousand dollars. She immediately invested it in the stock market.

Dad never knew Mom played the market or that she had any money. I was expected to keep this dark secret from him. Over the years, Mom did quite well in the market, in spite of the fact that she didn't know a damned thing about the market or stocks.

Her strategy was to go downtown to the Merrill Lynch, Pierce, Fenner, and Bean brokerage office and hang out. They had a room with nice seats where people could watch the trades on the ticker tape across the top of one wall. Mom had set up an account with Merrill Lynch and they had assigned her a broker.

She would observe the other players—mostly old men—and note which ones made successful trades. Often these guys had been captains of industry and they knew what they were doing. Men in such an environment tend to be very competitive and don't share their information or sources readily, but Mom would flatter them a little and follow up by asking what they thought were good stock picks. And they, being typical men and her no doubt being the only woman in the place, would share their analysis with her.

When such "confidences" paid off, Mom wasn't cheap. She would take part of her profits and buy a nice gift as a payoff. I remember one audacious case in which she learned from Dad that his shop had a job silver-plating metal champagne glasses. She made up some preposterous lie that I don't remember and conned him into *gold-plating* a set of eight and a tray for her. She used them as a payoff to one of her "sources."

Using this strategy, she was quite successful. First, she provided the down payment to buy the house we had been renting. The payments were no more than rent, so Dad agreed to the obligation. After a few years she bought the house next door. This was not kept a secret from Dad. She just made up some lie about the source of the money. In another couple of years she bought the house directly behind us on the next street over, and shortly after that the house next door to it. At one point we owned a group of four houses.

NO LONGER AN ONLY CHILD—1934

On the 1st day of September 1934, Mom presented *me* with a baby sister. She said it was because I had asked for one. Yeah, right! They named her Shirley Edna. The "Shirley" was probably from Shirley Temple, and the "Edna" was Aunt Mina's middle name.

Mom was not the motherly type and Aunt Mina was not around to act as her proxy, as had been the case when I was little, so Mom had no choice but to curtail her daily sojourns downtown to the stock market. As soon as I got home from school each day she gave me basic training for taking over her mothering duties.

I entertained Shirley—which was kind of fun, changed her diapers—which wasn't, warmed her bottles and fed her; none of which compared with playing outside with my friends. By summer vacation the next year I was a qualified "Nanny." Mom, then, routinely left Shirley in my care every day—I was nine years old—while she headed for the stock market.

I believe this contributed to a bond between my sister and me, because over the years we have never had a squabble and have always been the best of friends.

OFFICIAL CINEMATOGRAPHER

Dad rarely bought anything unessential or frivolous. However, shortly after Shirley was born, he brought home a movie camera. He said he had paid $10.00 for it in a hockshop. He believed that's where one shopped for the best bargains. It was a Stewart-Warner 16mm with a fixed-focus lens.

Mom had always been the photographer in the family, but she seemed apprehensive about operating this new contraption. Therefore, it fell to me to take an interest in it, which I did with enthusiasm. I became the family cinematographer.

Film—black and white in those days—was expensive. A 100-foot roll cost around $4.00, and it only provided 4 minutes of filming. Dad coughed up the money only on special occasions—usually on Christmas—or sometimes if we were going on a weekend trip to the desert. Mom would ride me a little about not wasting film on this or that, but Dad never applied any limits. We went to Boulder Dam on one trip during its construction. Mom wouldn't let me take pictures of the dam because "nothing was moving."

We needed a projector to show the movies, so after we had accumulated a couple of rolls of film, Dad brought home a used projector, probably from a hockshop as well. It was minimal. It was a Keystone, and had to be cranked by hand. A 60-watt bulb was used as a light source. The projected image was dim and the action jerky, but we were happy.

After a couple of years of making do with this projector, Dad took me to a local camera store to look for something better. I'm sure he took me along, even though I was only 10 or 11, because he respected my experience and thought I could help make a good selection. We picked out a brand new Keystone. This one was nice. It could handle 400-foot rolls, had a *500-watt* bulb, and it was motorized. It cost $69.95, and Dad had to arrange lay-away payments. When he finally brought it home, the family was delighted. The images it projected were so much brighter and clearer that it was like watching our old movies for the first time.

FOLLOW THE RED BRICK WALL—CA. 1940

As I mentioned earlier, Mom had bought the house next door. Over the years it became a burden on Dad. One year the roof developed leaks. It was a flat roof, and Dad had to get on top with buckets of melted tar and a mop to re-surface it. Dad was always saddled with plumbing, electrical and painting maintenance chores. The renter husbands seemed helpless.

As if that weren't enough, Mom would frequently dream up some "improvement" which, in her mind, would justify increasing the rent. Dad always got the job. One year she decided on a patio. Patios had become a sort of "in" thing with the wealthy. She envisioned, or more likely saw in a magazine, a deck made of cement, with a hole for a shade tree, and an umbrella'd table with chairs around it. Dad sweat a whole summer putting it in.

This patio was about 20 x 30 feet. It required a *lot* of concrete. These were the days before one could just call a cement company and have a mixer-load of cement delivered and poured into your forms. The work had to be done starting with the raw materials. Dad had ordered a truckload of sand and one of gravel. They were dumped in our driveway. It was my job to mix batches of concrete in a mixing trough and haul wheelbarrow loads of the mix to where Dad was working. He'd deposit the load into the proper area, finally leveling and smoothing the batch. It took many such batches and weekends to complete the whole surface.

The final touch was to plant a tree in the hole provided. Mom chose a pepper tree—a lousy choice because of dropping peppers that stained the cement. The nursery delivered it and helped Dad plant it. It was only about eight feet tall and gave no significant shade. Over the following months, even with frequent watering, it didn't grow. It just sat there. Early the following spring, I learned in science class that plants need nitrogen to grow. I thought about the dormant pepper tree, and about my large supply of potassium nitrate that I used for making black gunpowder.

Without consulting anyone, I took about a quarter pound of the nitrate and sprinkled it around the base of the tree. After that, I became occupied with other things and I essentially forgot about what I had done. Some months later at dinner, Mom said to Dad, "Have you noticed the pepper tree next door? It's grown like a weed." Dad hadn't noticed, but after dinner we all walked over to look. My

God! It looked like Jack's beanstalk. It must have grown 4-5 feet taller. Its canopy was significantly larger and its trunk was much bigger in diameter.

As they were standing there in amazement, I decided to confess. I just couldn't see how I could get into trouble this time, so I told them what I had done. Dad produced a Mona Lisa smile, indicating approval, I thought. Mom mumbled, "You might have killed it." I glowed, just a bit, in spite of her snideness.

The following summer Mom came up with her next "improvement." The renters couldn't enjoy their patio for lack of privacy. They needed a wall along the east side, toward our house. She reasoned no such wall was needed along the west side, since it faced a shrub-lined walkway.

The decision was made that it should be a brick wall—a red brick wall. I don't think Dad had ever laid brick, but he got a lot of satisfaction in having friends and acquaintances admire his various areas of expertise. He would gladly teach himself and add one more to his repertoire.

So a load of red brick showed up in the driveway along with some sand. Dad brought home some sacks of lime and cement. The next Sunday he built a form for the footing and filled it with concrete. The next weekend, as soon as he got home from work, around noon on Saturday, he continued. After running a taut string between two stakes to provide a level reference, he began his first course of brick. I kept busy mixing mortar for him.

Dad wasn't one to take a lot of breaks. He'd just work continuously, except for going to the bathroom or getting a drink of water. By Sunday evening he had finished laying the bricks. All that was left to do was to cap the wall with some flat terra-cotta tiles. That could wait till the following weekend. He stood in the twilight, admiring his work and his newly acquired talent. Finally, he came into the house to eat supper and then to listen to his Sunday night radio programs.

During construction, Mom's critical eye had spotted one red brick that was darker than the others were. She knew that complaining to Dad would have been pointless. He would never have torn out bricks to replace the offending one. As Dad left for work the next morning, he gave an approving glance at his handiwork. Yep, he was an acceptable bricklayer, maybe even an accomplished one.

However, in the kitchen, cleaning up the breakfast dishes, was the Wicked Witch of the West. From the window over the sink, she looked out upon the new wall.

There was that damned dark, offensive brick. The annoyance it caused her the day before had now grown into a full-blown obsession. It *had* to go.

Fearing that I might try to stop her (fat chance), she waited till I left the house. Then she headed for the garage where she found a hammer and a screwdriver, Mom's standard substitute for a chisel. The offending brick was 10 or 12 courses below the top, so she picked out a brick in the top course directly above it, and began pecking out the mortar holding it in. It was not totally cured and chipped away easily enough. In a minute she had the first brick free. Compulsively, she removed brick after brick until she had removed about 50, leaving a "V" shaped gash in the wall. At the very bottom of the "V" was that dark red block she was after. Out it came, like a painful wisdom tooth. After smashing it with her hammer, she threw the pieces into the trashcan.

I expect Mom spent the day dreading what Dad might say or do. He could get ugly when pushed beyond a certain limit. I had noticed the "V" shaped surgery that afternoon as I went to the garage for something. I had no idea that Mom had done it, and just assumed Dad had, for some reason. I didn't even ask her about it. Later, I was in my bedroom when Dad came home. Suddenly he was shouting at the top of his voice, using words that I had only furtively heard spoken among the older boys at school. I stayed cowered in my bedroom. I was a little afraid of him even in the best of times, but when he exploded I was terrified.

The tantrum went on for maybe ten minutes. I never heard Mom's voice; she must have decided to just clam up and play it safe. Then Dad stomped out of the house, got into his car and sped off. We didn't see him again until Tuesday night. I have no idea where he spent the night. Eventually he got over it, and a few weeks later put the wall back together, albeit with a slight telltale sag where the "V" had been. Mom never criticized the sag.

DAD'S OLD OBLIGATION

Dad had never been able to repay Aunt Mina for the money she had loaned him to start a newsstand back in the late 20's. Being very miserly, she added interest to the debt every year. Interest in those days was high, so the amount had increased substantially. To settle the debt, Mom signed over one of our rentals to her. I'm sure Dad was relieved. He must have realized he could never pay her back. Mom would have never been that generous on Dad's account, except it was to repay her closest sister.

Dad wasn't a deadbeat; he just had no discipline or know-how when it came to handling money. In fact, he was a very honorable person. If he said he would do something, you could rely on it being done. He was just the opposite of Mom in this regard. Dad was the most dependable person I knew. I honestly cannot remember him ever missing a day of work. I would have been more surprised if Dad missed a day of work than if the sun would have failed to come up. He would go to work when he was sick, had the flu, or a toothache. He never went to the doctor. Instead, he medicated himself using the U. S. Pharmacopeia book, which he had kept from the time he had worked as a pharmacist.

Well, I do recall one event when I was about six. Dad went into the garage, closed the doors, got into the car, and started the engine. After a while, Mom found him unconscious and called an ambulance. They took him to an emergency room, where he recovered. I never knew what that was all about. Mom would only say he had no intention of killing himself. He just wanted some attention. I have always believed that explanation, because if he were serious, he had a gun and access to cyanide from work.

NO SMOKING

Aunt Mina was addicted to smoking. On one of her frequent visits, she told Mom it was an expensive, filthy habit and she hated it. She said she had tried many times to stop, but sooner or later would always cave in to the addiction. I was in the room while this conversation was going on. She turned to me and said, "Mickey, if you don't take up smoking until you are 21, I'll give you my house on Alston Street." Even though I was 15 or 16 at the time, I still viewed myself as a kid. I had no desire to rush into the world of adulthood, and I never had any urge to smoke. I said, "Sounds like a good deal, Aunt Miney." I never did take up smoking, and for that I will always be grateful to Aunt Miney.

YERMO VISIT—CA. 1942

Sometime during the early war years, 1941 or 1942, Aunt Mina moved from Las Vegas to Yermo, California. This was a small town, population under 200, located in the desert near Barstow. It was a "railroad town," but it did have a restaurant in the depot, and that was where Aunt Mina worked.

One Easter vacation, Aunt Mina invited me to stay with her for the week. Sounded like fun to me, so I accepted. She didn't have room in her cramped quarters for me, so she got some old, retired desert rat who lived in a small shack to put me up.

He had spent his life as a prospector, but he never discovered much of anything—just enough to eke out a bare existence. His skin was like leather, and he had a sore on his nose that drained continuously. He was constantly blotting it with a large bandana. I learned many months later that it was cancer and that it eventually killed him.

I would walk over to the depot restaurant every morning for breakfast, then I'd spend much of the day exploring along the tracks, looking for rocks and minerals, especially for anything that had fallen off ore cars. At that time, I was into mineralogy. I had traded Melvin Lee the treasured specimen I had of a dog's skull for his mineral collection, and I had learned to use chemical tests to identify the various minerals.

One day I was wandering about the depot when I discovered they had a small library. It was for employees such as my aunt. I found a book on minerals there. It listed dozens of minerals, giving all their compositions, densities, colors, crystal types, etc. Boy, did I need that book! I got Aunt Mina to check it out for me. In a small general store nearby, I bought a spiral notebook, in which I planned to copy down most of its information.

My aunt had a small desk in her room that she told me I could use, so I set to it. I'd spend hour after hour, sitting there like a medieval monk. Mina was a heavy smoker and the room reeked with smoke deposits. After a couple of hours I would develop a "sick" headache. Apparently everything in the room—walls, curtains, furniture, etc—were coated with tobacco chemicals. She lived in this toxic chamber.

In spite of this, my compulsion drove me on until after a few days I had copied what I needed from the book. The ironic thing was that after I got home, every time I tried to use the notes I had so laboriously taken, I'd get that awful sick headache again. All that work had been a waste; damn Pavlov and his dog!

CALICO TREK

One day, toward the end of my stay, I told my aunt that I wanted to walk up to Calico. It was a silver mining ghost town of the late 1800's. I had been there a couple of years before with my parents on one of their weekend trips to the desert.

Early the next morning, off I started up this dusty, dirt road. I had walked maybe a mile when some guy in a pickup came by and gave me a lift. When we got to the old ruins, I ventured out on my own. I was interested in exploring around in the old mine diggings, hoping to find some minerals for my collection. I soon located one of the mine entrances. I couldn't go very far in—maybe 300 or 400 feet—before it got too dark see without a light. As usual, I hadn't planned that far ahead.

While I was rummaging around, I did come up with two keepers. First, I found a page from an old 1890's newspaper. It had strange ads for patented inventions, corsets, funny looking dresses, and various patent medicines. The irony was that after 50 years in the mine it was in perfect condition, but after I took it home it began turning yellow within a week and after a couple of months it was ruined and I threw it out.

The other find was a silver nugget. Well actually, it was a nugget of horn silver (silver chloride). You wouldn't know from its appearance that it contained any silver. However, its density gave it away. Back in the 1880's, it probably fell off a railed pushcart they used to bring out the ore. Because it looked just like any other rock, no one had noticed it since. I put it in my pocket, and by the time I got home the surface had developed a nice silvery shine from being rubbed against the cloth.

Many years later, Knott's Berry Farm bought the ghost town and made a tourist attraction out of it.

UNCLE GEORGE

A man named George Sicks came into the depot restaurant every day for his meals. He didn't work for the railroad like most. Rather, he was sort of a wheeler-dealer, always looking for a get-rich-quick scheme. Well, he and Aunt Mina became acquainted and my dear naive aunt began telling George about her savings and her real estate. By then Mom had signed over the two houses on Alston Street to her. I'm sure George's eyes widened and his mouth watered for the carrot that Aunt Mina was dangling in front of him. In short order, they were married. Mina was 48 at the time, as I remember. She quit her job—the only good thing from this marriage—and they moved to Yuma, Arizona.

George knew of some land with oil drilling equipment and partially developed wells on it. He had convinced himself that if he could come up with some money he could buy the land, find oil, and get rich. Well, he convinced Aunt Mina to sell one of her houses and turn the money over to him. Naturally, he ran out of money before he found any oil. So he persuaded her to sell her other house, which she foolishly did. He blew that money on dry wells too.

That ended any possibility of my being given either house for not smoking, but she had given me a big favor, even so. During this time, my friend Kenny Thompson, who was eager to become an adult, had taken up smoking and was trying to get me to begin. I would always say I didn't want to queer the offer my aunt had made me. As a result, I got through those vulnerable years, and never did take up smoking.

George was a heavy-set, weather-beaten, desert-rat type. Being macho was important to him, and he smoked big black cigars to support the image. He and Mina had been married only a few years when he developed cancer of the throat. He refused treatment because he was a Seventh Day Adventist. He didn't last long, and Aunt Mina was on her own again with no assets. In the early 50's she moved in with Mom. Dad had died by then.

Aunt Mina was a two-to-three-pack-a-day smoker. Over the years she developed a terrible cough. At times she would get into a coughing spasm and turn blue before she could catch her breath. One day Mom found her dead in the living room. She had died of a stroke.

_____TEENAGE TRIBULATIONS

✦

The Worm Convolutes—1938
A Perfect Crime
Goody, Goody
A Brand New School—1938
Settling In
The Cast

THE WORM CONVOLUTES—1938

I was an ideal kid, by the standards of the day, all through grammar school. I was polite, obedient—well, most of the things in the Boy Scout oath: Trustworthy, Loyal, Helpful, Friendly, Courteous, Kind, Obedient, Cheerful, Friendly, Brave, Clean and Reverent—and, I did what a lot of the "good" kids did: I joined the Boy Scouts when I was 12.

My parents thought it would be a good program for me. Dad sprung for a uniform. Mom took me downtown to get it. The one she picked out was two sizes too big, the standard practice in those days. Then she dragged me to a photo studio and had the oversized thing photographed, hat drooping into my eyes, shirt hanging over my knuckles, and pants wadded up on top of my shoes.

I attended meetings regularly, memorized the Boy Scout's motto, and generally was a dependable—if mediocre—scout. I was assigned to the "Beaver Patrol." Things progressed nicely. I earned my Tenderfoot badge and read the "Boy Scout's Manual" as if it were a modern-day Bible. It was full of wonderful advice such as "refraining from self-abuse" because it would reduce the hormones needed for you to grow up into a strong man. Of course every boy wants to grow up to be strong and manly, but good grief, they didn't seem to know what they were dealing with here!

Charley Heckman had managed to get several members of his gang to join the troop, and persuaded the scoutmaster to form a new patrol for them: the Mustang Patrol. Naturally, Charley was made patrol leader. His "gang in the scouts" was only kids, of course, but still they carried an aura of toughness. Nobody crossed them. To promote this image, they played extra rough when we engaged in outside games such as "Capture the Flag." Smaller kids often showed up at the staff's area for treatment of a bloody nose or other minor injury. Being a timid, non-violent, insecure kid, I tended to avoid the Mustangs as much as possible.

THE PERFECT CRIME

I had a close-encounter with Charley on a weekend outing to the Rio Hondo Boy Scout Camp. The camp's directors had provided two-man pup tents for everyone. They made assignments randomly, and I was paired with Charley. In the afternoon, all the kids set up their tents about fifty yards away from the council area where everyone sat around the council fire at night and sang an endless repertory of songs. The tents were arranged in a circle around our troop's staff tent so the Scout Master and his assistants could keep an eye on us. The staff tent was much larger. It consisted of several pup tents configured so that one corner of each was secured to the top of a common pole stuck in the sand and the other corners were staked to the ground to form a large circular enclosure supported by this pole. The result was rather like Arab tents in desert movies. The staff had hung all kinds of paraphernalia from the pole, including a lantern, several canteens, some mess kits, and several metal drinking mugs.

That night at the campfire, while everyone was singing "She'll Be Comin' 'Round the Mountain," Charley came over and sat down beside me. He said, "Follow me. I want to show you something." Apprehensively, I got up and disappeared into the darkness with him. While the troops sang on, we quietly made our way to "our" tent. Charley dug into the sand at the back of the tent and produced a coil of clothesline rope. It seemed Charley always had some rope handy. He was unusually innovative in using it, and quite expert at tying knots. He explained to me that we were going to take one end of it and tie a loop around the bottom of the staff's tent pole. Then we would cover the loop with sand so it couldn't be seen, and run the rope back to our tent, burying it as we went. I have always been a follower, never a leader, so I did as he directed. Besides, it was exciting. After we strung the rope and hid it well, we snuck back to join the off-key singing. We hadn't been missed.

It was winter, but being in California, the temperature was probably only about 35-40 degrees. Although not bitter, it was humid and bone-chilling. A light fog was coming in and settling on everybody and everything. The camp directors decided to call it a night. They said a benediction and sent us off to our tents. Everyone scurried around, laid out their sleeping bags and crawled inside. It was dark, except for the light from the lantern hanging from the staff's tent pole. The lantern became less and less illuminating as the fog continued to roll in. Finally, everyone bedded down and the lantern was turned off. For another 20-30 minutes we heard the usual buzz-buzz of kids talking. Finally, that died down; all was quiet and pitch-black.

Charley and I dared not speak. We just lay still as panthers crouched in the dark, waiting for the right time to strike. After another ten minutes or so, Charley nudged me with his elbow: the signal. We grabbed our end of the rope and pulled as hard and fast as we could. Crash! Clang! Bang! All sorts of racket came from the direction of the staff's tent. Then, muffled yells totally inappropriate for Boy Scout leaders emanated from under the collapsed wet, cold structure. I had only recently learned the meaning of the most taboo of all words, and here it was, being yelled at the top of somebody's lungs in a Boy Scout camp.

Everyone was awake now. Flashlight beams appeared from several pup tents and made their way in the direction of the commotion. Charley, under cover of the confusion, carefully rolled up his rope and buried it at the rear of our tent. Then calmly, with our flashlights, we joined the others to survey the results. It was the perfect crime!

GOODY, GOODY

A surprising number of boys, upon reaching the age of 12, wouldn't join the Boy Scouts because they saw it as a "goody, goody, two shoes" thing. However, goody-goody was no problem for me. I was a natural at it. Still, some dark clouds were forming on the horizon.

I discovered that male hormones were beginning to flow, creating strong urges that were totally in conflict with being angelic. Also, I had acquired new interests, such as science stuff, which resulted in "experiments" that often disrupted the calm of adults. I was uncomfortable around girls and probably sublimated my sexual drives into my pursuits of science.

I continued to have the countenance of a "nice" kid, but in actuality I had become two people: the old "nice" kid which was maintained and shown to the adult world; and now, this new obsessed kid that was becoming interested in doing things that were unacceptable and had to be hidden from parents, teachers, and other adults. I wasn't even aware of the double personality. It just naturally evolved.

You've read about how stunned people are when they learn that someone they thought of as a nice person gets arrested for murder, or perhaps even for being a serial killer. His acquaintances may say, "He was such a polite fellow…seemed so normal. I wonder what could have happened to him." I never understood their confusion. Such occurrences always made sense to me. I could almost identify with those criminals—not the killing of course, but the successful hiding of the unacceptable part of their personality. With this psychological asset, I moved on to junior high.

A BRAND NEW SCHOOL—CA. 1938

Our school district built two new junior high schools, due to overcrowding. Since the new schools had plenty of capacity, they took the 7th and 8th grades from the area grammar schools, along with the 9th and 10th grades from the only high school in the district: Montebello High. As a result, I became a seventh grader in the opening year of the new Eastmont Junior High. It was farther from home—over a mile—but at that age, I didn't mind the walk. A kid had borrowed my bike and gotten a stick caught in the front wheel. It stripped out all of the spokes. It was a couple of years before I had enough money to get it fixed.

SETTLING IN

These were exciting years for me. I went to different rooms for each class. The classes were taught by teachers who specialized in their subject. Subjects I liked were science, math and gym. Ones I didn't like were history, English and, oddly, shop. School "clubs" would meet once a week. I joined the Science Club. I got to show the class how to make fireworks. The next 2 years, I joined the Radio Club. By then I knew more than the teacher did about how radios operated. My final year I joined a Photography Club. I used it to make my science fair entry that year—a group of pictures taken through a microscope.

My obsession for electricity broadened to include science in general. I became a science geek, except that word wasn't in use yet. Most kids, especially girls, seemed to have a lot of trouble with science. I was pulling down straight "A's" in math and science, so I was frequently approached for help. It did a world of good for my feelings of self-worth. However, I was too naive to see they were just using me. I was too much of a geek for them to take any other interest in me.

This began a personal dichotomy in which my technical side was nurtured obsessively and my social side was allowed to atrophy. I felt comfortable, secure, and even a little superior in situations involving technical matters, but increasingly, I felt inadequate and awkward in social situations. I never went to school dances or performed in school plays. I never developed romantic relationships with girls and never learned to understand them. This led to increasing sexual frustration, since I had no idea of how to approach or appeal to girls. Most of my beliefs about females came from the distorted views of my mother.

In spite of the psychological damage going on, I was embarking on a very pleasurable period in my life. These years were full of discovery, excitement, and fulfillment.

THE CAST

During my years in junior high and high school, my closest friends consisted of a small group of rather odd kids. None could have been classified as entirely normal. Almost all were from one-child families, and this collection was particularly strange in that none of them cared much for any of the others. They didn't hang out with each other, except when I was involved. Let me introduce them to you...

Charles Heckman: I knew him from grammar school. He was a badly-spoiled only child, almost totally amoral, and willing to do just about anything—right or wrong. If you loaned him money, you would probably never see it again. He shoplifted anything he wanted, even though he got a generous allowance and always seemed to have spending money. His dad was a salesman for Pennzoil and made more money than most families in the neighborhood. They were the only 2-car family I knew of.

Charley's gift was that he was not a boxed-in thinker. He could dream up ideas I would never have considered or even imagined. Many included unacceptable, or even illegal activities. While still in grammar school, he had become adept at using rope and knots to accomplish many of his misdeeds.

Charley invented a device for breaking and entering. It was an "L" shaped piece of sheet metal that he used to open locked doors. He knew more about locks and keys than anyone I ever knew. He learned how to make a paraffin mold of a borrowed key and then to make a key from the mold. He knew how to bug a room, and bugged his parent's bedroom to learn what they were going to get him for Christmas. I was fascinated by his success at that and tried the same thing, but I heard nothing. Just as well!

After stealing some telephone equipment from an empty building, Charley fashioned himself a linesman's phone. He would climb a telephone pole, connect the linesman's phone to a neighbor's line and place long distance calls on their bill. To implement the pole climbing, he designed and built a pair of linesmen's climbing leggings, complete even with spikes.

Charley was fascinated with firearms, although as a kid he never owned anything other than a .22 caliber pump action rifle and a BB gun. However, due mostly to his innovations, he and I fashioned crude pistols, shotguns, and cannons using pipefittings and homemade gunpowder. Together, we learned a lot about explosives and bomb making. Later, as an adult, he founded the C & H Hand-loading Equipment Co. that manufactured equipment for firearms enthusiasts.

Kenneth Thompson: Kenny was easily the smartest of any of us. He probably bordered on genius. It's hard to figure where his intelligence came from. He was an only child of unexceptional parents. His father was a cop for the Los Angeles County Sheriff's Department; his mother was a typically average housewife; and other family members that I met were all ordinary as well.

I met Kenny when we were both taking General Science in Junior High. We both were getting A's in the class. His strong suit was chemistry. Mine was physics: electricity, radio, and optics. Kenny was hard to get to know, kind of standoffish. He lived about five miles from my place, which slowed the process of getting acquainted. One day after school he invited me to follow him home on my bike. He lived in a small frame house in a rural area that had been subdivided into half-acre lots. He and his dad had built a little shack on the back of their lot that Kenny used as a laboratory. I was impressed. Here was a kid my age, 14, with his own laboratory! He had a surprising variety of chemicals, glassware, and other apparatus. We quickly became close friends.

Our expertise hardly overlapped at all. I accepted his superior knowledge of chemistry, and he of my knowledge of electricity, optics and such. Except for biology, in which neither of us excelled, we nicely complemented each other's knowledge of science.

Kenny never finished high school. It totally bored him. When he was 17 (he looked much older), he got a job as a chemist at Gooch Labs in Los Angeles. He knew enough chemistry to pass as a graduate chemist and held the job for several years.

Jack Gretta: Jack was another only child. His mother was a wonderful person. She was sweet, caring, an organist for the local church, and one of the best mothers I ever knew. His dad was friendly, but sort of a wimp; a small, frail man, whose job was servicing an insurance debit for Prudential. In those days, insurance men would come around each month to collect premiums on policies they had sold. These premiums were usually about fifty cents or a dollar.

Although the family didn't have much, they spoiled Jack rotten. I remember once when he wanted to install a model engine test stand in his bedroom, he drilled holes in the hardwood flooring for the mounting bolts. Then he routinely spilled nitromethane on the floor, totally ruining the finish. That seemed to be okay with his parents; mine would have killed me.

Jack was rejected by almost everyone. At best, he was a "C" student. He often got "D's" or "F's," was lousy at sports, and had a sullen personality. No one wanted to be associated with him.

His parents sent him to summer camp one year. My parents sent me that year, too. Jack didn't fit in at all. He wouldn't swim, wouldn't do leather or bead handicraft—although I'm sure he could have done them better than most—and wouldn't sing at the campfires. It was the camp's practice for the counselors to present an achievement badge to selected kids each night around the campfire. By the end of the week, every kid was supposed to have one to wear when his parents came to take him home. Jack *never* got one.

However, Jack was a genius with his hands. He could make or fix anything. One time someone gave him a radio that had been in a house fire. It was a charred mess, a total loss, or so you'd think. But Jack cannibalized parts from other junked radios and amazingly got it working. Mind you, he didn't know anything about radio or electrical theory. These were academic areas requiring reading and studying, which Jack avoided if possible.

Jack was even better at mechanical things. He could repair almost any gasoline engine, electric motor, generator, or pump. He became a master at building gas-engine powered model planes. He even built a model pulsejet driven plane (like the German V-1 buzz bomb) that he flew from a U-control wire. It could be heard almost a mile away.

Jack was fascinated with aircraft. After he served a couple of years in the Navy, he built his own plane and got it FAA certified. He taught himself to fly, got a license, and eventually became a flight instructor and an FAA inspector. He joined Wheeler Aircraft in Connecticut, and the last time I saw him he was their vice-president.

Harold Lane: Everyone knew him as "Bud." He, too, was an only child. His father was a behind-the-scenes-politician and apparently raised Bud in the "Good ole Boy" philosophy of you-scratch-my-back-and-I'll-scratch-yours. His father had an aversion about working for anyone and was always looking for ways to make money, using his wits. He operated a dance marathon in the 30's. He "invented" a restaurant that was shaped like a large tamale. It was located in East Los Angeles and became something of a landmark. California had a number of such novelty restaurants. The Brown Derby was the most famous. One was shaped like a coffee pot, and several were shaped like fruit.

[Caution—Name drop ahead]

Bud's dad finally made it big when he stumbled upon a very dapper and distinguished-looking man who ran a haberdashery in Belvedere Gardens. His name was Chet Hollifield, and Bud's dad convinced him to run for the 19th Congressional District. Chet looked great on the political posters, so not surprisingly, he was elected.

For years, Bud's dad ran that congressional district from behind the scenes. He supplied the brains. Chet was the icon. Chet became head of a congressional Atomic Energy Committee and traveled to the Pacific to witness the Bikini Atomic Bomb tests. He took home movies and obtained copies of official footage from the Navy and the Atomic Energy Commission. Because Bud and I had passed out circulars during his election, we were invited to a private showing at the congressman's home in Montebello. I was stunned by those movies. They made my bomb-making attempts seem pitiful.

Bud was of average intelligence, but not very original or clever, and contributed little to our activities. Bud's mom, "Pete," as she was called, was a neat-freak and was strict about kids messing up her house. Therefore, Bud's place was never the center of any of our activities.

However, Bud was always anxious to join in and would do most anything you'd ask of him, but unless I lobbied the others on his behalf, he usually wasn't included. For the most part, he was included only when we decided to build, transport, and set off a bomb—an activity requiring manual labor that Bud eagerly provided.

Melvin Lee: Melvin was a Jew from one of only two Jewish families in our neighborhood. Melvin seemed to me like an only child, but he actually had an older brother who was already grown. His family was quite Orthodox and never encouraged any Gentile kids to come around.

However, I endeared myself to his family on an occasion when some ornery kids "pantsed" Melvin and ran his britches up the school flagpole. He was extremely embarrassed and hid in some shrubs. I went to his house and asked his mom for another pair of pants. After that, I was always welcome. They would invite me to stay for meals and take me along on outings that often included other family members from across town. However, it was made very clear to me, when I once took an interest in one of his cousins, that getting involved with her was a totally unacceptable thing. I knew nothing about Jews and their ways and was completely confused.

Melvin loved biology, and to some extent, minerals. These were our main links. He kept a collection of snakes in his bedroom, including a rattler. On one occasion he traded his entire mineral collection to me for a dog's skull that I had bleached and used as a decoration on my bedroom shelf.

Melvin was never drafted because he had a chronic ear problem. While the rest of my buddies and I were in the service, he went to UCLA and got a degree in herpetology.

Lynn Sarkissian: Lynn was, yep, an only child. He lived in a nice house in a newer part of town called Bella Vista with his mother. His father owned a raisin-grape ranch near Fresno. His parents were either separated or divorced. People rarely admitted to divorce in those days. In any case, plenty of money seemed to be available for Lynn to pursue his interests.

He designed and built prize-winning model planes that were marvels of detail. I remember one bomber he built with pilot and co-pilot controls that operated the various wing and tail surfaces. It had landing gears that retracted and bomb bays with bombs that it could release.

Our common interest was pyrotechnics. Lynn had learned how to make many different kinds of fireworks, including aerial starbursts. He was way ahead of

Charley and me in powder formulations. It was from Lynn that we learned how to make *good* gunpowder. I taught Lynn how to make pipe bombs—a fair exchange.

_____THE SKY's THE LIMIT

✦

Acid Indigestion—ca. 1939
Try, Try Again
Blackouts

ACID INDIGESTION—CA. 1939

For several years Charley and I developed and pursued many interests together. One of the earliest was a fascination with balloons. The 30's were the heyday of lighter-than-air vehicles. Both the Germans and Americans had built monster airships such as the Hindenburg and the Akron. That gave us the idea to make balloons that would rise and carry something (like a message).

Small balloons cost a penny apiece, and larger ones were a two for a nickel. We went to the dime store, bought five penny balloons and two nickel ones. We knew from the Hindenburg disaster that lighter-than-air vehicles were filled with hydrogen, so we began to consider how to get some hydrogen to fill our balloons.

Charley got a chemistry textbook that described how to make a hydrogen generator. This consisted of a flask, a thistle tube (a kind of small funnel), a rubber stopper with two holes, and some glass and rubber tubing. We had none of these things.

However, Charley's next-door neighbor worked in a factory that had a small chemical lab. Charley presented our problem to his neighbor, and in a couple of days the guy brought home enough glassware, rubber tubing, and stoppers to make the generator.

Next, the chemistry book said to put some zinc metal in the flask, add hydrochloric acid, and presto, hydrogen would form. We went to the drugstore and discovered they had none of these items. Being new at this chemical business, we had no idea where to find such materials. Now, it was up to our resourcefulness…well, mostly Charley's.

I did contribute the idea that common dry cells used in flashlights had a case made of zinc metal and I knew where an endless supply of them could be found—right behind the police station. Still, getting hydrochloric acid was a problem. Ah, ha! The answer was right there in the chemistry book.

It said hydrochloric acid could be made using the same apparatus, except the ingredients were sulfuric acid and ordinary table salt. Salt, we had. Charley knew that fire extinguishers—the soda-acid type—had a small bottle of concentrated sulfuric acid inside. So, true to Charley's character, we broke into Montebello Park Grammar school one weekend, took apart an extinguisher, and stole the bottle of acid. I had some misgivings about the fact that now the fire extinguisher wouldn't work, but Charley just ignored me. I meekly went along.

Back at Charley's place, we began setting up the apparatus in his bedroom, when a closer reading of the book indicated that for this reaction to proceed it required heat. Well, among the chemical equipment Charley had acquired was a Bunsen burner. Without a moment's hesitation, Charley grabbed up the flask, funnel, tubing, Bunsen burner, acid and salt, and headed for the living room. Here was a fireplace with a gas jet—exactly what was needed to operate the burner. His mom was out somewhere, and we decided to proceed with the project.

The fireplace was at one end of the living room. In front of it was a small brick apron about 4 feet wide and 2 feet deep. Around this brick apron and covering the entire floor was a *new*, solid green, wall-to-wall carpet. This was the first wall-to-wall carpet I had ever seen in a home.

Charley, with some help from me, began setting up the apparatus on the brick apron. The main reaction flask was supported on a ring-stand with the burner beneath. A glass tube and the small, funnel-like thistle tube were pushed through holes in the rubber stopper. The stopper was then pressed tightly into the neck of the flask that contained the salt. Rubber tubing was connected from the glass tube in the stopper to another glass tube immersed into a second flask that contained water.

The directions were to pour enough concentrated sulfuric acid into the thistle tube to cover the pile of salt, then light the Bunsen burner to heat the contents of the flask, producing hydrogen chloride gas. The gas would run through the rubber hose to the second flask and bubble through the water, forming hydrochloric acid.

Well, Charley—never one to worry about consequences—torched off the burner. Soon the contents of the flask were boiling, and hydrogen chloride gas was bubbling through the water in the second flask.

THEN SUDDENLY the rubber tubing, which had formed a nice arch between the two flasks, got hot and collapsed. A kink formed at the outlet of the reaction flask. Pressure built up instantly. The only outlet for the pressure was through the thistle tube. The bottom end of this was immersed in the sulfuric acid. The pressure caused most of the acid to shoot up and out of the thistle tube, hitting the ceiling and instantly turning it dark brown. Then acid began to drip from the ceiling onto the apron *and* the carpet. We could do nothing to stop it. It just kept dripping! Big holes began to form in the carpet. In 30 seconds I'd seen enough and bolted for home.

A couple of weeks later, I found enough courage to return to the scene. When Charley let me into the house, I spotted his mom sitting in a living room chair with the damaged end of the carpet over her lap. She was meticulously sewing in loops of green yarn, in a hopeless attempt to salvage her new carpet. We didn't speak.

TRY, TRY AGAIN

Well, as much of a disaster as that was, we weren't about to give up our fantasy of lighter-than-air flight. After all, we had a whole dime invested in balloons. However, we did give up the idea of generating hydrogen for them. We thought about using helium, but had no idea where to get any, and knew it couldn't be generated like hydrogen.

Then an ingenious idea came to mind: natural gas! It was piped right into the house; we had an endless supply! My house had gas jets in every room to allow the use of small portable heaters, so in the privacy of my bedroom we connected the rubber tubing to a jet, tied a balloon to the end of it, and turned on the gas. The balloon filled out slightly, but then stopped; the gas pressure was not strong enough to force the balloon to expand. However, we thought of a neat solution. My mom had a nasal pump that consisted of a simple rubber syringe. We cut the rubber tubing between the jet and the balloon and inserted a ¼" brass 'T.' (My dad had an amazing collection of pipefittings.) On one leg of the 'T' we connected the syringe. With a balloon tied to the far end of the tubing on the other leg of the 'T,' we began forcing gas into the balloon by first kinking the tube from the jet and squeezing the syringe. Then we kinked the tube to the balloon (to hold the gas in the balloon), un-kinked the other tube (letting more gas into the syringe), and repeated the process until the balloon was filled.

We filled and launched all of our penny balloons that day. It was a clear fall day with some high cirrus clouds. Totally fascinated, we'd watch a balloon ascend and become a black dot and disappear. We filled up the larger nickel balloons and tied notes to each that read, "If found, please send post card to Mickey McCoy,

6150 Northside Dr., Los Angeles, California and tell where it was found." Off they went!

We pooled our resources and bought more balloons. Launching the balloons was great fun, but the kinking and un-kinking was a real pain. Before long, Charley came up with the best idea yet. He reasoned that if we installed a bicycle tube valve on each side of the 'T' fitting, we could eliminate the tedious kinking and un-kinking procedure.

Charley, being an expert at making guns for our childhood gang wars, had collected a bunch of old inner tubes to cut into rubber bands for ammunition. These were piled in a corner of his garage. We extracted two valve stems, removed the springs from them (so the low-pressure natural gas would flow through), and installed one at the inlet and another at the outlet of the 'T' fitting. This worked just fine.

We launched the rest of our balloons—about 10—each with a note attached. Much to my surprise and delight, I received a postcard about a week later. It was from a woman in Covina, about 16 miles east of us. She said that when she had gone outside Sunday morning the balloon was snagged on her chicken coop. That indicated it had been up for 5 days.

We didn't realize it at the time, but the reason it stayed up so long was because we had used natural gas: methane. If we had used hydrogen, as first planned, it probably wouldn't have stayed up more than about a day. The hydrogen molecule is very tiny. It would have escaped through the pores of the rubber much faster than the larger methane molecules.

Over the next couple of years, we perfected the technique of clustering balloons. That allowed us to lift bigger payloads. These loads consisted of lightweight gliders that we suspended from the balloons by a thread. We attached a slow-burning fuse to the thread, causing it to burn in half, thus releasing the glider after a few minutes of ascent.

It took some research and many failures to develop the fuse. The main problems were weight and burning rate. Our available fuses were pulled from firecrackers (which burned much too fast) or were homemade with gunpowder twisted into a strip of tissue paper. These burned slower, but not slow enough, and furthermore, they were heavy.

Finally, one of us thought of using yarn. It turned out that soft cotton yarn worked perfectly.

We had great sport in sending these crafts up. The gliders, when released, would sail around over the neighborhood and we would chase after them on our bikes for blocks to recover them.

BLACKOUTS

The war with Japan was underway and the nation was gripped in fear that Japan would bomb the West Coast. The government had ordered nightly blackouts and had set up searchlights and anti-aircraft batteries up and down the coast. These pencils of light pierced the blackened sky and on a few occasions, when the people who monitored the equipment imagined they saw an enemy plane, they would shoot a few rounds at it. In support of this effort, they set up a system of neighborhood "block wardens" to enforce the blackout order.

Mr. Dane, who lived across the street, was our warden. He wore a warden's helmet and walked the neighborhood streets, looking for cracks of light shining through the windows of houses. He took his job seriously, and if as much as a sliver of light were spotted, he'd bang on the front door and order the occupant to fix it. His body language revealed that he was proud of his authority.

I suppose it was only a matter of time before a mind as devious as Charley's would come up with the next devilment. Charley suggested we launch a cluster of balloons at night and ignite it (after all, the balloons were filled with natural gas). It might cause a big commotion.

As we developed the plan, we first had to come up with an igniter; our old yarn fuse would never torch off the balloons. However, the solution was easy. We made a small tissue paper packet, like a miniature tea bag, filled it with flash powder, and ran the yarn fuse into that. It worked every time.

Charley, always anxious to push the limits, also suggested that since we would have some unused payload to spare, why not add a few balloons to the cluster that were filled with oxygen? Although they wouldn't add to the lift, they wouldn't weigh much either, and they *really* ought to enhance the resulting fireball.

We knew how to generate oxygen, using hydrogen peroxide and lye, and had previously attempted to increase our shot-putting distances by breathing our generated oxygen before each toss. It seemed to add a foot or two to our distances.

How could I resist the idea of using oxygen to enhance the fireball? That was pure genius at work. We proceeded to assemble the bundle. It consisted of seven nickel-size balloons filled with natural gas and three with oxygen, plus the yarn fuse and the "tea bag" igniter.

An important part of our plan was to wait for Mr. Dane to make his nightly rounds and time the release of the cluster so he would be over at our end of the block when it exploded. Charley hid in the backyard with the balloons and I stood out on the sidewalk watching for Mr. Dane to come down the street. Because of the blackout, it was hard to see much. A little light from a third quarter moon and the searchlights scanning about was just enough that I could make out Mr. Dane when he was a couple of houses away.

I gave the signal to Charley, who lit the fuse and let the contraption go. As it moved up over the house, I could see the red glow of the yarn fuse. My heart was pounding. The tiny glow rose higher and higher and drifted over the street where our proud warden strode.

All of a sudden, night became day, accompanied by a low boom like a blow on an enormous base drum. Then all was black again. Mr. Dane's jaw fell open as he gawked into the sky. He started back down the street, stopped, then headed for one of the houses, stopped, appeared totally befuddled, and finally took off running for his own house, no doubt to get to his phone to report an invasion.

In no time, emergency vehicles began showing up at Mr. Dane's place—two police cars and a fire truck—with sirens blaring. Neighbors began pouring out onto the street. More searchlights appeared in the sky. We mingled with the crowd, but shrugged our shoulders and looked as puzzled as anyone.

_____THE UNION PACIFIC

◆

A Great Playground
The Donkey Engine—ca. 1939
The Daisy Chain—ca. 1940
Terror on the Trestle—ca. 1942

A GREAT PLAYGROUND

The Union Pacific tracks provided the dividing line between civilization and open country for our neighborhood. One set of tracks was used for both east and west traffic. They started eastward from downtown Los Angeles and passed south within a half mile of my house.

"Across the tracks" were open fields where we went to shoot rabbits, birds and other helpless critters. This area was a great place to test our latest bomb designs without ruffling the neighbors' feathers, and the railway itself was a source of endless fascination.

THE DONKEY ENGINE—CA. 1939

A large area, zoned for industry, was located a couple of miles to the west of my neighborhood. Factories had located there to have access to the railroad line. Willard Battery Company was nearest to my house, and Goodrich Tire & Rubber Company was about a half-mile further west.

A switch had been installed on the track's main line (let's call it the main line switch) to provide a spur for servicing these two factories. Along this spur were several more switches (we'll call them spur switches). The first of these diverted freight cars to Willard Battery, and further west, three more were provided to direct freight cars to various parts of the Goodrich Tire & Rubber plant.

A small steam engine would be dispatched from the Los Angeles train yards to move freight cars about the loading docks whenever a factory was loading materials for shipping. This little engine was called a "donkey."

Charley was about 14 years old, and I was a year younger. One day we were playing along the tracks. In the distance, we spotted a donkey engine coming down the tracks. It was coming from the train yards, but moving slowly. We reckoned it was headed for the main line switch and then down the spur to one of the factories.

Charley had experience with train switches, based on a rather elaborate Lionel electric train set he owned. It had remotely operated switches that occasionally would hang up halfway, switching neither to the right nor to the left. When this happened, the train would derail at the switch.

With this invaluable knowledge, Charley's devious mind conceived the idea of setting the spur switch halfway between straight-ahead (to Goodrich) and to the right (to Willard) to derail the donkey.

Charley rummaged around the field until he found a suitable rock, ran over to the first spur switch, and started banging on its padlock. We had gained experience with railroad locks before and found them easy to break. In a few seconds he had the lock off and he was pulling the lever to operate the switch. When he had it rotated halfway, he called to me, "Let's go fix the next one too."

The donkey was still slowly puffing its way toward the main-line switch. I chased after Charley to the next spur switch (toward Goodrich). He handed me the rock, as if to say, "You're in this, too." So I banged away until the lock fell off. We set that switch halfway as well.

These switches were equipped with round flat steel discs mounted on a vertical shaft that acted as flags so the crew could tell which way the switch was set. When set for straight through, a green disc would be seen. When the lever was pulled to set the switch to turn, the shaft would rotate 90 degrees, and a red disc would be shown. With the switch set halfway between, as we had done, the engineer would see a partly red and partly green display.

I would have thought the engineer would simply look toward the switch, see that it looked odd, get out and set it right. Wrong. Charley had an intrinsic understanding of human behavior. All he said was, "Just watch."

So, hunkered down in the weeds, not far from our second sabotaged switch, we watched. After a while we could see the donkey stop on the main line. The fireman got out and operated the main-line switch (we hadn't touched that one). He waited for the engine to clear the switch, reset the switch, and got back aboard.

Here it came, backing up (because it had backed into the spur). The engineer was looking to the rear from one side, the fireman from the other. The tender (the car behind the engine that carries the engine's fuel oil) was leading the way.

Jeeze, I was getting jittery. All I could think of was getting out of there. The little donkey was clattering along about 10-15 miles an hour. It was almost to the first switch, where I fully expected it to stop because of the ambiguous display, but it *didn't*. One of them apparently looked at the flag, saw whatever color he expected to see, and continued. Charley was absolutely right!

Suddenly, we heard this sickening grinding of steel against steel and steel against granite (the roadbed). The tender's rear trucks (a group of 4 wheels) had derailed in the switch *between* the straight-ahead rails and the right-turn rails. The crew scrambled from the cab, looked at the derailed wheels, the tampered switch, and then the cuss words began to fly. I was almost peeing in my pants with fear. Charley, not surprisingly, was totally enjoying the show.

The engineer, after some deliberation, decided to try to pull the tender up onto the tracks by moving the donkey forward. They got into the cab, put the thing in forward, and slowly opened up the throttle. Steam spewed from the cylinders on each side. The donkey's four big driver-wheels squealed as they slipped on the rails, but bit-by-bit they gained traction and began to inch forward.

Again, there were all those horrible grinding sounds, but amazingly, the tender, after rocking precariously from one side to the other, climbed up onto the tracks. The fireman set the switch properly, hopped into the cab, and they were on their way again. They passed by us (lying in the weeds about 50 feet away) and might have seen us if they had looked, but they were occupied with the next switch en route to their destination.

I hate to ask you to believe that this whole scenario was repeated at the second spur switch, but I swear on my mother's grave, it was. Charley's insights regarding human nature were eerie. When we heard cussing again, we knew our victims were sufficiently distracted for us to snake our way through the grass to our bikes and escape.

THE DAISY CHAIN—CA. 1940

Playing along the tracks over the years, Charley and I had observed the relationship between the movement of the trains and the operation of semaphore block signals. The route along the tracks was divided into blocks, each about a mile long. A semaphore signal was placed at the entrance to each block. Its function was to notify engineers, by arms and lights, whether any rolling stock was on the tracks ahead. If something occupied the block immediately ahead, the semaphore arm would drop to a 90-degree angle and the light would turn red. However, if the obstacle was further up in the second block ahead, the semaphore arm would position itself at a 45-degree angle and the light would shine amber.

If an engineer saw a semaphore arm at 45 degrees (amber light), he would slow down, but was allowed to enter that block cautiously. As he moved through this "amber" block, he would eventually come to the next semaphore that would be indicating red, at which point he was under orders to stop his train and wait until the light turned amber, indicating that the equipment on the track had moved forward to the next block.

Normally, trains move along at cruising speed, seeing nothing but green lights because their schedules allow for adequate spacing between trains. The semaphore system is for safety purposes to prevent rear-ending a slow or disabled train (or other equipment).

Charley was unusually observant—and diabolical. He noticed that the mechanical movement of the semaphore arm caused the color of the light to change. The arm had three lenses (green, amber, and red) mounted on it, and as the arm moved to one of its three positions, the appropriate lens would move in front of the light source.

One day Charley climbed up one of the semaphores. The railroad had foolishly provided a ladder on each one for access by their maintenance people. He reached out, grabbed the semaphore arm and pulled it down to the red position. A small motor inside began to whine in an attempt to return the arm to its proper upright position, but Charley found he could hold the arm down against the motor's torque.

What Charley was doing was determining if it was possible to hold the arm down against the pull of the motor and how much force it would take. What *normal* kid would ever think of performing such a test? In the distance, he could see a train coming, so he released the arm and scrambled down the ladder. We waved innocently to the crew as the engine passed.

A couple of days later Charley began to implement his plan. He located a large rock. I expect it weighed about 25-30 pounds. Around it, he lashed a rope to form a sling and tied a loop on the loose end of the rope. Charley was clever at knots.

I was always nervous when we did the crazy things Charley dreamed up, but this time I was even more so. We waited until about 10 p.m., when it was totally dark. Charley was bigger and stronger than I was, so he opted to carry the rock on his bike. He tied it to the handlebars and off we went.

We arrived at the tracks by way of a dead-end road about fifty yards from the targeted signal. We trudged over to the semaphore, saw no train in sight, and began to climb the semaphore—Charley first, with me following behind, lugging up the rock. Charley pulled down the semaphore arm while I struggled to hoist the rock up so he could hang the loop over the end of the arm. When we were finally done, the large rock dangled from the projecting arm.

As we climbed down the ladder, we heard the motor groaning to return the arm to its proper position, but to no avail. The red light was glaring into the night. We waited—Charley with pleasurable anticipation, me trembling with apprehension.

Consider the amount of ingenuity involved in this effort. Charley had not only figured out a simple rig for setting a red light in order to stop a train, but he also conceived to do it in the dark, when the engine's crew could not see the rock dangling from the semaphore. Furthermore, he reasoned that the train would just sit there while they sent out maintenance people to see what the hell the problem was. And all during this delay, other trains would be stopped, one behind the other, at "red" blocks, which would form like a daisy chain back up the line. Near genius!

I would never have believed a demoniacal plan like this could work so well, but it did. Within an hour, the headlight of a train appeared on the horizon. Soon we could tell it was slowing down. It had entered the second block back, which was yellow. It slowly crawled forward until it was within about 50 feet of the semaphore—then stopped. It was a steam engine pulling a freight train.

We were hidden in the darkness near a dead-end road where our bikes were stashed, but we were close enough to the engine that we could hear the engineer and fireman talking loudly to hear each other over the sounds of the engine. We couldn't make out anything they were saying, but the inflections of their voices carried sounds of dismay and confusion.

By now, my trembling had progressed to mild shaking. Charley was enjoying every minute of the drama he had authored. I wanted to get out of there, but he absolutely insisted we stay. The rest of his plot was about to unfold. The engineer got out of the cab, walked toward the semaphore, looked up, but apparently couldn't see the rock. He climbed back into the cab. *Everybody* waited.

After a while, we saw another train's headlights approaching. Soon it had slowed down and stopped at the next semaphore up the track, which of course was red. Charley wasn't through yet. We kept out of sight for almost another hour, when way up the track we could see still another headlight coming. Now I *really* wanted to go. Finally, I rationalized that if they sent maintenance people out, they probably would come up the dead-end road where we were to get to the semaphore. That did it. Charley finally decided he'd seen enough, so we snuck down the road, got on our bikes, and took off.

TERROR ON THE TRESTLE—CA. 1942

Kenneth Thompson and I were the same age: sixteen. Our bomb designs had become sophisticated to the extent that they included the use of iron pipes for bomb casings. Because of the war, we knew about underwater mines and depth charges, and we wanted to duplicate such explosions.

The only body of water close to where we lived was the Rio Hondo River. It wasn't very deep. Most of the time a person could just wade across. During some previous "tests" we had discovered a desirable spot on the far side of the river where the water was about four or five feet deep—just right for our underwater blasts.

We started out to test our creation with Charley carrying the bomb and me carrying a 16mm movie camera that my dad had bought for taking family movies. Since we needed to avoid getting the camera wet, we decided not to wade across the river. The nearest bridge crossing was at Whittier Boulevard, almost a mile north of our selected spot. However, the Union Pacific Railroad crossed over very near the place we had chosen.

The span was about 150 yards long from one bank to the other and at its middle at least 70 to 80 feet above the river. It was a typical railroad trestle, consisting of a latticework of long telephone-like poles. On top of the poles were two parallel wooden beams extending across the river under the cross-ties. The cross-ties had been set very irregularly, with spaces between them varying from 8 to 12 inches, and the railroad tracks were spiked on top of them. No structure existed above or on either side of the tracks. There was only bare, empty space.

Such spans were never designed for anything but trains. Walking across one is extremely hazardous. Your foot might easily slip between two ties, and with nothing to grab onto you could lose your balance and fall off, but kids and common sense mix about as well as oil and water.

We made our way to where the tracks entered the span. We hardly noticed that the tracks made a rather sharp curve as they approached the crossing. This was intended to square the approach of the tracks to the river's course, minimizing the length of the span needed. As a result, one's view up the tracks was limited, but after a quick look and hearing no sounds we ventured out, carefully stepping on one tie, then the next.

The treacherous, uneven spacing between the ties and the awkward steps necessary to navigate them became more frightening as we proceeded out away from the bank. I looked down between the ties and saw the drop to the ground increasing. An uneasy feeling was growing in the pit of my stomach.

When we got about a fourth of the way across we heard a terrifying sound. It was a train blowing its whistle at the crossroad, a couple of hundred yards beyond the blind curve. Absolute panic struck. We froze in our tracks. One of us shouted to run back, pointing in the direction from which we had come. We took a few steps, and then both realized that the train would get there before we did.

I began to think irrationally, considered jumping (it was at least 40 to 50 feet up), and even hanging from the end of a tie. Then one of us saw a 55-gallon drum sitting on a small platform right in the middle of the trestle. The platform didn't appear big enough to hold us, but if nothing else we might be able to scrunch up on top of the drum. We yelled agreement and took off. I ran as fast as I could, probably twice normal, due to adrenaline. Each gazelle leap spanned five or six ties and landed squarely every time. One miss and I would have surely broken a leg, which would have ended my problems.

As the engine rounded the curve, the engineer spotted us and began blasting his whistle incessantly. He was probably as panicked as we were. As the engine entered the span, we could feel the ties under us shake and vibrate. We got to the platform with only a few seconds to spare and managed to squeeze onto the platform. It was square and the drum was round, leaving a small corner on each side into which we crammed ourselves.

Now the train was upon us, but feeling giddily safe, I looked toward it. I just couldn't miss this! I pointed my camera at the monster as it roared by. It shook us mercilessly and sprayed us with steam, but by golly, I stood my ground and caught the event on film.

After the train passed, we disentangled ourselves from the platform and drum and gingerly made our way across the rest of the span. In the future, we always crossed over the Whittier Boulevard Bridge.

_____DIVERTISSEMENTS

❖

The Electric Dog—1939
Limb Physiology
Articulated Salamander
The Gun Boat—1939
The Underground Highway—1940
A Weighty Endeavor—1940
Bye, Bye Birdie—1940
Pup in the Pot—1940
Trigonometry & Transits—1941
Unbreakable Code—1942
Tobacco Expose—1942

THE ELECTRIC DOG—1939

One morning a few of us kids, including Jack Gretta, were walking to school. It had been raining all night, and the ground was soaked. It was still sprinkling lightly as we came upon another group of kids standing around an electric power pole.

They had discovered they could touch each other and cause a shock. The pole was wet, and since the insulators on the pole were also wet that allowed current to leak from the wires above, down the pole, and into the ground below. When it reached the ground, it spread out in all directions from the pole.

If one kid stood near the pole and a second one stood farther away, there would be a difference in voltage between them. Since their shoes were wet, they only needed to reach over and touch each other to cause a very noticeable shock. Well, being kids, we didn't see the hazard in all this. It was just something different with which to have some fun.

Jack and I got into the act. We touched each other on various places. Touching the other's hand caused a mild shock—just enough to cause the hand to jerk away. Then I rolled up my sleeve and Jack touched me on my forearm. Two of my fingers curled up. He moved his finger to a slightly different place and one of my other fingers curled up. Hey, this was neat!

So of course he rolled up a sleeve and I did the same to him. Soon we found we could control the fingers individually by selecting the right spot on the arm. The other kids all started imitating our discovery. Quickly tiring of that, Jack tried touching me on the forehead. Wow! When I closed my eyes I could see black and yellow bands moving across my field of vision. We messed around, doing that to each other for a while. Then Jack said, "Let me touch your tooth." So obligingly, I parted my lips and he touched a front tooth. "Yeow!" I screamed. It hurt worse than when a dentist drills into a nerve.

We were all about to leave the site of our discovery when a small white dog came trotting down the sidewalk toward us. He was wearing a collar and dragging a chain. He'd broken his tether and was just enjoying his freedom. He came up to us and stopped. Jack immediately saw an opportunity. He reached down and picked up the end of the chain.

Now, the amount of voltage produced was proportional to the distance between two individuals. All of our previous experiments had been between two kids standing only two or three feet apart. However, in this case, with a chain about ten feet long, the voltage between Jack and the dog was considerably greater. Jack received a healthy shock and let out a yell as he threw the chain into the air. The dog jumped straight up a foot or so, and yelping all the way took off full speed down the street.

Deciding we had had enough fun for one morning, we all resumed our trek to school.

LIMB PHYSIOLOGY

Jack and I were fascinated with our newfound ability to cause our fingers to move. We decided to duplicate the phenomena at home. So, over at his house we discussed how we could use the 110-volt AC power to simulate the leaking power pole. We knew a straight connection would knock us on our can. That had happened to us accidentally several times before.

We concluded that we would need a very low-power device as a load to limit the current to which our bodies would be subjected. Our first thought was a low-wattage light bulb. Jack dug out a Christmas tree light bulb. It was probably about five watts.

So bravely, we hooked the bulb to an outlet. It lit. Next we disconnected one lead in order to put ourselves in series. I grabbed one lead and Jack the other. I reached over and touched Jack's arm. We both got a nasty shock—too much current.

Not to give up easily, we racked our brain for some lower wattage load. Soon one of us thought of using a neon bulb. We knew they drew very little current, and fortunately, we had one in our collection of electrical junk. In no time we had replaced the Christmas tree light with it.

With ourselves hooked up again, I reached over and very gingerly touched Jack's arm. We both jumped in anticipation of getting zapped again, but this time—as Goldilocks might say—"It was just right." Now we could continue our experiments in a more controlled, less hazardous, environment.

I probed around on Jack's arm, causing various fingers to curl. With a pen I marked the spot for controlling each finger. After that it was like playing a musical instrument. Just touching a spot caused the corresponding finger to curl up. We reversed roles, with him marking my arm. We eventually tired of that.

I remembered the colored bands I had seen when Jack had touched my forehead earlier at the power pole. We repeated that, and sure enough, those yellow and black bands moved across my field of vision again. I suspect that experiment cooked a part of my brain and may explain why my IQ dropped 20 points that day and my under-arm hair turned white—just joking.

ARTICULATED SALAMANDER

One day I happened to tell Melvin Lee about the experiments Jack and I were doing. Being the only true biologist among us, he was extremely interested and eager to see it performed. However, when I mentioned using him as a subject, he recoiled. He was terrified of electricity.

Melvin remembered an experiment Volta had performed in the early 1800's in which he caused a frog's leg to contract by applying a small voltage to the nerves controlling the muscle. Of course this was exactly what we had been doing to ourselves. Melvin wanted to see it happen for himself—however not to himself.

Aha! He didn't have any frogs to donate to the cause of science, but he did have several salamanders. He would provide a salamander for the experiment. After thinking about his pet salamander being exposed to electrical shocks, he pronounced, "It will have to be pithed." "Pithed?" I asked. He went on to explain "pithing" was the process of pushing a needle into the brain through the forehead and squishing it around, destroying the brain. This would prevent the salamander from feeling any pain during the experiment, without killing it.

On the appointed afternoon, Melvin showed up with his salamander in a box. I prepared the bench in the garage with a ring-stand and a burette clamp I borrowed from Charley Heckman. Additionally, I had some straight pins, wire, a six-volt battery, and a board with four homemade switches mounted on it. I figured if Volta could successfully use a 1.5-volt cell, that I could certainly get results with a 6-volt battery. It was a lot safer than using 110 volts and a neon bulb. The switches were my bright idea to control each leg separately and try to make it look as if it were walking.

Melvin, assuming the role of an experienced biologist, pithed his salamander—a rather unpleasant operation, but the salamander took it well. I mounted it in the burette clamp with its head and forelegs sticking out one side and its hind-legs and tail out the other.

This was followed by hooking up the battery to each switch, and from there to a pin. The burette clamp acted as a ground return for all the circuits. The mad scientists were now ready. I depressed one of the switches and probed around on the victim's back until I found a spot that caused one of his forelegs to move to the rear. I released the switch and proceeded with the next switch and its pin until I found the right spot to control another leg. Eventually we had all four pins properly located.

Action! With Melvin controlling two of the switches and me the other two, we soon could make the poor thing appear to walk. Well, to do a good job we would have needed four more switches and pins to pull the legs back and forward after each step. However, this was enough to satisfy us. Melvin retrieved his pet, took it home, and gave it a proper burial.

THE GUN-BOAT—1939

That summer I spent most of my vacation at Jack's Greta's house. It was a simple case of seduction. Jack's mom knew he had only a few friends. She was an extremely social person and wanted to help him become more social also.

One day I needed something Jack had and went by his house. In a matter of minutes, his mom produced homemade tollhouse cookies and milk. That was a real treat for me.

While we were enjoying the cookies, Jack said, "You know a lot about electricity and radio. What do you say we build a radio-controlled boat?" That pushed my ego button and I asked how we could do that. He said he could build the boat and install a motor and batteries to run it if I could come up with a radio receiver, some control circuits, and a portable transmitter. I falsely bragged that I probably could. I had seen a circuit for a one-tube AM transmitter. It was used for talking through a radio. I thought I could convert it to operate on batteries.

However, I pointed out a significant problem: all this equipment would cost much more money than we had. Jack's mom must have been listening nearby, because she appeared and said she could contribute $20.00—maybe even more if necessary. That was a *lot* of money, and the project seemed feasible, so I agreed.

We spent weeks preparing to build this. For practical reasons, Jack decided to build a barge. It would be more stable and could carry more weight—an important issue, since he had decided to use a Claxon-horn motor to propel it and a motorcycle battery to power the motor. Both were heavy.

I began scrounging through second-hand stores and junk shops, and eventually accumulated several old radios from which to scavenge parts. Two were portables from which I could get vacuum tubes designed to run from batteries. Radios in those days all used vacuum tubes. Both our transmitter and receiver would have to be powered by batteries, so I scavenged through the trash behind police stations for discarded batteries with a little life left in them.

In the meantime, Jack was building the barge. He limited the length to four feet so he could test it in the bathtub for buoyancy, balance, and leaks, and check the performance of the motor and propeller in water.

After a lot of trial and failure, I finally got a transmitter and receiver to work at the low end of the broadcast band (about 540 kilocycles) where no stations would interfere with our signals. Now, somehow I had to get the very weak signal from the receiver—just a two-stage RF amplifier—to operate a relay to control the boat's functions.

I remembered that Charley Heckman had received an electric eye (photocell) kit for Christmas. The kit contained a sensitive relay for detecting small currents from the photocell. I approached Charley about his relay. He had become tired of playing with the kit, and he just gave the whole kit to me.

Soon I was able to get the receiver to operate the relay whenever I keyed the transmitter. With proper tuning and adjustments I could make it work reliably from a couple of hundred yards away. Now we had to decide what functions the boat was to do and design control circuits to accomplish them. Jack found an old hex-barrel, single-shot .22 cal rifle in a junk shop. It didn't have a stock. Otherwise, it seemed okay. Jack bought it for $1.50. He wanted to mount it on the barge and be able to fire it remotely.

Our choice of functions and their positions on what would be a rotary switch were:

Position	Function	Position	Function
1	Forward half-speed	6	Left-rudder/forward
2	Forward full-speed	7	Right-rudder/reverse
3	Reverse half-speed	8	Left-rudder/reverse
4	Reverse full-speed	9	Stop motor/rudder reset
5	Right-rudder/forward	0	Fire gun

10. Rotary Switch Table for Radio Controlled Boat—ca. 1939

The next hurdle was to find a rotary switch. A couple of years before, I had bought a pinball machine from a junk store. The pinball machine happened to contain special electrical parts we needed for the barge, so without much reluctance I tore apart this old dog for its parts. The most important were stepping relays and latching relays. A stepping relay operates a rotary switch, and for each pulse the relay receives it steps the switch to its next position. A separate electrical pulse causes the stepper to return to its home position. A latching relay closes when it receives a pulse, and remains closed until its source of power is interrupted.

In our application, if we wanted the barge to go forward at half-speed we would send one pulse. The stepper would advance the switch to its first position. That position was wired to a latching relay. It powered the motor to drive the barge forward. Additionally, a contact on the latching relay would send a reset signal to the stepper relay, returning it to its home position, ready for the next group of pulses to be sent. To stop the barge, we would send nine pulses. This position of the stepper was wired to a relay that interrupted the power to all the latching relays, causing them to unlatch (which in this case, turned off the motor).

A slightly more complex scenario was turning the barge to the right while running in reverse. In this case, we would send seven pulses. This would cause the stepper to move its rotary switch to position 7. That position was wired to latch the motor-reverse relay *and* the rudder-right relay. As before, to terminate the command we would send nine pulses, unlatching both relays.

Finally, when we wanted to fire the gun we would send ten pulses. Ten was chosen to avoid accidentally firing it during maneuvering commands.

Designing a system to operate on pulses sent over one frequency (channel) was difficult. We sweat blood figuring it out and getting it to work.

The next problem was how to send a group of pulses reliably. Actually, we had already answered that question before settling on the relay logic. We used an old rotary dial we had salvaged from a broken telephone. These dials were designed to send a group of pulses, the number of which corresponded to the digit selected on the dial. We mounted the telephone dial on top of the transmitter. We would transmit various commands to the boat by simply dialing the corresponding number to send the correct sequence of pulses to the relays.

Jack had commandeered the bathtub to check out his barge's buoyancy, stability, and water-tightness, and to test the motor and rudder action in water. Eventually, he got the bugs worked out and we combined our efforts to install the relay control system. It contained one stepper relay, nine latching relays, and one de-latching relay. In addition, Jack had installed some relays for controlling the motor's direction and speed and two solenoids to operate the rudder to the right and left; and finally, one solenoid to pull the trigger on the gun.

All during the two months we labored on this project, Jack's mom would feed us snacks and fix tasty lunches to keep us going. Additionally, as promised, she paid for the necessary materials and parts. Her seduction was successful.

Finally, the day came when everything was assembled and working. Most of the ponds that had formed during the winter rainy season were dried up. This was the end of August. We had only two choices. One was a dirt-banked reservoir on the other side of the railroad tracks. It was small, only about 50 X 75 feet. The other was at the bottom of an abandoned brickyard in South Montebello. It was several hundred feet across and usually had mud hens floating on it. These would be targets for our gun. However, it was between two and three miles away.

Nevertheless, we decided that's where we would go. We put the barge and transmitter in my wagon and started out with one pulling and the other walking alongside. We took turns. It was hot. It took us a full hour of trudging. Once there, we checked out the controls to make sure everything was still working. All was okay. Jack loaded the gun with a .22-long bullet and cocked it. The barge was heavy, and it took both of us—wading into the water—to launch it.

I sent some commands with the homemade remote control, got the motor started and tried turning the barge. I soon learned I had no knack for converting my intentions to dialed commands. Jack, on the other hand, was a natural. He had lots of practice with his U-controlled planes.

In no time, Jack was sending one command after another, causing the barge to go wherever he wanted. Soon he had it headed out toward the mud hens. The barge didn't seem to spook them at all. It probably just looked like a log to them. Jack was going to see if he could hit one. Of course he had no way to take proper aim and just guessed where it was pointed. Finally, he dialed "0." Bang! It caused a small splash on the far side of the flock.

Jack turned the thing around, brought it to shore, reloaded, and sent it back to sea. Another bang! I never even saw that splash. Jack claimed he did. Back to shore for another reload and out toward the flock again. I noticed that the motor noise and gunshots didn't scare off the birds. They must have figured there was no danger. They were absolutely right!

Finally, the battery powering the motor began to poop out. I told Jack he'd have to fire the gun, as I didn't want a loaded gun pointing our way when he steered it back to shore. So, with no further aiming maneuvers, he dialed "0" to discharge the bullet. We began to worry whether or not the barge had enough power to get back. Ever slower, it inched its way toward us, finally making it—with scarcely any power to spare.

That was the only time we launched the barge. School was to start soon, and we became involved in other things. That was also the last summer I didn't have a full-time job.

THE UNDERGROUND HIGHWAY—1940

Some years ago a winter storm dropped more rain than the drainage system in Los Angeles could handle, resulting in extensive flooding. City officials decided something had to be done, so they constructed the Los Angeles Basin Storm Drain System—a vast network consisting of miles of large underground pipes that drained into the Los Angeles River and then to the ocean.

They lined the streets with curbs that had drain openings at every intersection. These drain openings connected to thirty-inch diameter pipes that led down to large, six-foot round drainage pipes. These six-foot pipes drained into even larger conduits, about eight feet square. These were not sewers; sewers were an entirely separate system. This system drained thousands of streets throughout the city.

An entrance to this drainage system was located between the edge of our junior high school's property and the end of a dead end street. The cover for this entrance was made of cast cement, about 4-feet square. Near each edge, a steel handle was imbedded in the cement for lifting it. The edges of this cover were tapered to match the opening in an underground concrete vault that was about fifteen feet square. The vault connected several six-foot round drainage pipes. A steel ladder was mounted on the wall of the vault for maintenance crew access. It worked just as well for kid access.

A kid named Bob Bruner told Charley Heckman and me that we could put our bikes down through the opening into this underground drainage system and go anywhere we wanted to go. He said he had been down there before and would be our guide. We agreed to meet at the opening the following Saturday. Bob said we would need flashlights, some chalk and a compass. I had a nice pocket compass my granddad had given me. I would bring it.

On Saturday morning we arrived at the vault with chalk, flashlights, and my compass in hand. Charley's bike was fitted with a headlight. However, it only lit when his bike was moving, since it ran off an alternator attached to the front wheel. Bob had a conventional flashlight. It was hard for him to hold the flashlight and steer the bike at the same time, but he could manage. I had my Boy Scout flashlight. It was designed to clip on a belt and shine forward—just what I needed. I also carried a couple of spare D-cell batteries in my pocket.

Bob had previously explained that the chalk was to mark a trail. The main hazard, other than a sudden rain, was not being able to find our way back to the vault where we started. The arterial nature of the drain made it easy to go southwest toward the Los Angeles River, but almost impossible to find your way back, as dozens of forks had to be navigated when returning. To preclude disaster as we toured south, we would need to mark every fork we passed through with our chalk.

We lowered our bikes down the opening, one by one. It was springtime. The likelihood of rain was low; however, weather forecasts were not available in those days. I had heard of kids being drowned in storm drains when an unexpected rain would occur, but such stories were from other areas like Fresno. Our storm drain system was new, and none of us had heard of anyone drowning in it—*yet.*

Nevertheless, when we entered the six-foot cylinder pipe, water was flowing in it about 5 or 6 inches deep. Bob explained some water always flowed in the system from lawns being watered and businesses hosing off their sidewalks. Bob led the way, with Charley right behind and me bringing up the rear. Right away the water became a problem. Not only did it require more effort to pedal through; it was splashing Charley and me from the bike ahead. We finally resolved these problems by oscillating from one side of the tube to the other, passing only through the water as we went from side to side. It was fun.

In no time, it became dark. We could only see whatever was illuminated by one of our lights and some spots of dim light coming down from curb drains, spaced at the ends of blocks.

After we had gone a mile or so, blazing our trail with chalked X's as we went, we began to wonder just where we were. Bob to the rescue. He said one of us could climb up through one of these curb drains, look out, and try to see an intersection street sign. It was Bob's idea, so he was elected. These drains were not too steep—about 20 degrees. Up he crawled. Soon he reported he could read "9th Street," but couldn't see the cross street. That told us we had traveled a couple of miles south. My compass had indicated that we were traveling south by southwest, so we were going towards the river, but we didn't know how far west.

We started out again and almost immediately entered an eight-foot rectangular conduit. This made the going easier, since the bottom was flat and the water spread out so it was less than an inch deep. We marked the tube we had just exited—then, off again.

After going another mile or so, we decided to take another bearing. This time I was selected to climb up the drain. The others boosted me into the opening. As soon as I was a few feet into the pipe, I got a flush of claustrophobia. For a few seconds I froze. However, not wanting to appear chicken, I forced myself slowly upward. As I got near the drain opening, I ran into spider webs. I hate spiders. That was another phobia. With light from the curb drain, I looked carefully—really carefully—for spiders. Not seeing any, I cleared the webs and moved on up. Finally, with great relief, I was able to peer out through the curb drain.

There it was! A street sign with the words "Atlantic Blvd." on it. Now we knew about where we were—close to the Union Pacific East Los Angeles Station. Wriggling my way back down, I dropped into the main conduit. With a big sigh of relief, I shook off my double-phobic encounter. Actually, we were all getting edgy being so far from our starting point. I had seen some clouds when I peered out, although they didn't look like rain clouds. Still, we decided to take a vote on whether to continue or go home. Home was *unanimous*.

Our chalk trailblazing paid off. At every fork, we looked for our mark—an "X". Often it would seem to be marked the wrong way. Darkness and fear can play diabolical tricks on your memory. However, we stuck with our chalk marks, and after about an hour we were relieved to find the original vault. We hauled our bikes and butts out of there, never to return.

A WEIGHTY ENDEAVOR—1940

Money was always a problem for us kids. Although Charley usually could get whatever he needed from his mom, he was proud and didn't like to "go begging." As a result, we were always on the lookout for ways to make some cash.

Charley had the most amazing sources of information. Somewhere he had heard that the Union Pacific had repair yards in a large industrial area just south of the city. Worn driver wheels were removed from steam locomotives there and replaced with new or refurbished ones. These driver wheels were large—probably six feet in diameter—and heavy. They had to be balanced, and this was accomplished at the factory by filling a cavity in the wheel's casting with lead.

Before a wheel was carted off for scrap iron, workmen would salvage the lead from it. They did this in an open field where they had set up a stand made of firebrick. They would place a wheel on the stand and light a gas fire below it. After a while, the lead would melt and run out through a hole in the wheel where it was caught in steel containers that looked like oversized bread pans. When cooled, these provided lead ingots for reuse.

The field was large—probably 30 to 40 acres—and was surrounded by a chain link fence to keep out kids. However, Charley and I had learned long ago that wherever a chain link fence had a gate over railroad tracks it was possible to wriggle under the fence between the tracks.

So one crisp winter day we biked our way to the yards—about ten miles. Looking through the fence, we saw no one around, so we hid our bikes in some weeds and did our wriggling act to get in. Once in, we spotted the brick furnace and made our way to it. These workmen were messy. There were patches of spilled lead everywhere. We could just reach down, grab an edge, and lift. Some contained up to twenty pounds of lead. We gathered as many as we could carry and hauled them back to our bikes, then we went back for a second load.

Charley, the much better planner, had brought along pieces of clothesline with which we lashed the pizza-like pieces of lead all over our bikes. When we started off, I was amazed how much harder it was to steer the bike with maybe sixty pounds of dead weight, compared to carrying a person weighing a hundred or more pounds. On the way home, pieces of lead would work loose and fall off. Stopping to pick up some of our dropped treasure and re-lashing it to the bike became routine.

We headed for my house (since my dad had a blowtorch and a ladle,) unloaded in the driveway, and washed the pieces clean of dirt. Now we needed a mold. Bread pans would be ideal, but my mom wasn't into baking, so Charley wheeled home and returned with one of his mom's bread pans.

I fired up Dad's blowtorch. While Charley held a piece of lead over the pan, I played the flame along the bottom edge until it melted and ran into the pan. Eventually, we had a pan full of lead drippings and pieces of lead too small to hold. Still, it was not an ingot yet. Mom was not home, so we took the pan into the kitchen, put it on one of the stove burners and turned the burner on high. Very soon all the lead was molten.

After it cooled a bit, the lead solidified, but was as still hot as hell. Being impatient, we pushed the pan off the burner onto a board, carried the pan outside and sprayed it with the hose. When it cooled sufficiently, we turned the pan over and our ingot dropped out. We repeated the process until we had four ingots, each weighing about 30 pounds.

Now we were ready to try to sell them. In those days, there were a lot of second-hand stores and junk stores. The second-hand stores sold useable stuff such as furniture, small and large appliances, clothing, tires, and tools. Junk stores, on the other hand, carried junk—stuff too broken to fix. These stores usually had a salvage operation. They tore things apart, separated the iron, copper, and brass, and threw them into separate piles. Eventually a scrap dealer would buy whatever they had accumulated.

Charley was able to get his mom's car occasionally. He wasn't old enough to have a driver's license, but he was big enough to pass for someone who might. One day he got the car; we loaded it with our four ingots and headed to our favorite junk store.

The owner knew us both. He told us the only lead he dealt with came from dead car batteries and he just paid a penny a pound. At that rate, our whole load would only be worth about $1.25. After some consideration he said, "Since it's in ingots, I'll give you $2.00 for the lot." No deal. We would try to do better elsewhere.

On the way home I remembered a radio repair shop in Montebello, owned by a bachelor named Ray Johnson. Ray was weird. He was so neurotic, people hated to have him work on their radios. However, in those days, having a working radio was a necessity and he had the only radio repair shop for miles around.

Ray picked up and delivered large console radios using an old 1917 open coupe car. White was the make of the car. It looked odd because he had the entire car chrome-plated: the body, wheels, and even the engine. Chrome plating was not cheap. It must have cost him a bundle, but it provided a lot of attention. So much so that people would run out of shops to watch him drive by—always quite slowly, of course.

I was in his shop one day looking for some parts when this woman came in to pick up her repaired radio. He looked in his log for the transaction and said, "Oh, I sold it. It was here over 30 days," and pointed to a sign on his wall stating: "Radios left over 30 days will be sold for charges." They had a furious exchange of words. However in the end she stomped out—no radio, no money. Ray smiled a look you might expect to see on the face of a Roman gladiator who had just run through his opponent.

Ray lived in a fantasy world. His fantasy was that some day he would sail off to the South Seas and live like a king with servants, luscious food, and luscious women. To this end, he was building a sailboat (or so he told me several times) and for the keel of the boat he needed lead—hundreds and hundreds of pounds of it. Collecting lead was such an obsession that he saved the lead foil from cigarette packs and the solder drippings from his workbench.

I convinced Charley to drive to Montebello to see if Ray would give us a better price for our ingots. We walked into the shop. Ray was working at his bench on a radio. He glanced up, but kept working. If we had been carrying in a radio for repair, he *might* have gotten up. However, for a couple of kids with no radio, he expected us to stand there waiting until he got finished.

Finally he walked over and asked what we wanted. I said, "Ray, are you still collecting lead for your sailboat?" He looked at us as though he was preparing for combat.

"What have you got?" he asked sharply.

Charley chimed in, "About 120 pounds." Ray said to get it and he would take a look. We carried in the four ingots.

After inspecting them, as if he knew what he was doing he said, "What are you asking?"

Charley and I had discussed what we would ask on the way over. We had decided on $10.00 for the four. Charley said, "Ten dollars."

Ray's lips twisted. He probably knew this was a fair price, but he wanted to steal it. He countered, "I'll give you five for the whole lot—that's it—no more." Charley and I walked to the far side of the shop to confer. Five dollars was a lot better than the junk dealer's $2.00 offer. We decided to take it. Ray's face lit up with that "skewered opponent" look.

Charley and I split the money and headed for home. As we licked our financial wounds, we resolved that stealing lead from the railroad was no way to make money.

BYE, BYE BIRDIE—1940

Kids at school seemed to have an innate ability to operate an underground-like network of information. Within this network our gang was getting a reputation for being weird, yet talented in certain ways. Stories about our experiences were being circulated throughout this grapevine.

This became apparent one day when a kid named Les Enz approached me at school. Les, I learned, lived down by the Union Pacific tracks in a rather nice ranch-style home. His dad was an engineer for the railroad and apparently wanted to live close to the line in order to enjoy the rumble of the trains going by.

Les raised pigeons as a hobby. He approached me because one of his pigeons had developed a growth on its throat and was getting to the point where it couldn't eat. It would surely die. Les had convinced himself from those grapevine stories that I had the talent to operate on his bird. Well, when you find yourself on a pedestal of admiration, you can't help being tempted to hold on to it, even if it requires a bit of bravado and bluff. Even though I never had done anything even remotely like this, I said, "Sure, bring your pigeon over."

Les convinced me that it was an emergency. He told me the growth was about the size of a chickpea. I had no idea what a chickpea was, so he showed me with his fingers, indicating it was about 3/16 of an inch in diameter. I told him it would take me a couple of days to collect the stuff I would need. We set a date.

I brought Melvin Lee into the operation. He had a scalpel we would need. Also, he could act as anesthesiologist. Because the neck skin was thin, I decided to close the incision with clamps instead of stitches. I set about making about ten clamps from a sheet of German silver Dad had in the garage. From the edge of the sheet I cut off thin slivers and bent each into a loop with the ends touching. I set up a shallow dish to hold alcohol, our antiseptic.

Melvin and I designed a method of administering ether. It consisted of a tube from a roll of toilet paper into the end of which we cut an arc to go over the bird's neck. With the bird on its back, the tube would be positioned vertically to surround its head. Into this tube we stuffed a wad of cotton.

On the selected day, Les showed up with his pigeon in a small cage. We showed him our set up and apparatus. He seemed impressed. Les removed his bird from its cage. It flapped a bit, but soon Les had calmed it and was holding it upside down. I could see the large lump on its throat. It reminded me of an aunt in Wisconsin who had a big goiter.

Les held the bird, with its back on the bench. Melvin put the toilet paper tube over its head, and with an eyedropper he dripped a few drops of ether down the tube onto the wad of cotton. Meanwhile, I poured some alcohol into the dish and placed the scalpel, clamps, and my fingers into it. This was to be an antiseptic operation.

In no time, the bird had gone limp. I began to worry that Melvin would kill the thing with too much ether. He assured me he wouldn't. I took the scalpel and made an X-shaped incision though the thin skin, from top-to-bottom and side-to-side of the growth. The skin peeled back easily exposing a white mass.

I decided to cut the mass into quarters. The stuff was hard, about like the meat of a Brazil nut. With a little effort, I finally managed to cut it into the four pieces. One-by-one I teased the first three loose and removed them. The fourth was attached to something. I trimmed away at the stubborn piece little by little until only a chunk about the size of a BB was left. This is where I should have stopped.

However, being compulsive, I was determined to get all of the growth out, so I kept trimming a little at a time when the scalpel slipped (just a little). It cut into the underlying tissue and into a blood vessel—the carotid artery! Immediately, blood began to fill the cavity.

We all just stood and watched. No one knew what to do. The bird's previously limp legs rose straight up, its claws splayed, then everything went limp. The poor thing had drowned.

Trying to appear sincere, I expressed my deepest regrets to Les. Watching his bird die under such circumstances caused a weirdly sad expression to come over his face. He mumbled, "Oh, it's OK," put his dead bird in the cage, and peddled off. I had tumbled off my ill-deserved pedestal.

PUP IN THE POT—1940

Ferguson Street ran parallel to the railroad tracks. Being close to the tracks, it wasn't very desirable property. Long stretches had only vacant lots along the side. After dark, it served as the neighborhood Lover's Lane.

One day, while riding my bike along Ferguson, I spotted a dead dog next to the curb. I'd gone about fifty feet past it when the thought occurred that its head would make a neat skull to display in my bedroom, so I wheeled around and went back to inspect the carcass. I laid my bike down and stepped over to examine it. I knew it hadn't been there long, since it didn't smell too bad yet. However, the flies had found it; maggots were sure to follow.

I set to work cutting the head off with my pocketknife. It would have been easier had my knife been sharp, but it was always dull from playing mumblety-peg.

Finally, the head came free. I picked it up by one of its ears, climbed on my bike, and wrapped the ear around the grip on my handlebar. Thus secured, I set off for home, its head swinging to and fro.

Mom had gone to the market, so I took my prize into the kitchen and looked for a suitable pot. I had heard the best way to get skin, flesh, and cartilage off bones for making skeletal displays was to boil the specimen. So, into the pot it went. I added enough water to cover it, set it on the stove and lit the burner. When the water began to boil, I reduced the heat to a simmer, covered the pot with a lid, and went out to the garage to pass the time.

About 45 minutes later I heard a shriek from the house. It was unmistakably Mom. She had come home from the market, entered the house by the front door, smelled something cooking and gone into the kitchen to see what it was. Lifting the lid from the pot, she looked in, and there was this dog's head staring back at her.

Her next utterance was, "MICKEY!" yelled as loud as she could. Up to this point, I had fantasized what a wonderful skull I would have and all the admiration it would bring from my friends. Now, suddenly, reality intruded. I ran to the back door, only to collide with Mom as she was trying to run out of the house. She was so discombobulated and upset, she began to sob hysterically. She sat down on the back steps and between sobs yelled, "What in God's name are you trying to do? Have you gone *completely* crazy?" I had no answers, at least not while she was in this state.

After a while, she calmed down a bit and I began to explain. It made, just barely, enough sense to her that she let me finish cooking the thing, but she made it clear that pot was never to enter the house again. After a couple more hours of simmering, I took the pot out to the garbage can and dumped all the loose skin. The brains were still mushy in the brain cavity, but I was able to rake them out by poking around with a screwdriver.

After hosing the skull clean, I inspected it and was rather disappointed. Although it was a fine specimen, it was *yellow*. I had expected it to be white, like in the museums. After I fretted about this for a while, it occurred to me that maybe I could bleach it.

So with skull and pot, I headed for the garage, where Mom did the washing. Here was soap, bleach, bluing—all the things the modern woman of the day used to put out a wash of which to be proud. I read the dilution instructions on the Clorox bottle, but ignored them in favor of a solution several times stronger. With the skull in the pot covered with this brew, I let it soak overnight.

First thing the next morning, I ran out to the garage and looked into the pot. The skull was beautiful: a gleaming white object of art. After being washed and dried, it assumed a prominent place on a bookshelf in my bedroom.

Surely Dad saw the skull soaking in bleach. It was sitting on his workbench in the garage. However, he never said a word to me about it. He probably satisfied his curiosity by asking Mom such probing questions as, "What in hell is that damned kid up to now?"

Skulls and skeletons hold an irresistible fascination for kids, and mine generated an abundance of ooh's and aah's over the next couple of years. The person most intrigued by it was Melvin Lee. He pestered me constantly to sell or trade it to him. Finally, one day he offered to trade me his *whole* mineral collection for it. I had developed an interest in minerals and he had a super collection. A deal was struck!

Oh, the pot…it was relegated to being a paint-mixing pail, never to enter the house again.

TRIGONOMETRY & TRANSITS—1941

I owned a cheaply-made (toy-quality) microscope I had found in a second-hand store. The body was cast of pot metal, the equivalent of today's plastic junk. One day as I was using it I tried to tilt it back for a more comfortable angle and it snapped in two. The base and stage broke into one part, the optics and focusing adjustment in the other. I was sick. A garage mechanic told me there was no way known to man for repairing broken pot metal. It couldn't be soldered, brazed, or welded. The glues of the day were worthless. So, I relegated it to my junk-treasure box, being unable to bring myself to throw it away.

I was in the 9th grade and taking trigonometry. The teacher, William P. Ball, had decided that as a practical trigonometry exercise the class would survey the perimeter of the school property. He told everyone to buy a simple protractor and bring it to class on Monday. He would provide soda straws to sight through, straight pins, and some scraps of wood from wood-shop, with which we could make simple transits for the exercise.

Immediately, I remembered my broken microscope. Over the weekend I retrieved it from my treasure box, deciding it should be far better for sighting than a lousy soda straw. However, microscope optics are designed to look at objects a fraction of an inch away. I needed a telescope that could focus out hundreds of feet. I didn't have a clue. While mulling over how I might convert the microscope into a telescope, I biked over to the J. J. Newberry store to get the protractor. A full circle protractor, 360 degrees, cost me 10 cents.

Back at work on the microscope, I soon realized the nosepiece (lens at the front) was of no use, so I removed it. Looking through the eyepiece toward the sky, I could see a clear circle of light with a sharp black perimeter. Lowering the scope to look at distant objects, I could see only a blur. Eventually, I reckoned some sort of lens was necessary up front, as in telescopes and binoculars. I remembered an old broken camera in my junk box. I had bought it at summer camp; it hadn't lasted a week before the shutter broke. Digging it out from among the other treasures, I could see its lens was in a metal cell just press-fitted into the camera body, and with a little effort I got it free.

Holding the lens in front of the scope tube, I was able to get images to form of distant objects—inverted, however. They would go in and out of focus as I moved the lens forward and back. Neat! All I had to do was make a cardboard tube to hold the lens and let it slide back and forth along the front end of the scope tube. Easy enough! Soon it became evident that when looking at distant objects the focus position of the tube didn't change perceptibly between looking at an object 20 feet away and an object much farther away. This meant I could slide the tube to a focus beyond 20 feet and just tape it into position—no focusing required. The image was still upside down. I had no idea how to erect it, but for this purpose I concluded it wouldn't matter.

Next, I had to figure out a way to mount the tube. Fortunately, a remnant of the "C" shaped arc—called a limb—remained above the point where the microscope had broken. I drilled through it at a 90-degree angle to the tube and mounted a bolt. With a bolt through this hole and one I drilled in the center of the protractor, the scope (well, now a transit) could swing to any horizontal position. I fashioned a pointer made of tin can metal and attached it to the transit limb. Now it could measure the angle between one sighted object and another—well *almost*. It was still necessary to guess exactly where the transit was pointing, as a wide field of view was visible.

My .22 rifle had a cheap telescopic sight on it with crosshairs to provide a reference to exactly where it was pointed. I thought, *That's the kind of thing I need here*. I had heard that crosshairs are made from spider web strands. No problem—the garage was full of webs. I remembered when I had removed the eyepiece from the rifle for cleaning that it had a metal stop, a washer-like item, a short distance forward of the eyepiece lens. I also recalled dust fibers on the edge of its hole being sharply focused when I looked through the eyepiece. That would be the perfect place to put the crosshairs so they would appear sharp. Handling spider web strands turned out to be much trickier than I thought. After a dozen or so attempts, I finally got a satisfactory set mounted across the stop hole and used model cement to hold them in place.

I was smugly satisfied with my effort and could hardly wait for Monday to show it off to Mr. Ball and the class. Well, Mr. Ball *was* quite impressed. He looked at it, through it, twisted the tube about to see the pointer provide readings, and asked, "Did you make this by yourself?" I beamed, "Yes, sir." I think he figured maybe my dad had helped me, but he seemed to take my word on the matter. After he instructed the class how to assemble their soda straw transits, we all went out onto the school grounds to start the surveys. Mr. Ball established a north reference with his pocket compass and everybody began taking readings. Accuracies were not precise, since we didn't have proper tripod mounts for our transits. We used wooden fold-up chairs on which the "surveyor" sat backward, steadying his instrument on the back of the chair during a reading. A professional would have an assistant hold a rod (like a long ruler) at the end of the distance to be measured on which to take readings. We took readings on our assistants themselves.

We spent the whole class hour taking readings, and homework was assigned to use trig tables to reduce them to a plot of the school grounds. Tuesday the class compared notes. Surprisingly, they were not too bad. The "error-of-closures" obtained was usually under 100 feet. Mine was in the 20's. I just knew I'd get an "A". I did. What else would you expect from a geek?

UNBREAKABLE CODE—1942

The Little Orphan Annie radio show used secret codes to provide clues to the next afternoon's show. They did this with a "Secret Decoder Button." Although I could not get my hands on a secret button, I was still able to "crack" the code. This introduced me to a life-long fascination with secret codes.

By now, 1942, the Japanese had attacked Pearl Harbor; we were embroiled in World War II; and military intelligence required secure methods of communication.

The Germans used a mechanical device called "Enigma." It was very much like Little Orphan Annie's magic decoder button in that it generated one character for each letter to be transmitted. However, whereas in Annie's code the key was changed each day in a simple manner, Enigma changed the key in a pseudo-random fashion for each character sent. The German's believed it to be unbreakable, and it *almost* was.

The Japanese had developed a code based upon the complexity of their printed language. They thought the Americans could never decipher it, but we did.

The Russians and the Americans often used codebooks. Both the sender and the receiver would have a copy of the same book, frequently an easily-obtained novel. Coding was done by scanning the pages for a word you wished to send. When found, its page number, followed by the word-count from the beginning of the page to the word provided a number grouping such as 37-92, meaning the coded word was the 92nd word on page 37. So long as the code-breaker could not identify the key book involved, the code was virtually unbreakable. The weakness was if a spy or a ship were captured, the codebook could be found and the key compromised.

With my interest in secret codes already established, I naively assumed I could come up with an unbreakable code. My goal was to avoid the need for a complex secret encoder/decoder machine and to eliminate the use of codebooks that could be captured.

I realized an unbreakable code must have the equivalent of a key that could be changed with each letter transmitted (as with Enigma, of which I was not yet aware). Otherwise, a frequency-of-use pattern would emerge, allowing the code to be deciphered. I reasoned any code that randomly generated a new key for every letter wouldn't work, because the receiver of the code would have no way to duplicate a truly random sequence of keys. The best compromise for this approach was to use a pseudo-random method of changing the key for each letter sent. The German Enigma used this method, and because of the pseudo-random algorithm, the British were eventually able to crack it.

I decided to use the old standard Morse code as its base. Morse code is easy to learn. Almost every Boy Scout learns it in order to earn a merit badge in signaling.

I divided the alphabet into three parts: a through h, i through p, and q through z to correspond to the three kinds of Morse code symbols. Morse code only transmits three kinds of symbols (dots, dashes, and spaces). In my code, a dot is represented by any letter from the first group (a-h); a dash is represented by any letter from the second group (i-p); and a space by any letter from the last group (q-z). Spaces are used to separate the groups of dots and dashes.

For example, if you wanted to send the message, "You are being watched," you would take the first letter "y," and from memory know in Morse code "y" was "-.-. " (dash, dot, dash, dot, space). Since the first symbol is a dash, it can be represented by any letter from the group (i-p). Let's pick "k." The next symbol is a dot. Since it can be represented by any letter from the group (a-h), let's choose "d." In similar fashion, letters representing the remaining dash and dot might be "m" and "a." We need to add another character to represent a space to separate this group of symbols from the next group. Any letter between q and z could be used. Let's pick "u." Now the first letter "y" in the message is represented by the group "kdmau."

This may seem like a lot of letters (five) in order to send one character. However, the advantage is great. Note that a dot can be represented by any one of eight letters—the same for dashes. And the space denoting the end of the dot/dash group can be represented by any one of ten letters. Thus the first letter "y" could be represented in $8 \times 8 \times 8 \times 8 \times 10 = 40,960$ different ways. Also, note that the selection of these ways can be totally random. No pseudo-random or algorithmic patterns are used which could be discovered to break the code.

However, this system has one shortcoming. Morse code represents characters with as few as one symbol (dot or dash) to as many as five symbols. A code-breaker could pick up this pattern and possibly deduce Morse code was involved. To camouflage this telltale pattern, I decided to represent every character in the text with a group of six letters. Space letters (q-z) would be used to pad the group of letters to make it always equal to six.

This modification provides another benefit. Originally, an "e" (which in Morse code is a single dot) could only be represented by two letters (one for the dot and one for a space). This reduces the mathematical ways of representing it to only 8 x 10 = 80 ways. By requiring all characters to be represented by six letters, this improves to 8 x 10 x 10 x 10 x 10 x 10 = 800,000 ways. Numbers (0 through 9) in Morse code are represented with combinations of five dots and dashes. In the case of a numeric, there would be 8 x 8 x 8 x 8 x 8 x 10 = 327,680 ways—still darned good. This means on average, every character can be represented in roughly a half-million different ways. In our example message above, the first word, "You" could be coded some 500,000 x 500,000 x 500,000 = 125,000,000,000,000,000 different ways.

If letters are selected in a random fashion, no frequency-of-use pattern will emerge. However, if you wished to be diabolical, you could make letter selections to simulate a normal frequency distribution. That ruse would be totally misleading.

When I was fooling around with these concepts during the war, computers hadn't been invented yet. Without them, I seriously doubt if this code could have been broken. Of course, with modern computers it certainly could. Still, I believe it would have given them a run for their money.

TOBACCO EXPOSÉ—1942

Annually, my school held an open house for parents to come and see examples of things their kids had been learning. It consisted of various projects, and in essence, open house evolved into a fledgling science fair.

I and other geeks now had a forum. Two years before, in the eighth grade, I had brought in my homemade telephone. I had a lot of trouble keeping it working, since I hadn't learned how to solder yet and the wiring connections were just twisted together—not a very reliable technique. However, parents are a tolerant lot, and I received many patronizing comments, in spite of the problems.

In the ninth grade, I took a bunch of photographs through a cheap student-grade microscope used by the biology class. The school had a small darkroom where I developed and printed these pictures. I mounted two dozen of the best prints on a poster-board and typed up an annotation for each print. That was it! Not much, but it received a lot of attention. In those days, many adults had never looked through a microscope, or even seen pictures taken through one. Close-ups of a fly's eye or a mosquito's proboscis were things they had never seen, let alone a paramecium or a human epithelium cell.

In the tenth grade, Kenny Thompson and I were discussing possibilities for that year's open house project when he came up with an idea for a joint project. He proposed we perform an extraction of some kind.

The previous summer, Kenny had taken a job as bottle washer in the laboratory of the California Flaxseed Co. Because of his precocious knowledge of chemistry, they had allowed him to learn—and run—various lab tests. Among these were extractions. These extractions were run in a three-part glass apparatus called a "Soxhlet extractor." It consisted of a Pyrex flask, into the opening of which was fitted a rather complex glass assembly (the extractor), and above it was a water-jacketed condenser.

The extractor assembly was fitted with a sample container having a tube extending from its bottom. The tube curved to a point near the top of the container and then bent back down below the container's bottom, where it emptied into the flask below. Another larger diameter tube provided a path from the flask, around the extraction container, up to the condenser. The condenser was supplied with a constant flow of water through its jacket to cool the vapors rising into it.

The way it worked was thus: the sample from which an extraction was to be made was wrapped in filter paper and tied closed with a thread. This was placed into the sample container within the extractor. Next, some solvent, appropriate for dissolving the desired component from the sample, was placed in the flask. Then, while water flowed through the condenser's cooling jacket, heat was applied under the flask.

Eventually the solvent would boil and the vapor would be conducted around the sample up into the condenser, where it would condense back to a liquid and drip down onto the sample. Slowly, as the extraction container filled, the components within the sample that were soluble in the selected solvent would pass through the filter paper with the solvent. When the container was nearly full, its liquid contents would flush (like a toilet) down into the flask below.

This process continued until all soluble components in the sample ended up in the flask. The apparatus was then disassembled and the solvent in the flask was allowed to evaporate away. The remaining material was the extracted components from the sample.

This apparatus made an impressive display. The entire Soxhlet was constructed of glass, which made it possible to observe the entire process. Watching the sample container fill up and flush periodically was fascinating.

Kenny and I decided to extract the nicotine and tar from a cigarette. We were ahead of our times. Tobacco was not considered a health hazard in those days. Kids couldn't buy it, mostly because kids were supposed to be kids. You weren't allowed to drink, smoke, go into bars or nightclubs, or gamble until you were 21. The only negative thing I remember about kids smoking was the coaches said it would "shorten your breath." This was one of hundreds of myths generated in those days, without any proof or other validation.

In preparation for our exhibit, Kenny borrowed a Soxhlet extractor from California Flaxseed's lab. We set it up in my garage. With running water for the condenser and natural gas for the burner, we were ready.

Kenny prepared a cigarette by doubling it in half, wrapping a filter paper around it, and securing it with a thread, then he pushed it down into the Soxhlet sample container. Meanwhile, I half-filled the flask with ether and placed it on the ringstand. Kenny followed by positioning the extractor above the flask and placing the condenser on top of the extractor.

At the first flush, the solvent was already turning brown from the tar. Nicotine is colorless. After about 40 minutes we decided we had extracted virtually all the solubles we were likely to get, so we shut down. We poured the contents of the flask into an evaporation dish (a shallow dish). Ether evaporates rapidly, so in short order the dish contained only the nicotine and tar we had extracted.

We knew we had a great exhibit, and wondered if we could do anything interesting with the residue. I had heard of mice being used to test the toxicity of various compounds. Their bellies were shaved and the product being tested was smeared on the shaved area. The skin is thin there and the material is absorbed quickly into the bloodstream.

Well, I had an endless supply of mice. Field mice had taken up residency in our incinerator in the back yard. I even had a cigar box trap I had previously built to catch them. I dug it out, baited it with cheese, and set it in front of the incinerator.

After about a half hour, we had a trapped mouse. I had already learned the hard way that you don't just reach in and grab a mouse. I had been bitten badly one time doing that. So I took some ether and dripped several drops through a hole I had made for the purpose in the top of the box. Soon the scurrying noises stopped and I retrieved the knocked-out mouse.

Kenny kept it unconscious by dripping ether on a wad of cotton held over its nose. I got my dad's razor, a Gillette safety, and began shaving the thing's belly. When done, we took some of the tarry gook and smeared it all over the shaved area. In about 45 minutes it began to convulse. After about 15 minutes more, it died. We decided to include this in our open house demonstration.

Our exhibit at the open house was a real success. Several parents came by, asked many questions, and were properly impressed with the glistening glass apparatus, the bubbling, and the flushing. We had made up a couple of placards. One described the setup, and the other stated that the effect of one cigarette would be tested on a live mouse at 9:00 p.m. Probably 90 percent of men smoked in those days—even doctors—and women were taking it up in droves in order to look sophisticated, imitating movie stars. No one was saying it might be unhealthy. Our display may have been the first time the thought crossed any of their minds.

By 9:00 p.m. we had a crowd. Oddly, it was mostly men. Only a few women were there, and hardly any kids. Kenny and I had our mouse in a jar so everyone could see that it was alive. We had previously shaved it belly. Kenny explained to the audience that we were going to put the mouse to sleep with ether so it wouldn't feel any pain. Everyone knew about ether; it was the standard surgical anesthesia at the time. Gee, we were *so* humane!

Kenny opened the jar, dropped in several drops of ether, and put the lid back on. In a minute or so the patient passed out. I laid him out on his back while Kenny kept him unconscious with ether and a cotton wad. With a flat ice-cream stick, I smeared the tarry extract on its stomach.

After some time, the convulsions started, and after a bit longer they stopped. An observant man noted that it had stopped breathing. We pronounced it dead. I wish I had had a camera to record some of the expressions in that crowd.

Epilogue:

Ether is one of the most volatile and flammable liquids known. To have it in the same room with a flame is extremely perilous and totally foolhardy. In both the garage and the lab at school, we had fumes everywhere and we were using a Bunsen burner to heat the flask. I have no idea how we avoided burning down one or both places.

Oh, yes, I washed my dad's razor, re-sharpened the blade—you did that in those days—and put it back in the medicine cabinet each time. He would not have been a happy dad if he had known where it had been.

Although this certainly wasn't the cause of problems for the tobacco industry in the following decades, it may have been one of the first shots across their bow.

_____BLACK POWDER

◆

Mini-disclaimer
The Recipe That Bombed—1939
Saint Sarkisian
Evolutionary Steps
School Grounds Fiasco—1939
Flying Fish—ca. 1939
Artillery (Of Sorts)—1940
Lights Out

MINI-DISCLAIMER

The following chapters contain some anecdotes about my adventures with explosives. I have used codes to obscure dangerous ingredients so parents of teenagers won't feel it necessary to ban this book from them.

THE RECIPE THAT BOMBED—CA. 1939

We, like many boys, were fascinated with fireworks. The Fourth of July was eagerly anticipated every year. In those days, fireworks were legal almost everywhere. All kinds of firecrackers could be bought—from ladyfingers to cherry bombs, skyrockets, Roman candles, fountains, and sparklers. Most kids, when their fireworks ran out, would go on to other interests. However, shortly after getting acquainted, Charley and I developed a long-lasting fascination with "making our own," especially things like cherry bombs.

We began with cutting open firecrackers and dumping the powder into a container. It took a lot of firecrackers to accumulate much powder that way. We made a few *super* cherry bombs, blew them up, and were soon out of our main raw material: black powder.

Not one to give up easily, Charley found a book that listed the ingredients for making black powder. We pooled our money and headed for Rexall's drug store to see what we could find. Much to our delight, they had everything we needed except charcoal.

While returning from the drugstore, it came to us that we could get charcoal from burnt wood. Soon we had a fire going in Charley's back yard. We could hardly wait for the charred boards to cool down. In no time we were scraping charcoal off the boards into a jar. Lots of chunks were mixed in with the powder, so we used Charley's mom's flour sifter to solve that problem.

Guessing at the proportions, we stirred the magical ingredients together. Next, we poured a little on the ground and lit it. Sure enough, it burned, but not nearly as fast and furious as the flash-powder we had been retrieving from firecrackers. No matter—it burned.

For a bomb container, Charley found a narrow-neck glass bottle. It held about three ounces. We poured some of our newly-made powder into it. Our next problem was that we didn't have any fuses left from our Fourth of July fireworks cache. What the heck! According to guru Charley, we could make our own. He went into the house and soon reappeared with some tissue—the gift-wrapping kind. He cut it into long narrow strips and creased one into a long "V" shape. Next he sprinkled some of our new powder along the crotch of the "V." We carefully twisted the tissue lengthwise so the powder was trapped in the center of this "tissue-twine."

This seemed clever of us (well, mostly of Charley), but the devil turned out to be in the details. We didn't test the fuse; the material was too precious. Charley stuck one end into the jar and we were ready to set off our first bomb, made with *our own* black powder.

We took the device out to our testing grounds—a vacant lot directly behind Charley's house. After setting the bottle on a flat spot, Charley struck a match and lit the fuse. We ran like hell, as we figured glass would be flying everywhere. Then...nothing! The fuse had burned fast (actually too fast for comfort), and died out right at the neck of the bottle.

The smart thing to do would have been to make another fuse. Right? Well, Charley may have been innovative, but he was also compulsive, impatient, and not always too smart. He had brought this box of kitchen matches—the big kind—to light the fuse, and stacked some of them up, tepee-style, around the bottle (bomb) so the heads met right above the opening. His idea was to light the bottom end of one of the matches and let it burn up to the heads where the flame would ignite all the heads and set off the bomb. It seemed like a fine idea to me, so, feeling secure, I stood about six feet away and watched.

Charley had recently learned to strike a match using his thumbnail. He thought it was cool. Well, that's what he did, and he was leaning directly over the bottle when he lit the match. The tip ignited, but broke off and flew *directly* into the center of his "tepee." It ignited the group of match heads and instantly set off the bomb. All this happened so quickly Charley didn't have a chance to move.

Luckily, this amateur gunpowder didn't cause an explosion. What it did, though, was shoot up a stream of sparks like a Fourth of July fountain. The stream hit Charley directly in one eye before he had a chance to close it. He screamed and ran for the hose in the back yard. He stuck the nozzle in his eye and yelled at me to turn on the water. I did. By this time his mother had heard the racket and came running, so leaving him in her care I took off for home.

Charley was out of school for a couple of weeks. The next time I saw him, he was wearing an eye-patch. His eyelashes, eyebrows, and the hair to the top of his head were burned off. He took off the patch to show me his eye. It looked like the moon, craters and all. Since our homemade powder had small granules of charcoal in it (the size that could pass through the screen in the flour sieve), these tiny, red-hot cinders had exploded into his open eye, making the craters. One would suppose that would be the end of our gunpowder-making efforts...No way!

Saint Sarkisian

Sometime after Charley's eye had healed, I was discussing the whole affair with a kid in gym class. His name was Lynn Sarkisian. Lynn chuckled when I told him how we had made the gunpowder. He said, "You guys were going about it all wrong. Here's what you have to do," and he proceeded to explain the tricks of the trade:

After mixing the ingredients together, the next step was to add enough water to make a paste, then we were to grind the mixture in a mortar and pestle until everything was fine and intimately mixed, pour the slurry onto a cookie sheet and put it in the sun to dry. After the slurry had dried to a "cake," we were to scrape it off, break it up, and put it back into the mortar; then dry-grind it to a fine powder. That would produce *real* gunpowder.

Charley and I wasted no time gathering the materials to make a batch. We soon encountered our first problem. Lynn said we must weigh out the ingredients; we couldn't just guess at the amounts. Well, neither of us had $5.00 for even a cheap balance, so we decided to build one.

After some creative thought, we decided to make a balance, using a wooden coat hanger as the beam. We pulled out the metal hook and filed a "V" notch in the bottom, across the hole left by the hook, then we built a base and support by nailing together pieces of scrap wood. On the top of the support we sawed a fine slit horizontally and mounted a small piece of sheet metal in it (cut from a tin can) to form a vertical edge for the beam to sit on.

For weighing pans, we used the lids from coffee cans. In each lip we poked three equally-spaced holes. Then, using kite string, we suspended a pan from each end of the beam. We balanced it by wrapping a loop of solder around the beam on the light side and sliding it along the beam till it was balanced.

It was crude; it was rickety, but it worked. The next thing needed was weights. Someone told us that a penny weighed 3 grams and an ounce was equal to about 30 grams (10 pennies). Now all we needed was a mortar and pestle.

Neither of us could come up with a way to make one. We'd seen one in science class and thought briefly about swiping it. Lynn had bought his at Caulkin's Chemical Co. downtown for about $3.00. However, we were short of funds, having spent all we had for more chemicals. Lynn felt sorry for us and loaned us his. Now we were on our way.

It was hard to contain our enthusiasm. We were making *real* gunpowder like the pros. The process went like clockwork—the weighing, the wet-grinding, the drying of the cake, and finally the dry-grinding of the cake. We put a teaspoon of our new product on the driveway and lit it. Wow, this was *The Real McCoy*! Sarkisian was a saint! With a reasonable supply of good gunpowder, we were ready to return to the task of making big cherry bombs.

EVOLUTIONARY STEPS

All firework casings for sale to the public were made of paper or cardboard to eliminate the possibility of shrapnel fragments. Since this was the commercial method, it established our mind-set (i.e. to make the bomb casing of paper).

We tried making several cherry bombs by wrapping layer upon layer of newspaper around a core of our new powder. They did explode, but never made as impressive a bang as the manufactured ones—or for that matter, the ones that we had made earlier from powder collected by cutting firecrackers open.

Obviously, more factors were involved in making an impressive explosion. First, of course, is size. Less obvious is the speed at which the powder burns and the strength of the casing. We were aware that powder extracted from firecrackers burned faster than ours did. We never understood why, but we noticed that their powder had a silvery look. Ours was just dark gray.

We concentrated on making stronger casings. We seemed to have reached a limit, using our primitive methods of rolling layers of newspaper. Wisely, we decided not to go back to using bottles. I remembered that my dad had a roll of copper tubing stored in our garage. We would use that.

We quickly found the roll and sawed off about a 5" length. It was 1/2" tubing and would make a nice size bomb. We pinched one end closed in the vise, crimped it over, and pinched it again. Then in went some powder, followed by a similar crimp on the other end. All that remained was to drill a small hole in the middle for the fuse. This could have been a disastrous step if the drill bit had developed enough heat to set off the powder, but drilling soft copper doesn't develop much heat, so we lucked our way through that one.

Back at Charley's place, we set the thing out on the back lot and placed a tin can over it. The standard kid's test, in those days, of a firecracker's power was based on how high it would blow a can. I, who had now become the fuse lighter, lit the fuse and off we ran to watch. BLAM! A big flash and a good-sized puff of white smoke, but neither of us saw the can blow away.

After a couple of furtive glances to make sure no neighbors had been attracted, we went back to survey the damage. A fist-sized crater was still smoking a little, but we saw no sign of the copper casing or the can. We immediately began a search; kids must have relics of their escapades. Soon we found both. The copper casing had split lengthwise through the fuse-hole, but being copper it had not fragmented. It would make a fine souvenir. The tin can got the worst of it. It was split, twisted, and mangled. How marvelous!

This became our standard bomb design for several months. During that time we probably made a dozen of them and we were inviting friends to watch the shows. We became quite celebrated. Then one night at the supper table Dad said, "I can't figure out what happened to my copper tubing. It's nearly half-gone. Mickey, do you know anything about it?"

"Gee, no, Dad," I lied. But after that, the supply of tubing remained undiminished.

Yet the effort had to go on. We had developed an admiring audience of five or six kids, who were always approaching us at school to ask when we were going to set off another one. We just couldn't let such fans down, so we began scrounging about for a substitute casing. In no time we spotted an old curtain rod stored high up in my garage. It was about ¾-inch in diameter, hollow, and made of steel. Even we knew we would be upping the ante using steel for a casing.

SCHOOL GROUNDS FIASCO—CA. 1939

We sawed off about eight inches from one end of the rod, and using the same techniques as with the copper tubing, fashioned what seemed to us like a monster-bomb. Fortunately, we did have the sense to drill the fuse hole *before* filling it with powder. We were getting smarter, you see.

At school I ran into Lynn Sarkisian one day and told him about the great bombs we had made, using his formula for black powder. Since he lived a long way from us, he had never seen any them. When I told him about the monster we had just made, he pleaded to let him watch it blow.

That night I talked it over with Charley. I told him I wanted to set it off at school during gym class so Lynn could watch. (Lynn and I had gym class together.) Charley objected, because he would be in social studies at that time, but finally he agreed. Actually, I think he probably reckoned he would have an alibi by being in class when it went off. In such political matters, he was a lot smarter than I was.

The next day I brought "it" in my lunch bag. Gym class was second period, so my nervousness wasn't protracted too long. During gym, Lynn and I snuck off from the others and headed for the track & field area. We selected a spot at the far end of the infield and placed it on the ground.

I lit the fuse and we ran to hide behind a handball court. I say "hide," because we had picked that spot, not so much to protect ourselves from flying shrapnel but so anyone who looked toward the explosion wouldn't see us. BAAROOOM! It was much noisier than I had expected. We stayed hidden as the gym class came running past us toward the mushroom cloud. They were followed by huffing, puffing, overweight Coach Lewis, and finally, by several teachers—including Principal Freese!

Someone found the twisted casing carcass and gave it to Mr. Freese. As the crowd dispersed, we blended in, acting as innocent as possible. Fortunately for Lynn, he didn't have a reputation with the kids as a bomb-maker, as did Charley and I, so he didn't get fingered, but we did. However, when Mr. Freese got back to his office, he apparently did a little detective work and decided that since I was in second period gym class and Charley wasn't, I alone was the culprit.

That afternoon I got called to report to the principal's office. I started formulating lie after lie to get off the hook. Nothing seemed credible. With my stomach churning, I headed for his office.

"Mickey, did you set off that bomb?" he began.

"No sir, I just heard an explosion and went over with the other kids to see what had happened," I lied.

Figuring that I was lying, he said, "No matter. But listen to me and listen closely. If a bomb goes off on this school grounds EVER again, it will be your last day here. Do you understand? You'll be kicked out of school!"

"Oh, yes, sir," I blurted, and he let me go. We had a very clear understanding.

FLYING FISH—CA. 1939

One day, a few weeks after the school grounds blast, I got itchy to make another bomb, using the curtain rod for the casing. I decided to make a smaller version of the one Lynn and I had set off at the school grounds. I cut about a five-inch length from the rod. I still had a short piece of commercial pyrotechnic fuse Lynn had given me. He had told me it would burn underwater. How neat!

I assembled this medium-sized bomb using the curtain rod, our new black powder, and the pyrotechnic fuse. I hadn't thought far enough ahead to consider where I would set it off. The closest body of water I knew of was a small reservoir across the tracks, then our fishpond popped into mind. Without any consideration of possible consequences (a marvelous facility of the pre-adult mind), I immediately decided on the pond.

Dad had built our fishpond from colorful desert rocks he and Mom had collected on weekend trips. It sat in a rear corner of the back yard, about four feet across and maybe two feet deep. For a homemade project, it was quite attractive. Dad had stocked it with a half-dozen goldfish and some water lilies.

Mom was downtown, and I was alone except for my sister Shirley, who was playing with her friend down the street. So robot-like, I compulsively strolled into the back yard, lit the fuse, and tossed the thing into the pond. I hurried into the house and watched out the window.

Whooom! I heard this muffled explosion. A geyser of water shot into the air, drenching the whole back yard with water. With heart pounding from excitement, I ventured out to inspect the results. The first thing I noticed was all of the goldfish lying around the back yard—dead. Then I looked up into the apricot tree and saw all of the water plants, hanging there like Spanish moss. Inspection of the pond revealed that instead of the usual two feet of water, only about two inches was left in the bottom.

Panic struck. I had to clean up the evidence before Mom got home. I got the hose, dragged it over to the pond, and began filling it back up. Then I climbed around in the apricot tree, retrieving water plants, and tossed them back into the pond. Finally, I gathered all the dead fish and threw them into the pond. I thought everything would look normal and my parents would just think bad water had killed the fish. Everything went well. Even the back yard dried off in an hour or so. I removed the hose and put it away. I figured that if I just played dumb about the dead fish, I would be home free.

Mom came home and never noticed the fish. No questions; no lies. Later, Dad came home. He didn't look outside. Wow, this was easier than I thought! The next day was Saturday. Dad worked half-days on Saturdays. When he got home, he wandered into the back yard, noticed the fishpond was empty, with plants and dead fish laying in the bottom, and soon determined the cause; a crack ran down one side, and all around the bottom where the bottom joined the sides. All the water had leaked out.

He called me out of the house. I saw him standing next to the pond, and being a smart kid, knew I was in big trouble. He said, "How in hell did this happen?"

Lying to Dad was not the brightest thing to do, but I came up with a fib. I answered, "I threw a cherry bomb into the pond. Gee, I didn't think it would hurt anything."

He told me to come with him, and headed for the garage where he got out a hammer and a chisel, handed them to me, and said, "Fix it." Then he walked away, shaking his head.

Well, I spent the rest of that day and all the next chiseling out the cracks. On Monday, Dad brought home a small sack of cement. After he inspected my chisel-work, he told me to mix up a batch and trowel it into the cracks. I complied. The following day I filled the pond with water. It held. Hallelujah, I was off the hook!

ARTILLERY (OF SORTS)—CA. 1940

Charley was fascinated with guns. I was also, but to a lesser extent. Charley wanted to try building a simple cannon, using a water pipe. The design would be a muzzleloader, modeled after those that had been used during the Civil War, and as was the tradition, it would have a small hole in the breach through which to ignite the powder charge.

Since we were going to use pipe, that meant we would have to fabricate it at my house. My dad had a good supply of water pipe and fittings. He also had a large die for cutting threads on half-inch pipe and a pipe-vise mounted on the wall to hold the pipe when cutting or threading it. Dad did all the plumbing for our house and some for our rent houses, too, so he was well equipped with plumbing tools.

We mounted a length of pipe in the vise, and with a hacksaw cut off about a fifteen-inch piece. I mounted it in the vise, and with a lot of grunting cut some threads on one end, using Dad's die. A half-inch cap would work well for the breach. Dad had a large wooden box full of pipefittings he had collected over the years. Hunting through them was a dirty job because of the accumulated dirt and rust, but soon I came up with the right cap. We screwed it on the newly-threaded end and tightened it with a pipe wrench.

I located Dad's electric drill (a real rarity, in those days), fitted it with a small bit, and drilled a small hole in the breach for fuses.

Back at Charley's place, we guesstimated two teaspoons of powder was about right for a first attempt. In went the charge, followed by small wads of cotton that we rammed home with a piece of dowel. Charley dug into his supply of marbles and found one just the right size for a cannon ball. In it went, followed by more cotton and tamping. Finally we inserted a fuse from a firecracker in the breach. We were ready; this was getting exciting!

For a target, Charley drug out a heavy-gage cardboard box in which his dad's cans of Pennzoil had been shipped. Foolishly, he set it up against the side of the garage. We placed the cannon on a sawhorse (in those days, every household had a couple) and aimed it point-blank at the box.

Charley, still traumatized from his previous accident, handed me the match. Nervously, I lit the fuse and jumped away a few feet. BLAMB! A puff of white smoke rose skyward, and the cannon recoiled backward about fifteen feet. We ran to examine the damage to the box. It didn't look too bad—just a half-inch hole in the front, and another in the back. But then we pulled the box away from the garage wall and found about a three-inch circle of stucco missing. The marble was nowhere to be found. Being glass, it must have just disintegrated.

We were delighted with the results, and no neighbors descended on us since they had become accustomed to hearing cherry bombs and the like go off in the area. During the following year or so we fired our homemade cannon many times. We were always looking for projectiles to use in it. We tried old penlight cells, ball bearings, shot made from steel punchings from a factory nearby, and our favorite: shot made by cutting up solid solder into very short pieces. These came from a five-pound can of solder Dad had bought to repair the radiator on his car. The shot was great for shooting at blackbirds sitting on telegraph wires near the tracks. I say *at*, because we didn't dare hold the thing to aim it, so we never hit any. We always laid it on the ground and propped it into position with rocks.

LIGHTS OUT

We tried improving the aim of our cannon by cementing a thumbtack (with point upward like a gun sight) at each end of the barrel. Our confidence in this upgrade was so great that we relied on it for our next act of delinquency.

Our subdivision had been laid out by the developers to be very upscale. The developers had even offered a prize for the best street layout. It was won by some Frenchman. Some of the streets formed large concentric ellipses. Northside Drive, the street I lived on, was divided with wide parkways down the center. All the streets were lined with trees, sidewalks, and handsome fluted-column street lamps made of simulated granite.

During the depression and subsequent years, the property lost value and the lots were sold to builders who constructed modest homes intended for middle-class parents. However, the amenities such as the beautiful streetlights remained.

These lights were always a temptation to young boys. While walking home from school, it was standard practice for them to fling dirt clods at the large glass fixture sitting on top. The glass was thick enough to resist dirt clods, so not much damage was done; however, BB guns were another matter. They could punch a small hole in the glass and often would hit the light bulb inside, breaking it. This kept the maintenance crews busy.

During that time I learned that a time-delayed fire could be set, using glycerin and another chemical. It required about a teaspoon of one chemical to be placed into a small mound. On its peak, a small depression was needed on top—about the size of a fingertip. Into this depression a couple of drops of glycerin would be poured. The other chemical would slowly oxidize the glycerin, heating it up. After fifteen to twenty minutes, spontaneous combustion would occur and the pile would burst into flames. What a neat way to provide adequate time to get away before a bomb or cannon went off. Inevitably, a correlation developed in Charley's mind between the omnipresent temptation of the street lamps, our new cannon, and the time-delay.

Once we succumbed to the temptation to do this act of vandalism, we decided it had to be a "night" job. We selected a street lamp in front of a vacant lot just a few hundred feet from Charley's house. A large Pepper tree with a crotch about four feet off the ground stood nearby. It would be a good a place to set the cannon.

In Charley's garage we prepared the cannon with a marble projectile and Charley mixed up a batch of very thick mud in some dirt next to the garage. Southern California dirt contains a lot of clay, so the resulting batch was almost the consistency of kid's modeling clay.

With our chemicals, mud and cannon in hand, we tiptoed down the driveway, past the living room where Charley's parents were listening to the radio, and on down the street to the targeted light. Charley packed his mud into the tree's crotch and mounted the cannon, taking careful aim with our new thumbtack sights.

Using the clay-like mud, I affixed a small cardboard square to the barrel close to the fuse hole and poured some potassium permanganate onto the cardboard surface. Then I placed a fuse between the pile and the ignition hole in the cannon's breach. After making the necessary depression in the pile, I took an eyedropper and placed two drops of glycerin into the crater.

We trotted back to Charley's house like Indians, making as little noise as possible as we crossed his front lawn and went up the driveway to the rear door. As we entered, we began talking about things photographic, hoping his parents would assume we'd been in the garage developing film. Without hesitation, we went into the living room; we wanted to be in plain sight. Charley got out a board game and placed it on the living room floor. We set out the pieces and began to play.

After about ten minutes we heard a big bang. Everybody looked up. Charley's dad looked at us momentarily, and then went outdoors. We followed, but his mom stayed behind. Other neighbors had come out as well. Finally someone noticed the street light was out. Charley's dad and a couple of other men walked over to the street light. They looked up at it, saw the fixture was missing, then looked down and saw that the ground was covered with broken glass. No one happened to wander near the tree.

One man thought the light had blown up. Charley's dad didn't think so, but he didn't offer any theories (which, no doubt, would have included an explosive). After a while, all the people went back into their houses. Charley and I resumed our board game. All evening, Charley's dad kept eyeing us, but we knew we had gotten away with this one.

The next day Charley casually walked by the tree, found our cannon nearby, and retrieved it; no point leaving evidence lying around.

_____MORE POWER

♦

CHEMISTRY TO THE RESCUE—CA. 1940

Although Charley and I had a lot of success and fun with our black gunpowder, the bombs we made were never as powerful as we would have liked. We seemed to have hit a limit. Of course we'd heard of dynamite, nitroglycerine, and TNT, but we had no knowledge of how they were made. That stuff seemed out of our league—and it was. Now, as was often the case, something fortuitous occurred to help us along.

I ran into a young fellow named Roland Mott at school. He was a short, over-weight kid who just made you smile when you looked at him. I remembered Roland from grammar school, where at lunchtime a group of a dozen or so kids would gather around him on the grass. There he would entertain everyone with stories he would simply make up as he went along. This kid had a real talent.

I bumped into him in the hall and we stopped to chat. I told him Charles Heck-man and I had been making black gunpowder with some success. He said his older brother had made pipe bombs when he was in high school, but now he was in the service. Although Roland never messed with explosives himself, he remem-bered the main ingredients in his brother's bombs. He said they were ingredient "X" and sugar (about 50-50, he thought). I will refer to this oxidizer as ingredient "X" so young readers won't blow off a hand—or worse.

I wasn't familiar with ingredient "X," and the use of sugar in an explosive seemed ludicrous. In any case, I figured Kenny Thompson—my chemically knowledge-able friend—would know. When I next saw Kenny in science class, I told him what Roland had said. He thought for a few seconds and then said, "[Ingredient "X"] is what they use in chemistry class to make oxygen for demonstration pur-poses." In Kenny's small collection of books was a high school chemistry text he had all but memorized. It mentioned ingredient "X," but Kenny didn't have any of the stuff in his lab.

That afternoon when I got home from school I looked in my dad's old *U. S. Pharmacopeia* to see if I could find this chemical. Sure enough, it was listed. It gave the formula as [xxxx], and said it was used in mouthwashes.

By this time I had been picking up odd jobs and doing a little baby-sitting, so I wasn't quite as strapped for money as in the past. I hopped on my bike, headed for the drug store, and asked the pharmacist if he had any ingredient "X." His immediate response was, "What are you going to do with it?" This pharmacist wasn't as dumb as I thought. I was prepared with my lie and said my dad wanted it to make some mouthwash. He was completely duped, and sold me 4 ounces of the white powder for a quarter.

As soon as I got home, I took a half teaspoon of the stuff, mixed it with an equal amount of sugar, and formed a pile with it on the driveway. I didn't know what to expect, so to allow myself a couple of seconds to get away I put a fuse from a firecracker in it. Carefully, I lit it and jumped back. It didn't blow up. It just burned furiously with a purple flame—weird. The real test would be in making a bomb using it.

Charley and I were beginning to drift apart. He had become interested in girls, and our pranks—as much fun as they were—simply couldn't compete with sex. As a result, I began spending more and more time with Kenny Thompson. The next day at school I told Kenny what I had done. He was interested and followed me home after school. I repeated the experiment, using the same quantities as before. He was duly impressed and said the purple color of the flame was due to the ionization of the elements in ingredient "X." That was its spectral color. We decided to make a test bomb.

EXPLOSIVES TUTORIAL

Explosives are used for three basic purposes: firearms, destruction (like bombs, mines, and torpedoes), and blasting.

For use in firearms—from pistols to naval guns—a material is needed that produces a large quantity of gas at a controlled rate. This means the material should burn at a steady rate during the period the projectile is being pushed through the barrel. A material that burns too fast could build up excessive pressure and blow up the gun. For centuries, black gunpowder served this purpose well. After the Civil War, Alfred Nobel invented more powerful explosives. These would shatter a firearm because they produce gas at a very high rate. However, special slower burning formulations were eventually developed for use in firearms and are known as smokeless powders.

Destructive war weapons—such as bombs, mines, and torpedoes—need the fastest burning formulations to produce extreme pressures with which to shatter and destroy the target. Organic explosives are ideal because they burn (actually decompose) extremely rapidly. Examples are TNT and gun cotton. These have been used very successfully in wars.

Blasting requirements lie somewhere in between for these different types of explosives. Enough pressure must be created to split and fracture rock, but not enough to pulverize it. Black powder was used for years. Dynamite was formulated for this purpose, and it is much more powerful.

The basic burning rate for a given material is mostly established by its formulation and the pressure developed during burning; however, the effective burning rate can be further determined by the size of the grain. In the case of black gunpowder, the size of the grain is controlled during the grind and sieving process of the dried carbon cake. If it is ground to a very fine powder, it will burn quite fast. This is used for blasting. If more coarsely ground, it might be appropriate for pistols and rifles. For cannons, the grain would be quite coarse. The same is also true, not only for black gunpowder, but also for more modern nitrated organic formulations. For example, large naval guns use grains with dimensions that are measured in inches.

As kids, we didn't know any of the above, except our experience with black gunpowder indicated the finer we ground it, the faster it burned and the better the bomb it produced. Additionally, we observed the improvement in the use of ingredient "X" over potassium nitrate, but just chalked it up to its being more "powerful." Actually, the radical in ingredient "X" is much less stable than nitrate. It gives off its oxygen more easily and completely, so it can oxidize such unlikely things as sugar. The explosive this produces is more powerful, but also more dangerous to handle.

TEST BOMBS

For the casing, we settled on a piece of half-inch iron pipe about five inches long. It was already threaded on both ends, so that saved some time and effort. After locating two end-caps in Dad's dirty box of fittings, we screwed one on one end and we drilled a small hole for a fuse in the center of the other cap. After filling the casing with a 50-50 mixture, we screwed on the second cap. Now all we needed was a fuse, but getting fuse was always a problem. Our homemade fuse was too unreliable and dangerous to use with pipe bombs. Andrew's Hardware store downtown sold commercial supplies such as dynamite, caps and fuse, but wouldn't sell such stuff to minors. We learned this after wasting 40 cents on bus fare. Our last hope was Lynn Sarkisian.

Lynn had two sources. One was his dad who owned a farm near Fresno where he grew raisin-grapes. His dad kept dynamite, caps, and fuse in a shed. He used these to blast out stumps. Dynamite fuse came in 100-foot rolls, and when Lynn visited his dad, he would occasionally snitch a few feet for his own experiments. Additionally, he knew some folk near Los Angeles who manufactured fireworks. He got a different kind of fuse from them.

Lynn was always generous, and he gave us five feet of each kind of fuse. The fireworks type was about 1/10 inch in diameter, made of cotton woven around a gunpowder core and coated with something that made it glossy and stiff. Since this was safe and dependable, we cut off a few inches to use in our first test. We headed for the other side of the tracks where there were open fields for miles. I was carrying the bomb, looking for a suitable spot, when I noticed a small hole in the ground. It was probably an old gopher hole. I stuffed the bomb down the hole, lit it, and ran.

After ten to fifteen seconds there was a loud blast. It was considerably louder than an equally-sized black powder bomb would have been. We ran over to examine the results. It had created a hole more than a foot in diameter. I immediately began searching for pieces of the pipe. (When telling other kids of your exploits, it is always more effective if you have some relics to show.) Down in the crater, I found one of the end-caps, and nearby, most of the pipe. It was split and shattered, with sharp edges—quite impressive for show and tell.

A couple more experiments followed, using one-inch diameter pipe, but soon our supply of ingredient "X" was exhausted.

Logistical Problems

Realizing that we had used all of our supply of ingredient "X," our first thought was to head back to Rexall's where I had purchased the first supply, but I couldn't use the "mouthwash" fib again. This was just 2 weeks later. A Thrifty drug store was located just a couple of miles farther away. That's where we headed. When I asked the druggist if he had any ingredient "X," he said he would check. In a few seconds he came back and asked, "How much do you want?" That was music to our ears. We asked how much it would cost. He looked it up and informed us it would be 65 cents per pound. We bought the whole one-pound jar.

With great anticipation, we raced home and opened the jar, but instead of a fine powder, we found crystals. Gads! We knew crystals wouldn't burn right, and since we had broken the seal on the jar, we couldn't return it. Now what?

Then I remembered Charley's mortar and pestle. Charley had bought a set so we could return the borrowed one to Lynn. With the mortar and pestle we could just grind the crystals into a fine powder as we had done with the carbon granules. It was a bit of a bother, but it was a solution. I hurried to Charley's place. Kenny stayed behind, because he and Charley were never on very friendly terms. Charley gave me the set and said I could keep it until he wanted it back. With girls on his mind, he probably saw no further use for it.

RESEARCH CONTINUES

One afternoon Kenny brought me some samples of different kinds of chemicals he thought might be suitable candidates to mix with ingredient "X." One by one we tried each of them by burning small samples. After completing the burning-rate tests we followed up by performing tests using some small (1/2-inch pipe) bombs. All of these created about the same size explosions and craters. The big difference was the antimony trisulfide bomb. We could never find any sizable pieces of the pipe casing after the explosions—just a few small fragments imbedded in the crater.

Fortunately, our research revealed that when ingredient "X" is mixed with any oxidizable material (something that burns), then the mixture becomes sensitive to friction or grinding. We did some crude experiments to get a feel for just how sensitive it was. We found when mixed with sugar it was not sensitive to ordinary handling, but it could be set off if ground or hit with a hammer. Everything else we tried mixing with ingredient "X," was more sensitive and could be set off with the slightest grinding or impact. Now we knew why sugar, as ludicrous as it sounded, was chosen for the original formula.

BUMPS & GRINDS FORBIDDEN—CA. 1941

One afternoon, during a three-hour time slot between when I got home from school and when my dad got home from work, I was in the garage, about to make a batch of bomb powder. Fred Keyes wandered by, saw what I was doing, and wanted to help, so I dubbed him my "lab assistant."

Fred was an odd duck. His hair was never combed and his clothes were usually rumpled, and sometimes even smelly. Fred was amiable, but not too fastidious. The most attractive thing about him was his sister, Vivian. Fred wasn't part of our inner sanctum, but I knew him because he lived nearby.

I had never been convinced that sugar made the best bombs. After all, sugar had a lot of water crystallized in it and when burned, it produced even more water from the hydrogen and oxygen in its molecule. So on this occasion, I was going to build a "sulfur" bomb.

I got out the mortar and pestle and set Fred to grinding some ingredient "X" crystals into powder. I told him, when he was finished, to put the powder into a cardboard container, to add in an equal amount of sulfur, and finally to stir them together carefully.

In the meanwhile, I was preparing the bomb casing. The hardest part was drilling a hole for the fuse in one end-cap. Dad had an electric drill we always used, but the bits were old and dull. I didn't realize I could buy a new bit for only a dime.

While I was drilling into the cap, the thing exploded with a big flash. The garage immediately filled with white acrid smoke. I could hardly see Fred as he raced out into the open air. I was right behind him. We were both choking from sulfur dioxide fumes.

When I got a look at him, his face was scorched, his eyelashes and brows were missing, and his hair was singed off several inches above his forehead. Fred had thick lips, and they were beginning to swell and blister, but unlike Charley's case, Fred's eyes were spared. All in all, he wasn't hurt too badly; he just looked like hell.

He told me that after he had ground up the crystals, he added the sulfur to the mortar and was mixing them together with the pestle when it happened. Big surprise!

After the smoke and gas cleared out of the garage, we ventured back in and Fred washed his face in the service tub, but he still looked terrible. His face was starting to burn, and he decided to go home to put some ointment on it. After that, Fred stopped coming around.

That was a painful lesson for Fred, but a lifesaver for me, because this made it clear that when assembling a bomb, if any powder were left on the pipe threads the friction between the pipe threads and the end-cap when being screwed on could set the thing off. After that, we made sure to clean the threads _very_ carefully before assembly.

Over the next couple of months we built several bombs, using various mixtures. We settled on the use of two-inch pipe about six inches long, since that size could be purchased from plumbing supplies, already threaded, with end-caps to fit. No one dreamed we were making bombs with these.

AQUATIC ADJUNCT—CA. 1942

Kenny and I were fascinated with setting our new bombs off underwater. With the limited supply of dynamite fuse we had obtained from Lynn, we were in a position to give it a try. Dynamite fuse is waterproof, and it will burn under water as well as in the air.

Our first attempt was made using our (now standard) two-inch pipe design, filled with ingredient "X" and an acidic mixture. After assembling the thing and fitting it with an eight-inch fuse, we waterproofed the whole bomb with airplane dope. I took movies of the preparation.

After it dried, we headed for the Rio Hondo River several miles away and crossed over the Whittier Boulevard Bridge to the opposite bank. That would put us out of reach of the Montebello Police in case anyone reported an explosion.

Looking for a suitable spot (deeper than the usual 2-3 feet), we walked south almost a mile. There we spotted a place that appeared to be 5-6 feet deep. The banks were covered with tall reeds and rushes, great for hiding if necessary.

I found a shallow place and waded out to the middle of the river with my camera. When all was ready, Kenny lit the fuse, tossed the bomb into the deep spot, and ran to a place where he could watch. Dynamite fuse has a very predictable burning rate, so I counted off…"one chimpanzee, two chimpanzees, etc." until just a few seconds were left. Then I started the camera; this technique was to conserve precious film.

The explosion produced a muffled boom, immediately followed by a geyser of water and a plume of smoke. It was fun, but not nearly as impressive as the depth charges we had seen in the newsreels. (Naturally, since naval depth charges use about 300 pounds of high explosive.)

We made several more underwater bombs, trying different mixtures, but the results were much the same. On one occasion we took along a couple of girls that we had previously taken ice-skating. The best part of this outing was that we got the girls to take off their shoes and wade out in the river. In those days, girls wore long dresses that were just high enough to expose their bobby sox. How titillating, seeing them hoist their skirts above their knees!

PATRIOTIC DISPLAY—CA. 1942

Eventually, the Fourth of July arrived. Here was our chance to replenish our supply of fireworks, especially firecrackers for their flash-powder and fuses. This year Kenny wanted to make some formulations that would produce colored smoke when burned. He had learned from Lynn that by adding certain dyes to the powder mixture, brightly colored smokes could be generated.

In no time we had red smoke, blue smoke, yellow smoke, and green smoke. We decided we would make a mortar that would fire up three aerial bombs at once. These would explode high in the air—forming red, white and blue smoke clouds. Great! How patriotic!

But wait! We had a problem. There was no such thing as a white dye. So what else could we use to produce a bright white cloud? The wartime newsreels of the times provided the answer; however, I'm not going to reveal what this stuff is; it's too dangerous to mess with. For the story, I will refer to it as ingredient "Y."

By this time Kenny and I had found better sources for our chemical needs. One was National Chemical Co. in the industrial area of Los Angeles. There we found ingredient "Y" in one-pound cans. It wasn't exactly cheap, but we bought one.

Sometimes the gods seem to watch over you. We somehow sensed that we were dealing with something dangerous. Kenny knew of a method of mixing dangerous chemicals without the friction of stirring. Since ingredient "Y" was new to us, we took only a very small amount (about the size of a match head), put it on a sheet of paper; then added an equal amount of ingredient "X" next to it. Kenny then picked up the corners of the paper, one at a time, causing the two powders to mix by rolling over each other.

That went well. Kenny picked up the paper with the mixture and carefully placed it on the garage floor. Then he got a kitchen match (the old wood kind nearly 3 inches long), lit it, and touched it to the little pea-sized pile on the paper. CRACK! A very loud, very sharp report like a 45 cal. pistol went off. A big puff of the whitest smoke appeared. Tiny pieces of paper were floating everywhere. Kenny recoiled backwards, still holding the match—well actually, its stub. The match had shattered, leaving only what was between his finger and thumb. Then blood began to ooze from the tips of his two exposed digits.

What we wanted was to produce nice bright white smoke, which we did, but what we had stumbled on was an explosive mixture that burned so incredibly fast it exploded without the need for *any kind* of casing. What a great find, or so we thought.

JUST HOW DANGEROUS?

We immediately knew that this stuff could make a great blasting cap, but we had no idea how dangerous it was to mix or store. So, for a test we made a second tiny batch as before. Again, we set it on the garage floor, but this time, instead of setting it off with a match, we decided to grind it a bit with a stick to see how sensitive it was.

I took a yardstick and gingerly reached over to stir the powder. It tolerated stirring for a second, then the stick lightly ground some of the powder against the floor. CRACK! It went off as before, taking a corner of the yardstick with it.

We should have given up on the stuff right there, but we rationalized that it was safe enough to mix if we didn't stir it. In those days, the Dixie Cup company was making small disposable paper cups for use at water coolers. They were tapered cylinders with a flat, round bottom. We had a package of these and used them for weighing out small quantities of chemicals. It occurred to me that if we put the two ingredients into one of these cups and slowly rotated the cup while we held it tipped at an angle (sort of like a cement mixer), we could mix the ingredients without stirring.

This seemed to work well, and it would allow us to take the two ingredients separately to a test site and mix them there—much safer than carrying the mixed ingredients around. So that's exactly what we did for our first field test.

Kenny's parents had moved from Bandini to a house in South Montebello. Behind the house was open acreage, with a tree here and there. It became our test area for small to medium amounts of explosives. We headed there to make a moderate-sized batch of our new find. Using a Dixie cup, we mixed about a teaspoon of each ingredient together and poured it on the ground. We carefully stuck in a fuse, composed of a soda straw filled with a slow burning powder. Then we spotted a tin can and placed it over the pile. Finally, Kenny found a wooden box nearby and put it over the whole thing.

I had managed to get a roll of color film for my movie camera, so I set up a safe distance off to capture the explosion. Kenny lit the fuse and ran. In a few seconds, BLAM! A blast of dust rose from the ground. Wood flew in all directions. We ran back to look at the hole and gather up the debris. It was kind of disappointing. It had created a lot of shattering energy, but not much of a blast. After a bit of thought, we concluded that this kind of explosive doesn't produce much gas (hence little blast effect), but what gas it does produce it generates extremely rapidly, causing the shattering effect. One learns something new every day.

A Panic Call—CA. 1942

One summer afternoon Kenny and I had been mixing up small quantities of our new "Devil's Mixture" in my garage. After running some tests, we still had a teaspoon or so of the powder left in a Dixie cup. We decided to put it up on a small, high shelf, figuring it would be safe enough—not too smart, as it turned out.

The next morning I caught my bus and headed for Sherwin-Williams. It was summer vacation, and I was working full time in the lab now. It was washday for Mom. Her washing machine was located in the garage, next to a service tub, about three or four feet below the shelf where we had stashed the paper cup of powder.

Mom was making trips to and from the house with armloads of clothes, then to the back yard to hang the washed ones on the clotheslines. At about 10:30 that morning she happened to be in the house when she heard this loud explosion. She ran out the back door to see a big cloud of white smoke coming from the open garage doors.

Immediately, she ran to the phone. Did she call the fire department? No! She called *me* at work. Over the very loud PA system someone bellowed. "Mickey McCoy, answer line 3. There's been an explosion at your house!" I grabbed the phone. It was Mom screaming hysterically, "You've blown up the garage. Get home, *now*!"

So I ran out of the building; caught a bus; made a transfer to another bus; and finally got home—about 45 minutes later. Mom had calmed down some. She just pointed to the garage. I went out to inspect the damage.

First, the shelf on which the Dixie cup was sitting was gone—disintegrated—no sign of it anywhere. Beneath it had been a second larger shelf on which Mom kept her box of Rinso soap chips. It was blown off, but I found it lying on the garage floor, brackets all bent. The box of Rinso had been blown to bits. Soap chips were everywhere. It looked as though it had snowed. To the right of the shelves was a window; the glass had been blown out into the yard. Further to the right, were some wide shelves. They were still intact. It was where Mom stored her Mason jars. Only a couple of jars remained on the shelves. The rest (about 2 dozen) were scattered and broken all around the garage. And finally, Dad had mounted a porcelain light socket on a two-by-four stud above the shelf where the explosion occurred. It was sheared off cleanly, just two wires left dangling.

I hurriedly cleaned up the mess before Dad got home. Still, he couldn't miss the window, shelves, and light that were gone. Strangely, I don't remember him saying anything to me about this mini-disaster. Apparently he got whatever explanation he wanted from Mom. He probably figured he could get a straighter story from her.

From this experience Kenny and I learned that this stuff is totally unpredictable. With a little further research, we learned that every State in the Union had outlawed the mixing or manufacturing of this explosive. The reason? Every explosive and fireworks company that had ever set up to make it had been destroyed in a disastrous explosion! Did that deter us? Of course not; we were still adolescents, you know.

THE BUCKING PACKARD—CA. 1943

By the winter of 1942–43 Kenny had dropped out of high school, gotten a full-time job as a chemist (at Gooch Labs), and bought an old 1928 Buick to get around in. However, we still saw each other frequently.

One evening we were discussing our super burning mixture (ingredient "X" and ingredient "Y") when a devilish thought occurred to one of us. If we took a *small* amount of this mixture and put it on the street, eventually a car would run over it, causing it to explode with a loud report. The driver would think he had a blowout and pull over. Hee, hee, ho, ho—we chortled at the thought. So we got the containers of both ingredients and a Dixie cup and got into Kenny's old Buick. It was about 9:00 p.m.

At first we thought we would put it on Whittier Boulevard, but as we considered that, we realized there would be too much traffic for comfort, and since the boulevard was illuminated by streetlights, someone might see us. So we settled on a street in the neighborhood: the intersection of Alston and Hendricks. That intersection had no streetlights. Great!

We proceeded to the intersection and stopped. I got into the back seat with the two ingredients and a Dixie cup. Kenny turn on the interior lights so I could see what I was doing, but the dome light was so dim I could hardly make out anything. Just the same, I opened the bottle containing one of the ingredients and poured out what seemed like a small amount into the cup. I repeated this with the second bottle and put the lids back on both bottles. Things were going along just fine.

Then I took the Dixie cup, tilted it to the proper angle and began to turn it slowly. I could feel the powders tumbling over each other, and I suddenly realized that more powder was in the cup than I had thought. In fact, there was *way, way* more powder than I thought. Panic took over. It felt like enough to kill us if it went off, and this stuff was extremely sensitive. I told Kenny what had happened and he said, "Dump it out in the street, but be damned careful." So I opened the door, stepped out of the car and *carefully* dumped it on the street.

As it happened, Bud Lane lived about five or six houses down the street on Alston. We decided to go there to hide out. Bud and his girlfriend Gerry Doyle were in the living room. Bud's parents were gone somewhere. While we waited, I began to imagine the worst. I feared that someone might cross the street and step on the pile, blowing off a foot or worse.

After a short while, we confessed to Bud and Gerry what we had done. They didn't seem to appreciate the seriousness of it all. As the minutes ticked by, my mind was fantasizing all kinds of horrible scenarios, and I was getting more and more nervous. Kenny's face was sallow, revealing that he was plenty nervous, too. Bud and Gerry were listening to records, showing no apparent concern.

Finally, shortly after 10:00 p.m., we heard an enormous BOOM. Bud ran to the front door and looked toward the intersection. He decided to go down to the corner to see what had happened. Gerry stayed behind. Kenny and I peeked through the partially open door. All up and down the street house lights were turning on. I could make out some headlights at the intersection. They were illuminating an ever-increasing crowd of people.

After about 15 minutes, Bud returned. We anxiously awaited his report. Believe it or not, this is what he told us. "A man (about 25 or so) said he was driving along Hendricks when there was this enormous explosion. The front of his car, a Packard, jumped into the air like a bucking horse; then slammed back down on the ground. When he got out to see what had happened, he found *both* front tires blown out. While he and some others were standing in the street discussing the event, someone noticed a patch about three feet in diameter on the street under the car, eerily glowing in the darkness." Bud verified that he, too, had seen the glowing patch.

Eventually, someone called a tow truck that hauled the Packard and its driver off. Soon the lights in houses up and down the street began to switch off and the neighborhood returned to normal.

Neither Kenny nor I was ever able to explain how both front tires could have blown out. We did, however, know why the street had a glowing spot. That was due to a property of ingredient "Y."

_____CHRONIC FUSE PROBLEMS

◆

Again with the Acid—1942
Dress Rehearsal
Act One
Act Two & Finale

AGAIN WITH THE ACID—CA. 1942

Eventually, we ran out of dynamite fuse, which ended the underwater experiments. We were too embarrassed to ask Lynn for any more. After all, he'd had to steal it from his dad when he went to visit him.

So Kenny and I set our minds to work on alternate methods. We considered using electricity, and eventually we did, but at this time a novel idea occurred to us. Kenny had learned that sulfuric acid could set off ingredient "X" explosive mixtures. I recalled that a certain acid eats through cotton, so we conceived the idea of having the acid slowly eat its way through a cotton plug and then into our explosive under the plug, setting it off.

Brilliant! For the bomb, we envisioned a 2-inch pipe with the usual cap on one end—the bottom in this case. At the other end, we would reduce the diameter to 1/2-inch with a nipple. Into the nipple we would screw a 4-inch length of 1/2-inch pipe.

Next we would ram a predetermined wad of cotton into the 1/2-inch pipe. Then we would take the bomb across the tracks, dig a hole into which we could set it upright, and finally pour in the sulfuric acid, screw a 1/2 inch cap on the top, and run.

Great idea, but over the years we had become cautious. We had no idea how fast the acid would eat through cotton, how much cotton to use, how hard to pack it, or how much acid it would take to eat its way through.

DRESS REHEARSAL

Kenny came up with (8) 6-inch by 1/2-inch test tubes. Their bore was the same as the 1/2-inch pipe we planned to use. We put a tablespoon of sugar in the bottom of each and lined them up in a test-tube holder. This would simulate the explosive mixture and give us something against which to ram the cotton. Next, we measured out three different size wads of cotton, forming two of each size. By this time Kenny had acquired a beam balance that was sensitive to about a hundredth of a gram. We used that to determine the size of the cotton wads.

Accompanied by some scratchy notes, we put the wads into the test tubes and rammed them in place. Then into one of the test tubes we put a measured amount of acid and timed how long it took the acid to eat its way to the sugar. One by one we repeated the test, using different amounts of acid with different size wads of cotton.

In one case, the acid was absorbed before it made it through. In another case, the acid made it through a small wad in only a couple of minutes (too dangerous). But just like Goldilocks, we found one combination that was "just right." It took about 10 minutes. As we watched the acid eat its way through the samples, we saw that it moved in fits and jerks as it exploited "worm-hole" like paths through the cotton. This made us nervous, so we went with the slower configuration.

ACT ONE

Now we were ready. We decided on a small test bomb, using 1/2-inch pipe about 8 inches long. It wouldn't require a nipple, since it would all be one diameter. We filled it about half full, using an ingredient "X" and sugar mixture, then we weighed a specific amount of cotton. I carefully tamped it into place. Kenny pre-measured the proper amount of acid into a small glass-stopper bottle, and we set off for the tracks.

The ground was soft from a recent rain, so we just pushed the pipe into the ground to make it stand vertically so the acid would drip through the cotton. Kenny poured in the acid, screwed on the cap, and off we ran. Immediately, we started timing it with our watches.

Tick, tick, tick, tick…on and on…then…BOOM! According to our watches, it took 16 minutes. Great—total success! We felt like true scientists.

ACT TWO & FINALE

A couple of weeks later we decided; enough with the testing; let's go for a full-size one this time. So we bought a 6-inch length of 2-inch pipe threaded on both ends, a 2-inch end-cap, a 2½-inch nipple, a 5-inch length of 1/2-inch threaded pipe, and a 1/2-inch end-cap.

We screwed the larger end-cap on the bottom of the 2-inch body, filled it with our standard powder, carefully cleaned the threads, screwed on the nipple, and then the 1/2-inch pipe. Finally, we weighed out a wad of cotton and carefully rammed it home.

We headed back to the railroad tracks. When we got there, I looked around for a gopher-hole and soon spotted one. Into it the bomb went. Kenny removed the stopper from the bottle containing the acid and poured it into the top. Immediately, I put on the end-cap and in my nervousness got it cross-threaded. Kenny didn't see any need to wait around and took off. Finally I got the cap screwed on, tightened it as tight as I could, and ran.

From a safe distance away, we started to time the fuse with our watches. Ten minutes approached and finally passed...no explosion. We kept waiting...15 minutes, 20 minutes. What the devil had happened? The minutes crept by about as fast as grass grows. After an hour, we began to assume the acid had all been absorbed before it got to the powder.

Since these bombs represented a fair amount of investment in money and time to us, we began to talk *insanely* about going back and disarming it.

We were impatient. Finally, the slightly more insane of us (me) led the way to the bomb. I kneeled down, pulled it out of the dirt, and laid it down on the ground. With my nearly as stupid buddy standing a few feet behind me, I unscrewed the bottom end-cap off. As I leaned over the thing, having just set it back down on the ground, it went off with a brilliant flash and a horrible explosion. The pipe casing recoiled violently and bounced along the ground 75, or maybe even 100 feet. With the bottom end uncapped, it had acted like a cannon instead of a bomb. Fortunately, the pipe didn't fragment; that would have made a messy funeral.

There I was, lying on my back, gasping for breath. It felt like someone had hit me in the solar plexus with a four-by-four. Kenny came over, looked down and said something...no doubt something insipid like, "Are you OK?" I couldn't make it out. My ears were ringing like a Chinese war gong.

When I was able to get up, we gathered up the casing and slowly made our way home. Hours later, after the ringing subsided in my ears, I noticed that if I held my nose and blew, I could hear air leaking out of my right ear. This condition lasted for six or eight months. I feel sure the blast cracked an eardrum. Fortunately, it seemed to have healed up on its own.

It was a brilliant idea for a fuse, but all the same, we decided not to make any more.

_____HIGH-SCHOOL HIGH JINKS

✦

Paint Fight—1942
Glowing in the Dark—1942
Shirley's Halloween Party
What a Gas—1943
Wheels—1943
Snapped Sac
Pool Hall Caper—1943
Science Award—1944

PAINT FIGHT—1942

During the summer of 1942, I got a job at Sherwin-Williams Paint Company as a "bottle washer" in their research lab. Bottle washing in a paint company is dirty work, but fortunately, paint companies have tons of solvents of every kind. Through my efforts, Fred Keyes got a job there too. I managed to slip the dirty jobs off onto him while I learned how to run various tests used in a paint lab.

One afternoon the lab got word the warehouse was receiving a lot of returned paint from stores around the city. The lab's job was to investigate the problem and hopefully find a way to correct it so the stuff could be salvaged. One of the chemists went over to the warehouse and brought back a sample and the story.

The product was aluminum paint. Something was wrong with the formulation and gas was forming in the cans, causing them to swell and blow off their lids. The chemistry behind this is as follows: Aluminum pigment (finely ground aluminum metal) is stable in an acidic (low pH) varnish. However, in a basic (high pH) varnish, aluminum reacts to form hydrogen, and this batch had mistakenly been made with a varnish that had turned basic.

Trucks were picking up this paint from all around the city and bringing it to the warehouse. The cans were all pregnant, and lids were popping off at random. Because of the mess, this was being transported to the back of the factory into what was known as the "intermix room." Bad batches of paint were stored in this room until the lab could devise a way to intermix it with good batches to "work it off" (get rid of it).

It was late in the afternoon by the time all this bad paint had been picked up and put in the intermix room. The head chemist approached Fred and me and said that if we would like to work late, they would give us overtime pay. We never turned down money. The job was to go to the intermix room, open these cans and dump the contents into fifty-five gallon drums. The cans varied in size from half-pint to a gallon.

After everyone else left for the day, we started to the intermix room to make some easy extra money. When we got there, we could hear the occasional "pop" of a can blowing its lid. An old wood table and bench were in the room, both multi-colored with layers of old paint spills and splashes. Each of us, armed with a pry-type can opener, sat down at the table and began our task. We dumped the cans that had already popped their lids into a drum. The others would blow their lid with the slightest pry from our openers. They would fly up and hit the ceiling, often leaving rings of aluminum paint where they hit.

This was fun, but it was getting messy. Whenever a lid flew off some paint would spatter out. With every pop we were getting sprayed. Being kids, when one of my cans caused some paint to land on Fred he would say, "You did that on purpose," and would dip his finger into a can and flick some paint on me. Well, that led to a full-fledged paint fight. Soon we were flinging handfuls of paint at each other, and in no time we were both covered. Since this was aluminum paint, we looked like the Tin Man from the Wizard of Oz.

After a few hours we finished opening and dumping all the cans into two drums. We elected not to put lids on the drums, for fear of blowing the place up. Cleaning ourselves up was a mess. Probably the toughest paint to clean up is aluminum, because the particles of metal are ground to an exceedingly fine state. We stripped off; washed ourselves down with a couple of gallons of mineral spirits, and then washed our clothes in a five-gallon pail full of lacquer thinner. It took several rinses to get most of the aluminum out. After our clothes were dry we went home, happy as clams. We had each made about $3.00 in overtime.

GLOWING IN THE DARK—1942

While working at Sherwin-Williams, I learned the ingredients in luminescent paint. The pigment that caused it to glow in the dark was calcium sulfide. It was a special variety, containing certain impurities which enabled it to store up energy when exposed to light and then to release the energy back as a blue-violet light in the dark. The phenomenon is called "luminescence."

Recently I had been on a school trip to the Griffith Park Planetarium. I was impressed with their star projector. I thought it would be neat to paint dots of this luminescent paint on the ceiling of my bedroom to make it look like stars when the lights were turned off. I brought home a quart can of this pigment and mixed some of it with varnish. Then I marked the ceiling with a pencil, using a star chart to locate the winter constellations and other stars. Finally, I painted a dot on each mark. I varied the size of the dots depending on the brightness of the star.

Anxiously, I waited for darkness that evening to see the results. When darkness finally came, I turned on the room lights to charge up the dots. When I turned the lights off, I was stunned by the degree of realism achieved in the effect. It looked exactly like the house had no roof and you could see directly up to the night sky.

Even my parents, who rarely expressed any interest in my endeavors, thought it was quite impressive. I, like any kid, bragged about it to my friends, and some came by to see if I was making it all up or not. Every night when I went to bed I marveled at the realism. I got my money's-worth of pleasure for my effort.

SHIRLEY'S HALLOWEEN PARTY

My sister Shirley had a few friends her own age, but her forte was acting as a kind of leader of the little neighborhood kids. These kids were generally about five or six years old. Shirley's self-appointed role was similar to that of a camp counselor. She organized and supervised games for them after school and during summer vacation. She was the undisputed head honcho of a troop of about ten kids. They loved the structure she provided, and she obviously loved her role as well.

The year Shirley turned eight, she decided to host a Halloween party for her little kids. She and Mom decorated the house with witches and ghosts and Dad set up a washtub of water in the back yard for apple dunking.

The evening of the party arrived and here came the kids, dressed in their Halloween outfits. As would be expected, Shirley had planned all kinds of games. The games were followed by dunking for apples. The kids were mostly too small for dunking, so Mom tied apples to a string and they tried to bite them "on the swing." Some did a little better at that.

Then Shirley decided to take them all into my bedroom, where she planned to tell them ghost stories in the dark. Like lambs to the slaughter, they followed her into the bedroom. The door was closed and the light switched off. Being little tots, they saw the stars and thought they were somehow outside. From the hall next to the bedroom, I could hear them chattering about the stars above.

Immediately, Shirley began telling them a story—probably a bit too scary for such little kids—and every so often I could hear little yelps of fright. That's when I thought of a clever idea. I went out into the garage, got some of the luminescent pigment and brought it into the bathroom. Here I powdered it onto my face and hands, and then standing close to the light bulb, I charged it up. When I had finished, I turned off the bathroom light and looked at myself in the mirror. Holy crap! I even scared myself. My head looked like a glowing skull. The eyes were just black pits. My hands look like luminous bones.

I recharged myself again with the light, and then turned it off. I had already prepared the hall by shutting all the doors and turning off its light. Then, as quietly as possible, I went into the hall, carefully opened the bedroom door a crack, and slowly slithered both hands into the room. No response. They were too engrossed in Shirley's spook story, so I decided to make some low moaning sounds to get them to look my way. Immediately, there was a solitary scream. I opened the door further and stuck my head in. The kids broke into a cacophony of terrified yells and cries for their mamas. A scramble ensued that sound like a stampede.

I realized this had gone too far, so I reached in and turned on the light. Kids were glued against the walls, screaming; two were trying to get the window open to escape. A couple of brave ones ran past me to get out. Still, several were missing. We found them under the bed. One by one each kid bolted from the house and ran home, most of them screaming.

Boy, did we catch it in spades from the parents. Most of the kids insisted a light be left on at bedtime. Several couldn't sleep. Some had nightmares. None of the parents would let their kids come play at our house for months (in some cases, never again).

WHAT A GAS—1943

In Southern California, natural gas was used for heating. It was dirt-cheap. The underground deposits seemed endless. No one used electricity or oil for heating, and I never ever saw a piece of coal in California. Every home, school, and business had gas piped to it by the Southern California Gas Co.

Natural gas has no odor, and since leaking gas presented the very real hazard of fire, explosion, or suffocation, an odorant was added by the gas company to give the gas a characteristic smell. Everyone who lived in that part of the country knew that smell. Most thought it was the natural odor of the gas.

Kenny, now working part time for Gooch Labs as a chemist, had become acquainted with Jack Mazelli, who was a chemist working in the laboratories of the Southern California Gas Co. Jack was an interesting guy. He could hold your attention while talking about even the most mundane things.

Kenny and I were bumming around one Saturday when we stopped by Jack's place and got to chatting about natural gas. Jack said that the added odorant was called "Calodorant." The odor was so strong it required only a few parts per million to give gas it its characteristic odor.

Then Jack said, "Would you like to see some?"

"Sure," we responded. So, Jack shuffled down to his basement and brought back a bottle. It was about a pint—enough to odorize Los Angeles, I thought.

Immediately Kenny asked, "Could we have some?"

Jack said, "Sure, why not?" and again shuffled down the stairs and retrieved a vial. It was a sample container from the lab where he worked. He opened the larger bottle. I expected the room to smell of the stuff instantly, but it didn't, at least not right away. Apparently the chemical has a high molecular weight and evaporates slowly. He filled up the vial, capped it, and handed it to Kenny. By now, the room did smell as though there was a bad gas leak. It was fall, and Jack opened the windows to vent the smell away.

On the way home, Kenny admitted why he wanted the sample. He could play pranks on people, making them believe they had a gas leak. Ho, ho, pretty funny.

At this time we were both juniors at Montebello High. Kenny hadn't dropped out of school yet. One day we were eating lunch together and Kenny pulled the vial out of his pocket. He said he'd come up with a great idea. The school had scheduled a pep rally for the big football game to be played that afternoon. The rally was to be held in the auditorium—a large, theater-type hall—where the whole student-body would be present.

At the appointed time, Kenny and I filed in with about a thousand others and took some seats next to the aisle along the right side. We were about half-way down. Kenny had planned ahead. He had brought a paper towel from the "Boys room" and had torn off about a 2 by 2 inch square. He handed me the square and told me to fold it length-wise several times and then crimp it in half. When finished, I had a sort of "V" shaped rod of paper.

To start the rally, they dimmed the lights enough so kids would focus their attention on the well-lit stage. After the principal made a few routine announcements, the rally began. Cheerleaders came out with their pompons, kicked up their legs, and led the audience in shouting out M-O-N-T-E...B-E-L-L-O...Rah...Rah...Rah. The kids were getting into the spirit. Maybe, if we shouted loud enough, we could spur our team on to beat our nemesis, South Pasadena.

At about this point, Kenny leaned over with the vial and removed the lid. He told me to dip the crotch of the "V" into it and then quickly flick it down the aisle as far as I could.

I did as instructed, except my aim wasn't very good. The missile landed about eight or nine rows down, but had landed among the seats. The lights were dim, so no one saw me flick it, and since it didn't hit anyone, no one was aware of its flight or landing either.

This was a big auditorium. It was packed with kids, and along each wall—on the left and right sides—were gas heaters spaced about every 15 feet. The auditorium lights had been dimmed, but it wasn't actually dark—a safety requirement so people could find their way out in an emergency.

Soon some kids in front of us began sniffing. Everybody recognized that smell, and concern was developing. Finally a couple of kids got up and walked to the rear of the auditorium. That's where the teachers stood to better monitor the kids. Soon they returned with Mr. Brock, the chemistry teacher.

Mr. Brock, being a very intelligent, analytical guy, began sniffing around the nearby heaters. By now the odor had spread enough to include several of them. He sniffed and sniffed...got down on his knees at each one and sniffed some more. He checked all the shut-off valves. It was fall and none of the heaters had been turned on. The odor was spreading rapidly. The crowd was becoming very nervous and restless. By now several more teachers were in on the search. They were checking the heaters along the left wall as well.

Finally the principal got the word, came out on the stage and stopped the rally. He announced, "Now don't panic, but everyone must evacuate the auditorium immediately. Return to your classes." He didn't say what the emergency was, but by then the word "gas" had spread though the crowd. There was a mini-stampede. Fortunately, no one was hurt.

WHEELS—1943

Fred Keyes and I had been hitchhiking to and from high school every day. Catching a ride was iffy, and sometimes we'd be late to class. One day, Fred had had enough. He took some money he had saved and started shopping around for a car. What he came up with probably didn't quite qualify as a car; "clunker" is a more accurate description.

He picked up for $25.00 a 1928 Chevy coupe. It didn't run, so he tore down the engine in hopes of cleaning it up and getting it to go. He and I spent over a month scraping out carbon deposits, grinding the valves and putting in new rings. Finally we got it going. Now we would have some wheels, if only we could get gas for it.

This was during the war, and gas was rationed. Gas sales were controlled by coupons. Driving to school didn't qualify for a gasoline coupon book. However, kerosene wasn't rationed, so we tried running the engine on kerosene. It wouldn't even start.

Here's where Jack Gretta came to the rescue. His model airplanes used nitro-methane. That wasn't rationed, but it was too expensive to run a car. Jack's idea was to use the nitro-methane to start the engine and then see if it would continue running on kerosene.

We began by squirting some nitro-methane into the carburetor as we cranked the engine. It started easily. Sometimes the engine would continue to run on the kerosene and sometimes it would stall. Stalling was most common on cold days, but after a few starts it would warm up enough to run rough, then finally smooth out.

Once we knew this technique would work, we ran a copper tubing line from the carburetor to a hole in the dashboard. Using a pump-type oil can, filled with nitro-methane, we could start the engine from inside the car. It became our standard method of starting the car.

The engine knocked a lot, had little acceleration and left a trail of black smoke, but it got us to school and back each day.

SNAPPED SAC

Cars of that period had wood frames. The doors were mounted on hinges that were screwed to the car frame. On Fred's car, the hinge screws had all worked loose, been tightened, and worked loose again. This cycle had been repeated over the years until the wood was so chewed up by the screws that they wouldn't stay tight. Naturally, the doors didn't open or close properly. In fact, on the passenger side we just left the door closed and climbed in and out through the window. Fred decided to pound pieces of dowel into the screw holes, and then saw the dowel off flush. This was to take up the slop so the screw would hold better.

One Saturday we did just that. We got the driver's side door mounted, and it worked much better. Then we began working on the other door. This didn't go so well. The dowels had shifted the positions of the screw holes enough that it was hard to get the screws started. I was bent over, holding the door from the bottom and pulling up to position the hinge. Fred was trying to get a screw started through a hole. He yelled, "Higher, higher." I lifted as hard as I could. Soon I was lifting almost the weight of the car. Crack! It sounded like someone breaking a pencil. I couldn't straighten up and a severe pain was running down my right leg. I was through for the day. Still bent over, I limped several blocks home.

In those days people didn't take their kids to the doctor for every little complaint. To justify a $2.00 office visit it had to be a broken bone or worse. The prevailing wisdom was that given time, it would heal by itself.

Sure enough, in a few weeks I could stand up straight and walk without much of a limp, but when I swung my right leg forward, with each step I felt pain down my leg. It was about six months before I could jog or run. Eventually, I learned to ignore most of the pain. However, this event resulted in my having back trouble all my life.

About 10 years later I had to wear a steel brace for a couple of years. Then about 10 years after that, I had surgery to correct two herniated discs. Moral: Kids aren't invincible. They just think they are.

POOL-HALL CAPER—1943

It was February, 1943. By this time Kenny had dropped out of school and had become a full-time chemist for Gooch Labs. Sometime during the previous fall his dad had taken leave from the County Sheriff's Department to volunteer in the Army. Although he was much too old for the draft, he was accepted, and because of his experience as a police officer, he was given a temporary commission as a lieutenant in the Military Police (MP). Immediately, he was shipped off to the Italian Theater.

Kenny's mom had a job working second-shift in some company making defense materials. So Kenny was very much on his own, especially in the evenings, and had gotten into the habit of coming to our place every night for supper after he got off work. Sometimes he would hang around all evening, and other times he'd go off to be with other friends.

One place he frequented was a pool hall in Montebello. Kenny was only 17, but he was in a hurry to become an adult. There he smoked, played pool, and felt very grown up. It was there that he ran into Jerry Hall, who was a year older. Jerry and his friend Phil, another 17-year-old kid, had come up with this neat plan to burglarize the pool hall. Supposedly, Jerry had cased the place and had learned where the owners hid their operating cash. His plan included breaking into the pinball machines and emptying the coin boxes.

He had noted that the rear door dead bolt lock didn't work; they simply barred the door with a 2 x 4 dropped into a "U" channel mounted on each side of the doorframe. Breaking in would simply involve drilling a hole in the door above the 2 x 4, reaching in and lifting it out of its channels, and opening the door.

They wanted Kenny to join them. Now Kenny had done his share of delinquent acts, but he had never gone so far as breaking and entering or burglarizing. I didn't understand his motives. I expect that it had to do with feeling grown-up, or something, and for some reason he wanted me to join in with them. I said, "No way," but over several evenings he kept pressing me. Peer pressure can be a powerful thing, and finally I said I would, but that I didn't want any of the money and I would only act as a lookout.

So the die was cast. The day selected was Friday, because that was when most of their customers got paid and when they spent the most. The time was to be 2:00

a.m. in the morning, when the city was nearly deserted. I was to walk up and down across the street from the pool hall, watching for anything that looked like a police car coming. If I saw anything I was to light a match as though I was lighting a cigarette. Phil was to be positioned inside the pool hall at the front window, watching me for any signal.

Next Kenny informed me that they needed something to drill a 4-inch hole in the door, through which they could put their hand and grab the 2 x 4. He reminded me that my dad had a hand brace, and more important, an expansion bit that could be adjusted to cut a hole that big. I was in this deep, so I agreed to take it along.

To the average crooked mind, this must have seemed like a foolproof plan, but it turned out to be more of a proof-of-a-fool plan. Jerry, the mastermind, never observed that *right next door* to the pool hall was the office of the "Montebello News," a small local paper that printed a weekly rag. They ran their press once a week—on Friday night. This run would last until about midnight. In the early morning hours they would sort and bale the papers for pickup at around 5:00 a.m. Their distribution day was Saturday.

On the appointed night, Kenny and I drove over to Montebello and parked on a side street a couple of blocks from the pool hall. Kenny took the brace and bit and headed to the rear of the building, where he was to meet Jerry and Phil. I walked out onto Whittier Boulevard, where I began my surveillance. I noticed a faint light in the newspaper office, but assumed it was just a nightlight for the police patrols. I was right. *But* also, there were two men working in the back. The door between them and the front office was closed.

After about 20 minutes I saw Phil's face against the window; they had gotten in. We waved a quick acknowledgment, then I began walking (suspiciously) up and down the street, across from the pool hall.

The two men in the back of the newspaper office heard sounds from next door.., probably the greedy attempts to break into the pinball machines. One of them went to their office window, looked out, and saw me walking back and forth. Any moron could see that I was a lookout, so while the one guy watched me from his front window, the other called the police.

In a few minutes I spotted the headlights of a car coming from the center of town. I lit a match and kept watching. As it got closer, I could see the chrome siren on the roof. I assumed it was just on a routine patrol, but to be safe I walked a short distance to a gas station to hide in the men's room till it passed. It stopped in front of the pool hall.

Two cops were in the car. One stayed inside; the other got out and headed for where I was hiding. The men's room was small, with no place to hide. I thought about just coming out and turning myself in, but I couldn't imagine how he knew anyone was there. I knew he couldn't have seen me enter from a couple of blocks down the street.

I was skinny (about 135 pounds) in those days, so I decided to hide behind the door. The door opened about 90 degrees, then it stopped against a wall. I slipped into the narrow space between the door and the wall. I could see through the gap between the door and the frame and watched the officer approach. I splayed my feet like Charley Chaplin and turned my head sideways to make my profile as thin as possible. When he got to the door opening, he scanned the interior with his flashlight. Seeing nothing, but having been told that someone was in there, he pushed against the door. I sucked up my stomach, but my head was too wide. The door compressed against my ear. He pushed a couple times more—same thing. Then I saw the chrome plated muzzle of his .38 special pointing at me through the crack. "Come out with your hands up." I did.

He cuffed and frisked me and led me to the police cruiser. In the meanwhile, a second cruiser had blocked escape from the rear alley. They gathered up the other three and we all headed for the police station. When we got there, they removed our cuffs and got our names, our parent's names, addresses, etc., and put us each into a separate cell.

Each cell was equipped with a commode and a steel plank that was connected by hinges to the wall. A length of chain was connected at each end so it would be horizontal when in the down position. It served as a bench and a bed. The only other thing in the cell was one army blanket. There was no heat, and this was a cold, damp February night. Fortunately, we were all dressed for the occasion, with heavy clothing and jackets. I used my blanket as a thin mattress.

The next morning they took us one at a time into an interviewing room, where we were faced with a guard, an officer who also was a local preacher, and our parents. They asked all the usual questions. Then, the best news was when they explained their policy to our parents.

It seems that prior to the war, felonies such as ours were put on the court's docket. A judge would review the case. First offense juveniles under 21 were usually given a short stint—three months or so—in the reform school that was located a few miles east in Whittier. Adults were charged with a felony, and if convicted, usually were sent to prison.

However, during the war—because of the draft—efforts were made to liberalize the system. First, laws were enacted by Congress to reduce the age of legal majority from 21 to 18, obviously to provide more men for the draft. Secondly, to empty the jails and reform schools as much as practical, again to augment the draft, all but serious cases were given probation. My parents appeared much relieved.

All of us, including Jerry, although he was 18 and therefore an adult, were given 6 months probation. Every Friday afternoon I had to report to the police station. The preacher-officer would spend about 20 minutes with me, trying to point me toward a proper life. It wasn't necessary, though. I had been converted *completely* by that one night in jail. I absolutely decided that crime was not for me, in any shape or form. In any case, after 3 months they decided I was cleansed enough and they dropped the probation requirement.

SCIENCE AWARD—1944

When I was in high school, Bausch & Lomb—an optics company known for its microscopes, binoculars, and other scientific equipment—sponsored an annual science contest for high school senior classes. It was held near the end of the school year so the award could be presented at the Awards Assembly just before graduation.

Being a science geek, I had heard of the award, but that was about it. On my own, I would never have competed for this or any other award. However, my chemistry teacher, Mr. Brock, had taken a shine to me and suggested I enter. I wasn't very enthused, but with his encouragement I finally decided to give it a shot.

The competition consisted of three written examinations: chemistry, physics, and biology, and a thesis on a subject of your choice. I had gotten A's in chemistry and physics classes, but only managed to drag down a C in biology. I was weak when it came to memorizing random information like names. Latin names were the worst, and in those days, that's mainly what high school biology was.

I knew my main competitor would be Chuck Hammond. He was a straight A student with an unbelievable memory. Several other science geeks were competing as well. One was Hal Weston. He knew minerals and chemistry, but not much else. Then there was Jack Garner. His dad was an M.D., and he planned on becoming one, too. He had taken Latin instead of Spanish, and could impress you with his Latineze. He was very good at biology, knew some chemistry, but didn't know beans about physics. Other kids had entered the competition, but each had some weakness or other. Chuck Hammond was the guy to beat.

The tests were to be held in the appropriate classrooms, supervised by the senior teacher of that subject—Mr. Brock, chemistry; Mr. Walker, physics; and Miss Compton, biology.

Miss Compton was about 50, significantly overweight, wore her hair in a bob, and no make-up. From this and her drab clothing, it was obvious she had long ago given up the game of trying to attract men. Her only attempt to improve her appearance was that she wore a girdle.

That girdle was her constant enemy. When she lectured before the class, you'd see her squirm a bit. Then as the binding worsened, she would attempt to tug it down through her dress. Finally, when the binding became unbearable, she would grab the crotch of the offending thing with both hands and pull it into submission. This display would elicit a giggle or two from the less sensitive boys. The girls would avert their eyes. I think over the years this act had been relegated to Miss Compton's subconscious. When presenting her lectures, she never skipped a beat while accomplishing such relief.

I didn't bother to study for either the chemistry or the physics test. I figured I should spend as much time as possible brushing up on biology. I reasoned my best chance of beating Chuck Hammond was to come up with a thesis that would outshine his. I thought I had a chance there, because he was a scholarly type, whereas I was a more pragmatic, hands-on type. Finally I settled on using my homemade spectroscope to measure the wavelength of light.

My spectroscope was a diffraction grating type. These used a diffraction grating, rather than a prism, to analyze the light source. A diffraction grating consists of some base—usually a glass plate—on which very fine parallel lines have been ruled with a diamond tool into the surface. Generally, they would have either 15,000 or 25,000 lines per inch. To manufacture this required precision equipment. Because of the precision required, diffraction gratings were extremely expensive, and therefore prisms were more commonly used.

However, someone had come up with the idea of making replicas of these gratings by pouring collodion, a thin clear plastic solution, on an original grating. After it was dry, the collodion was peeled off. This thin membrane was then cemented to a thin glass plate for support. Such replicas were very affordable—just a few dollars.

I had obtained a 25,000 line per inch replica grating and constructed a spectroscope in a small wood box. Light to be analyzed would enter through a vertical slit at one edge of the box, pass through the grating, and then diffract at an angle, depending on the wavelength of the light. The effect was that white light would be spread into a spectrum like a rainbow.

For the thesis, I planned to measure the wavelengths of the light emitted by the sodium atom when sufficiently heated. I chose sodium because its emission consists of two very bright lines in the yellow portion of the spectrum. They are close together and easy to see.

A formula relates the variables (grating lines per inch, wavelength of light, and the angle of diffraction). All I needed to do was measure the angles at which these two yellow lines were diffracted by the grating, then I could calculate their wavelengths.

Previously, I had built a carbon arc that I used to heat specimens—usually minerals I was trying to identify. After charging the carbon rods with a small amount of sodium chloride (table salt), I turned on the power and observed the light with my spectroscope. I saw and recognized those two bright yellow lines. Although it was kind of cumbersome, I measured the angles to each line with a protractor. I took the average of about ten readings on each line. Using these averages, I calculated the wavelengths from the formula in the *Handbook of Chemistry & Physics*. Then I wrote my thesis in the format I had learned in science classes.

After turning in my thesis, I took the three examinations. I felt I did well in physics. That exam had only one question I wasn't sure of, and I knew I had aced the chemistry exam. But that damned biology exam…Miss Compton had written questions that were purely esoteric. She didn't teach reasoning in her classes, just memorization. I figured I was screwed.

Several weeks later, it was time for the awards presentations. The whole student body was assembled in the auditorium. First they presented the sports awards: letters for football, then for baseball, next for basketball, and finally for girls badminton. Finally they presented awards for typing and other piddling things.

Everyone expecting an award was sitting in the first few rows so they could trot up on stage when their name was called. These hopefuls were dressed nicely for the occasion. I sat up in the balcony in this big auditorium with a couple of classmates.

Finally, almost as though it were an afterthought, the principal said, "Oh, yes, we also have an award here for the science competition." As if to justify it, he read, "It's an award provided each year by the Bausch and Lomb Company." His voice trailed off, revealing he had little or no knowledge of the company or its award. Then he turned over his notes and read, "This year the winner is Mickey McCoy."

I turned to my friends and asked, "Did he say me?" By then, the principal was shielding his eyes with his hand as he scanned the first few rows, looking for someone getting up to come claim his trophy. No one moved—not even me. Finally, some mouthy kid sitting near me yelled, "He's up here." and pointed at me.

I have always been a phobic about attention being directed at me, and here were a thousand kids, all twisting around in their seats looking up at me. I felt like running out the exit and not stopping, but instead I ran out the exit, down the stairs to one of the big double-door entrances to the auditorium's main floor. Being on a trot, I had flung the doors wide open, accompanied by a flash of bright daylight. What an entrance! I jogged down the aisle and up the stairs to the stage.

I walked over to the principal. He handed me the award, with an insincere, "Congratulations." With cowed head, I mumbled, "Thanks," took it and disappeared off the stage, up the aisle, and out of the building. I never returned to school that day.

Nevertheless, I've always been proud of that award, mostly because I beat out that damned Chuck Hammond. I just know he was sitting in the first few rows, fully expecting to scarf it up. It was a nice bronze medal in a hinged olive wood presentation case. The award also included a certificate with my name on it.

When I got home that afternoon I showed it to Mom. She, always careful not to give me a swelled head, said, "That's nice." I never did show it to Dad. It didn't seem worth the risk.

Now, looking back, I see my dad in a totally different light. Although he was proud of me, I didn't realize it at the time. Much to my surprise, he came to my graduation that year and gave me a wristwatch as a graduation gift.

Bausch & Lomb

HONORARY
SCIENCE AWARD

THIS nationally recognized award for high scholastic attainment in science studies will be presented to the member of the graduating class who, in the faculty's estimation, has shown the greatest progress in science during his or her high school career. The award is sponsored by the Bausch & Lomb Optical Company to further interest in, and understanding of, the sciences.

11. Bausch and Lomb Science Award—ca. 1944

12. Bausch and Lomb Certificate—ca. 1944

13. Bausch and Lomb Medal—ca 1944

_____SCHOOL-YEARS EMPLOYMENT

❖

Informal Jobs—ca. 1938–39
Roots and All
Apprenticeship
Genuine Employment 1941 to 1944
California Flaxseed
Sherwin-Williams Paint

INFORMAL JOBS—CA. 1938 TO 1940

Like most kids, I tried making money any way I could. With all my experience nanny-ing for my sister Shirley, I was a natural for babysitting, but times were still tough as the country struggled its way out of the depression. Most people didn't have money for outside entertainment.

Fortunately, one couple who lived across the street seemed to have a little money to spend. They had two kids: a boy and a girl. The man was a commercial photographer and had built a darkroom in his garage. I used to ask his advice on using my movie camera—lighting, exposure, etc. So I got their business. Kids who babysat usually got 10-15 cents an hour, but this couple was generous and always gave me a half-dollar, even if they were out only 2 or 3 hours.

Charley Heckman had babysitting jobs from one of his neighbors, too. Charley hated being left alone with those kids, so he would get me to go with him. For dealing with the kids, he would split his fee with me, but Charley was amoral. He would poke around under the cushions on the couches and chairs, looking for coins that had fallen out of people's pockets. Surprisingly, he always seemed to find some. Worst of all, he raided the kid's piggy banks, shrewdly leaving enough so they wouldn't notice.

ROOTS AND ALL

I became acquainted with a freelance landscaper-gardener, who performed odd jobs around the neighborhood. He was old—probably near sixty. He generally worked alone, even though this was hard work for someone his age. However, occasionally he'd get a job to take down a tree and haul it away. For that he simply had to have help, so about once every month or two he'd bang on the front door and ask for me.

"Would you help me take down a tree?" he'd asked. I knew from previous jobs he expected me to work most of the day for a dollar, but I would always agree.

My part was to climb the tree with a rope and tie it around the main stalk, about three-quarters of the way up. Then I'd climb down and the two of us would chop a notch in the trunk about six feet above the ground. To make that possible, he'd back up his old 1920's Model T truck to the tree to give us something to stand on. After we had chopped a notch about two-thirds of the way through the trunk, he'd move the truck off, maybe 50 feet. Then he'd get me to crawl under the truck and tie the rope to the frame.

Next, with me warning any oncoming cars, he'd put the miserable old thing in low gear and give it the gas. Eventually the tree would let loose a loud cracking sound and topple into the street. With axes, we would chop it into pieces to fit on the truck's bed.

With that done, we'd begin digging out the roots. That was a tough job. I don't know how he managed. After a couple hours of digging and chopping roots, he would decide it was time to pull it out with the truck and rope so, after tying a secure knot around the top of the trunk, he would start up the truck again. This was always harder—lots of burning tire rubber and horrible clutch noises. Sometimes we'd have to stop and dig some more around the roots.

Eventually, the old man and his old truck would win. After getting the stump in the truck, he'd take me home, reach into his pocket, pull out a sweaty leather purse, and from it retrieve an old, crumpled dollar bill (which he would uncrumple enough to make sure it wasn't a fiver) and hand it to me.

APPRENTICESHIP

The next summer (1940), I decided to find some less back-breaking work. I got acquainted with a guy who had a refrigerator repair shop on Whittier Boulevard. He was looking for an assistant, so I would drop by his shop each morning to see if he needed any help. On the average, every couple of days he would have an appointment for a service call. On those days, he would hire me at 15 cents an hour. He didn't pay much because he reasoned that I was getting free training: the old-world apprentice system, I guess.

I'd go out on these service calls with him. In those days, before Freon, they used either sulfur dioxide or ammonia as refrigerants. Home refrigerators used sulfur dioxide. Ammonia was used in large commercial systems such as air conditioners for theaters and department stores.

Both gases are horrible to work with. Sulfur Dioxide has an extremely strong acrid odor. I think it's trying to warn that it can wreck you. Sulfur Dioxide turns into sulfurous acid when it combines with the moisture in your lungs, producing a painfully burning sensation. The acid then proceeds to destroy your lung tissue.

Whenever he had to "break" a line in the system, sulfur dioxide would come rushing out and the occupants would have to dash outside until it dissipated. I learned to get out fast. After repairing the system, he would fill the system back up from a cylinder of sulfur dioxide he carried in his truck.

The less hazardous part of the job required learning the names of all the tools and parts he carried and being able to produce them on command, just like a nurse in an operating room. He also expected me to help him hoist refrigerators on and off his truck. I was never what you would call a strapping kid, but I was strong enough for my size.

This guy would pay me only at the end of the week. I guess that was to make sure I didn't skip out on him. I never made even $5.00 in one week.

GENUINE EMPLOYMENT—1941 TO 1944

I guess Dad had observed (without comment, as usual) that my working career was floundering. Apparently he discussed with the owner of Deluxe Furnace Co. where he was the foreman of the Electro-plating department that he had a 14-year-old kid whom he would like to put to work. After setting the job up, he told me I could spend the summer working there full-time. It required that I get a Social Security Card and the pay would be minimum wage ($0.25 an hour). I jumped at the offer. Not only did it figure out to be all of $10.00 a week, but also I would be working with my dad. I was overjoyed that he was showing that kind of interest in me.

The electroplating department consisted of a separate building from the rest of the manufacturing operations. It was probably 50 feet wide and 75 feet long. At the rear was a large sliding door, into which handcarts of castings and stampings were pushed in and unloaded for plating. The other end of the building opened onto Western Avenue. Near the rear, along one side, were several grinding-wheel stations, powered by overhead belt pulleys. Next to them were several buffing-wheel stations, also powered by overhead belts.

Opposite these stations at the back of the building was a large motor-generator. The motor was 25 horsepower. It drove a 6 volt, 1000 amp, DC generator which provided the current used in the electroplating process. Between the motor-generator and the front of the building were half a dozen large tanks. The first of these tanks contained a pickling solution where iron castings were cleaned of scale and rust. This was followed by five electroplating tanks: copper, nickel, chrome, bronze, and a smaller one for electroplating precious metals such as silver or gold.

Three white men, the grinder/buffers, worked at the grinding and buffing stations. Both jobs were bad. Grinding caused them to become covered in fine iron and silicon dusts. They wore no masks and they breathed in tons of these pollutants. Buffing was not quite as bad. Here they applied a polishing compound to a cloth wheel and buffed out the marks left by grinding. Of course they would become covered with that compound, too. These poor guys stood on their feet 8 hours a day doing these dirty jobs. They made 60 cents an hour.

The plating tanks were manned by two Mexican men. They loaded the racks with castings and stampings that were lowered into the tanks. In those days, good electroplating consisted of cleaning the object in a pickling solution then washing off the solution under a spray of water. Immediately, the object was lowered into the copper plating tank and given a generous coating of copper. After that, it received a layer of nickel in the next tank. Finally, it would be given either a final layer of chrome plating or bronze. All these tanks contained dangerous chemicals. The pickling tank contained hydrochloric acid. All the other tanks contained cyanide, in one form or another. The Mexicans were paid only 45 cents an hour.

Dad, having a lame leg and being foreman, was allowed to have a straight-back wood chair. He'd walk about the place, observing how the work was going, then sit in his chair for a while. In 10 or 15 minutes he'd repeat the process. He seemed easy-going. The men respected him, and I never saw any confrontations or arguments with his men. He never told me what he was paid, but I figured it was about a dollar an hour.

My job was operating the spray booth. The booth consisted of a small room, probably six by ten feet. At one end it had a waist high shelf on which items to be sprayed were placed. A large exhaust fan was mounted overhead and one wall held a compressed air fitting to which a spray gun was attached. The compressor was installed outside the booth, for safety reasons. Again, no mask or other protection was provided. In those days, a worker's health and safety were simply non-issues.

I sprayed all the bronze plated items with clear lacquer to protect them from corrosion. Chrome plated items didn't require such protection. Within a week I became quite proficient with a spray gun, and since they paid me 25 cents an hour, my take-home pay was $9.92 after they deducted 8 cents for Social Security.

CALIFORNIA FLAXSEED

In 1942, I had just finished Junior High. By that summer the spray-booth job had been filled by a permanent employee, so I looked elsewhere. Kenny Thompson had worked for a company called California Flaxseed the previous summer, but he had lined up a better paying job for this summer. He suggested I go talk to them.

Well, I was a shoo-in. Kenny was well-liked by the chemist there and recommended me. The chemist's name was Jolly Joe Taylor, and I had a problem keeping a straight face whenever I called him "Jolly Joe." He said they paid 40 cents an hour for a bottle washer. Great! I'd get to work in a chemical lab and get paid 15 cents an hour more than as a spray-booth operator.

This was an odd company. It was owned by a British fellow with a thick Cockney accent. All summer long he went around shirtless and excessively tanned. He was unmarried and had a strong prejudice against women. He wouldn't allow women to work for him. All his office help were men. He insisted on being called "Captain Bush." Everybody complied.

Now Captain Bush was a brilliant chemist. He was always performing experiments that were ground-breaking in his field, such as using organic oils. His lab consisted of a building with six rooms. Half of these were filled with chemistry and technical books. His library was the best in the city, and many researchers came from miles around to use it.

Jolly Joe put me to work washing glass apparatus. It was tough, since many of their experiments consisted of oils which would polymerize (get thick and gooey) and often scorch the inside of flasks. Captain Bush wouldn't use glass beads as was standard practice in many labs, but he did use strong solvents such as ketones and ethers, which eventually enabled me to get the job done. Captain Bush was a perfectionist, and he wouldn't start an experiment with any glassware that wasn't spotless.

Before summer was over, Jolly Joe had taught me to run a number of sophisticated tests, such as measuring the refractive index of oils, performing volumetric analyses that required the preparation of accurate normal reagent solutions, and using their precision balance, pipettes, and burettes. These precision operations were performed in an air-conditioned room. That room was kept at a constant 68 degrees—very refreshing in the summer time.

SHERWIN-WILLIAMS PAINT

At the end of summer, I quit to return to school. Kenny had spent the summer working in the Sherwin-Williams Chemical Lab; however, he didn't quit his job, as I had. During the summer he bought an old 1928 Chevy to support his ever-maturing lifestyle. The car and his other activities cost money, so he continued working part-time at the lab.

Kenny told me about a problem Sherwin-Williams was having. During the previous year, two of their chemists had been drafted, leaving only two. Finding Kenny had been a big help, since he knew almost as much as a graduate chemist, but he was only available part time, so Kenny spoke to the head chemist and told him about my experience at California Flaxseed. With that background and a recommendation from Jolly Joe, they offered me a part-time job in the lab, too. They only wanted to pay 40 cents per hour, but eventually I got them up to 45 cents.

That job was a neat arrangement. After school Kenny and I would drive to the Sherwin-Williams plant. Usually we arrived about the time everyone was punching out. The deal was that we would punch in, go to the lab where the chemists would leave a list of tasks and/or tests they wanted done. We'd work until we had to leave, and then punch out. They paid us for whatever time we put in. They understood there would be times when we couldn't show up, due to studying for tests, etc.

Kenny did the lab tests, since he had learned them during the summer. Mostly I did bottle washing. In a few weeks I had learned to do distillation curves, flash points, and the determination of non-volatiles. The lab had two miniature (laboratory) grinding machines; one was a three-roll mill and the other was a stone mill. They were used for making lab-size batches of paint (paint has to be ground). Both were considered extremely valuable to the company, since they were irreplaceable during the war. It had taken nearly all summer for Kenny to convince the chemists to let him operate them.

So, probably with trepidation, our task list would sometimes contain instructions for grinding a sample batch of paint. At first the instructions would always specify that Kenny operate the mill, but operating a mill is slow and tedious, so after Kenny would get it set up, adjusted, and running, he would turn it over to me. Eventually, the chemists became aware that I was operating the mills and they quit specifying the operator.

This arrangement had been in place for a couple of months when Kenny announced he had found a job at Gooch Labs—a testing laboratory downtown. He had convinced them he was a graduate chemist; he told them that he'd gone to USC. The job was full-time, so Kenny dropped out of school. School had always been a big bore because it was too easy for him. Now, he was finally all grown up and on his own.

So I lost my ride. I had to start taking the bus—a 45-minute trip each way. Still, it was a good deal for me. I was doing work that I enjoyed. I could work as much, or as little, as I wanted, and after Kenny left they offered me a nickel raise, to 50 cents per hour, so I continued working there. After Christmas I managed to get Fred Keyes a job there as well. Having no previous lab experience, he got stuck doing all the dirty work. This included bottle washing and getting lab quantities of the various raw materials used in the factory.

Getting these raw materials was the hardest of our jobs. Retrieving samples of most liquids (oils, solvents, varnishes, etc.) usually meant climbing up on a stack of drums, maybe three or four high, and wrestling a drum down to the ground where we could open it and get a sample. Those devils weighed between 400 and 500 pounds. We had no hoists or cranes—only a skid that we positioned and worked the drum onto, allowing it to slide to the ground. There was a yard crew of several big, burley guys, but they never offered to help. However, it was their job to get the drum back on the stack.

One of the bottle-washing jobs was a chronic problem. It involved the cleaning of distillation flasks. These were shaped like a bulb, about the size of a billiard ball.

They had a long narrow neck with a small tube attached to its side. They were used to run distillation curves on various solvents. Since the paint industry used commercial-grade solvents, a small amount of oil or resin was always dissolved in them. To run a distillation test, a sample of a solvent was put in the flask, then the flask was heated to boil away the solvent. At the end of the test, the contaminating oils and resins remained in the flask and turned to a varnish. Sometimes they even charred.

During the past 30 or 40 years, the only known way to clean out these flasks for reuse was with glass beads. Several spoonfuls of small glass beads would be put into the flask and swirled around. It was easy to spend 20 or 30 minutes on one flask. Eventually, this procedure would remove the varnish, but the inside of the glass would be ground rough by the glass beads. The next time the varnish would bake into that ground surface and be even harder to remove. After about three cleanings, the flask would be trashed and replaced with a new one. Labs all over the country cleaned their flasks this way. Glass beads were a standard cleaning item stocked by labs.

Now comes Mickey to the rescue. After using beads to clean a few flasks, I figured there had to be an easier way. With my experience with explosives, I recognized that oxidation was the answer. I could just oxidize (burn) that crap out of there. One night, when I was in the lab alone, I got out my favorite oxidizer (ingredient "X") and put a couple of teaspoons into a particularly dirty flask. It even had some material that was charred black.

Next I fired up a Bunsen burner and held the flask over the flame. After 20 to 30 seconds I noticed ingredient "X" beginning to melt. Then WHOOSH, a blue flame shot out of the top of the flask, clear to the ceiling, where it left a brown smudge. That was seriously close to an explosion. A little more varnish and the flask would have blown up in my face.

After the flask cooled down, I took it over to the sink and rinsed it out. It looked like new. Not a smidgen of varnish left; even the charred stuff was gone. Well, this was the answer, but I needed to find a way to make it safer. Since the varnish was always located on the very bottom of the flask, I reasoned that after I put in ingredient "X", if I tipped the flask on its side (i.e. 90 degrees) the oxidizer would not be in contact with the varnish. Then I could heat the side (now on the bottom) until the oxidizer melted. Once melted, I could simple rotate the flask, very slowly, back to upright. As I did, the melted oxidizer would burn the varnish only at the edge where it made contact (like the edge of a grass fire). Eventually, when the flask reached vertical, all the varnish would burn away. Brilliant!

I was eager to show off my new procedure, so I came in to work early the next day. I demonstrated my idea to Asa Pollack, the head chemist. Now Asa wore glasses that looked like the bottoms of Coke bottles. Whatever he looked at, he either had to adjust its distance from his eyes by moving it—or himself—to just the right distance away. After I rinsed the flask out, I handed it to him. He went through this focusing procedure and was obviously impressed by the like-new condition of the flask.

Nevertheless, he was against using ingredient "X." He thought it was just too dangerous, but after he watched me clean a couple more "toughies," he finally decided that with proper precautions, it was practical. The other chemist, Henry Hamilton (everyone called him Ham), thought it was a fabulous solution to the problem. They decided to adopt its use in the lab. Good news travels fast. I understood by the following summer, when I got drafted, that virtually every lab in the city was using my method.

After I graduated in June, I continued to work at the lab, now full time, until I was called by the draft. In September I took a leave of absence to go into the service.

PART II
STORIES OF WORLD WAR II

_____MILITARY MANEUVERS

❖

Greetings—1944
Anchors Away
Boot Camp—1944
The Singletree
Well-Seasoned Traveler—1944
Christmas
The OGU—1945

GREETINGS—1944

During my senior year I volunteered to take the "Eddy" test. This was an aptitude test, devised by a person named Captain Eddy in the Navy, and its purpose was to identify students with technical aptitude who were soon to be drafted. These students could then be selected for training as electronic technicians (repairmen). Those who passed the Eddy test were guaranteed an assignment to the Navy's electronic schools. This would be much better than being assigned to a ship headed for a war zone. I was way ahead of the curve on this one. Of course I passed. Finally, graduation came.

The war was in full swing, and all the males were being drafted when they reached eighteen and had finished high school. I had satisfied both conditions. Therefore, it was just a matter of time.

The first thing I should have done was head downtown to the Navy recruitment office, with Eddy test results in hand. Naively, I assumed the Navy would contact me. A month went by, and then another. Finally, I did go to the Navy recruitment office to find out what was going on. The jerk who looked at my Eddy test letter obviously didn't know what it was. He informed me, bureaucratically, that Navy enlistment was filled for the month, and I could try again the following month, if I hadn't been drafted in the meantime. Drat! Well, being young and stupid, I supposed that was what I should do.

Naturally, the next month I got my "Greetings;"…a "personal" letter from President Roosevelt, directing me to report to an induction examination center. On the stated date I showed up at this warehouse-like building downtown. I got a physical, along with hundreds of other kids. As the joke of the times went, "If you were warm, you passed." I guess I was warm enough. I was sent home to await the next bureaucratic missive.

In a few days I received a letter with a date to report for induction at Fort MacArthur, near Long Beach. The family drove me down for a patriotic sendoff. We waved goodbye, and I entered the gate. Immediately, some Neanderthal—with a mouth the size of a mixing bowl—began yelling, "Line up over here. No talking. Now hear this." After he ran out of memorized babble, he produced a clipboard and began calling out our names, to which we were to answer "Here" or "Yo." With muster completed, he herded us into a room that was empty, except for an American flag standing in one corner. An officer appeared and pronounced that we were to be sworn in. No choice was offered. We raised our right hands, and in less than a minute we were in the Army. We were marched, if one could call it marching, off to a barracks and told to pick out a bunk.

In my slow-witted way, I was beginning to ponder, "I'm in the Army—what happened to the Navy?" I couldn't think of anything I could do about it. "I'll just sleep on it," I thought. The next day we were rousted by a loudspeaker blaring what I think was supposed to be a bugle. While we were getting dressed, the Neanderthal reappeared. It was off to the infirmary to get shots. God, I hated shots! I just knew I would pass out, but somehow I got through the ordeal without ending up on a stretcher. Then we were sent to the mess hall for breakfast.

About 10:00 a.m. we were lined up and marched to a building that smelled like a laundry. It was set up like a cafeteria to issue GI clothing. First we were issued underwear and shoes, then dungarees and dress uniforms. We were told to take the stuff back to the barracks and change, and to put our civvies (clothes we wore in) in a box they provided. Rumor had it they were going to issue us rifles the next day. Crap! This was getting serious. These guys were fixing to send us to Europe to augment the liberation forces. I had to do something—*now.*

ANCHORS AWAY

In desperation, I made my way to a pay phone. Dialing "Information," I called Bud Lane. Once he had told me his dad had connections and if I needed a "string pulled," maybe he could help. I explained my dilemma to him about the Eddy test. He assured me he would tell his dad, who would do what he could.

The next morning the Neanderthal ordered us outside the barracks. He lined us up and marched us to a building. Once inside, we were told to strip. Then, one-by-one we were led into a hall where desks were lined up on one side about every 25 feet. Along the middle of the hall, in front of each desk, was a small pedestal. Seated at each desk was an officer, representing various service specialties. A Marine colonel was at the first one. He was looking over these naked recruits for suitable physical specimens for the Marines. If he saw one he liked, he stamped the soldier's papers "MARINES" with a rubber stamp, and they led the guy off to be transferred to the Marines. If the colonel wasn't interested, they directed the recruit to the next platform and passed his papers on.

The second desk was selecting candidates for the Army Air Corps Paratroops, and at the next one a Navy Lieutenant Commander was looking for Submariners. Eventually, I entered this gauntlet. I could almost hear the Marine colonel sneer as he looked as my scrawny body. An orderly took my rejected papers to the next desk—same story with the Army colonel. Again, my papers were moved on.

[Warning—Name drop ahead]

Then, as I stepped up on the next platform (still buck naked, of course), the Navy officer looked at me, and then down at my papers, then to some other paper on the desk. Finally, he bellowed, "Do you know a Congressman Chet Hollifield?"

I knew where this was coming from, and I had been told that going around the chain of command in the military was a court-martial offense. I had to lie, but effective lying requires at least a minuscule amount of self-assurance and poise to pull it off. These evaporate when you're standing, naked and vulnerable, on a pedestal. Nevertheless, I managed to blurt out, "N-n-n-o, Sir."

Then he asked, "Did you receive a letter stating that you had passed the Eddy test?"

"Yes, sir," I responded as I straightened up displaying some relief. He took a large red rubber stamp and imprinted "NAVY" on my papers. I was in (or out, if you prefer).

What had happened, of course, is after receiving my phone call, Bud had called his dad at the Nineteenth Congressional District Headquarters in East Los Angeles. Bud's dad, Harold, had all but put Chet Hollifield into that Congressional seat. The voters had played only a small roll, as Chet ran unopposed. So a call to Chet in Washington resulted in a call from Chet to the Department of the Navy. Chet did what all Congressmen do: he did favors for constituents that would enable him to call in some chips later.

Back at the barracks, they had gathered up all the boxes of civilian clothes with our names and home addresses on them. The next day a truck was to haul them to the post office to be returned to our homes. An orderly came by with my new orders, stating I was being transferred to the Navy. He also had a train ticket to Green Bay, Wisconsin. I scrounged among all the boxes of clothes, and finding mine, I changed back into my civvies. Soon, a jeep came around to take me to the Los Angeles Union Station. I had been in the U. S. Army exactly 3 days.

BOOT CAMP—1944

The train was coach and, as I recall, took four days to get to Chicago. It took another day to get to the Great Lakes Naval Station at Green Bay, Wisconsin. This naval station served as an additional training center associated with the Great Lakes Naval Station north of Chicago.

After arriving, I was herded into an auditorium with about a hundred others for orientation. We were told we were all being put into a special company where we would be billeted together. Everyone in that company had passed the Eddy test, and because of the urgency for electronic technicians, we would be pushed through boot camp in eight weeks, instead of the usual sixteen.

Boot camps are run by regular Navy personnel, never wartime draftees. They were career men and were known as "Boot Pushers." They taught classes in the Navy way of doing things, drilled us in how to march, and ordered us around. Most of them had worked their way up from Apprentice Seaman to Seaman Second Class and had been in the Regular Navy from two to four years.

Now comes some real irony. Upon being sworn in, we were given the rank of Seaman First Class. This was a concession that Captain Eddy had received from the Navy brass to attract high school seniors to take his test. So, here we were—a bunch of geeks who had been in the Navy all of one day and who outranked all the "Pushers." It's hard to appreciate how much that must have galled them, and I'll leave it to your imagination as to how far they went out of their way to make our lives miserable.

In boot camp, Navy procedures and cleanliness are everything. They form the basis of Navy discipline and control. Every Boot washed his own clothes by hand. Each piece of clothing, except shoes and socks, had eyelets on their edge through which short lengths of cord, called clothes stops, could be threaded. These looked like short white shoestrings, used to tie the garment to a clothesline. It's a good system, since ordinary clothespins would never do on ship in a stiff wind. Don't ask me about the socks; I was never on a ship.

The use of these damned clothes stops was made into a fetish. All knots had to be square—well, that's probably OK—but you couldn't have any more than an inch left over after you tied them. Anything longer was called an "Irish Pennant" and was a sin on a par with picking your nose while in formation for an inspection. I remember trying to tie those damned things, sans Irish Pennants, in sub-zero weather.

Beds had to be made so tight (taut) that the inspecting officer could bounce a quarter on them. Bunks had to be lined up in a precise straight line. We used a stretched string to accomplish this. All of our clothes, except what we were wearing, had to be rolled into a tight roll and each end tied with a clothes stop. They had to be tied tight enough an inspecting officer could bounce it on the floor.

A sea-bag was used to store all of our clothes and other possessions, and it had to be hung from a horizontal timber exactly the right height above the floor, using exactly the right hitch (knot). Our white dress uniforms ("whites") were almost impossible to keep absolutely clean while stored with other items in our sea bag. As a result, they had to be scrubbed every week to make them snowy white. Some clever guy in our company came up with the idea of storing our whites in condoms. What a brilliant idea! On Saturday mornings we would remove the condoms for inspection and replace them after inspection. This was winter, so our whites were never actually worn—just inspected.

The barracks had to be kept spotless. The floors were wood to simulate old-time ship's decks. They were unvarnished, and just walking on them would leave black scuffmarks from rubber-sole boots. As a result, they had to be cleaned every morning by means of the "Great Lakes Shuffle." That consisted of about half of the company lining up at one end of the barracks wearing their dress shoes (leather soles), and with a large piece of steel wool under one shoe, they would scour the floor as they moved forward. Each person would clean one board, about 4 inches wide, the whole length of the building. Then with push brooms we would sweep up the wood dust and carry it outside. Next, all the bunks were carried (not slid) to the freshly cleaned center, and the process repeated where the bunks normally stood. The barracks were two-story, so the other half of the company was upstairs doing the same thing. This exercise, I was told, resulted in the floors having to be replaced about twice a year. We did all this, and other chores, before breakfast yet! The enforcers of all this nonsense were dubbed "Chicken Shit" by the enforcees.

Spot inspections could occur at any time. These were generally at a personal level, and punishments for discrepancies were meted out on an individual basis. However, the big inspection was once a week on Saturday morning. These were white glove inspections. The inspecting officer wore white cotton gloves that he wiped over every unlikely place he could think of. Even the slightest sign of dirt resulted in demerits for the company. Ten companies (in ten barracks) all competed every Saturday. The highest possible score was 4.0. The winning company was given some perks, such as getting out of marching practice, and allowed to display a broom: the Navy symbol of a "clean sweep." Except for the first week of sizing things up, our company of "Geeks" flew the broom every week we were there. You see, Geeks were just cleverer than the average seaman was when it came to beating the Chicken Shit system.

THE SINGLETREE

A crucial part of every sailor's training was firefighting. About the worst thing that can happen aboard a ship is a serious fire. It ranks up there with taking on water and sinking. At Great Lakes, some equipment had been set up in a remote field for training Boots in firefighting.

The first facility was a concrete, full-sized mockup of a ship. It had a super structure in the middle (mostly to make it look like a ship), but the deck was like a large swimming pool, filled with about 3 feet of water. The instructors would select six Boots who would climb a ladder to get into the aft part of the "ship," then they were separated into two teams, with three men on each team. Each team manned a fire hose, with one person controlling the nozzle and the other two holding the hose to keep it from recoiling back. They stood there in water up to their crotches.

The exercise began as the instructors turned on a valve at the bow. This allowed gasoline to float out on top of the water until all the water was covered with about a half-inch of gasoline. Of course it was getting on the trainees, as well. Then they closed the valve and torched off the gasoline near the bow. Flames shot up about 20 feet and rapidly began to work their way toward the aft end of the ship.

During this training, the two teams were expected to advance toward the bow, fighting the flames back. If you messed up and let the flames get past you, they would surround you and you would become burnt toast. The instructors had prepared us well and I never heard of anyone being fried. I don't know what they could have done if things went awry.

However, the concrete ship was just preparation for the Singletree. This fiendish device consisted of a ten-inch diameter pipe that stuck out of the ground about eight feet. The top was capped off. From about a foot above the ground to about a foot below the cap, a pattern of half-inch holes had been drilled up and down its length and all around its circumference—surely more than 50 holes. It was to simulate a ruptured, burning fuel line.

In this exercise, six teams surrounded the Tree, each team manning a fire hose. When set, a pump would be turned on and gasoline would squirt out of all the holes, then the gasoline would be ignited and the crews had to *try* to put out the resulting inferno. They weren't always successful. Sometimes things would get out of hand and a crew would drop their hose and run for it. Their hose would lash around the ground like a mad python. Other crews had to jump over it as it whipped by and sometimes lost control of their own hose and ran. When things got that bad, the instructors would shut down the pump and let the Tree burn out.

Our firefighting training took place in December, and it was between 20-30 degrees below zero. The first day out, I thought my feet were going to freeze solid. The pain was awful. The next day I put on all of the twelve pair of socks I had been issued. That helped a tiny bit.

The cold weather was bad enough, but being wet from the cement ship's pool and the spray from all the fire-hoses made things excessively miserable. Everybody not engaged in an exercise would run over and stand as close as they dared to each fire being fought. When the teams would put out their fire, the bystanders would yell out a chorus of "boo's." There were no buildings, no shelters, nothing—just these short-lived fires for relief.

WELL-SEASONED TRAVELER—1944

Mercifully, boot camp lasted only eight weeks, as they had promised. They gave us all three-week passes so we could go home for Christmas. Also, they handed each of us our two months pay: about $100.00. I bought a ticket to Los Angeles and caught the train for Chicago, the rail-hub of the nation.

When I got to Chicago, I knew I had to change trains, and that required going across town from one station to another. Young and naïve, I had never asked what time the train to California was scheduled to depart; I just started walking across town. When I got to the other station, my train was just leaving. I just stood there, helpless, watching it pull out of the station. The clerk at the desk told me the next one out would be the same time the next day. Drat! Well, actually Boot Camp had taught me some stronger words than that.

I found myself in a strange city with 24 hours to kill. I began by taking in a movie. That barely used up two hours. Then I found a small library, or so I thought. I went in and a woman handed me a bunch of brochures. I sat down at a table and began to look through them. Eventually, I learned that I was in a Christian Science Reading Room. Although I was somewhat fascinated by a "scientific" religion, I finally got bored and left.

By now I was starting to get hungry. Here I was in a great city and had no idea where to find something to eat. I had never been in a restaurant, except for a roadside diner with my parents, so I just walked around. Eventually I came upon this shabby building. In the window was a sign, "Free Coffee & Doughnuts." That sounded good to me, so I went in. It was a trap. They told me that I had to sit in one of the chairs they had lined up in rows and listen to a preacher. After he was finished, everyone would get coffee and a doughnut. I should have walked out right then, but being insecure and polite, I stayed. It was almost an hour before I got my doughnut. I didn't drink coffee yet, so I just choked it down.

That's all I ate that day. I killed more time walking around, looking in store windows. As the afternoon wore on, I began to worry where I would spend the night.

Continuing to roam about, I eventually wandered into the seedier part of the city. The long shadows of the buildings were cutting off the sun, and it was starting to get cold—colder, that is.

Just as the streetlights came on, I happened upon a building where some men were entering. These guys were dressed like bums. On closer inspection, they *were* bums. The door they were entering had a sign over it "Beds-50 Cents." Getting desperate, I walked in. It was dark and musty. I followed a couple of guys who seemed to know where they were going, up a stairs to the second floor. At the top was a door guarded by a fat, ugly woman whose gravel voice was demanding fifty cents before she would let you through the door.

I fished out a half-dollar and gave it to her. As I entered the room—actually the whole second floor of the building—I could see rows and rows of iron bunks, like those used in the service, and folding cots. It was a "Flop-House." Everyone was scrambling to claim a bunk with a mattress. I had arrived early enough that I managed to get one too. It was starting to get dark and the only light was provided by a couple of low-wattage light bulbs connected to wires dangling from the ceiling.

Most of the men stripped down to their underwear and crawled under the smelly blankets provided, using their clothes as a pillow. I kept my clothes on. I was afraid someone would steal them during the night. After a while the ugly woman turned off the lights. I was plenty tired, so I had no trouble falling asleep. Once during the night I woke up to a chorus of snoring, but somehow managed to get back to sleep.

The next morning I woke up, feeling grimy. I couldn't think of anything but to get to the station and wait for that train to load. I didn't try to find food or a place to clean up. I just wanted to make sure I didn't miss that damned train again.

Christmas

I caught the train OK and in a few days arrived in Los Angeles. From letters I had written, the family knew about when I was coming home. In those days, nobody called long distance. It was considered just too damned expensive. If something was urgent enough, they might send a telegram. I didn't think this qualified. So after gathering my luggage (a sea-bag), I took a streetcar to the east edge of the city. There I caught the 5-cent Montebello bus that ran on Whittier Boulevard. I got off at Findley Street and walked the two blocks home.

I didn't knock, just walked in. Shirley spotted me and ran to give me a welcoming hug. Mom came from somewhere and joined in. Dad was still at work. It was a weekday. We talked for a while. Shirley was full of questions about the Navy. Mom seemed more subdued. I think she was wondering how long it would be before I would be sent off to a battle somewhere—mother-type worries.

Soon Dad came home. He seemed genuinely glad to see me, sticking out his hand for me to shake. I accepted cautiously, as he had never shaken my hand before. I felt grown up. He talked to me as though I was an adult, asked if I needed any money. I still had about fifty dollars left, so I declined. This was a different family. I had respect. No one was bossing me around. I was the center of attention. How strange!

Eventually, Christmas arrived. There weren't many gifts. I hadn't brought anything with me. I snuck a peak and saw most of the presents under the tree were for Shirley. I was relieved. The best part was that Dad was going to cook. Navy food was a lot better than Mom's was, but now I was back on her turf again.

Dad and I went shopping for a turkey. In those days you didn't just go to the market and pick out a frozen turkey. We went to a turkey farm. This place had hundreds of them in a large fenced-in yard. The owner invited us to pick one. Dad consulted me about a good-sized one he had spotted. I nodded, having no opinion except to agree with his judgment. He pointed it out to the owner, who picked up a long pole with a wire hook on the end. With practiced skill, he snagged Dad's turkey by the leg and hauled him out of the flock.

He dragged him, squawking, into a shed. Then I heard the unmistakable sound of an ax; the squawking stopped. After a bit the owner brought out our turkey, stripped of his feathers, feet, and intestines. He placed the carcass on a platform scale, calculated the price, and put it in a shopping bag. My dad got out his wallet, peeled off a couple of dollars and exchanged them for the bag.

When we got home, I noticed that the bird was covered in pinfeathers. This was normal, and in past years it had always been my job to pull them out with tweezers, so I set about making my traditional contribution. In my opinion, Dad was a great cook. This opinion had surely come from years of eating Mom's terrible cooking, being relieved only on weekends and holidays when Dad would take over. Certainly he was no gourmet, but he could roast a succulent turkey, stuffed with the best dressing I have ever had.

On Christmas day Aunt Mina and Uncle George drove in from Yuma. I always thought George was an insufferable blow-hard, but Aunt Mina made mince-meat pies just the way I liked them. That made it worthwhile. Uncle Raymond also showed up. We only saw him twice a year: on Thanksgiving and Christmas. He was a life-long bachelor, and I know he had only these two decent meals each year. Dad didn't like him at all because he was unkempt and a political fanatic.

However, you wouldn't have known, as Dad was always civil to everybody, but he did avoid being cornered by Raymond as much as possible.

The OGU—1945

After Christmas I returned to duty. My orders specified that I return to the Great Lakes Naval Station at Green Bay. I was to report to a facility there called an "Out-going Unit" (OGU). This was a holding area where they housed Navy personnel until their next assignment was ready. In my case, they were waiting until the next class started for my electronics training.

To keep us busy, we were assigned all kinds of menial work: shoveling snow off walks, mess hall duty, trash pick up, etc. I was lucky, probably because I had a Seaman First Class rating. I was assigned mess hall duty inside, where it was warm. Outside it was 20-30 below.

This mess hall was run by a female officer—the first one I had seen. She was a lieutenant and every bit as Chicken Shit as anything I'd seen in Boot Camp. Even though it was winter, she made us wear our summer whites. We had to report to duty at 4:00 a.m., then we were kept busy, carrying food supplies to the cooks and hauling prepared foods to the serving line. A half-hour before opening the mess hall doors, she'd order an inspection. We'd all line up and she would pass along in front of us. We were expected to extend our hands as she approached. She would examine our nails for signs of dirt, and then rap the underside of our hands with a baton to indicate we should turn them over for her to examine the palm side. When she got to the end of the line, she would bark, "Bow over." This meant to bend over at the waist while she went down the rear of the line, looking at everyone's seat for signs of soil. Soiling there was a sure sign that you hadn't put on a clean uniform, or that you had been sitting around goofing off. An orderly followed along and took down the names of those who failed.

During serving time, some of us were assigned as chow runners and some as servers. I always got to be a server. Serving hundreds of men each meal gets boring, but we found ways to make it less so. One day I was given the job of passing out the butter. Eons before, a clever way of serving butter had evolved in Navy mess halls. The butter "station" was always the last in the serving line and was always preceded by a station that handed out biscuits, bread, or sometimes a cookie.

Serving lines consisted of stations that were heated by hot water, into which trays of food were placed to keep them warm, but butter was a different matter; you wanted butter to stay cold. The solution consisted of putting pats of butter into a shallow pan filled with ice water to keep them from melting until they could be served. If the pats got too soft, a new cold tray was brought in to replace them.

The final part of the process was to dispense the pat of butter without picking it up. Now this was clever. They would take a fork and bend the two middle tines back about 90 degrees and the two outside tines forward the same amount. With this instrument the server could stab a pat of butter in the ice water and lift it out. The second part of this neat system was that the pat could be released onto the tray by simply banging the fork against a knife held in the other hand. The knife was held crosswise to the fork and the impact caused the butter to fly off from inertia.

With very little practice, a server could learn the art. When a tray came by he would stab a pat (click), pick out an empty spot on the tray, strike the fork against the knife (clack), and the pat would land on (and stick to) the targeted spot. Every swabby (Navy troop) soon got to know the characteristic sounds of the butter server: click-clack, click-clack. It was like Pavlov's dog. When you heard that sound, you knew you had a pat of butter *somewhere* on your tray.

Now for some fun…. Every butter server soon learned from his predecessors that the stabbing and dispensing motions were too fast for a casual eye, and the average swabby had been conditioned to move on as soon as he heard the click-clack sounds. So the joke was that a server would stab at a pat (click), but deliberately miss it; then immediately strike the knife (clack). The victim would move out into the mess hall, sit down at a table and soon realize he had no butter. Immediately he'd be back, complaining that he hadn't got any butter while the others in line were yelling at him for breaking into line. Great sport, right?

One day we were serving dinner. I was manning the butter station. Among other stuff, they were serving mashed potatoes and gravy. The butter pats had been on the table long enough that they were slightly softened, but not yet a problem to serve. Along came this big guy. He had his tray extra full—a big eater. It was winter, so he was wearing his heavy P-coat. When he got to me, I surveyed his tray for a spot to place his butter pat. Gravy had run off the side of his potatoes and along all of his piled up food. Only one tiny area of metal tray was showing.

I took careful aim and fired. He moved the tray slightly between the click and the clack. The pat landed at the bottom edge of one of the embossed dividers into a run of gravy. The pat slid up the gravy-covered divider full speed and flew up the sleeve of his P-coat sleeve. He stopped and glared at me accusingly. I contemplated death—with luck, maybe only mutilation. While meekly apologizing, I placed *two* pats carefully on the tiny clean spot I had missed. No more attempts at artillery here.

This one is the best. It's rare when one gets to witness an inspiration of genius occur. This day we were serving lunch. I was doing the butter station again. The trick of clicking and clacking but no butter had gotten old. Besides, the possibility of pulling it on someone a second time and pissing him off was always a concern. The fellow manning the bread station next to me had watched me pull the click-clack-no-butter trick on previous days. Then, the line stopped because they had run out of a main-dish upstream and were waiting for a chow-runner to bring a new tray from the kitchen. During the interlude, "bread-man," who was actually serving cookies this meal, leaned over and said, "Stick a pat of butter to the bottom of this cookie." Then he explained that when the next guy in line came by, he would place the cookie on his tray *and* I would do the click-clack-no-butter routine. When the guy came back complaining that he didn't get any butter, I was to pick up the cookie and show it to him.

So here comes our victim. Bread-man puts a cookie on his tray. I do my click-clack thing. Our mark took a couple of steps, whirled around and faced me. He said, "You pulled that trick on me before. Stop messing around and give me my butter." I reached over, picked up his cookie, and showed him the butter. His aggressiveness morphed into apologies as he started walking away. Then he stopped again, as he realized there wasn't any way I could have launched that butter pat to land under the cookie. He shuffled on to a table, shaking his head. We pulled that routine many times while we were in the OGU. Some of the "second takes" were priceless. I feel sure that trick has become part of Navy lore. I feel honored that I saw its birth.

I had spent three weeks in OGU—it seemed like three more weeks of Boot Camp—when I got my orders. Finally I was to begin electronics training. That afternoon I found myself on a train for Chicago.

14. High School Graduation—ca. 1944

15. In the Army—ca. 1944

16. In the Navy—ca. 1944

_____ NAVY PEDAGOGY

◆

WRIGHT JUNIOR COLLEGE—1945

The Navy had taken over the entire Wright Junior College for the duration of the war. Dozens of classes were being taught on all kinds of subjects in which Navy personnel needed training. They had converted the gymnasium into one big barracks full of double-decker bunks. The class I had been sent to attend was called "Pre-Radio." In those days the term "Radio" covered just about anything wireless or electronic. The course was only one month long, but attending eight hours each day for one month is almost equivalent to taking a one-hour class for a year in college.

The purpose of this particular course was to provide a review of algebra and basic electricity, but most importantly, to filter out those who would have trouble keeping up in the accelerated classes that would follow. It was designed to eliminate about 50% of the students. Most of those who flunked out would be assigned to ships destined for war zones—a strong inducement to do your best.

None of the material being taught was new to me. They spent quite a bit of time teaching the slide rule; most had never learned to use one, but I had that down pat years before, when I had built my own slide-rule in junior high, so it was an easy gig for me.

THE MAYOR'S KID

For many, it was tough going. One guy who sat at the desk directly in front of me was doing poorly. He soon noticed that I was getting good marks, so he began turning around during tests to peek at my paper. At first I didn't do anything about it, but after a few days I began pulling my paper away from him. During one recess, he took me aside and pleaded his case.

He was taking the class a second time. He had flunked the previous month. His dad, who was the Mayor of Chicago, had pulled some strings, and the Navy was giving him this second chance. I was surprised, since the whole idea of this class was to eliminate those who lacked the necessary aptitude. However, I spotted an empty desk in the back and moved to it. The coddled son flunked again.

BLISS ELECTRICAL SCHOOL—1945

After breezing through Pre-Radio, I was shipped off to "Primary Electrical & Electronics" classes at Bliss Electrical School, another school that had been taken over by the Navy. It was located in the suburbs of Silver Springs, Maryland. This was a first-rate technical school in the Ivy League style. It was two-story brick, all covered with vines, and had dorms and a cafeteria for resident students—ideal for Navy use. The Navy had retained all the civilian teaching staff—a very wise decision. One middle-aged chief was the only Navy personnel other than the students. He had a habit of humming everywhere he went and had been given the nickname, "Sixty Cycles." Those were the days before "Hertz" was used to designate frequency.

This place was no breeze for me. The course material was college-level and difficult. Magnetic theory was especially hard for me. Relationships of current, turns of wire, hysteresis, and inductive coupling were so complex, many of the concepts had to be treated empirically, but I loved it and studied hard.

They had assigned us students two to a room. The rooms were just large enough for two beds and two small desks. Everyone spent their evenings studying in their rooms. Being in the Navy meant you could not leave the premises without a pass. Our room was on the second floor.

AMAZING GRACE

One night my roommate, Mead (In the service everyone went by their last name), was gazing out our window. After a bit he said, "McCoy, come take a look at this." I went over to the window. Across the street was a building with an illuminated window on its second floor. The window was covered by sheer curtains, but you could make out a person in the room. The person seemed to have long hair (in those days, a woman), and as best we could determine, was seated in front of a vanity. Periodically her hair would be pulled to one side or another, but we couldn't see what was pulling on it. We watched, fascinated, for a while, then the person appeared to get up and move across the room. The light went out.

The next night Mead was back at the window. This time he caught the act a little earlier and saw what looked like a snake wriggling out of its skin. Mead went next door to look out McCracken and Nelson's window (rooms had been assigned alphabetically) for a better angle. A branch of an oak tree was in the way, so they all came to our room. Now four of us were gawking out the window, trying to figure out this veiled display. Soon the hair routine was repeated, yet no one could make sense of what he was seeing.

Finally the mystery was solved. One afternoon Mead spotted a woman walking along the sidewalk and entering the spied-upon building. She had no arms! That night we all played Peeping Toms again and quickly decided that she was brushing her hair, using her leg and holding the brush with her foot.

Mead decided he wanted to get a date with her, so he watched for her every afternoon and soon concluded that she came home at about the same time each day. One day he timed things to run into her deliberately. He had to leave the school property to do so, but he figured it was worth a Captain's Mast—a disciplinary court—to meet her.

By golly, if it didn't work! He got his date. Later, he told us she was born with no arms, she was married, her husband was in the Army in Europe, she worked in an office as a file clerk, and she could write and type with her toes.

It seemed especially incredulous that she could write and type. A couple of weeks later, I boarded a trolley going to downtown Washington, D. C. At the next stop, she got on. She wore a dress with a full skirt, about mid-calf length. Her purse was on a long strap, hung over her shoulder. When she got on, she slipped one foot out of its slipper with unbelievable gracefulness, reached into her purse, took out a dime, and deposited it in the coin box. Amazing…absolutely amazing! After witnessing that, I was convinced she could file, and my doubts about her ability to write and type were dispelled as well.

[Caution—Name drops ahead]

THE ROOSEVELTS

I had been in the Navy five months and still hadn't learned how to feed myself. Oh, I could take food from a dish with a fork and put it in my mouth, but I was still too insecure to enter a restaurant and get a meal. My usual solution, if I was going into town, was to eat breakfast at the mess, go in to town, forgo eating until late afternoon, then come back to the base (school) and eat dinner at the mess.

I was talking to my roommate, Mead, one day about things to do in Washington. He said he always went to the USO to dance. Mead loved the girls. Well, as dorky as I was, I had never learned to dance, so that didn't sound at all appealing. However, he also mentioned they served snacks and other food that volunteers brought in. Now, this sounded more tempting, so I resolved that the next time I was in town I would stop by the USO.

It was mid-March when I first made my way to the USO. As I was approaching the entrance, it was beginning to get dark. Just as I got close enough to reach for the door handle, the door burst open. A tall, skinny woman dashed out and slammed into me. She stopped and apologized. "Gee, I'm sorry. I was in kind of a hurry." I just answered, "It's OK," and she went on to a waiting car.

I thought, *That sure did look like Eleanor Roosevelt.* When I entered, a sailor was standing near the door. I asked him if that was Eleanor Roosevelt who had just left. He said, "Yeah, she comes here pretty often." For a few moments I felt quite special. After all, the First Lady had almost knocked me over and had even spoken to me.

Almost exactly a month later, April 12, the world received the news that President Franklin D. Roosevelt had died of a stroke. At the time, he was at Warm Springs, Georgia: his favorite retreat. FDR, as he was generally known, was serving his fourth term. This, of course, was unprecedented. His second term was up in January 1941, but the Democratic Party had chosen him to run for a third term in 1940. The rationale was that the world was very unstable, Europe was at war, and "we shouldn't change horses in mid-stream." Congress bought this argument. The same thing was repeated four years later, in 1944, after we had gotten into the war. He had served a little over one year of this fourth term when he died.

Being nearby, I went into Washington and joined the crowds on Pennsylvania Avenue who watched the funeral procession and his caisson roll by.

WARD ISLAND—1945

After finishing at Bliss, I was sent to the Navy's radar school, located at Corpus Christi, Texas. Well, actually, the school was located on a small island known as Ward Island, about halfway between the town of Corpus Christi and the Naval

Air Station. This site had been selected because of the extreme secrecy surrounding radar technology at the time. Nothing else was on the island other than the Navy base. The entire perimeter was enclosed by a chain-link fence capped with barbed wire. Along the fence, a motorized patrol was maintained.

Within the fenced island was a concentration-camp-like area that contained the classrooms and electronic equipment. This area was surrounded by a double fence. Between the fences was a continuous foot patrol with attack dogs. It had one guarded entrance through which the classes entered and exited each day. Each class consisted of about 100 students, and there were 39 classes. A new class started and an old one ended each week. The course lasted 39 weeks—nine months.

In the morning the classes would form by companies, each being eight columns by twelve rows. We would march through the gate to the playing of a band stationed just outside the gate. At the gate were monitors who counted the number in each company as they entered, and companies with discrepant counts were marched to a holding area where the company chief was required to account for the discrepancies. At noon we marched out the gate to the chow hall, and then back in after we had eaten. At the end of class in the afternoon we marched out again.

Each barrack housed one company. Each was provided with showers and a recreation room. Waves—female Navy personnel—worked in the administration offices, although none attended classes. The Waves were all housed in one barrack.

Security was a big deal. We weren't allowed to use the words radar, magnetron, klystron, plus some others outside of the fenced class area. On weekends, when we were given liberty (leave passes), they had unidentified monitors milling around all the bars in Corpus, listening for any "loose" talk. Getting caught meant being "kicked out and shipped out" and assigned to a war zone. I never heard of it happening to anyone.

Sometime after the war the island became the campus of Corpus Christi State University.

CURRICULUM

All classes were set up assuming you knew electrical and electronic theory. Of course this did not include theories concerning the new secret technologies. These technologies, including microwave theory, were taught at Ward Island. Microwave theory covered the design of magnetrons, klystrons, waveguides, and parabolic antennae, all common stuff now. This school taught technology only as it related to airborne equipment (i.e. equipment operated from aircraft). Shipboard equipment was taught in other Navy schools.

After a month of such training, we began classes concentrating on the theory of operation of a particular radar, navigation, or communication set. Four weeks were devoted to each piece of equipment. The first two weeks were conducted in a classroom where we learned the circuit designs and the function of every component in the design. The second two weeks were in a laboratory where they had several complete sets of the equipment to be studied. This equipment was fully powered and operational. Here the first few days were used to teach the operation of the set. The remainder was spent troubleshooting various problems the instructor would insert into the equipment. Let me assure you, after four weeks (eight hours per day) of this training you were a true expert on that particular model of electronic equipment.

At first, because it was considered easier to understand, we were taught older British-designed radars. These operated at 600 MHz and used Yagi antennas (like UHF TVs). Eventually we worked our way up to the latest and greatest: the 3-centimeter wavelength, 9000 MHz, X-band equipment. Generally, such equipment was installed in the actual aircraft for which it had been designed. About ten airplanes were kept in a hangar for this training. Our final months included servicing the electronics in these aircraft.

With tons of stuff to learn, I was eating it up. The secrecy involved made me feel like an insider—someone special. At that time, radar and other new electronic developments were symbols of U.S. leadership (as later were nuclear bombs, missiles, and the Space Program).

Inertial Navigation

One of the first circuits we were taught generated a linear voltage ramp—a voltage that increases linearly with time. This ramp was used to cause the electron beam in a cathode ray tube (CRT) indicator to deflect linearly from one point to another. Its position on the display represented the position of the radar pulse that had been transmitted through the air toward a target. When the radar pulse hit a target, a part of the energy would be reflected back and detected by a sensitive receiver. This tiny signal would be amplified and used to brighten the CRT electron beam. Because the beam was being moved across the face of the CRT linearly, the brightened spot would occur a distance along this movement exactly proportional to the distance to the target, thus the target and its distance could be determined.

Originally, such ramps were generated by simply charging a capacitor through a resistor from a fixed voltage. However, these ramps had a slight curve to them and were not very satisfactory. Eventually some designer realized if the capacitor were charged using a fixed current instead of fixed voltage, its voltage would rise linearly—exactly what they needed. A vacuum tube circuit was designed to provide such a fixed current source.

This process is mathematically known as integration. Integration is the major function in calculus. I had begun taking Calculus at USC night school, but had only attended about two months when I was drafted. I knew what integration was, but that was about it. Nevertheless, I was fascinated by the ability to model a mathematical function using electronics.

I was already aware of the difficulty ships and planes had in determining their positions. Historically, sextants were used to determine latitude and chronometers were used to determine longitude. Sextants could be used only in clear weather. Neither sextants nor chronometers provided much accuracy. These were replaced by radio-direction finding methods that depended on the known location of ground-based radio stations. Better, but still not good enough. During the war, an improved ground-based radio system was developed called "Loran." It used a worldwide network of ground-based beacon transmitters and a special receiver on board the ship or plane. This was better yet, but still slow. It took 15 to 20 minutes to take readings from the Loran, which then had to be translated to corresponding intersecting curves on a special map.

This is where things were during the war. I began to dream of a better way—one that was more accurate and could provide continuous, instantaneous positions. My old high school physics came to mind. There I had learned that velocity is equal to the integral of the accelerations applied during a given period, and distance traversed is equal to the integral of the velocities occurring during a given period. Did you hear that word "integral"? It is the result of the same integration function described above.

My mind began to whir. If one could connect an electronic integrator to the output of a device that sensed fore and aft acceleration, the resultant voltage would be proportional to the velocity of the ship or plane. If this voltage were fed to a second integrator, its output would be proportional to the distance traveled by the ship or plane. Wow! All we needed was a device to sense acceleration: an accelerometer. None existed.

I put a lot of untalented thought into how an accelerometer might be constructed. After a number of dead-ends, I finally decided on a weight (mass) suspended within a box by two wires—one above and one below—and then similarly, a pair of wires from the right and left, and finally, a pair from fore and aft—six wires in total, orthogonally arranged. The idea was that these wires would comprise six strain gages. The strain gages would measure the stresses caused by any accelerations along the three axes.

But now, two new problems appeared. First, the vertical wires would be under stress continually from gravity. This would result in an erroneous altitude value. Somehow gravity would have to be subtracted out. The other, more serious, problem was that the box would have to be maintained perfectly level. The slightest tilt would cause some stress to occur on each of the horizontal strain gages, resulting in errors. I saw both of these as engineering problems that could be solved.

A slight digression…I had become acquainted with a fellow in my class named Sidney Alderman. Sid was from a wealthy family in Washington, D.C. His family lived in a mansion, with servants, chauffeur, and gardener. This was not the wealth of a family dynasty such as the Rockefellers, DuPonts, or Vanderbilts. Rather, they were nouveau-riche—his father simply made a very large salary. He was an attorney and the First Vice-president of the Southern Railway, the top legal authority for the company. Sid told me his dad received a salary of

$250,000 per year. By comparison, my dad earned less than $2,500 per year—a hundred-fold difference.

Germany had surrendered earlier this year (in May 1945). An International Tribunal had been formed to try the German High Command for war crimes. These trials became known as the Nuremberg Trials. Sid said that his dad, because of his high status in the legal profession, had been selected as one of the prosecuting attorneys at Nuremberg. He had agreed, at a token salary of one dollar per year, to perform this rather unsavory job. These trials were actually underway in Germany as Sid was relating all of this to me.

Sid told me that he had attended one semester at MIT before he got drafted. Sid and I became good buddies. We had similar interests (photography and science), and he loved hearing about my childhood adventures. His life had been very different from mine.

I described my idea to Sid, who thought it was clever, but saw a lot of problems in making it practical. However, while at MIT he had become friends with an associate professor of physics. He thought we might get some opinions or suggestions from him, so I wrote a description of my idea and Sid enclosed it with a letter to his professor friend.

After a while Sid got a reply. It was very discouraging. The prof agreed that a stable level platform was necessary, and he stated that it would be virtually impossible to implement, because there was no way to differentiate the gravity component from the acceleration components. But even more serious, he pointed out that an electronic integrator would inherently accumulate an "error of integration" which would increase with time. He estimated that the best circuitry could not maintain adequate accuracy for more than a few minutes. That punctured my balloon. I dropped the whole approach as impractical.

Footnote: Nine years later I got a job as an electronic technician at Firestone Tire & Rubber Co. They had a contract from the Army to build an artillery missile called the "Corporal." My job was to run checkout tests on its various electronic components. One of these components was the Range Corrector.

During flight, the missile was tracked by radar. When it reached a predetermined velocity, its engine was shut down and it coasted in a ballistic path to the target.

This method of establishing range to the target wasn't accurate enough for the Army, so the Range Corrector was devised and installed. This functioned by having the radar continue to track the missile while it was coasting above the atmosphere. This allowed a better prediction of the impact point, which was then compared to the desired target location. Once the magnitude of range error was determined, a radio signal was sent to the missile. The duration of this signal—a matter of seconds—was converted to a voltage that was proportional to the range error that needed to be corrected.

This Range Corrector contained a *strain-gage accelerometer* that was connected to two *electronic integrators* (the output of the first being fed to the second). The output of this "double integrator" was sent to servos, which controlled the rocket's pitch vanes. The result was that the missile would be directed a shorter or greater distance while it traveled back through the atmosphere.

When I saw this exact use of accelerometers and integrators, I made a beeline to the company's engineering library. There, in the manual for the Range Corrector, was the design organization, Massachusetts Institute of Technology. To quote Tom Lehrer, in a cynical reference to achieving recognition in academia "Plagiaries, plagiaries—let no one else's work evade your eyes."

A DIRECT HIT

That summer a big storm came up. Storm warning systems were virtually nonexistent in those days. However, we had received a report from the Naval Air Station, a few miles down the coast, something that looked like a hurricane was headed our way. As a precaution, the Air Station was tying down all their planes.

Back then, Ward Island was technically an island. It was surrounded by water, albeit just a small bay. Two bridges had been built for accessing the island: one on the road to Corpus Christi, the other on the road to the Air Station. Both were small wooden bridges.

In no time, the storm was upon us. Classes were closed and we all hunkered down in our barracks. With such short warning, there had been no time to provision the barracks with food. The winds became stronger and stronger. Soon the flimsy building was shuddering with each gust. This continued all night. The next morning the winds had increased to well over 100 mph. One of our windows blew in near the storm's peak. The rain poured in and we had to set up a mop and bucket brigade to control the flooding. Eventually we boarded up the opening with a mattress and a portable blackboard. These were held in place by some bunk beds we pushed up against them.

Everyone was getting hungry. By now the candy machine in the rec room had been emptied; all that was left in it were the display bars. A couple of guys broke the glass to get them. Now we were out of food. As we scrounged around, even the cockroaches began to look appetizing.

Then a startling thing happened—at least I thought so. The winds suddenly subsided, the rains stopped, and the sun came out. This was the first hurricane for most of us, so someone who hailed from Florida explained that the eye was passing directly over us. He went on to say that the calm would last less than an hour and then the storm would start up again, except it would blow from the opposite direction. *Amazing*, I thought.

Seizing the opportunity, someone said, "Let's send a couple of runners to the mess hall to see if they can find any food over there." In less than a minute, two volunteers ran out the door toward the mess hall. In about twenty minutes, they were back. All they had were two boxes of saltines and several pounds of sliced processed cheese. We divvied them up in a civilized manner. I got two saltines (eight squares) and one-and-a-half slices of cheese. They tasted like cuisine. It was all I had to eat for three days.

As predicted, the skies darkened and the wind and rain returned. Unbeknownst to us, when the hurricane was approaching it had pushed a lot of seawater into the bay behind the island. When the winds reversed, it pushed all this backed-up water out toward the ocean, creating a torrent and washing away both of our bridges. We were stranded. It was three weeks until construction of a temporary bridge reconnected us with Corpus Christi.

CANNONS OF GOLD

One evening, while in the base's small one-room library, I happened across a book about lost treasures. It was all about lost mines and treasures in the Southwest. It grabbed my curiosity immediately. One of the stories it related was about some pirates working the Gulf of Mexico. Part of the booty they had acquired was some small wooden barrels of gold findings. Gold findings are the small pieces, flakes, and dust of gold—gathered by panning or sluicing—that have not been smelted.

According to the story, circumstances developed whereby they had to hide this gold. But gold findings presented a problem, because the wooden barrels would surely rot and allow the gold to disperse, so they came up with a clever solution. They would take three of their cannons, seal up the firing holes (in the breach) with lead, pour the gold down the muzzles, and then seal the muzzles with lead plugs. They reasoned that ought to secure the gold for many years. All this was clever and fascinating, but the real clincher was that they had decided to bury the three cannons on a barrier island not far from where we were stationed.

Over the millennia, a string of barrier islands formed along the gulf coast. A particularly long one—known as Padre Island—extends from a little north of Corpus Christi south to the Mexican border. Barrier islands are basically long, narrow, sand bars. On the ocean side, generally nice beaches form, while inland from the beach are sand dunes. In some areas the sand is partially anchored by scrubby plants, but in most areas the sand just blows about, changing the appearance of the dunes from day to day. Between the islands and the mainland is a strip of seawater, about three to eight miles wide, that is often navigable.

At the north end of Padre Island, the pirates decided to bury their gold-filled cannons, so the story went. To make things even more enticing, the book went on to say that Spanish gold and silver coins often wash up on the barrier island beaches during a hurricane. Wow! We'd had a hurricane blow through just last month.

I cornered my buddy Sidney Alderman and excitedly told him the story about the cannons. I also mentioned the way old Spanish coins washed up on the barrier islands after hurricanes.

Well, how could a couple of young bucks, with more imagination than brains, resist? No way! With virtually no preparation or planning, the two of us made our way to Aransas Pass on the north side of Corpus Christi Bay. A causeway crossed from the mainland to Port Aransas on the northern tip of the island. Oddly, no road had been constructed on the causeway—only a railway track. Its purpose was to enable a small supply train to make a once-a-week trip to the port. At the port was a tiny fishing village, consisting of several wooden shacks and a dock. The main building was a bait-and-supply store for fishermen heading out into the gulf.

We began to walk the few miles across the causeway. Our timing and luck were good, because after a few minutes a couple of guys in a pick-up truck came bumping along. It was straddling one of the tracks. They stopped, offered us a ride, and we hopped in the back. I thought my kidneys would surely tear loose, but much to my relief nothing of the sort occurred.

It was late summer, but still rather hot and plenty humid. We bought a couple of soft drinks at the bait-house and told the owner we were going to walk along the beach for a ways and come back. No advice was offered, so off we started. No canteens, no food, no plan, no sense, no nothing. We were going to walk along until we spotted a cannon, while watching for the glint of gold or silver coins in the surf, washed up by the hurricane.

We probably walked six or eight miles, getting hungrier and thirstier, but not actually in trouble. All the while, we scanned the dunes and investigated anything that looked promising. Eventually it began to get dark. We knew we couldn't make it back in the dark, so we decided to spend the night.

We were afraid to sleep on the beach, fearing that the tide might come in and soak us. A nearly full moon was shining and visibility was moderately good, so we picked out a spot on the endless dunes of sand and laid down fully clothed. We were both tired and quickly fell asleep.

After a while—maybe an hour at the most—Sid woke me up. He was nearly shouting. "There's crabs everywhere! They're all over me!" I awoke with a start. As soon as we moved, the crabs took off. They were small—their shells were perhaps an inch and a half across. We discussed what to do. Neither of us had been pinched or bitten, or whatever crabs do. We couldn't think of anything, so we both went back to sleep. In no time the little pests were back, but by now we weren't all that afraid of them. Anytime we'd move, even a hand or foot, they would scatter, but in less than a minute they would return. We finally figured they just wanted to share our body heat. We decided just to ignore them. Oddly, they didn't move around too much and we were able to get some sleep.

The next time I awoke, I was about half-buried in sand. A slight breeze was blowing the fine sand everywhere. My sweaty face was covered with the stuff, and it stuck tenaciously. Sand was in my ears, my mouth, and even in my eyes. Sid was in the same shape. We walked over to the beach and splashed our faces in the surf. That provided a welcome relief. We tried using our rayon neckerchiefs to dry off; that was a laugh. We ended up using our jumpers, then we returned to the sand dunes to try again to get some sleep.

About midnight (I reckon, since the moon was directly overhead), I shifted from one side to the other. My little pets scattered, and then returned. As I was facing this new direction, I saw something moving along in the sand several feet away. I could tell that it was *big*—as big around as a broom-handle and almost a foot long. As I watched closely, I could see that it had dozens of short legs propelling it along. It was some sort of centipede or millipede, I thought. I woke up Sid for him to look. We wondered whether it might be poisonous and agreed to assume that it was. Deciding *To hell with sleep*, we walked back down to the beach, squatted, and spent the rest of the night watching the surf roll in.

When morning came we started back toward the port. We had lost all of our enthusiasm. We probably could have stepped on a gold doubloon and never noticed it. When we finally dragged ourselves back to the Navy base, we were dirty, wrinkled, smelly, sunburned, and hungry.

Nevertheless, we were so consumed by our delusions that we continued to be puzzled as to why we hadn't seen at least one cannon sticking up out of a dune. However, in spite of such strong delusions, we never did venture back.

STRIKING OUT

In the Navy enlisted ranks (everything below commissioned officer level), promotions are obtained based upon years of service-in-grade, test scores, and performance evaluations. The process of petitioning for a promotion is called "striking." For example, a seaman second class could strike for a seaman first class. In support of this process, the Navy had published a separate manual containing all the naval knowledge necessary to pass the test for a given rank. These manuals had titles such as, *Striking for Seaman First Class* or *Striking for Petty Officer Third Class.*

By a quirk in the rules, due to Captain Eddy's desire to funnel men with high electronic aptitudes into Navy schools, we all were seamen first class without striking for that rank. After a certain amount of schooling, the Eddy plan was to allow the students to strike for petty officer third class, and then at the end of their training, to provide another striking opportunity which could improve their rank to petty officer second class.

About midway through the course, our class was notified of the impending opportunity to strike for petty officer third class. Manuals entitled, *Striking for Petty Officer-Third Class* were passed out to everyone—well, everyone except me. Mine was titled, *Striking for Seaman Third Class*. I, endowed with my neurotic mental processing, read the title as *A Striking Manual for Seaman Third Class*, which of course I was. That made *perfect* sense to me, and I set about studying it. It wasn't very difficult—mostly Navy jargon, Naval ranks, some "who's who" in high ranks, etc. I had heard that the test questions were based *exactly* on the material in the manual. I couldn't miss.

The time came to take the test. I looked over the questions—what the hell is this? Not a question I recognized anywhere. The test had questions about naval history, great admirals, ships' names, etc. I had no idea what the problem was. Everyone else was rapidly scribbling down answers. Finally, in confused desperation, I started answering the few I knew and guessing at the rest. Of course I failed. Only one other guy (out of 100 in the class) didn't pass. At least he had a good excuse. He'd been home on emergency leave and hadn't had a chance to study.

Well, at the end of our training they offered another striking opportunity. With the proper study manual this time I managed to pass. So I spent the rest of my Navy career as a petty officer third class; the rest of the class moved up and sported the two chevrons of petty officer second class. Sigh!

[Caution—Name drop ahead]

KIDNAPPED

During my schooling at Ward Island, I became acquainted with an affable young man. His name was George Weyerhaeuser. He was an excellent student, and we frequently discussed interesting aspects of the course material. We never became close buddies—as I had with Sidney Alderman—but I got to know him fairly well. He was the same age as I and was from Tacoma, Washington. That was about all I knew, as far as his personal life was concerned.

One weekend he wanted to go into town (Corpus Christi) on liberty, but was short of money. I was always low on funds as well. My net pay was only $30.00 per month, but I liked and trusted him and happened to have an extra five dollars. I offered it to him, saying I planned to stay on base that weekend and wouldn't need it. He accepted the money, promising to pay me back the next payday, which he did.

Then, a couple of weeks before our class was to graduate, I happened to be shooting the breeze with Sidney. I casually mentioned the small loan I had made to George. Sid said, "Did you know his family is extremely wealthy?" This, coming from a kid who was raised in a mansion with servants…When I replied in the negative, he went on. "Haven't you ever heard of Weyerhaeuser Lumber? They own just about all the lumber in the northwest part of the country. They even have their own steamship lines to ship their stuff around the world." I answered that Weyerhaeuser Lumber did sound a little familiar. I seemed to remember seeing it stamped on some lumber that my dad had bought once.

So I asked, "Why do you think he needed to borrow money from me?" Sid had a quick reply. "His family wants to raise him properly, just like my parents with me. They know money can spoil a kid rotten, so they never send him money. He has to make do like the rest of us." He went on. "In fact, both of our families were in a position to keep us out of the service, using their political connections. However, both families saw that as coddling and unpatriotic, so they didn't interfere with our being drafted."

Then Sid hit me with a bombshell. "I'll bet you didn't even know George had been kidnapped when he was a kid. It was big in the news in the mid-thirties." I answered that I didn't know about any kidnappings except the Lindbergh baby. He went on. "The Lindbergh case was sensationalized by the press because of Charles Lindbergh's fame. In that case, a $50,000 ransom was demanded. In George's case, a ransom of $200,000 was demanded. It was paid, and as you can see, they got him back."

"Did the kidnappers get caught?" I asked. Sid didn't know. But, a recent check in my World Almanac indicates they were caught.

GRADUATION DAZE

Since the course was thirty-nine weeks long, with thirty-nine classes spaced one week apart, a class graduated every week. Friday was always graduation day for the oldest extant class.

A tradition had evolved whereby the graduating class (a company of about 100 men), on entering the training compound on Friday morning, would throw their pocket change at the band at the entrance to the training compound. This resulted in some disruption of the selection being played as the band members scrambled for the coins. The enlisted men thought this was hilarious, as it represented a minor act of rebelliousness.

During the war, military officers were quite intolerant of any act of defiance, pranksterism, or other forms of rebelliousness. They saw such behavior as a threat to their authority and control. Generally, anyone involved would get punished by being assigned to a work group for a week or two. These groups would get stuck with unpleasant chores such as picking up trash and butts or painting the buildings during their personal off-duty time.

However, in this case, the offense occurred on their last day, when not much could be done about it. By then the men's orders had been cut to send them off to their next duty station and no time was left for any punishment. Besides, about a hundred men were involved, making it even more difficult to apply any discipline. In this case it was begrudgingly tolerated.

Eventually, the class ahead of us came due to graduate on the coming Friday. We, of course, were scheduled to graduate the following Friday. Now in every group (especially, one containing a hundred people) there are bound to be a few who rise to a kind of pseudo-leadership, the rest following their lead. The "leaders" of that graduating class decided to carry the now-tolerated rebellious act to a new level, just like kids testing their parent's limits. They decided to forgo the coin toss and use the money to buy supplies to build a large shaft—a large *corkscrew* shaped shaft—a large *purple* corkscrew shaped shaft.

Why? Well, every period seems to come up with some word or phrase that universally symbolizes a repressed angst of the times. In those days the expression was "Getting the shaft." To add a little emphasis, one might say "I got the *purple* shaft." In the service, this could be applied to any arbitrary decision made which seemed detrimental to your interests, so the artisans in the company busied them-selves fabricating their shaft. Somehow they managed to fashion it into a large corkscrew about twelve feet long and painted a bright purple (what else?).

When Friday arrived, they smuggled their shaft into the middle of their company formation then marched to their position in front of the other companies that were lining up along the street leading to the training compound. The band started playing, and all the companies began their routine march toward the compound gate. As the graduating company approached the band in front of the gate, the formation parted slightly in the middle, allowing the eight men carrying the shaft to move forward so they were leading the procession.

The band members, who were all prepared to scramble for coins, were dumb-founded. They totally lost their places in the score. It sounded like band practice for ten year-olds. The chiefs' (the ones who call out cadence) mouths dropped open. Everyone, in the first three or four companies lost step; then broke ranks in order to see better; and finally burst out in applause and laughter. The guards called for help. Soon the base commander drove up, accompanied by several jeeps with guards. They quickly herded the offending company off to the holding area. We didn't ever know what happened to them, as they all were transferred out over the weekend, but apparently not much. The following Friday would be our turn to graduate. We were eager to take advantage of the crack just made in the ruling authority.

Our inspiration came from the fact that the band played the same sequence of songs every day, beginning with one called "Colonel Bogey." I believe it origi-nated in the British army. It was popularized years later (1957) as the theme music for the movie, *The Bridge on the River Kwai*, with Alec Guinness. As with many military marching tunes, enlisted men had added their own lyrics which they sang as they marched, and quite often the words were intended to shock (or at least express) rebellion. In this case, the words began, "Horse shit; it makes the grass grow green."

Now in the military, "horse shit" had a specific meaning. It applied to any supe-rior who made decisions which benefited himself and who didn't give a rat's ass how it affected his subordinates. So every officer knew the words of this song were intended to strike back at those superiors who would "make their own grass greener" by being "horse shit." However, this form of rebellion was tolerated, because officers were taught that so long as the troops were bitching (venting), things were still under control. Quietness in the ranks was regarded as a danger sign.

We decided to dress two guys in a horse costume—one being the head, the other the hind-end. We figured we could hide them in the middle of the formation, as had the last class. Furthermore, we would construct a hole under the tail through which the rear guy could push out a potato every few feet. Finally, a third man would follow behind the horse, with a broom and dustpan, sweeping up the "horse shit."

In a few days Friday arrived. We were ready, and so was the administration. Virtually all the officers, including the commanding officer, had shown up. If anything was going to occur, they didn't want to miss it.

We smuggled the horse and street sweeper into the middle of our formation and marched into position to lead the other companies. Soon the band started playing, and our chief gave the order, "Forward Harch, Hut, Tu, He, Fo." We started up, and at the same time broke out singing the lyrics, "Horse shit; it makes the grass grow green." The formation parted enough to allow our horse and the sweeper to move out in front. Plop, out came a potato. And then plop, another. The sweeper began his lowly task, but allowed enough time for everyone to see the string of potatoes lying on the street. The band didn't miss a beat; this was better than scrambling for pennies. Everyone was cracking up, even the officers and the base commander. The jeeps full of guards were never ordered to intercept us, and we moved unimpeded into the compound.

The next day, with no reprimands, our company was on its way to various duty stations. In my case, I went to an Outgoing Unit on Coronado Island, off San Diego.

NAVAL DUTIES,
Everyday Navy Life—1945–46

❖

Guard Duty
Counting Points
Lame Lock
Subconscious Help
Close the Door after You Leave

GUARD DUTY

I spent only three weeks at Coronado Island before being assigned to Alameda Naval Air Station near Oakland, California. It was now January 1946 and the war had been over since the bombing of Hiroshima and Nagasaki in August. As a result, the intense effort to support the wartime maintenance of aircraft, for which I had been trained, had now been redirected to storing these aircraft—referred to as "mothballing."

So at Alameda that's all I did for the three months I was there. It was dull work, pulling electronic equipment out of the planes, then wrapping and labeling the parts for warehouse storage. I longed to be able to put all the neat training I had received to better use.

Alameda, like most Naval Air Stations, was located at a coastal site. These facilities were positioned close to a seawall, into which a ramp was built to allow flying boats such as PBM's and PBY's to be pulled up onto land and then moved to a nearby hangar for maintenance.

One day I drew guard duty. My watch was from 2000 to 2400 (8:00 p.m. to midnight). I was to patrol the area between the waterfront and the hangars. As soon as I left my barracks to report for duty, I noticed a thick fog had rolled in. I was able to find my way to the guard shack—similar to those you see around the palace in England—by following a road with an occasional street light. Once there, I relieved the previous guard, who turned his guard-belt and pistol over to me. I strapped on the belt and gun. It was a standard military issue—45-caliber automatic. The ex-guard left.

As I began to walk my beat along an access road, I noticed that the fog was getting thicker. I could barely see my feet. As I moved away from the lighted guard shack, it became darker and darker. I couldn't see anything now, not even my feet. I had shuffled (certainly not strode) along for about 10 minutes, when I heard the sound of waves lapping against something. I couldn't see anything in that soup, so I gingerly put one foot forward at a time, feeling the ground with my toe as I went. Suddenly my toe felt nothing. I was at the edge of the seawall (which incidentally, had no railing). My heart pounded when I realized that I could have easily stepped off the edge and nobody would have known.

I retraced my steps to the guard shack, where I stayed put the rest of my watch. At midnight my replacement showed up. I transferred the guard-belt and gun to him while I gave him some precautions about the unprotected seawall. I noticed that he was a kid about my age, 19, and seemed apprehensive. However, I left and made my way back to the barracks to get some sleep.

The next day, while pulling equipment out of a PBM, one of the other guys asked, "Did you hear about the kid who killed himself on guard duty last night?"

"No," I responded, "Which beat?"

He said it was in the ramp area on the Midnight to 0800 shift.

"How did he do it?" I asked, suggesting that he might have fallen off the seawall.

"No, no. He shot himself."

Later that morning I was called into the Security Office. The officers asked me some pointed questions such as, "Did you know him?" and "Did you two have an argument?" Apparently, they thought since I was the last one to see him alive, I may have had something to do with it. I told them what I knew. Finally, the officers concluded that the kid must have been depressed, perhaps his depression was intensified by the fog, and he just committed suicide. They let me go and I never heard any more about it.

COUNTING POINTS

Relief came in March when we were told they were looking for volunteers to be transferred to Norfolk, Virginia Naval Air Station. Norfolk (the city) had a terrible reputation among enlisted men. The city had been overrun for years with drunken sailors on liberty from the three naval installations in the area. The merchants and residents were sick of sailors. I had heard, and later saw for myself, some tavern owners had put signs in their windows saying, "No Gobs or Dogs Allowed." "Gob" is slightly derogatory slang for "Sailor."

In the service, one soon learns never to volunteer for *anything*. As a result, no one volunteered—well, except me. I was tired of "mothballing," and had heard that at Norfolk, they were still doing maintenance work. So in a few days my orders were cut and I was soon on my way to Breezy Point Naval Air Station near New-port News on the north side of Chesapeake Bay across from Norfolk, Virginia.

I was driven to a bus stop in Oakland that took me across the bay bridge to San Francisco, where I was dropped off at the train depot. My ticket put me on a train with passenger cars painted olive drab. These consisted of special sleeper cars, designed for the military to transport a maximum number of troops, yet provide bunking accommodations. They were known by GI's everywhere as "cat-tle cars."

I didn't know the geography of the area, so never questioned why I had been bused west across the bridge to a peninsula when I was being transferred to the *east* coast. The train started up. It went for miles, past one town after another. We'd spent the whole day clipping along when I looked out the window and noticed that we were approaching Oakland. My God! That's where I had started from that morning! The fools had traveled several hundred miles, only to return to Oakland! It was a lesson in military logistics. Then our cattle cars were put on a siding where we sat for a couple of hours. Eventually we were connected to a train that actually headed east.

For four or five days we clickity-clacked across the country. To kill time, almost everyone played card games. During the whole trip I played penny-ante poker. I can't recall how we were fed, but I think it was box lunches. I'm sure the train had no dining car. The toilets were exactly as I had remembered from my trips east with my mom in coach cars: a commode and a sink that was it. One could wash their face, hands and teeth, but taking a sponge bath was next to impossible in a lurching train from a soup bowl sized sink. I gave up trying.

When I got to my quarters at Breezy Point, I headed for the showers. As I stripped off, I noticed several bugs crawling on me. Gad, I had never had "bugs" before! They hadn't bitten me, although they surely had the opportunity. I have no idea what they were after. Nevertheless, the shower was delicious, as was get-ting into clean clothes.

The next morning an orderly came by to take a group of us to our job assign-ments in the maintenance hangars. My assignment was in a radar shop in one of the hangars. This was going to be great. It was filled with the latest test equip-ment, and on the workbenches were several radar sets in need of repair. Well, being only a petty officer third class, I got the hard jobs such as pulling equipment from the planes and reinstalling them after they were repaired. That didn't last too long, as I was compulsively inquisitive and always making suggestions for tests and repairs. Soon I became recognized as repair-capable and was given sets to work on. Since the war was over, almost everyone was just counting points until their discharge. There was little eagerness to advance in rank. The only competition came from a Chief and a petty officer first class. After a piece of equipment was repaired and reinstalled, they got the fat job of checking it out during a test flight. This resulted in receiving flight pay, which they greedily coveted.

LAME LOCK

This radar shop (like most, I was told) was located in a vault-like room within the hangar. It even had a regular bank-vault door with a combination lock. During the war, radar and other electronics were *secret*. However, somewhere along the line the combination lock on this door was miss-set and no one knew how to unlock it. It had a safety feature, whereby if anyone was locked inside by accident he could twist a handle to free himself. That's how we operated the door. During off-duty hours the door was left unlocked and a guard was posted to secure the room. I became compulsively fascinated with the miss-set lock and asked the lieutenant if I could fool with it. Much to my surprise, he gave me an OK.

The rear of the lock mechanism was covered with a thick round steel plate held in place with eight odd-looking screws. Their heads had a round hole lined with ribs. I had never seen anything like them before. Later I learned that they were called "spline head" screws. I soon found that a regular screwdriver or an allen wrench wouldn't turn them. It was going to take a spline driver or a spline wrench. The Navy didn't use them, and I had no idea where to get one. There was nothing to do but make one.

I began with an over-sized allen wrench that I ground down, forming one end into a cylindrical rod. Allen wrenches are made of hardened tool steel and they can lose their temper if allowed to get too hot against the grindstone. I spoiled a couple before I learned. After making one with the correct diameter came the hard part: filing the splines. That took several days of tedious work with a jeweler's file. Eventually I made a tool that worked, and removed the cover-plate.

Inside were the tumblers. Six, I think. If that *was* the number, then the lock had a billion different possible combinations; it was pretty secure. I had no idea how such a lock worked, so I spent hours tinkering with it until I finally figured it out. Like many things, it was rather simple once you understood it. Soon I was able to recover the lost combination. Now we could operate the door normally and dispense with the guards. Everybody thought I was some sort of Houdini. I didn't try to convince them otherwise.

SUBCONSCIOUS HELP

One of the cutting-edge technologies we were taught during training at Ward Island was radar bombing. During most of the war, bombers determined their bomb-release points using optical-mechanical bombsights. The Norton bombsight was the most accurate and most famous. Near the end of the conflict an electronic method had been developed that allowed the bombardier to identify a radar target, lock on to it, and when that target passed through a bomb-release circle on the radar display the bombs would be released. This electronic system could be used at night or in cloudy weather, whereas the Norton optical-mechanical system was limited to daylight and good visibility.

This radar bombsight required several mathematical calculations to be made electrically. The Norton used mechanical devices, such as gears and cams, to accomplish this. The concept that simple mathematical equations could be solved electrically totally fascinated me, and I made mental notes of how this was accomplished. Now that I had some time on my hands, I set about to design an electric calculator.

I had kept in contact with Kenny Thompson by mail throughout the time I was in the service, and with the war over I felt free to discuss such secret concepts with him. His response was enthusiastic. He was much better at math than I was, but he didn't know much about electricity. On the other hand, I had just finished a first-rate electrical and electronic education, so I would attempt to design circuits to accomplish mathematical functions, and when I had problems involving math calculations Kenny would often come to the rescue. We were exchanging five-to-ten page letters twice a week.

My first design effort was a circuit that—on paper—could plot quadratic equations (i.e. $ax^2+bx+c=y$). However, it was limited to values of a, b, c and x, which were positive numbers. This led to a second design that included both positive and negative numbers. With this design, one could solve for the roots of the equation (where y=0). Unfortunately, quadratic equations have two kinds of roots: real and imaginary. I never was able to design a circuit that would find imaginary roots, but I was gratified with what we had done.

I never actually built either design. I didn't have the resources. The device required a special arrangement of three potentiometers on one shaft. The Navy radar bombsight had several double potentiometers (two on one shaft), and even if I could have gotten my hands on those, they wouldn't have sufficed. There was another problem with implementing this design: "loading." The circuit required several potentiometers to be connected in a manner whereby one was loaded by the next, and these two were loaded by a third. This loading was detrimental to accuracy that wasn't too great to begin with.

So things ground to a halt, other than extending the concept to graph/solve higher order equations such as cubics and fourth degree. Then an idea occurred to me. Why not go electronic by using vacuum tubes and eliminate the potentiometers. No circuits existed for vacuum tube potentiometric circuits; I was sure of that. Being excessively optimistic about my own capabilities, I decided to invent one.

Immediately, I ran into a swarm of problems. Vacuum tubes are much more complex devices than resistors, from which potentiometers are made. They have unique characteristics such as transconductance, secondary emission, thermal effects, non-linearity; and they are inherently unipolar (current flows only in one direction), requiring biases to handle bipolar signals. These characteristics can all be described mathematically. The radio industry had already done that, but they were extremely ponderous, especially in this case, in which I was attempting to combine them with my own equations. Eventually I came up with a monster relationship, incorporating the necessary equations, but neither Kenny nor I had been able to solve it in terms of the variable we needed. We tried for several weeks, communicating back and forth feverishly—but no luck.

About this time I was in the PX (Post Exchange), buying some toiletries when I saw a brand new kind of pen. It was called a ballpoint. It was made by Reynolds—the aluminum people—and cost about $7.00. To me, this was exorbitant; it was as much as I made in a week—but I bought it.

Back at the barracks, I marveled at it for a while and then decided to use it for my calculations. It had bright purple ink and was easy to read. Of course there was no way to erase anything; I just had to cross out mistakes. Finally it got late and I undressed for bed. I laid the notepad and pen on the floor next to my bunk and fell asleep. A couple of hours later I woke up. The solution to the monster equation was in my head. I remembered the pen, found it in the dark, and began writing out the equation on the inside of my left forearm. As soon as I finished, I put the pen down and went back to sleep. The next morning, I awoke and saw all this bright purple scribbling on my arm. I looked at it, and by Jove, it looked like the solution to the equation we had worked so hard on.

What did I do with this magical solution? Nothing. It was all just a fanciful and fruitless exercise at that time. Nearly twenty years later, after transistors had been invented, the operational amplifier was designed. Finally, electronic analog computation became a possibility and a reality. I tell this tale because most people, including me, wouldn't believe that the mind is capable of such higher-order thought while asleep unless it actually happened to them.

CLOSE THE DOOR AFTER YOU LEAVE

By July 1946 I had accumulated enough points to get discharged. I got my orders to return to Fort MacArthur, packed my gear, and headed for the train station. In a few days I was back in California. At MacArthur, I was debriefed and paid off. They let everyone keep their uniforms—as souvenirs, I guess. I called my parents, who came that evening and retrieved me from the totalitarian arm of the government.

PART III
STORIES OF CIVILIAN LIFE

_____POST-WAR ACTIVITIES

◆

What Next?—1946
Back to Paint—1946
Dad Leaves Us—1946
The Ceremonial Last Bomb—1946

WHAT NEXT?—1946

After I was discharged and returned home, I mostly bummed around during the summer. I was very conflicted about going to college. I had taken college prep courses in high school and my grades were adequate, but I was still emotionally immature and needed counseling and direction. None was forthcoming from my parents. Neither they nor I had done any real planning or saving for such an endeavor. I'm sure Dad saw high school as a totally adequate amount of education. However, I think if I had been more self-reliant and assertive I could have gone to a university in town on the GI Bill, and I'm sure my parents would have been willing to provide support in the form of room and board. However, the perceived expectation was that I would find a job. I never followed up on college seriously until 1954.

BACK TO PAINT—1946

Lacking the aggressiveness to pursue a higher education, I took the easy route; I decided to return to the paint manufacturing business. When I left Sherwin-Williams for the service, I was making 60 cents an hour. According to law, all businesses were required to accept returning servicemen back into their old jobs. That's what I thought I would do. However, my mom's friend, Opal King, who lived next door, mentioned to Mom that her husband, Bob, who worked for W. P. Fuller Paint Company, knew of a job at his company's laboratory. He thought it paid more than Sherwin-Williams had been paying me.

Fuller's was located on the north side of Los Angeles. Using public transportation, it took over an hour to commute each way, but getting paid more was the main issue. With my laboratory experience at California Flaxseed and at Sherwin-Williams, I easily landed the job. It paid $175.00 per month (equivalent to $1.00 an hour).

The job was testing products in a control laboratory that were being manufactured in a lacquer factory across the street. Others in the lab—mostly women—tested paint products being manufactured in the main factory. Sherwin-Williams did not manufacture lacquers, so I had some things to learn in this new position; however, I enjoyed working with lacquer. Its properties were more predictable than paint.

DAD LEAVES US—1946

I had been working at my new job only a few weeks when one Saturday afternoon, as usual, Dad was working in the back yard. He spent a lot of his free time out back, adding a few desert rocks here and there, according to some design he carried in his head.

On this day, November 16, he came back into the house, perspiring more than justified by the weather or his activity. He complained about having bad indigestion. The standard treatment for that was a glass of water with a spoonful of bicarbonate stirred in. Mom fixed him a glass. He drank it and decided to go into the bedroom and lie down on Shirley's bed.

About this time, Kenny Thompson and I came into the house. Kenny had recently returned from the service and had bought an old used car. Mom told me Dad wasn't feeling well and he thought he might be dying. He had asked her to get out the registration for the car so he could sign it over to her. The house was already in both their names and he had no other assets. I went into the bedroom. He looked pale, but he was conscious and able to talk. After he signed the registration, he became less communicative. Mom said, "You better go get a doctor."

We didn't have a family doctor. I can only remember one doctor ever being in the house, and that was when Shirley was sick, years before. Kenny and I took off to look for a doctor. We zoomed down the street, heading for an area where we thought we had the best chance of finding one. Just as we were approaching Whittier Boulevard, I spotted a shingle hanging in front of a residential house. It said, "Dr. Paul Resnick." We stopped, went in and saw some patients sitting in a reception area. My last look at Dad had convinced me maybe he *was* dying, so I said to the receptionist, "I think my dad's dying. Can somebody come quick?"

She ran into the back, got the doctor—who came running out, and got into Kenny's clunker. We raced home. Dad was still breathing, but going in and out of consciousness. The doctor told everyone to leave the room and asked where the phone was. Mom showed him, and he called the Fire Department. They showed up in a matter of minutes with a cylinder of oxygen and worked on him for about a half an hour. Finally the firemen left and the doctor came out and told Mom that Dad had died. He was only 52. She sat down on the couch and began to cry hysterically. Dr. Resnick asked me if we had a preference of funeral homes or churches. We didn't, so he called a funeral home from a number he carried in his wallet. In a short while an ambulance came and took Dad away. Fifty years later (yes, 50), I was doing some genealogy research and got a copy of Dad's death certificate. On it was Dr. Resnick's signature, "L. Paul Resnick, DO." My Dad was dying of a heart attack and I had brought home an *osteopath*!

The next day, Mom was still crying uncontrollably, but she was starting to verbalize her grief. "What am I going to do? What am I going to do?" she kept repeating. Eventually, Ray Lacado, an old friend of Dad's, dropped by. He offered to take me to the mortuary to pick out a casket and to the cemetery to pick out a lot. Mom was in no condition to go.

With those essentials out of the way, it was necessary to come up with cash to pay for them. I called in an ad to the Herald Express newspaper and advertised Dad's 1941 Pontiac for $1100.00. Cars were still in short supply after the war, and it sold quickly. It took all the money to pay for the casket, the cemetery lot (actually two lots—one for Mom), and a gratuity for the minister.

I had only recently begun to develop any closeness to Dad. He had always been sort of standoffish and even a little scary as I was growing up. I wasn't too surprised that his death didn't evoke many strong feelings. Nevertheless, at his funeral I felt badly that the minister was only saying stock banalities about him. If I hadn't been so ignorant about funerals, or Mom had been in better shape, maybe someone could have given the preacher some crib notes about Dad's life and work. At the cemetery, the same preacher repeated the same trite words. Then they lowered Dad into the ground.

I honestly think the person who felt the loss of Dad most was my sister, Shirley. He had been her "guy" and she was only twelve at the time. Fortunately, I was living at home then and she was able to transfer many of her feelings for him to me. After the funeral Mom suddenly stopped crying. There were no more lamentations.

THE CEREMONIAL LAST BOMB—1946

In early December Kenny and I decided to build one last bomb—a really big one. We acknowledged that building bombs was rather adolescent for anyone our age—twenty—and went on to rationalize that this could serve as a ceremonial passage to adulthood. Even we couldn't find much logic in this, but it *sounded* good. We further decided that, since it was to be a ceremony, we should invite our old bomb-making friends to participate.

This included Charley Heckman, Lynn Sarkisian, Jack Gretta, Bud Lane, and Melvin Lee. Charley declined. He had found two new consuming interests: making money and pursuing girls who were attracted by it. Everyone else wanted to be "in" except Melvin, who was off on a tramp steamer seeing South America.

We all met at my place to agree on the kind of bomb and the financing. First, we agreed we would share the cost equally, with a limit of ten dollars each. Next, we agreed it would be a much larger pipe bomb than we had ever made before. Lynn suggested we go downtown to Andrew's Hardware and have them cut off a piece of seamless steel tubing for the casing. He knew Andrew's could provide that service, since he'd been there with his dad in the past to get large irrigation pipe and fittings.

Kenny, Lynn, and I took off for Andrew's Hardware. We ordered a 12" long piece of 6" diameter pipe with a 1/2" wall thickness. It took three men to haul in a length of heavy-walled 6" pipe from the storage shed. They laid it on a long table, with a large motor-driven hacksaw at one end. The clerk said, "Are you sure you want only a one foot piece? After it's cut, it's yours." We nodded our agreement. It took about fifteen minutes for the saw to cut off our piece. The cost was between $10.00 and $15.00, as I recall.

We decided against threaded fittings like those that we had used on smaller pipe bombs. Instead, we would have a plate welded on each end. On the way home we stopped at a welding shop in Belvedere Gardens. The owner suggested that for maximum strength he could cut a circular plate for each end and weld them inside the tube about a half inch from the ends. We agreed and selected some scrap 5/8" thick plate. The welder proceeded to scribe two 6" circles on it and cut them out with a torch, then we had him drill a 1/2" hole in the center of one circle. It would provide a hole to pour in the powder and serve as a location for the fuse. Finally, he welded the two plates in place, and our casing was complete.

Next, we had to choose the explosive mixture and a place to set it off. I proposed that we use ingredient "X" and charcoal for the explosive. The charcoal wouldn't be quite as powerful as some acids, but it would be relatively safe to mix and handle. I would mix a batch at home and we would load it into the bomb at the explosion site. We surely didn't want to carry a loaded bomb of this size around with us. Kenny and I suggested we set it off next to the Rio Hondo River in East Montebello, about a quarter mile north of Beverly Boulevard. From experience, we knew that this area was totally isolated. Everyone agreed. We set a date.

On the agreed date, I mixed the batch of powder. The five of us piled into Kenny's car and we headed for the river. Since I planned to take movies of the event, we elected to bury the bomb on the west bank and to observe (and film) from the east side. No obstructions would block our view from that direction. At this location the river was about 75 feet across, but only a couple of feet deep.

Lynn had brought along a 10' piece of dynamite fuse. Dynamite fuse burns at an almost constant predictable rate, but if accuracy is required, you need to burn a short length and time it. We needed to run such a test in order not to waste a lot of movie film, or worse yet, miss the explosion. Jack had a stopwatch he had snitched from the Navy. He was elected to run the test. After measuring and cutting off a 1' length of fuse, Jack moved a safe distance away to make a test burn. In the meanwhile, Bud and Lynn waded across the river with a shovel and began digging a hole for the bomb. Kenny and I were busy loading the explosive mixture through the small hole in the end of the casing, using a funnel.

Bud came back and reported that they had made a hole about five feet deep in the sand. Kenny stuck one end of the fuse into the casing hole, measured off 6' of fuse and cut off the excess. Jack's test had indicated the fuse burned at 16 seconds per foot, so the 6' length should take about 96 seconds. With this information, we all waded across the river. Kenny carried the bomb and I carried the camera. I took some shots of the bomb being buried. An old railroad tie was lying a couple hundred feet away. We placed it over the buried bomb—like in the old days when we would put a tin can over a firecracker to see how high it would go.

Everyone waded back to the east bank except Jack. Being the owner of the stopwatch, he had been elected to light the fuse, start his watch, and run across the river to join us. I yelled to Jack that we were ready, and took some footage of him lighting the fuse and running across the water, then I turned off the camera. Jack kept his eyes glued to his stopwatch and counted off the seconds. When he got to 90 I began filming again. Like clockwork, in a few seconds there was an enormous explosion. It was the biggest we had ever seen. The railroad tie flew into the air, and I tracked it with the camera until it splashed into the river. South, on the Beverly Boulevard Bridge, we could see that cars had stopped and people were looking at the rising mushroom cloud, trying to determine what had blown up.

We all splashed across the river to view our handiwork. A hole had been carved out of the bank, big enough to hold a Volkswagen. Our ceremonial event had been a success. Now we could all leave our delinquent childhoods behind.

_____RECONSTRUCTION

❖

The Madam of Manipulation—1946 to 1948
The Wishing Well
The Plan

THE MADAM OF MANIPULATION—1947 TO 1948

After Dad's funeral, Mom began to contemplate her future. She thought things out on her own, and any consultation with me was minimal. She decided she would take on housekeeping and baby-sitting jobs. Her first job was with a family who wanted a Nanny to look after their pre-school twin girls and do housekeeping. She would "live-in" for several days at a time.

However, Mom realized her income would be insufficient to provide any real security, so early in 1947 she decided to take in boarders. The first were four female college students who were attending East Los Angeles Junior College. What a setup!…if only I had any idea how to take advantage of the situation…I didn't!

One semester of that was enough for Mom. The girls were messy, left the bathroom filthy every day, and stole her linen. Her next experiment was to take in two working women boarders. It wasn't a disaster, but we lost our privacy, as they took over the house. By the end of summer 1947 she evicted them. They were followed by a married couple. That arrangement lasted till spring of 1948. Then Mom decided that to regain our privacy and get some income she would build an apartment addition onto the house. That decision led to a series of unintended adventures.

The following Saturday I was sleeping late. It was about 8:00 a.m., when suddenly I was awakened by a BAM, BAM, BAM. The pictures in the room were jiggling and I could feel the thuds through the mattress. I jumped up and looked out the window. There was Mom with a sledgehammer, pounding a hole in the side of the house. I yelled, "What the hell are you doing?" (After a hitch in the Navy, I could now say "hell" and get away with it.)

She stopped, looked up, and with sweat rolling down her face replied, "I'm starting on the apartment. Get out here and help me." Although I had outgrown her total control over me, she still regarded me as someone to do her bidding.

Now, Mom was one of the first feminists. She despised the inferior role women had in society, believing women should be allowed all the privileges men had, yet she strongly clung to convenient beliefs, such as men should do the hard, physical work because they were bigger and stronger, and they should perform such tasks as repairing cars, plumbing, appliances, etc., because the male brain had mechanical aptitude.

Dad had always been a hard worker. After working 44 hours a week in a factory, he spent his weekends doing projects around the house. He was not a couch potato. Even so, Mom had a need to control certain aspects of his efforts. Although she could employ several different tactics, messing up something to the point-of-no-return was a tactic she often used successfully. The banging outside my window was exactly that. She had made a big hole in the house that could not be ignored. *Something* had to be done. Being the only man around, I was the object of this cunning stratagem.

However, Mom soon had to face the fact that I wasn't Dad. I didn't have anywhere near his experience in plumbing or cement work. Eventually, seeing my limitations, she caved in and hired a contractor/carpenter: Mr. Goodrich. Still, I wasn't entirely off the hook. To keep the cost down she planned that Goodrich would lay the foundation, build the structure and install the cabinets. I would have to install the plumbing and electrical wiring and provide a lot of the manual labor needed by Goodrich. Eventually, she had to hire others as well to install sewers, plaster, and shingle.

THE WISHING WELL

One of the first obstacles to be dealt with was the wishing well. Some years before, Dad had built a wishing well using different colored desert rocks. He had made it look rustic, with a shingled roof supported by two poles. It featured a hand-crank, and was fitted with an axle, a rope and bucket. It was attractive, and I'm sure he was proud of his efforts. However, the wishing well sat right in the way of Mom's new apartment. It had to go! She ordered me to take the sledge-hammer and break it up, then she went off to her housekeeping/nanny job.

I wasn't enthusiastic about tearing down Dad's hard work, but Mom's orders prevailed. I took the sledge (a 12-pounder), wound up, and struck the thing a mighty whack. A little piece of rock chipped off. I tried again in a different spot…same result. I banged away for about twenty minutes. Blisters were starting to form on my hands, and the biggest chunk I had knocked off was about the size of a golf ball.

When Dad built the well, he had dug a round shallow hole and filled it with cement. This was the foundation. He used a cylindrical carton, about 20" in diameter and 4' high, as a form for the well's central opening. Next he placed a course of rocks around the carton, but spaced about 4" from it. In this space he poured cement and let it harden. Then he repeated the process, adding courses of rocks until it was about 4' high and formed a "well." This excessively strong structure was refusing to break up and was giving me blisters. Of course, there are Neanderthals out there who would have compulsively chipped away for hours or days until they finally succeeded in breaking it up, but not me. Physical ambition and effort were not my forte. After all, I was an "expert" on explosives that could do the hard work. Right?

The "lay of the land" was as follows: our house was located on a block situated between two streets—Northside Drive (my street) and Alston Street (the next street south). That was usual enough, but at our end of the block Alston merged into Northside. To accommodate this, the block was shaped like a bullet. The last house on the block was located on the "nose" of this bullet, facing the end of Alston Street.

This was Mr. Gerwitz' house. Mr. Gerwitz was a Jew—one of only a few Jewish families in this predominately Protestant neighborhood. Craving acceptance, he was a model of amicability. However, he had bought the house during the previous year and soon learned that the neighborhood kids habitually cut through his backyard to get from one street to the other without going all the way around the "nose of the bullet." His solution was to build a cement block wall from his garage down our mutual property line to the sidewalk on Northside, thus effectively blocking off the kid's shortcut. To minimize the eyesore, he painted the wall white and capped it off with red Spanish-style roofing tiles.

Even though I was 21, the decision to use explosives caused my brain to go into an obsessive mode. Consequences were not an issue. I decided to use a mixture containing my familiar ingredient "X." I knew it would explode without the confinement of a casing. I had read that blasters often used mud to direct the force of an explosion by providing the blast something against which to push. I had never tried it, but that's what I decided to do.

So after making a trip to National Chemical for supplies, I mixed up a two-pound batch, wrapped several layers of waxed paper around it to keep it dry, and inserted a length of dynamite fuse. I placed this in the bottom of the well against the side facing our house (to direct the blast in the opposite direction) and packed several shovelsful of mud over the package.

All was ready. I lit the fuse and ran into the house. The first time I considered any consequence was during the 20 seconds the fuse was burning. Then I thought, *The noise will attract a lot of attention. What will I say? Maybe it will break windows in our house. Better not stand in front of one.* Then BAROOM! No windows broke, and I ran outside. A big white cloud was making its way skyward. The wishing well was gone. I walked over to examine my work. Soon, neighbors came running over. From experience, they knew where explosions originated in the neighborhood. In this case, a mushroom cloud was there to guide them as well.

I was explaining to the onlookers about blasting the wishing well to make room for an addition when Mr. Gerwitz showed up. He was badly shaken, could hardly talk, and he was spattered with mud! Eventually I learned that he had been standing in his front yard, watering the lawn. His front yard was on the opposite side of his house. The force of the blast had thrown the mud over his house and showered it down on him.

As I was apologizing profusely to Mr. Gerwitz, I noticed for the first time that a section of his new block wall was leaning like the Tower of Pisa. At each end of the leaning section were large vertical cracks where it had separated from the rest of the wall. All the red Spanish tiles had been blasted into shards and were lying in his yard. Added to the apology was a solemn promise to repair his wall. With amazing composure, Mr. Gerwitz left to clean himself up.

A professional blaster could not have done a better job (well, forgetting Mr. Gerwitz' woes). The blast had broken the well into pieces just the right size for me to put into a wheelbarrow and haul away. Dad probably turned over in his grave.

THE PLAN

At first Mom decided on an addition that would consist of a bedroom, its own small kitchen, and a bathroom. This presented a problem. The neighborhood had been zoned for single-dwelling homes and a few apartments. The apartment locations had been clearly represented on the original subdivision maps to limit their construction. All such locations had been built upon. None were left. An exemption would have required a petition to be presented to the County Planning Commission. That was not Mom's way. She had learned to get what she wanted through guile. Lying or cheating was never an obstacle for her.

Her devious obsessive mind began to work. First, the construction had to *look* like an addition to her home. Another bedroom and bath would probably be OK, but a second kitchen would never fly. Even if she could fool nosy neighbors, she could never get it past the county inspectors, who would monitor every phase of the construction. Somehow, Mom would find a way to have an apartment with a kitchenette.

The new structure could not be closer than three feet from the property line (per code), so its east edge would run along this line. Our lot was small, and Mom wanted to get as many square feet as possible. Unfortunately, the property line separating our lot from Mr. Gerwitz' was at a sharp angle, due to the bullet-nosed shape of the block, thus the shape of the addition would be a trapezoid—odd looking, if not downright ugly—but it didn't matter. Mom had to have the space for her kitchen and bath, so she directed Mr. Goodrich to lay out the foundation accordingly.

The foundation was dug and poured. That much was cast in concrete (pun intended). The inspector came and OK'd Goodrich's work. While the inspector was there, Mom casually mentioned she planned to put a window in the diagonal wall. (In her mind, it would be over her kitchen sink.) She was told she couldn't do that. Even though the code allowed a wall within three feet of the property line, walls with windows had to be back at least eight feet. This added to the growing list of things Mom would have to connive around. She *would* have her window.

The first immediate problem was Mom's determination to have a kitchen and a bath. Both required plumbing in the form of water supply and sewers. Even though she could have legally had a bathroom, she decided to hide all plumbing from the inspectors. This tactic eliminated the need for any kind of plumbing inspection that might expose her deception. On her plan, the bathroom became a closet for my bedroom. To pull this off, she had Goodrich put in a door from my bedroom to this "closet."

Goodrich then proceeded to put in floor joists, wall studs, and ceiling joists. At this point, Mom decided she wanted a second floor. It would be the bedroom. The downstairs would be a living room, with, of course, a kitchen and bath. First, she had Goodrich put a dormer window in this new bedroom. For balance, she also had him install one in the old part of the house from the attic. Next, she told Goodrich to install a spiral staircase. I was impressed that this independent carpenter could do it, but it turned out to be very attractive.

After Mom decided where she wanted overhead lights and wall outlets, I ran wiring to these points, then Mom called the building inspectors out. The electrical inspector wasn't happy that I had used the old "knob & spool" method of installation, but it was still legal, so he passed it.

A much more serious problem arose when the structural inspector spotted the stairs and second floor. He told her he couldn't allow it—that the foundation was not wide enough, per code, for a second story. He also stated that the roofing structure Goodrich had put up over the second floor would have to be dropped down to a level commensurate with a single-story dwelling. Mom immediately realized that complying with a change to the roof would doom her plans for an upstairs bedroom. She broke down in tears. Not everyday sobs and sniffles—these were wails. The inspector was totally taken aback, as were Goodrich and I. Between outbursts, she lamented that it would totally spoil the appearance of the house; the dormer windows wouldn't be level, etc. She twisted the argument to be one of esthetics. After some minutes, the inspector became so unnerved he capitulated with one proviso (mostly to save face, I suspect). She would have to include a hip to match the original roof style. The uncontrolled lamenting subsided to a whimpering. Mom nodded agreement. She knew she had won. She *would* have space for her upstairs bedroom.

Next, a massive cover-up was launched that only Mom's audacity could have engineered. She instructed Goodrich to take out the stairs and the upstairs subflooring. Then she hired a plumber to install sewer drains from the illegal kitchen and bathroom and connect them to the main sewer line that ran directly beneath the new addition and to install water pipes for the kitchen sink, bathroom sink, and toilet. Then I measured the position of each water pipe outlet and sewer line connection by using xy coordinates from the floor up, and laterally from a wall. These measurements were carefully recorded on a secret copy of the construction plan. Finally, Goodrich installed the first floor sub-flooring (which covered up the sewer connections) and gypsum wallboard (which covered up the water supply pipes in the walls). I wrapped the exterior of the new addition with tarpaper and chicken wire.

Back came the inspector. I was as nervous as a cat. Mom seemed normal, except for a grim poker face. He saw only what Mom had intended him to see. No plumbing, and the stairs were gone. Except for a few minor comments, he passed the inspection. The rest was routine. Mom had a plasterer come in and plaster inside and out. After that, Goodrich laid down hardwood flooring. A roofer came out and shingled the new roof (with a hip, of course). All was ready for the final inspection. It went without a hitch.

Mom elected to lay low for a while, just in case the inspector returned for some reason. After a few weeks she decided it was safe, and the last leg of her deception was initiated. I got out my treasure map, showing the locations of everything hidden behind the walls and under the floor. I measured and marked, measured and marked. Then, with hammer and chisel, I punched holes to expose the plumbing connections. Everything was where it was supposed to be.

Goodrich rebuilt the stairs, added hardwood flooring upstairs, and installed a kitchen counter, plus some cabinets. Mom decided to play it safe and not install the kitchen window yet. She was afraid the inspector might drive by some day and spot it. It was over a year later when she had it put in.

From the outside, the house was an abomination, with that large trapezoidal wall and all, but it served her needs for many years by providing a steady income. Years later, when she sold the place, it brought a good price. The original house was only five rooms with 900 square feet. With the addition, it was now eight rooms with about 1400 square feet.

Once again, Mom demonstrated that cunning, driven by obsession, could provide her with solutions to her problems.

17. Revisiting Ray's Childhood Home—ca. 1986

_____LOST GOLD

◆

*The Superstition Mountains' Lost
Gold—1947–49
The Lost Dutchman Mine
Out of Water
Weaver's Needle
The Square of Stones
The Circle of Trees
The Hunt is On
Bonanza Gold
Back Again*

THE MOUNTAINS—1947–49

The Mazeli's were a family of three: Ray, his wife, and their son Jack. They lived in Belvedere Gardens just off Whittier Boulevard in a small frame house. Their house had a basement. I cannot remember any other house with a basement in California.

Kenny Thompson had met Jack Mazeli in 1944 because of their common occupations as chemists. Jack was an only child and was about four years older than Kenny or I. He had earned a degree in chemistry at USC, and was employed by the Southern California Gas Co. Jack was plump, wore thick glasses, and for reasons I never learned did not serve in the military during the war. He was disinterested in sports and was an inveterate reader: a couch potato. He seemed entirely content to live at home. It wasn't too difficult to see why.

His mom's role in the household was like hired help. She not only cooked and cleaned, but also served as a personal servant to her two men. Either of them might call out, "Mom, bring me a beer and some chips." No matter what she was doing, she would jump up and obey the command. She never seemed to resent this role. Actually, she seemed to get gratification from being useful to them.

Jack had taken over most of the basement, where he had set up a darkroom, storage shelves, and several filing cabinets. He subscribed to several photography magazines and chemical journals. Being rather lazy, he had trained his mom to be his private secretary. Her secretarial duties included filing his magazines, correspondence, photographs and negatives, and like a good Girl Friday, she took enough interest in his activities to know what-was-what and what-was-where. I remember examples where he might say, "Mom, get me that issue of Modern Photography with the article on exposure meters." By golly, in a few minutes she would have retrieved it. And, as if he were in a library, when he was finished he'd just set the magazine on his end table, then, she would re-file it.

Jack's Dad, Ray, was a heavy, swarthy, very Italian-looking man. He loved to play poker. That provided a common interest between Jack, Kenny, me, and him. Every Friday night Kenny and I would head for the Mazeli house to play nickel poker with Jack and his dad. Mrs. "M," of course, played the role of maid, making runs to and from the kitchen all evening for beer and snacks.

Other than being Kenny's friend, I had no prior connection with the Mazelies. Nevertheless, I was easily accepted into the group, probably because I wasn't a very good poker player. It was usual for me to lose between two and ten dollars a night. Every poker group needs (and values) a consistent loser.

Jack was a slow, deliberate, pipe-smoking player. He would analyze his cards for seemingly endless periods, driving his dad crazy. The standard mantra of the old man was, "For Christ's sake, Jack, play! It would be nice to finish this hand before the sun comes up." Jack would just ignore him. If he saw that he was starting to aggravate his dad, he might proceed to reload his pipe *before* he played his hand. This involved a ritual in which his dad would put down his cards, lean on his hands, and *glare* at Jack. Jack would methodically tap, tap, tap his pipe in the ashtray, empty out the ashes, and with a tool, he would ream the remaining ash from the pipe. After this, he'd reach into a jacket pocket for his tobacco pouch, carefully open it, and scoop out a load into the bowl of his pipe, fold up the pouch and return it to his pocket—all in slow motion, of course. As his dad's glares continued, he would tamp the loose tobacco into the bowl, eventually lighting, drawing, relighting, more drawing, and *finally* exhaling a cloud of smoke, much like the Vatican indicating the conclusion of the ceremony. By this time his dad was so livid he was speechless.

During one Friday night game, Jack and his dad informed us there wouldn't be a game the following week. They were going to take a trip to Phoenix that weekend. Kenny asked, "What're you going to do in Phoenix?"

Jack replied, "Dad wants to take me flying around the area." That was when I first learned that Ray knew how to fly and had a private pilot's license. He didn't elaborate further, and we went back to playing cards.

THE LOST DUTCHMAN MINE

Jack had read the book *Thunder God's Gold* by Barry Storm, about the Superstition Mountains and its lost gold mines. Then he had discussed with his dad the concept of finding the Lost Dutchman Mine by flying over the area and taking photos. With the photos they might be able to spot the mine, then hike in and locate it. Neither Jack nor his dad knew beans about hiking, camping, or surviving in the wilderness, but they had a friend, Bill Wells, who went camping and deer hunting every year. Because of this expertise, they had brought Bill into their venture. Other than Bill, they intended to keep it mum. After all, if they found the mine, they didn't want word to get out.

In preparation for this effort, Jack and Ray had gone to a military surplus store and bought a WWII aerial reconnaissance camera and a case of film for it. This big camera produced 5 x 7 inch negatives. They planned to drive to Phoenix, where they would rent a Piper Cub. Ray was then to fly them to the Superstition Mountains, about 50 miles east of Phoenix. Here he would fly a grid pattern about 2500 feet above the ground, within the area where the mine was supposedly located.

This was not an easy assignment. Holding the plane on a straight, level course, while compensating for wind driftage and turning around at the end of each pass to a new course that would slightly overlap the previous one, these were real challenges. Jack had to assume an uncomfortable position, hanging out the window in the wind with this big heavy camera while counting off pre-determined seconds between each exposure. Somehow, however, they pulled it off. When they got back to Los Angeles they had the film processed and enlargements made by a commercial lab, since none of Jack's darkroom equipment could handle such a large format.

While waiting for the processing, Jack, Ray, and Bill began to plan the provisions needed for the trip. It soon became clear to Bill that for a five or six day trek into the wilderness, it would take one—maybe even two—pack animals. How on earth were they going to arrange for pack animals at the Superstition Mountains? After mulling this over for a while, one of them suggested they hire some help to pack in the provisions. After considering the expense and the problem of secrecy, they decided to ask Kenny and me if we wanted the job as "sherpas."

Being young and adventurous, we accepted. The deal was that we wouldn't have to share any of the travel expenses or provision costs, but we would have to provide our own backpacks, sleeping bags, and canteens. We agreed that we wouldn't be paid anything, but if the mine were found we would each get a 5 percent cut. Sure. Why not?

Finally, the enlargements came back. We moved all the furniture out of the Mazeli's living room and Jack began laying out the 8 x 10's on the floor. They almost covered the entire room. The prints were already sorted in the order of their negatives on the rolls, so it wasn't too hard for Jack to get them into a mosaic layout. There were hardly any gaps between images, and the overlap was tolerable. Jack and his dad had done a creditable job of aerial photography. Jack proceeded to identify each print (A1, A2,...B1, B2,...etc.) That turned out to be a lifesaver later when we got lost in the mountains.

According to Barry Storm's book, the Dutchman mine was located on the side of a cliff. The digging had formed a small cave, not easily spotted from the trail below. After scooping up the prints, everyone took a stack and began scanning for anything that looked like a cave, especially on the side of a cliff. Jack had a ten-power magnifier, and when any of us saw something of interest he would scrutinize it under his glass.

Eventually, someone spotted a cave-like structure in one of the prints. Jack and his dad looked at it from all angles. Gold-fever and rational thinking don't mix well, and discussions about lost mines or lost treasure tend to make those involved a little "nuts"—sometimes a lot! Soon Jack pronounced this *was* the Dutchman's lost mine. There was no doubt!

So a date for the expedition was set (in December 1946). We all arranged for a week of vacation and began our preps. Kenny and I bought some backpacks, sleeping bags, boots, and canteens from a surplus store. I still had a mess kit and flashlight from my Boy Scout days.

After work on the agreed upon Friday, we all assembled at Mazelies' place and packed our backpacks. Since there were five of us, there wouldn't be any room in the car for the provisions, so Ray had rented a small trailer. We stuffed our packs into it, piled into the old man's car and set off. We drove all night and got to Phoenix early in the morning. After eating breakfast at a roadside cafe, we headed east toward the Superstition Mountains.

Jack was the researcher. He had the maps, the pictures, and knew the stories about the lost mines. Naturally, he would be our guide, notwithstanding, of course, that Jack had never been to the place before except from 2500 feet above in a plane.

There are two customary ways to get to the interior of these mountains. The one most prospectors and treasure hunters used was an old easy-going trail that enters from the west. The other was to enter from the south and climb over a several-thousand-foot ridge. Jack had decided that since it was only about half as far, according to the map, we'd take this southern route in. He didn't seem to realize each of those little contour lines on the map represented a 200-foot climb.

The Quarter-Circle U Ranch was located near where we planned to enter the mountains, so we turned off the main highway and took the ranch road, eventually passing the ranch house. It was a shack. Nobody came out to welcome us or to ask why we were there. They were sick of prospectors, treasure hunters, and the problems they caused. But since the ranchers only had grazing rights—no mineral rights to the land—they couldn't prevent anyone from prospecting on the property.

We drove on to the foot of the mountains, unloaded, packed up, and headed up a faint trail leading toward the top. I was not only carrying 60 to 70 pounds in my backpack, a canteen, and a miners pick, but had drug along my new Bolex H-16 movie camera and my dad's old 25-20 Winchester rifle. Having both hands full made climbing a lot more difficult.

Soon the two overweight Mazelies were calling for a rest-break. Kenny and I were happy to stop, too, but that damned Bill Wells just kept on climbing. After several more rest breaks with Wells continuing ahead, Kenny tagged him with the nickname "Billy-goat Wells." It stuck.

After several hours, we finally got to the top. It *was* a fine view. About four miles to the north was a great valley running northwest and southeast. Jack said it must be La Barge Canyon. Immediately to our left was a prominent peak: Miner's Needle. Dozens of canyons and arroyos were running every which way to the northwest. Our cave was somewhere in this maze. Jack, confidently referring to his compass and maps, pointed the way.

The mountains had been formed by upthrusting, causing a lot of shale-like rubble. Every step was hazardous. Cactus was everywhere, and avoiding it required a lot of agility. Everyone except Jack's dad, Ray, managed reasonably well, but Ray was just plowing through the stuff. At one point he lost his footing and tumbled down a ravine into an old dead cactus. Whenever we stopped to rest, Jack would have to pull thorns out of his dad's jacket and pants—and him.

Navigating some of the canyons was especially difficult, due to large boulders strewn along their bottoms. Some were almost as big as a house. To work your way up (or down) such a canyon required climbing over these huge rocks. Eventually we worked our way out of one of these canyons, but the going had been tough. Down in these canyons, distant landmarks were not visible. This prevented Jack from taking bearings on various peaks. We were beginning to worry that we may be getting lost.

It was starting to get dark. One of us spotted an outcropping low on the side of the canyon that formed a level place, so we set up camp and started to fix supper. Wow! Billy-goat had provisioned well. We had a large iron frying pan, a coffee pot, canned food, potatoes, and a cooked ham. My god, no wonder my pack weighed over 60 pounds! We were famished, and it tasted wonderful.

OUT OF WATER

All day no one had been mindful of our diminishing supply of water. We each had refilled our canteens several times from the three one-gallon cans of water we were packing. Now we were almost out of water, and it was only the first day out. First thing in the morning we would have to look for water. We spent most of the morning browsing here and there, hoping to find a tributary with some water flowing in it. Everything we found was bone dry. Then about noon, someone spotted a small pond. It was about twenty feet across, full of algae, and covered with scum. Yuk! On closer inspection, it had mosquito larvae swimming in it. We figured that was a good sign, since if the water were poisoned with alkali the larvae couldn't live. So, using our sweaty kerchiefs as filters, we filled our canteens and storage cans and were on our way again.

WEAVER'S NEEDLE

According to Jack, we needed to head northwest to get to the canyon with the cave shown in the photograph. A couple of miles further we spotted Weaver's Needle, a famous landmark in the area. The Spanish called it "El Sombrero" because it looked like a hat. That was encouraging, because according to Jack it was an important clue to the Lost Dutchman mine and most of the other lost mine stories in these mountains. Jack took a bearing on it. This told us we were *somewhere* along that bearing line, but where?

After hiking further northwest(?), Weaver's Needle disappeared and again we were just guessing as to our whereabouts. Toward the end of the day we came upon a spring. It was a blessed sight. The water was clear and cold. We washed the brackish water from our canteens and storage cans and filled them with the precious liquid, then we set up camp for the night. Once again, we ate heartily—ham, beans and canned fruit.

In the morning, Kenny pointed out an odd-shaped mountain on the horizon to the north, but Jack couldn't identify it on his map, so it was of no use for taking a bearing. We just kept wandering, guided only by the sun. We were getting deeper and deeper into the morass of canyons, becoming more and more lost, and it showed on Jack's face. On the trip over from Los Angeles, Jack had related several stories about treasure hunters having gone into the Superstitions who were never seen again. These stories were no doubt on everyone's mind, although now we didn't discuss any of them. By noon even Jack had to admit we were in trouble. Ray, who always seemed to take pleasure in criticizing Jack, began to grumble and make snide remarks about Jack's navigational skills and judgment. Jack's defense was to clench his mouth and ignore him.

THE SQUARE OF STONES

As Kenny and I trudged along, we began to exchange comments about never finding our way out. Fortunately, these were interrupted when Billy-goat yelled, "Hey guys, come look at this!" As usual, he was about a hundred yards ahead of the rest of us. Hoping for any good news, we all trotted up to him. He was standing next to a stone wall. It was about three feet high and formed a square, maybe fifty feet on a side.

Jack, the researcher, said, "I think I know what this is."

His dad snapped, "Well, don't keep us in the dark, professor."

Ignoring his dad, Jack explained, "It's an old Spanish corral. They didn't have wire fences and used stone for fences—you know, like in the old world." He went on, "The story goes that before this area became part of the U. S., the Spanish and Mexicans prospected here and found several rich gold deposits. These deposits were mined by expeditions that brought along cattle for food. That's the reason for the corral. But more important, I'm sure I saw a square in one of the aerial photos. If we can find that picture, maybe we can figure out where we are."

The stack of photos was in my backpack, so I opened it up and dug out the thick stack of 8 x 10's. We divided them up and everyone started looking. No luck.

Jack insisted he had seen a small square on one of them. He took everyone's stack and started scanning through the pictures again. Jack was near-sighted. He took off his glasses and brought each print close to his eyes for a sharper view. After looking through 20 to 30 pictures he exclaimed, "Here it is, here it is!" And there it *was*...a faint little square, less than a quarter inch across.

Quickly, Jack got out his mosaic grid, a crosshatch drawn on a map of the area. He soon located the print by its coordinates and made an "X" on the map where we were. What a relief to feel "unlost"! It turned out that we weren't too far from the cave we were looking for, so off we started, with renewed vigor and optimism.

In a couple of hours we spotted the cave up in the side of a steep canyon wall. I didn't know beans about the Lost Dutchman story, but I could tell it was not a digging—just a large weathered-out cave, but Ray didn't want to leave without climbing up to make sure. So he and Jack (and of course, Billy-goat) climbed up to examine it while Kenny and I rested below.

It was getting late and everyone was exhausted, so we agreed to camp nearby. The next morning we decided to head back by following La Barge Canyon southeast, rather than attempting to retrace our torturous path in. We thought Miner's Needle was tall enough to be seen from the eastern part of the canyon, so when we spotted it we could turn south and climb out of the mountains.

We lumbered along the bottom of La Barge for several hours. Ray was completely pooped. Worse than that, he had plowed through so much cacti that needles had penetrated the toes of his boots. At one point, we stopped while he took off his boots to see if he could get the thorns out. His toes looked like hamburger! Up to this point, I was unaware he had brought along a hipflask of whiskey, which he was using to anesthetize himself. We all began to worry that we might have to carry this 200-pound man out of there.

Ray had slowed our progress by needing a breather every few hundred yards. I didn't need that much rest, so while Ray was recuperating, I walked along the canyon bed looking for float—pieces of ore that had washed down from veins located in the canyon walls. I took a few samples and put them in the pocket of my backpack.

It was late afternoon when Jack pointed southward and yelled, "There's Miner's Needle!" Immediately we turned south and began climbing over some low hilly ground. Ray needed more frequent rests. During one of these, Kenny and I put down our packs and began exploring around. A short distance away was an east-west fault line I decided to examine.

THE CIRCLE OF TREES

On the way over I spotted an odd clump of scrubby trees. It appeared so different from the rest of the surrounding growth that I decided to walk over and look. The clump turned out to be scrub oak trees forming a circle about 10 or 12 feet in diameter. I parted some branches to look in. The ground was flat, with some wild grass and weeds growing on it. I looked around for Kenny. He was not far away, examining some rocks. I called for him to come over. We both wondered how such an unusual circular growth could have formed.

Soon the group was calling for us to start again. As we were hiking to higher ground, I mentioned the circle of trees to Jack. Jack mumbled, "Circle of trees; circle of trees—that sure sounds familiar." At our next rest stop he asked, "What did they look like?" Kenny and I described what we had seen. He went back to mumbling, "Circle of trees; circle of trees. I know I've heard of that somewhere."

It was getting late in the day and we could see we weren't going to make it out of the mountains before nightfall, so we began to look for a flat area to make camp. Finding a likely spot, we stopped. It was twilight, and as we were laying out our bedrolls someone spotted a tarantula about twenty feet away. While we were all looking at it we saw another, and another. They were coming out of the ground—hundreds, probably thousands, of them. I have a phobia of ordinary spiders, but *tarantulas*…I was terrified! We decided to build a fire and take turns, staying awake in two hours shifts, watching to keep them away. I knew I couldn't sleep, so I volunteered for the first watch.

Fortunately, a nearly full moon rose in the east, making the critters easier to monitor. During my watch I began to see that they weren't interested in us; maybe the fire kept them at bay. I began to relax a little. After two hours I woke up Jack, who was to take the next watch. I shook out my sleeping bag and cautiously climbed in. In no time, I fell asleep.

The next morning there were no signs of the arachnids. They seemed to be strictly night stalkers. We broke camp, packed up our gear, and climbed south toward Miner's Needle.

Kenny had brought along his 35mm Argus C3 camera. Soon after we broke camp, he snapped a picture that happened to include the foreground, the canyon below and the horizon beyond. This shot became our main clue during an attempt to locate this area in a later search.

We climbed and stopped, climbed and stopped, eventually reaching the south ridge of the mountains. Shortly after that we were back to the car and on our way home. Ray had kept himself going by nipping from his hip flask at every stop. We all looked like hell—unshaven and un-bathed for six days. In Arizona, we only got casual glances, as prospectors were a common sight there, but in California it was a different story. At one roadside cafe in Riverside, we were scrutinized as though we were escaped criminals. Late that night we finally got home, cleaned up, and returned to civilized existence.

The next afternoon I got a call from Jack. His voice was an octave above normal with excitement. He was yelling, "I found it, I found it! I found the story that mentioned a circle of trees!" I didn't know anything about the Superstition Mountains, its stories, or its legends, but I sensed this might be big. Then he said, "Come on over and I'll show you." So I called Kenny, told him about Jack's find, and suggested we should go see what he had. We agreed to meet at Mazeli's house in 30 minutes.

When we got there, Jack had a table covered with some maps and books. First, he showed us a map on which he had drawn our path down La Barge Canyon to where we had seen Miner's Needle and turned south. Then he pointed to a page in the book, *Thunder God's Gold* by Barry Storm. It was a map of the same area, and it showed a trail leading to exactly the same area our route had taken us. This page was a part of a story called "Wagoner's Lost Ledge."

In that story, in 1894 a man named Wagoner was returning from an area north of the Salt River, where he had spent time prospecting. Although not a true prospector (he carried only a bedroll and a suitcase), he spent much of his time searching for gold. Wagoner had tuberculosis and originally came to Arizona for his health. In those days, a dry climate was the only treatment known.

On this occasion he decided that instead of hiking his usual route out of the mountains through Apache Gap to catch the Mesa-to-Pinal stage, he could save a day's hike by taking a shortcut through the Superstition Mountains. He knew his stage passed south of these mountains.

Wagoner intended to locate La Barge Canyon and follow it to a trail leading out of the southern edge of the mountains. However, he misjudged the time this route would take and nightfall forced him to make camp in the canyon. In the morning he noticed he was due north of Miner's Needle. Being reasonably familiar with the area, he reasoned that the shortest exit from the mountains would be by hiking due south.

Turning south, he began to climb over some low hills—the same ones we had climbed. Not far along this route, he came upon an outcropping of rose quartz. On closer examination, he could see gold all through it. Using his pick, he knocked off as much of the exposed quartz as he thought he could carry, put what he collected in his suitcase, and continued. When he got to Pinal (now called Superior), he had it assayed and sold it.

Wagoner returned to his mine many times. The ore was so rich he could live for many months on the small amounts he could carry out in his suitcase. When he would leave the mountains, he always flagged down the same stage to get back to town. As time went on, his illness worsened and he came to realize he couldn't continue these trips into the mountains, so he decided to make one last trip in, collect as much ore as he could carry, cover over the shallow workings, and plant a circle of trees around the mine to camouflage and mark it.

During these many treks, he had befriended the stagecoach driver, Fred Mullins. On his last trip out he confided the existence of the mine to Fred, and even drew him a map of its location. He also told him that he had planted a circle of trees around it to mark the spot. Of course Wagoner soon died, and over the years Fred Mullins made many attempts to locate the outcropping, but was never successful. Eventually, the story and the map were exposed and were even published by Barry Storm in 1945, but no one had yet found the circle of trees—except, of course, me!

Jack, Kenny, and I decided we *had* to go back in and find this lost mine; however, none of us had any vacation days left. We agreed to wait until spring (April 1948). Our plan was to make a quick one-day trek in and out. We wouldn't take backpacks and we would carry only one canteen each and some beef jerky. We were sure we could get in and out in one day.

THE HUNT IS ON

Finally, spring arrived. Kenny, Jack, and I decided we would make the trip back to the Superstition Mountains, using my car. I had become tired of using public transportation to get to and from work and had bought a 1937 Ford. It was an oddball model with a tiny 60 HP V8 engine. Although a coupe, it was big enough for the three of us.

As before, we left on a Friday evening, drove all night, and arrived in Phoenix early the next morning. After a quick breakfast, we drove the last fifty miles to the Superstitions, past the Quarter Circle U ranch, and parked at the foot of the mountains. We got out and started our climb up the now-familiar trail. When we got to the ridge, we looked north, as we had on the last trip. In the distance we recognized La Barge Canyon and Picacho Butte, but *absolutely* nothing else looked familiar.

It took us a while to understand what the problem was. We had last seen this vista in the fall. Now it was spring, and the foliage and colors were entirely different. It was as though our memories had been rendered useless. We had thought we could just walk to our last campsite, guided by memory. We found that in the wilderness, cues are vague, ambiguous, and deceptive. However, we had Kenny's photo (actually a color slide) to help guide us.

After heading north for a while, but recognizing nothing along the way, we thought surely we were *somewhere* near where Kenny had shot the picture. He had brought along a slide viewer that, with the slide loaded into it, could be held up to one eye, while the other eye viewed the terrain directly. However, we were never able to match the terrain with the slide.

We never found anything—not the circle of trees, not the fault line Kenny and I had both noted previously, and not even our last campsite that we thought would be easy to spot. After wasting the whole day meandering around, we finally gave up and hiked out of the mountains.

As we approached the car, I noticed the right-rear tire was flat. As I opened the trunk to get out the spare, Jack said, "Hey, there's another flat on this side, too." We examined both tires for damage, but didn't see any.

After pondering the situation for a few minutes, Kenny said, "We'll just have to drive on one flat tire till we get to the ranch house." We changed the spare to the right-rear wheel, and I began a slow drive back over the unpaved rocky trail toward the Quarter Circle U ranch house. The tire was making a "flump, flump, flump" sound, and we knew that it couldn't last long before it would be ruined.

After a couple of gingerly driven miles, we came to the ranch house. One of my hangups is that I hate to ask for assistance, even directions, from strangers, but there was no getting out of this—it was my car. I walked up to the door of the shack and knocked. A tall, lanky man appeared (probably Tex Barkley, the owner). "Wud'ya want?" he growled.

I answered, "Can somebody give us a lift to the main highway? We have a flat that we need to get fixed."

He snarled back, "Yer'all found yer way in; now find yer way out," and slammed the door in my face.

Back at the car I said, "I guess we'll just have to drive on the flat back to a gas station." So off we went—flump, flump, flump. After another mile or so, the tire shredded and came off the wheel. We were now riding on the rim, but we had no choice, so we just kept going. Eventually we got to the highway and turned right toward Apache Junction.

A quick examination of the rim revealed it was too banged-up to support a tire ever again. We decided not to be concerned about the wheel and just drive on to the first gas station. The rim, rolling along the hard pavement, created a loud, strident, anxiety-producing racket. Our nerves were on edge when we finally spotted a gas station on the outskirts of Apache Junction. They put the car up on a lift where we could see that the rim had been flattened almost to the brake drum. They didn't have a replacement wheel. A check of the flat tire in the trunk revealed no leaks. That told us someone had simply let the air out of the two tires. So we filled the flat with air and mounted it in place of the ruined wheel.

Now we were back on the road, but with no spare. We drove the 50 miles to Phoenix, where we found a tire and wheel business. Fortunately, they had a replacement wheel and a tire, but most fortunate was that Jack had enough money to pay for them. Kenny and I together couldn't have come up with enough money. It took me several months to pay Jack back.

BONANZA GOLD

A month or two after the last trip, I went downtown to buy a book at the Technical Book Store. While walking back to the bus depot, I chanced across a shop that bought and sold gold jewelry, numismatic gold coins, and mineral samples containing gold. In their window I spotted a small quartz specimen containing visible gold—a sure sign of bonanza quality. On impulse, I bought it for a couple of dollars.

I showed it to Kenny, who was never much interested in minerals. He suggested we show it to Jack and tell him I had found it on the first trip into the Superstitions. Since the gold was so obvious, I made up a story that the gold wasn't visible until I broke open the rock, and that I had collected it from La Barge Canyon. That lie would have never flown with any prospector or miner, but gold fever can distort rational thinking. Jack bought the story completely. It was my intention to fool him for a while and then fess up, but he took it very seriously—even asked if he could borrow the sample. So, I gave it to him. Then the Devil took over.

By now, Kenny was in a serious relationship with a woman, whom he eventually married, and our Friday night poker games had petered out, so we no longer saw the Mazelies on a regular basis. However, after several weeks of not hearing from Jack, Kenny decided to contact him about something. He called their house. Jack's mom answered. When Kenny asked for Jack, she got flustered and finally admitted that Jack and his dad were in Arizona again, looking for lost gold. She said she wasn't supposed to tell.

It didn't take a brain surgeon to figure out that my sample of gold ore had made them go gold crazy. They probably had it assayed and learned it was hundreds, or even thousands of dollars per ton. Anything over $50.00/ton in those days was considered "bonanza ore." I'm sure they reasoned that since they had financed that first trip, anything found on it was theirs. They decided to return to the mountains, sans Kenny and me.

They, along with Billy-goat, had gone in from the western approach—the longer, but easier way in. Upon locating La Barge Canyon, they set up a base camp near the place where we, in the first trip, had entered the canyon. They spent four or five days, prospecting the canyon for the source of this fabulous specimen. Finding nothing, they became increasingly weary and disillusioned, eventually packing up and returning home.

This story leaked out slowly to Kenny and me over the months, but Jack never admitted it had anything to do with my golden stone, which incidentally he never returned. Deciding they got what they deserved for ditching Kenny and me, I never told them the true source of my trouble-causing rock. This silly affair resulted in our drifting apart from the Mazelies.

BACK AGAIN

For all practical purposes, Kenny and I had given up trying to find the circle of trees. Oh, we fantasized briefly about flying over the area to look for it—even considered using a new contraption called a "hopicopter" which strapped on your back, but we knew we couldn't finance these ideas.

Nonetheless, we got a lot of pleasure in telling our tales to friends and anyone else who would listen. At work, I became a center of attention whenever I would tell anecdotes about the Superstitions. I was surprised at the number of otherwise intelligent people who were willing to invest their money in any venture to search for lost mines in the area. But, never the entrepreneur, I refused all offers. Besides, if I didn't find anything, I could never handle the guilt of blowing their money.

Two of our friends, Bud Lane and Melvin Lee, took a different tack. They thought it could be the basis for a fun camping trip, with the lost gold mines just providing some interest and intrigue. With such limited expectations, Kenny and I decided to make another trip back, this time primarily as a vacation, but with a minor effort to relocate the circle of trees.

The four of us agreed upon a weekend in November 1948. We planned to spend one night in the mountains, which meant packing in some equipment and supplies. Earlier, Kenny and I had jointly purchased a surplus two-man tent. This would be a chance to check it out. On the first trip in, we had learned canned fruit was a good choice to take. It was easy to pack, contained a lot of nourishment (sugar), and provided much needed water, so we mostly loaded up on various canned fruits.

As on previous trips, we left Friday evening and drove all night. This time we used Kenny's car.

As we approached the turn-off onto the Quarter Circle U ranch, Kenny and I began to have trepidations about what the ranch owner, Barkley, might pull on us this time. As a precaution, Kenny had put a tire-pump in the trunk. We drove past the ranch house. No one was in sight, and we kept going to the foot of the mountains. We helped each other load the packs on our backs. Melvin looked wobbly. He was a very non-physical person, even worse than Jack was. Furthermore, he wasn't very coordinated. I began to wonder if he could make the climb.

Eventually, we got to the crest. Since it was November, the same month we had first seen the circle of trees, we thought we might have a better chance of making our way to them. Kenny pulled out his 35mm slide and viewer and looked over the landscape. Except for the distant peaks, nothing seemed to line up. It provided no indication as to which direction to go.

With little else to go on, we just headed due north. But, once down in the canyons, we were pretty well forced to follow the line of each canyon, wherever that took us. In late afternoon, we stumbled upon a nice spring. We drank, filled our canteens and bathed our feet. It was like finding an oasis in the Sahara. Mounting our packs again, we kept bearing north, thinking something might appear familiar to Kenny or me. Nothing ever did.

Late in the afternoon, we knew we would have to stop and make camp, otherwise we might go too far to be able to climb out of the mountains the next day. We found a likely spot and made camp. Kenny and I set up our tent, although it wasn't cold enough to justify. We didn't see any tarantulas around, and we bedded down for the night.

The next morning, we got up and decided to cook sausages someone had brought. We built a small fire and boiled them in a metal mug. They were delicious. We packed up, and even though we hadn't gotten to La Barge Canyon where a glimpse of Minor's Needle might have steered us near the circle of trees, we headed back south by compass. At this point, we were most concerned about finding our way out before nightfall.

To my surprise, Melvin held up quite well. He huffed and puffed a lot, but he hadn't slowed us down. Eventually we got to the southern crest and made our way down the mountain to the car. A quick examination of the car revealed nothing amiss. Apparently Barkley hadn't sabotaged us again; maybe he didn't even know we were there.

18. Lost in the Superstitions—ca. 1947

Ray is looking through his old Boy Scout compass. When I became interested in astronomy, he gave this compass to me so I could always align the telescope with true North. I still have the compass and consider it a treasure. —Thelma

_____NEW TECHNOLOGY,
Spectrol Labs—1948–1950

✦

A New Color Film
A Business Venture
Miracle Worker
Our Lab
Campbell & Co.
The Final Superstitions Trek
A Turn of Events

A New Color Film

After the war, Kenny bought a 35mm camera—an Argus C-4. He used it to take color slides. In those days, Kodachrome was the only color film available. Kenny had accumulated a fair-sized collection of such slides. However, in about 1947 a new color film appeared on the market. It was called Agfa Ansco Color, and had been developed by the Germans during the war. It differed from Kodachrome in that it could be processed easily, whereas Kodachrome could only be processed by Eastman Kodak in one of their "million dollar" labs.

Furthermore, Agfa Ansco had also put a kit of chemicals on the market which any amateur photographer could use to develop their film. The kit consisted of pre-weighed packages of dry chemicals the user would mix with water to form various solutions needed for processing the film.

Jack, always the researcher, learned about the new product and convinced Kenny to test it. Jack was a serious amateur photographer, but he had never gotten into color. He shot everything in black and white with a 2 1/4 x 3 1/4 Speed Graphic, a news reporter's kind of camera. Kenny purchased a roll of film and took pictures of various subjects around town. To perform the processing, he bought a processing kit, a 35mm daylight-developing tank, and several bottles in which to store the solutions. Jack had all the necessary measuring paraphernalia and a dark room where they could load the tank.

The three of us met at Jack's house. Kenny and Jack went into the darkroom to load the tank. Neither had ever loaded one before. Loading color film had to be done in total darkness. Eventually, they emerged with the loaded tank. Meanwhile, I had mixed the six solutions from the packages of chemicals in the kit. Finally, we were ready.

The first solution is called "the First Developer"…into the tank it went. Developing time depends upon the temperature of the solution, so we inserted a thermometer into a tank receptacle. After developing for the number of minutes indicated on a time-temperature chart, we emptied out the developer and poured in a stop-bath to terminate the developing action. At this point, if you were able to see the film you would see a negative image. The next step was to remove all the silver that formed this image. We did that with a bleach solution that dissolved the newly developed silver image. This left the unexposed silver halide that was a complement of the original image (i.e. a positive image). After washing away all traces of the bleach, the developing tank was opened in order to expose this remaining silver halide to light.

Now comes the clever part. The Germans had invented a way to produce a light-sensitive silver halide that had a dye molecule attached to it. These dye molecules remained colorless until they were processed in a special solution called "the Color Developer." The film consisted of three layers of emulsion, each with the halide attached to a dye molecule that would develop into a different color. The colors were cyan, magenta, and yellow (the complements of the primary colors: red, green and blue). After exposure to light, the Color Developer solution was poured into the tank, where it developed the remaining halide image to the appropriate color for each layer. The process is known as "dye coupling." Finally, a Fixer was used to remove any remaining halide, followed by the Hardener, to toughen the gelatin emulsion. Everything went well. Kenny's roll looked great. We had actually developed our color film. We were exuberant.

A BUSINESS VENTURE

Processing of our color film was slow. It took a couple of hours to mix the chemicals, mainly because the Color Developer contained a small amount of an oily liquid that was very difficult to mix into the solution. The processing itself took an hour and a half. All in all, it was a three-and-a-half to four-hour process. It didn't seem worth it, on a routine basis.

Kenny and I were discussing this cumbersome process when he said, "What if we start a business making processing kits that are already mixed, ready for use? That would cut the time at least in half." I had to agree that it sounded good. He went on. "I'll bet we could sell kits to every photo-shop in town." Immediately, we spotted a problem. In the instructions with the dry kit it said the life of the solutions was only two weeks after they were mixed. Being chemistry-fluent, we decided we could figure out why that was so, and then somehow fix it. We agreed to give it a try.

First things first…We had to know what the formulas were for the various solutions, so Kenny, oozing with self-confidence, called Ansco Chemical Co. (the American branch of the German Agfa Ansco) and asked them what the formulas were. Well, it seems the company was far more interested in selling film than chemicals. The kits were just a side business to get people to use their film. They would be happy to tell us the ingredients in all their solutions, which they did. The ingredients were all commonly available chemicals, except the oily liquid. The Germans had developed this special organic compound, dicholamine, for dye coupling. Ansco sold it to commercial labs in one quart and one gallon sizes. They would sell it to us, too.

That solved the formula problem. Now we had to address the two-week limit on the solutions after they were mixed. We felt our kit should have a shelf life of at least a year. We reasoned that all the solutions except the developers should keep indefinitely. By now, we knew that the First Developer was just a variation of an ordinary black and white film developer. This kind of developer was sold in photo stores in bottled solution, so it shouldn't present a problem for us. However, the Color Developer was a different matter. We confirmed that once the dicholamine was added, the solution lasted only the two weeks, as stated. We decided we would package the dicholamine in a separate vial, as Ansco had done, and achieve our goal of a one-year shelf life.

With a capital outlay of $25.00 each, we went into business. First, we took care of the legal stuff: putting our money into a bank account, obtaining a business license and a resale permit, advertising our fictitious firm name—Spectrol Labs, and buying a ledger binder and some pages. Next, we needed some equipment and supplies. At this point I witnessed a miracle—at least to me it was. In my world, everything was paid for in cash except a mortgage on your home. We had less than $30.00 of our original $50.00 investment left. However, Kenny seemed to have an innate knack for business. He said, "We'll go to Braun Chemical first and get some glassware and other lab equipment." All I could think of was, *We'll run out of money before we get started.*

MIRACLE WORKER

At Braun, Kenny asked for a salesman by name. He had gotten acquainted with him through his job at Gooch Labs. They shook hands and Kenny said, "Ray and I are starting a business, manufacturing color processing chemicals. We need some equipment to get started. Can you help us set up an account?" Always looking for new customers, the salesman replied, "Come with me." He took us to the Accounting department where we filled out a few forms. In a few minutes we were told our account was approved for $250.00, then we went to the order desk, filled out an order for glass tubing, glass mixing containers, porcelain funnels &

scoops, and an Ohaus chemical balance. At Receiving, we picked up everything and put it in the car. We hadn't plunked down a nickel! I had witnessed the beginning of the miracle.

Next we headed for National Chemical Company. Here Kenny repeated the same pitch with one of their salesmen, although Kenny didn't know him. At Accounts, we encountered a little reluctance; the manager preferred some references. With total aplomb, Kenny gave him the name of our Bank and mentioned we had an account at Braun. Well, it happened that National Chemical and Braun were fierce competitors. The manager said, "Braun? You have an account at Braun?" Kenny nodded. We were approved with an account limit of $500.00. I was flabbergasted. We took our chemicals list to the order desk and filled it.

I watched Kenny repeat this routine twice more that day—first at a bottle company where we got several cases of pint-sized bottles, 10cc vials and caps for them, and second, at a cardboard box company. Here we ordered some custom-cut cartons and separators to hold six bottles. They easily gave us an account, but insisted on a $25.00 deposit because it was a custom order. A week later, we picked up our gross of cartons. The miracle was completed. If ever I had any doubts, I was now convinced that Kenny was a real genius.

We still needed labels for the bottles and the cartons as well as instruction sheets. My neighbor across the street, Bill Kershner, owned a printing business. We approached him. He seemed happy to get the job. It was now May 1948 and we had everything needed to start up the operation.

OUR LAB

Since Dad had died, the garage had become mostly a storage area. We agreed it would be the location of our business. Dad had built a workbench along one side. It would serve as a place for our mixing equipment and balance. We decided we would need a new bench in the center of the garage for a filling area. Above it, we would install some shelves to support six 5-gallon water bottles. These bottles would contain the solutions needed for the kits, and being above, would provide gravity pressure for filling. Next, we built another workbench along the opposite wall. This would provide a place to pack a kit of solutions into cartons and seal them.

All this fit in the front two-thirds of the garage. We planned to divide the rear third, build a darkroom on one side, and an office on the other. Since I knew much more about photography than Kenny, I was to operate the darkroom, where I would be in charge of Quality Control. We would test each batch of solutions by processing some standard exposed film in them. Kenny was to be Chief Chemist for research.

We were so cash-strapped neither of us could afford to give up our regular jobs. As a result, the manufacturing of solutions, filling of bottles, and packaging were all done after we got home from work. Saturdays were reserved for sales and deliveries.

I had a strong aversion to sales and felt uncomfortable in the role of salesman. Nevertheless, each Saturday we went to various photo stores and pitched our product. The storeowners generally treated us shabbily. They'd let us stand around endlessly while they waited on customers: *their* highest priority. Only when the store was empty would they talk to us, often rather rudely. One thing I learned was that I was a better salesman then Kenny—actually a surprisingly good one. Kenny, with all his self-assurance, approached the owner with how users loved the kits, how much money they could make selling them, etc. The owners ignored this as just so much hype, but when they asked questions, especially technical ones, I gave them the honest, knowledgeable answers they wanted. As a result, most sales were made based upon my answers. Eventually, some money began to come in and we plowed every nickel of it back into the business.

Kenny spent most of his research efforts trying to eliminate the need for the user to have to add the Dicholamine to the Color Developer. No matter what he tried, the stuff would go bad after two or three weeks. After listening to his complaints about how oxidation was the problem, I had a bright idea. I suggested that perhaps instead of trying to neutralize the effects of oxygen, we could just eliminate it.

He replied, "But how?" My first thought was to purge the air out of each bottle, using an inert gas. He thought that was great. Certainly that would eliminate the source of the oxygen.

We checked into buying a cylinder of nitrogen to use for the purge. It was rather expensive, so thinking on the problem a bit, Kenny said, "We might be able to use natural gas. That's next to free." To test the idea, we mixed up a quart of Color Developer with the Dicholamine mixed in. Next, we purged two bottles with natural gas and then filled them with the developer. We set the bottles aside, with plans to test the first in one month and the second in two months.

After the month was up, I ran a test on a sample of film that had been given a standard exposure. The results were fine. We commented, "Hey, maybe we've got this problem licked." The second test (after two months) was a failure. The color balance was off. We knew we were on the right track, but we needed a developer that would last longer—a year at least.

We racked our brains as to where the remaining oxygen might be coming from. As I've said before, Kenny was a much better chemist than I was, but I had a better grasp of physics than he did. I suggested the oxygen was perhaps from air dissolved in the water we used to make the solutions. Kenny thought a second and then stated, "That's it, that's it, that's gotta be it!" Immediately, we set about making up a second test. We boiled the water to drive out all the dissolved air and then prepared two test bottles of Color Developer from it. It would be two months before we could test it, so in the meanwhile we continued with business as usual.

Sales were slowly increasing, especially reorders from dealers who had bought kits earlier. We even interviewed a young fellow to handle sales and deliveries during the week, but we couldn't agree on terms. Eventually, the two months passed and I tested the first bottle of developer. Bingo! It was perfect. Now, we figured we should wait a year to test the second sample. Impatience set in. About the only complaints we were getting back from the dealers was that their customers had trouble getting the Dicholamine to dissolve properly. To alleviate this, we decided to gamble and change the process without waiting out the year.

Kenny had determined we could avoid the necessity of boiling the water by simply bubbling natural gas through the water for about an hour. The natural gas seemed to displace the air completely. To implement this in production meant we needed a closed mixing vessel. At a surplus store, one of us remembered seeing a large stainless steel oxygen tank, used in bombers for emergency oxygen. We decided to check it out as a possible mixing vessel. One look convinced us it would do fine. This 7.5-gallon tank would be just right for mixing 5-gallon batches. Scrounging around the store some more, we located several stainless steel valves and fittings we would need. Luckily, we found a small stainless steel pump we could use to pump the contents of the tank up into the storage bottles over-head. The toughest item to find was a 6-inch diameter pipe coupling and plug made of stainless steel to provide a port in the top through which to pour in water and chemicals. We had to go to a specialty tubing company for that, and it cost more than the rest of the items all together.

A trip to a welder, one who could weld stainless steel, completed our new mixer. In its final form it had a sealable port on top, a bearing on a slant for a motorized mixing propeller, a valve in the bottom, two purging connections, and legs to hold it upright, since the bottom of the tank was round.

After revising our instruction sheets, we made the changeover. Everything hummed along nicely. However, this was the business world, and soon we became aware that we had a competitor: National Chemical, the same company that was selling us our bulk chemicals. For some years, they had been in the business of manufacturing photographic chemicals. Most photo stores sold their bottled developers, fixers, etc. Now that someone (Spectrol) had put a color processing kit on the market, they wanted to get in on the action too. They knew, as we had, that demand for such kits depended on their being in solution form…Ansco would always be the first choice for dry kits. National began selling an imitation of our first kit with the vial of Dicholamine, even plagiarizing much of our instruction sheet.

Shortly after they came on the market, we came out with our improved kit. They scrambled to compete. The head chemist at National knew Kenny from his job at Gooch Labs. He confided to Kenny that he had contacted Ansco for the formulas and that their kit was probably identical to ours, but he couldn't duplicate our new development. He admitted that every time he added the Dicholamine to the developer it would go bad in a little over two weeks. He asked, "How do you guys do it?"

Kenny smiled and told him we weren't telling, that we had put a lot of research and money into the method and considered it a trade secret. National's chemist further admitted they had analyzed our upgraded kit and couldn't find any new or special ingredients. Kenny didn't say any more, but he knew there were no special ingredients to find, just one less—oxygen! Within a few months, National pulled its kit off the market. It couldn't compete with our upgraded version.

CAMPBELL & CO.

In July 1948, our business activities led to meeting Bob Campbell. He owned a photo studio and a processing lab in Whittier. Bob was bright, articulate, and an obsessed entrepreneur. Although he made portraits in his studio, he possessed a minimum of right-brained, artistic talent, and so didn't get much business. Nevertheless, his processing lab was a going success. It involved making runs around Whittier and the surrounding area to pick up photo finishing from several dozen stores. These were brought back to his lab where he and his wife, Ginny, worked all night, processing them. The next day the processed photos were returned to the stores and a new batch of orders picked up. The two of them couldn't handle the workload alone and they had hired two young men, both in their early twenties.

These two, John and Philip, were Quakers, as were most people who lived in Whittier, a Quaker town whose most famous resident was President Richard Nixon. The Quakers do not believe in killing, even in wars, so the draft-aged men all claimed to be "conscientious objectors." The wartime U.S. Government hated the concept, believing everyone should be patriotic and willing to fight in a national conflict. Not being able to intimidate the Quakers, the government elected to send these objectors to serve in northern lumber camps—a sort of hard-labor punishment for not knuckling under.

As a result, John and Phil had spent the last few years at a camp in Oregon. Bob had found them upon their release the year before and had trained them to do darkroom work. They worked all night, six days a week (60 hrs). Bob paid them each $50 per month. That was much less than the $0.25/hr. minimum wage. Actually, Bob was not a mean-spirited person. He was just obsessed with his business, and such wages seemed justified, based upon the company's income.

THE FINAL SUPERSTITIONS TREK

Kenny and I became semi-friends with John and Phil. Both were fascinated with our stories about the Superstitions and its lost gold mines. Also, both were interested in photography, and especially in taking color pictures of landscapes. They hankered to take a trip to Arizona and take professional scenic pictures such as were seen in *Arizona Highways* magazine. They believed they might even make a career of such photography. With some prodding, Kenny and I were persuaded to go along on a trip with them to Arizona. The trip would be photographic in nature, but they wanted to climb into the Superstitions as well. We went in Phil's 1939 Dodge coupe.

Our first stop was at the Superstitions. Kenny and I selected our previous route in. We climbed to the southern crest. The weather was nice and clear, so everyone took pictures of the vista. Both John and Phil used 4 x 5 view cameras they had picked up cheaply. By this time, I had acquired a 6 x 9 cm Voightlander. It was a circa 1930, German made, cut-film camera which created great images. Although color film of this size wasn't available, I made do by cutting up sheets of 5 x 7 inch film for it.

We spent a few hours in the mountains and then decided to drive around the mountains to Apache Junction. We took the turn-off and headed northeast past Tortilla Flat to Roosevelt Lake. This was a spectacular area of steep barren canyons with clear blue water backed into them by the dam. We had a field day taking pictures. We followed one canyon to a desolate area with a lake called Canyon Lake. We stripped and took a swim in the cool, refreshing water. After climbing around in the mountains all day, it felt delightful.

Our trip then took us north to Utah, where we spent a couple of days photographing Zion and Bryce Canyon National Parks. By now we were out of film, out of money, and out of stamina. We headed home.

A TURN OF EVENTS

Bob Campbell had invented a clever new photographic process for black and white film. He had combined developer and fixer into a single solution. This single solution would develop the film at the same time it was fixing it and cut the usual processing of black and white film from three steps to only one. He called the product "Kontrol-X." The resulting negatives had a characteristically extended exposure range. That means the process provided more detail in the shadow and highlight portions of the scene than did regular processing. This was an advantage for portraiture and scenic pictures, since the additional gradations of gray could more accurately represent the subject. However, for photofinishing it caused the prints to lack "snap." Customers wanted their prints to look like lithographs—mostly black and white with minimal shades of gray. Bob received a lot of returned prints because of this. He corrected these by using a higher contrast printing paper. This was accompanied by a lot of grumbling about the customer's lack of taste. Nevertheless, he was wedded to his process and was determined to continue using it.

Bob had to mix up batches of the solution every couple of days, and he resented spending the time it required. He wanted to turn the task over to Spectrol Labs—Kenny and me—but he was paranoid. He feared someone would steal his Kontrol-X formula. After much cyclic neurotic reasoning, he finally decided to give us the secret formula, but made us sign a secrecy pact. In return, Kenny and I agreed to provide him our solutions in five-gallon bottles so that he could begin processing color film.

In those days, most people who used color film wanted slides. Bob obtained the equipment to cut the film frames and mount them in cardboard slides, thus he expanded his business to include color slide processing. About this time, Eastman Kodak, who during the war years had fallen behind the Germans in dye-coupled color technology, came out with a competitive product called "Ektachrome." Its main advantage over the Ansco product was the Kodak name. In fact, Eastman had copied it so completely that Kenny and I found we could use our Ansco formulas successfully to process it. Kenny did adjust the chemistry and processing times to get the best results.

Shortly thereafter, Eastman came out with a new color system based upon the German dye-coupling concept, except it did not involve a reversal process. The film would contain color negative images that, as in black and white photography, would be printed as positive images on paper. The process was named "Kodacolor." Bob wanted to be able to do this process, since everyone was starting to demand color photos. Black and white was on the way out for casual photography.

Spectrol Labs developed the new products that Bob needed and supplied them in five-gallon units. However, we never put any of them in kits to sell on the retail market. This much business was keeping us hopping, and we were now facing the reality that one or both of us would have to quit our regular jobs in order to continue. Kenny had gotten married. I had begun dating Bea, and was spending more and more time with her.

Then, in June 1950, North Korea invaded South Korea. It looked like we would be back at war again, this time with the Russians, and maybe the Chinese. We thought if that happened, the country surely would go back on a wartime footing with rationing. We also knew our products were non-essential and demand for them could plummet. After a long discussion, Kenny and I decided to sell Spectrol Labs to Bob. Bob was delighted to get our capital equipment, supplies, and formulas. A deal was struck. Kenny and I were both happy to be out of the business.

_____PRE-COMMITMENT PERIOD

❖

The Dating Game
First Communion—1949
Getting To Know (All Ten Of) You
Philco
Linking Up Again
Off to Japan
Tokyo: The First Night
On to Johnson AFB
The School
Overseas Jobs: Why?
Life on Base
A Sayonara Party—1951
The Odd Triple
Soup and Salad—1951
Sex and the Single Man

THE DATING GAME

Beatrice "Bebe" Waring graduated from high school in 1948 and began working at Fuller Paint Company's lacquer factory, where I also worked. Her job included calculating formulas for the lacquer factory to produce various size batches of the company's products.

I noticed Bebe during my walks back and forth to the factory, but except on business matters, I was too insecure to approach her. I taught her how to use a slide rule to make her formula calculations. This relieved her of performing the tedious long division and multiplication by hand. Bebe had been raised to be reserved and to play "hard to get." She didn't know how to flirt. One of her cousins, Dorothy "Gee" Coats, who also worked there, noticed the problem, took me aside, and asked if I would like to take Bebe out. I said "Yes," so Dorothy set us up and we began dating.

Bebe was the oldest of nine children. Her father, John Graham Bell, was named after Alexander Graham Bell, because family tradition held that the Warings were somehow related to Bell. Nevertheless, everyone called him "Chick." He had converted to Catholicism, probably as a pre-condition to marriage. Bebe's mother, Helen Everaldes [Ryan], was a devout Catholic. She was intent on raising good Catholic children and therefore, the family was heavily involved with the church and its activities.

Because of this focus upon the church, I found myself becoming exposed to Catholic life and ritual. Soon Bebe's family saw me as the one whom Bebe would marry, and assumed I would convert to make a proper Catholic union. Her mother and several of her aunts who lived in the Los Angeles area worked diligently to convince me Catholicism was the one true religion. I was flattered by the attention, and I read all the literature they brought to me. However, in my mind, religion and science couldn't be reconciled. It always confused Bebe's mother that I could be such a nice person and not believe in God. In her view, bad people were that way because they had not received a firm foundation in Christianity. I was always an enigma to her.

FIRST COMMUNION—1949

About 15 kids were going to have their First Communion at the church Bebe attended. I had been asked to take photos of the kids and make prints for their parents to purchase. I selected a nice background of shrubs and set up my Voightlander view camera outside the church. When the kids filed out of the church, they were led over to my setup. First I took some shots of the whole group, after which I planned to take a set of individual shots.

Like a pro, I had one of the taller kids stand on a mark, put my head under the black dark-cloth, centered and focused the image. After taking another light-meter reading, I set the aperture and exposure. I was ready. I took a shot of the first kid. Then the next one stood on the pre-focused spot and I snapped her picture. After about the fourth picture, Father O'Malley came out of the church. The parents of the next child in line asked, "Can we have Father O'Malley stand next to Bobby in his picture?" I was preoccupied with changing the film plates, checking the exposure, and re-cocking the lens, and without thinking, I said, "Sure, we can do that." The good Father walked over and stood next to Bobby. Naturally, every mother after that wanted Father O'Malley to be in the picture with her child. I took all the rest of the pictures with the cooperative Father sharing the spot.

That evening in my darkroom, I began processing the negatives. The first few looked OK. I had the exposure and focus right. Then, I lifted out another plate and held it up to the light. OH MY GOD! It was the first shot that included the Father. His head had been cut off! Instantly I realized he would be headless in all the rest, as well. A knot formed in my stomach as I realized I had forgotten to reposition the camera to include the top of Father O'Malley. With excessive apologizing, I gave the prints to the parents—no charge. Although very disappointed with their pictures of the decapitated priest, the parents all went out of their way to try to mollify my humiliation.

GETTING TO KNOW (ALL TEN OF) YOU

I got along famously with the family. Chick and I became quite close. We especially enjoyed sharing his hobbies of ham radio and photography. Bebe's mom always seemed to like me, but I wasn't able to share in her main interest: religion.

The kids (Bebe's brothers and sisters) loved me. To them, I was a breath of fresh air wafting into their stuffy, religious lives. The family had very limited resources, so the kids never received personal spending money. Recognizing this, I made up tasks and tests, often about minerals, astronomy, and other sciences. For right answers I'd give them a few pennies or a nickel. They ate it up. Another favorite was the coin-toss. Often when I came to visit I would have them line up on the front porch and I'd throw my pocket change onto the front lawn. We all thought it was great fun as they scrambled around, collecting the coins.

Bebe and I soon learned one of our common interests was Broadway Musicals. We frequently attended the Hollywood Bowl, Greek Theater, and Philharmonic Hall. We bought sheet music for some of our favorite showpieces and Bebe played them on an old, beat-up upright piano. As we became more serious about our relationship, we decided to buy a spinet as our first common purchase. The family gave away the old upright and our new—newly refurbished, that is—Baldwin became the centerpiece of the living room.

Bebe and I had our ups and downs as we tried to adjust to each other's personality. Our first tug-of-war was caused by a difference in the amount of time we wanted to spend together. Bebe was not comfortable with entertaining herself and wanted me to spend most of each weekend with her. I was involved in many things and found it difficult to arrange as much time to be with her as she craved. Bebe's response to such vying was to pout or engage in a silent treatment. I had little tolerance for that. It seemed to me like a character flaw I didn't want to live with, and often I would decide to break it off. Once we had broken up, Bebe would always compromise to bring about a reunion.

During this period I was not making much money. Dating, maintaining a car, and ordinary living expenses kept me uncomfortably broke. I began looking for a better paying job. Since I loved my work in the paint lab, I was in conflict about the idea of changing jobs. I had been promoted from the factory control laboratory to a position as chemist in their general laboratory. This was where all the research was performed. It was a great job.

PHILCO

I saw an ad in the paper saying Philco Corp. was holding interviews in Los Angeles for technical representatives to go overseas. It said a prerequisite was military electronics training. I had that, so I went to be interviewed. There was virtually no interview—just a test. I scored high on it and they offered me a position on the spot. The job required traveling to Philadelphia for two months training in the latest radar systems and other electronics. Following that, each person was to be assigned to an overseas duty station as a consultant or an instructor. They paid $525.00 per month. That was almost double what I was making at Fuller's lab. At this same time, Bebe and I were in one of our tug-of-wars and again I wanted out, so I accepted the position, quit the laboratory job, and Bebe and I parted ways.

Philco provided a first-class ticket to Philadelphia, where someone met and took me to their operation at 22nd and Lehigh Ave. It was next to Shibe Park, the old Athletics Ball Park. Still near penniless, I found a place to stay within walking distance of the job site—a room in a turn-of-the-century row house. The owner, Mrs. Nichols, was an old widow lady whose son and daughter still lived with her. The son was nice-appearing and friendly, but he had become an alcoholic in the service and could not hold down a job. The daughter provided the only income, other than that from the room I was renting, which brought in only $7.00 per week. She was absolutely a baseball fanatic and never missed a game at Shibe.

Mrs. Nichols and her husband had emigrated from Ireland. They were dyed-in-the-wool Catholics. I rather enjoyed listening to her thick Irish brogue, but had trouble not snickering whenever she made any reference to her dead husband, because she would ritualistically cross herself, bow her head, and recite, "May God have mercy on his soul." Their row house was situated directly across the street from an old stone Catholic Church. Mrs. Nichols spent a lot of her time praying there. On my first Sunday morning, while still in bed, an enormous clanging began, nearly jolting me onto the floor. The church was calling its six o'clock mass. My god, they could have heard it downtown 22 blocks away! When Mrs. Nichols returned from church that morning, I mentioned how the bells had nearly tossed me out of bed. She looked at me unsympathetically and made a slight scowl as if to say, "Ya moosn't creeticize the Choorch."

Philadelphia was fascinating to me. I'd never seen cobbled streets, policemen on horseback, gaslight illumination, and streets so narrow that streetcars passed within a foot or two of each other. The windows were barred to keep kids from getting their arms ripped off. I was so taken by these oddities, I used my first paycheck to buy a camera—a used Zeiss Rollicord—and spent much of my spare time walking the city and taking pictures. Since this was July, Philadelphia's hottest and most humid month, I often returned to my room sweaty and exhausted. No relief was available by showering, since old row houses didn't have such modern facilities. I tried taking a bath in the cramped tub, but the plumbing was so inadequate it took almost an hour for the water to drain. After one try I gave up and went to the YMCA to take showers. My room was like a furnace, so I spent no time there except to sleep. Occasionally I would sit on the front stoop and listen to the alcoholic son tell his wartime stories.

LINKING UP AGAIN

One day I received a letter from Bebe. She needed transportation to get to work and wondered if I was willing to sell her my car—a 41 Ford Coupe. Since I had no further use for a car, I agreed. Oddly, her letter lit a spark of interest in me. Bebe had the ability to express herself much better in letters than in person, and living alone had caused me to become lonely. We began a correspondence that seemed to repair our old differences, and I began to look forward eagerly to her letters and to seeing her again.

Philco had contracts with the Air Force to provide technical representatives at any location that the Air Force requested. These technicians were often called TechReps, or more commonly, just "Reps." These contracts required Reps to wear Air Force uniforms while on the job or when in the Officer's Club. The Air Force brass didn't like the idea of men dressed in "civvies" being assigned to their bases. To comply, Philco sent all their Reps to a high-end men's store, where they were each outfitted with two tailored Air Force uniforms.

One oddity was that everyone who was assigned to such a military contract overseas was subject to military law; they could be court-marshaled. Fortunately, they were provided with passports. Therefore, they could leave any time they wished…well, unless they had been arrested and were being tried in a court-marshal.

OFF TO JAPAN

With the two months training completed, I was assigned to Johnson Air Force Base in Japan. After getting a passport and shots, I was given a first-class ticket to California, and another—not-so-first-class—to Japan. Working for Philco was great in the sense that they treated their staff first rate whenever possible. However, their contract with the Air Force required them to use MATS (Military Air Transport Service) for the flight to Japan.

In Los Angeles, my mom and Bebe met me. Bebe looked great and it was obvious she wanted to get back together. From Los Angeles I flew to Travis Air Force Base, outside of San Francisco, to catch my flight to Japan.

Soon I was boarding a Cal-West four-engine prop plane. Cal-West was under contract to MATS to provide trans-Pacific flights for the military. Off we went, leaving the California coastline behind. We were told the plane cruised about 200 MPH and our route to Japan was about 6700 miles. The plane had one hostess. She had large, eye-catching boobs, and apparently was on the make for anyone that took any interest in her. Her job consisted of handing out box lunches at mealtimes and providing blankets and pillows. The first leg of our journey was to Hawaii, where we landed about 12 hours later—around midnight.

After refueling, we took off for Wake Island, another 12-hour flight. I slept soundly, wrapped in the drone of the engines. The next morning I looked out my window to see only water and more water. After becoming totally bored looking at the featureless ocean, I decided to visit the navigator's station. At Philco I had studied the latest navigation gear (Loran APN-7), and I was curious to see it operate in the real-world environment. The navigator was a friendly chap and seemed happy to talk with me. Since I understood his equipment, he offered to let me take the next bearing, which delighted me.

As I was going through the steps, the hostess pulled aside the curtain, stepped in, and leaned on me as she peered over my shoulder. "What're you guys doing?" she asked coyly. We answered that we were taking a bearing. With her body squashed against my back, I tried to concentrate on the task. In spite of the distraction, I finally completed the steps. The navigator recorded the results in his log and plotted our position on a map. Not getting much response, the hostess said, "Keep up the good work, fellows," and left.

Wake was a tiny speck of an island, just big enough for an airstrip. During the war it had been the site of a fierce battle. I began to understand the ferocity of this battle as I walked around during our plane's refueling. The island was a terrible mess.

Rusting hulks of military equipment were everywhere; miles of underground tunnels had been blown open; a number of destroyed Japanese tanks lay about (what good was a tank on a tiny spec of land like this?), and there was not a sign of a tree anywhere. Then it was into the air again toward Japan. After another ten hours, we finally arrived at Haneda airport in Tokyo. Flying for 33 hours over a single body of water makes one realize how enormous the Pacific Ocean is.

TOKYO: THE FIRST NIGHT

Philco maintained a small office in Tokyo. They had sent someone to the airport to pick me up. No limo here, just a jeep. En route downtown, I was told I would spend the night in town—it was already dark—and someone would pick me up in the morning to take me to my assignment at Johnson Air Force Base. In the darkness, I was unable to see the devastation that had resulted from air raids during the war six years earlier. Finally, we arrived at the building where I was to spend the night. The driver told me it was the remains of a bombed-out bank.

The only part of the building remaining was the basement. It had a bathroom with running water, and a few lights were strung here and there. The floor was covered with about an inch of water, and mosquitoes had taken up residence. In one area, six or eight steel army cots were standing in the water, each with a rolled up mattress and one sheet. After pointing out the bathroom, the driver disappeared. The mosquitoes had already found me—fresh imported blood. I could see it was pointless to undress. It would be like setting out a feast for these damned parasites. Keeping my clothes on might provide *some* protection against the swarms. I put my suitcase on one of the empty bunks, crawled into another that was standing in the shallowest water, and pulled the sheet over me. The mosquitoes saw this as a pathetic defense—an easy mark. After the first few dozen bites, my mind just ignored the incessant buzzing and biting and I fell into a shallow sleep.

ON TO JOHNSON AIR FORCE BASE

The next morning, covered in itchy bumps, I ventured up to the street. Now I could see the building was gutted and only the floor of the first story was serving as a roof. No wonder the rain had collected in the basement. It was the first time I had ever seen the destructiveness of war with my own eyes. I was aghast and fascinated. Soon a station wagon drove up, asked if I was Ray McCoy, and we were off for Johnson Air Force Base. On the way, I learned Johnson was an F-86 Fighter Base that provided training and support to fighter squadrons that were based around the Far East.

Upon arrival, I couldn't help but notice how attractive the base was. It was beautifully landscaped and the buildings were of permanent construction (in contrast to typical military clapboard). I soon learned the reason; during the last years of the war, this had been the Kamikaze base. It was truly suitable for the many ceremonies conducted prior to sending off their carriers of the "Divine Wind." In front of the Headquarters (HQ) building, the Air Force had mounted one of the latest rocket-powered Kamikaze planes for display. Well, it was actually a bomb; it had no landing gears!

The driver took me to some quarters located next to HQ. Later, I learned these were the officer's quarters where Kamikaze pilots lived while in training. There I was introduced to Bob Hartman. He supervised the Reps assigned to the base. Bob found an empty room for me and I unloaded my stuff. He explained that a civilian-run electronics school was located on the base and that it trained Air Force students in the latest radar, communication, and navigation gear. The school was situated in two hangars located adjacent to the runway. I was to be an instructor in airborne radar and bombing equipment. Tomorrow he would take me down to the school and introduce me around. He reminded me to be in uniform.

THE SCHOOL

The school was located in a couple of converted hangars, partitioned into classrooms, offices, and an instructor's lounge. About 30 instructors were teaching about 15 classes. Each class had a senior instructor and a junior instructor. The classes were eight hours per day, four days per week. Wednesday was a half-day (Air Force tradition). Each instructor taught only 18 hours per week. Add a few more hours for making up exams, correcting student input, and doing miscellaneous tasks, and you still have a soft workweek. In addition, we had a lot of latitude. An instructor could get a day off, or even several if he could arrange with his co-instructor to teach his classes.

About half of the instructors were Reps and the rest were Civil Service Employees (civvies). Philco provided most of the Reps in the Far East, but some were from other companies such as GE, Sperry, and Fairchild. The civvies weren't required to wear uniforms, so of course they didn't. Ergo, it was easy to identify them from the rest. Administratively, the civvies had their own supervisor and the Reps (irrespective of what company they worked for) had their own. Bob Hartman was my supervisor. Technical responsibility for the school's operation was divided between the two supervisors, based on the type of equipment. The instructors who taught radio or communications equipment classes reported to the Civil Service Supervisor. The rest, who taught radar, navigation, and identification equipment classes, reported to the Rep supervisor. Teaching assignments were based strictly on background and had nothing to do with which company employed you. I was assigned to teach APQ-13 (radar and bombing equipment). My senior instructor was a civvy, thus many instructors (but not all) had two bosses. It would seem totally unworkable, but in the more than two years I worked there we never had a problem with it.

This Air Force school was classified as an Advanced Electronics School. A prerequisite for attending it was prior graduation from one of the Air Force's primary electronic schools—about a year of instruction. My classroom was equipped with four operating radar sets. These were used for teaching maintenance and repair techniques. Our classes ran for five weeks, and then a new class would begin immediately. No breaks or vacations were scheduled between classes. I spent my first five weeks monitoring the APQ-13 class and taking copious notes. I was expected to begin instructing at the start of the next class.

Eventually, I found myself on stage, instructing. At first I was a little shaky, but I managed. After cycling through a few classes, I had become technically knowledgeable, having memorized all the circuits, several hundred components, and their functions. There is probably no better way to learn than having to teach others. Once I became comfortable, I found I had a knack for teaching. At the end of every five-week class, the students were given a questionnaire in which they could praise or criticize the course and the instructors. After six months or so, based on these questionnaires, I had become the school's top-rated instructor; however, no medals for this.

OVERSEAS JOBS: WHY?

The men had many reasons for taking overseas assignments. The first was money. Certainly that was why I was there. The pay was good, and so long as you stayed a minimum of 18 months, what you earned was tax-free. In those days, the U.S. was trying to persuade technical people to work overseas. The intent was to provide technical aid to war-decimated and poor countries. The laws were poorly written and there was a lot of abuse. Movie companies would go to foreign countries to make films. Everyone involved, including the actors, avoided income taxes. Our situation was almost as hokey, but Congress thought any support of the Korean conflict totally justified the benefit. There were endless other reasons for individuals to take jobs overseas: avoiding alimony payments, running away from marriage or family problems, and staying out of reach of the law (usually, state laws which didn't justify extradition). At any rate, the result was an odd collection of people.

My first roommate, Jeremy Mencher, was escaping from a tyrannical father. His dad was a very successful lawyer and determined his only son would follow suit. To accomplish this, he had sent Jerry to Yale, his old alma mater. Jerry was a bright kid, but he had no self-esteem, and along the way he had become a terrible stutterer. His most difficult word was his own name, Mencher. (Isn't that one for psychiatrists to chew on?) In order to avoid stuttering, he had developed an impressive vocabulary to provide synonyms for problem words. This worked so well most people didn't know he stuttered. However, whenever he had to introduce himself, there was no substitute for "Mencher." With his best effort it would come out, "M-M-M-M-M-M-M-M-M-M-**Mencher**." His intense exertion caused the "Mencher" to explode forth when finally released. Oddly, Jerry only stuttered when representing himself. He could act a part in a play with no problem; he was being somebody else. He could read from text OK, as long as he hadn't written it. As a result, he instructed his classes from notes copied from other instructor's material. It seemed to work well.

LIFE ON BASE

Everyone in our quarters had a houseboy. Actually, they were not boys. Most were about our age and some had families. They would clean your room, wash and iron your clothes, shine your shoes, and run errands. You paid them whatever you and they agreed on. In our case, Mencher and I hired a Japanese fellow named Nagashima Shiro. "Nagashima" was his family name and "Shiro" his given name, just the reverse of our occidental way, as are many things in the Orient. We settled on 5,000 yen/month ($13.89). Shiro spoke good English. It was certainly far better than any of the Americans could speak Japanese. He was a hard worker and at the end of a year we doubled his salary to 10,000 yen. Apparently that was too much. He bought a motor scooter. No one in the small town of Inariyama Koen had a motorized vehicle. He had assumed an ostentatious lifestyle.

I ate my meals at the officer's club and soon noticed that everyday at breakfast one of the civvies named John Hedlund got the same order. The Japanese waitress never asked what he wanted. It was always the same: three sunny-side up eggs, bacon, toast, and a stack of pancakes. They never brought butter or syrup, because he never ate the pancakes. When he finished his eggs, etc., he just stuffed the pancakes into his jacket pockets and left. I learned that Hedlund (being a military base, everyone was known by their last name) had been doing this for many years. He was one of the earliest instructors at the school when it began in 1947. Everyone called him "The Pancake Man," but no one had any idea what he did with his pancakes.

A Sayonara Party—1951

There was frequent personnel turnover because, after complying with the IRS requirement to stay overseas 18 months, many would return to the States. Shortly after I arrived at the school, the staff threw a going away party for one of their colleagues who had completed his 18-month hitch. This party was to be held in the nearby town of Hanno, where a very charming old Japanese hotel was situated next to a scenic lake.

Having no transportation, I was offered a ride by Hedlund, the Pancake Man, I only knew him from his idiosyncratic behavior at breakfast each morning. I noticed he had an overall "seedy" look, but he seemed nice enough. I piled into the space behind the two seats of his Ford coupe. It was cramped and I found it was necessary to sit sideways. Off we zipped. Hanno was only about ten miles away, and soon we were there. It was evening and the place was lit up with paper lanterns. You could see their reflections on the lake as we drove up the road to the front of the hotel. The hotel was built entirely of wood. It was a very large structure, built on a low plateau providing a view over the lake. In the front, heavy timber steps led to the main entrance.

At the entrance we were greeted by the owner and his staff. Americans called all white-haired Japanese men "Papasan." They bowed repeatedly. It seemed they would never stop. Before entering, we were asked to remove our shoes; one of the girls lined them up in pairs on the stoop. Once inside, we were taken to a large room where pads were set on the floor in a large circle for us to sit on. Japanese, when provided with a pad, sit with their legs folded back on each side. Most Westerners are not flexible enough for that position and sit Indian style (cross-legged).

Next they passed out funny little cups and small bottles of hot sake. This was my first taste of sake. It was delicious. While we were drinking it, three geishas, with lavish hairdos, did a traditional dance while a fourth played music on a samisen (a funny looking 3-string lute). After we finished our sake, we were beckoned to another room. There was a very large sunken hot tub. The old timers said we should get undressed and the girls would bathe us. I began to have apprehensions. I was shy and didn't want to get naked in front of everybody, and to be bathed by one of the girls—oh my! Peer pressure is an amazing force. Reluctantly, I undressed and a Japanese girl disappeared with my clothes. Immediately, another was sudsing me down in an area a short distance from the tub. I was confused. I thought tubs were where you washed. Not in Japan! There you bathe first and then you get into the hot tub to soak and relax. In a couple of minutes I was clean enough and was waved over to the tub. When my toe touched the water, it recoiled from the temperature. That water was too damned hot. Certainly hot enough to boil meat in, I thought. The secret, I was told, was to immerse yourself inch-by-inch. This deadens the nerves little by little, and eventually you were in.

There is probably no way to convince anyone who has not been in a hot tub (really hot, not just the 105 degrees Americans use) just how delightfully relaxing it can be. I think it's a marvelous Japanese tradition. Of course GI's and others returning from the Orient brought the idea back home and it became a booming new business in the States. But Americans, being adverse to a little pain, reduced the temperature, and by so doing reduced the benefits.

After our soak, we were helped out of the tub. The high temperature is so relaxing that most people need help. We were provided with cotton kimonos, divided into several groups, and led to separate rooms. Each room had a low table, around which we all sat cross-legged. They were going to feed us, and I had never eaten Japanese food before. I'm not much of an experimenter when it comes to food. I feel safer just sticking with "meat and potatoes." First, a young girl came in and set everyone up with sake again, then another prepared the meals at the table on a hibachi. She prepared sukiyaki for us. Whenever any of the girls entered the room, they dropped down and walked on their hands and knees, or sort of duck-walked, if they were carrying something. It was all very gracefully done.

After dinner we were led back to the large room. Now the actual party began. Sake began to flow liberally. The geishas returned to provide song and dance. Soon everyone was feeling "happy." The geishas invited the guests to get up and dance. These were probably children's dances, as they were easy to imitate. Even I, an avowed dance-hater, got up and learned a few steps.

Finally it was time to leave. Geishas are entertainers. They are not prostitutes as some of the Americans thought. Some of the guys tried their best to seduce them for the night, but had no luck. We left the hotel through the front entrance and down the steps. I got into Hedlund's Ford coupe again. I didn't know it, but Hedlund was smashed. He and his other rider got into the front seat and he started up. Instead of heading back down the road, he positioned the car about fifty feet directly in front of the hotel. To my horror, he put the thing in low gear, stepped down on the gas and headed toward the timber steps. At the top of the steps was a large round vertical column that supported a second-story overhang. Up the steps we bounced and clattered. CRASH! The car hit the heavy column and stopped abruptly. The old wooden structure shook. Hedlund, mumbling something unintelligible, threw it into reverse and rumbled back down the steps to the ground. The Papasan and his female staff came running out. They all stood on the platform and began bowing and pleading. It was to no avail. Hedlund backed up to make another run. The Papasan and his girls all fled inside when they saw the car coming. Again, clatter, bang, and then CRASH, as the column withstood the second onslaught. As soon as Hedlund bounced back down the steps for another try, I began yelling, "John, let me out. Let me out!" He mumbled something about missing all the fun, but he opened the door and I leaped out. Some of the others hadn't left yet, staying to see what Hedlund was going to do. I got into one of their cars and was glad to get out of there.

THE ODD-TRIPLE

A couple of months after I arrived, a new Rep named Charles Burney was assigned to the school. He was given quarters two rooms down the hall. Almost immediately we became close buddies. I soon observed that Burney had sadistic tendencies. One day, when I came back to my room, I found my houseboy hand-cuffed to the steam radiator with the steam turned on. Nagashima told me Mr. Burney had done it. "No reason, just mean man."

Before Burney came to Japan, he had been studying medicine. He planned to become a surgeon—good career choice for a sadist! But he had run short of money and dropped out of school. As if preordained, Burney, Mencher, and I became an Odd-Triple. In Mencher, Burney had found the ideal masochist. I found myself relegated to the task of keeping Burney from accidentally killing Mencher.

SOUP & SALAD—1951

During the week, the three of us ate all our meals together at the officer's club. Burney didn't pick on Mencher much during breakfast or lunch, but at dinner, which was a semi-lavish affair (soup, salad, wine, main course, & dessert), the games would begin. As soon as the waiter set out the soup and salads, Burney would take Mencher's salad and dump it into his soup. The first time I saw this happen, I fully expected Mencher to dump the mess in Burney's lap, but instead, without any hint of angst, Mencher just ate the mess. He would not give Burney the satisfaction of showing anger or revulsion. Each assumed this stubborn posture, and every night Burney would dump Mencher's salad into his soup and Mencher would impassively slurp it up. This game was repeated every dinner for over a year. I know it seems unbelievable, but it really did happen. Eventually, Mencher was reassigned from the Far East to Spain, putting an end to the nonsense. In all that time, Burney, Mencher, and I remained the best of friends.

SEX & THE SINGLE MAN

Sex in Japan is viewed in a totally different way than in western countries, especially the United States. The Japanese see it as a normal, healthy, pleasurable part of life. They have no silly, religion-based taboos attempting to control it. That doesn't mean Japan is one huge singles bar where everyone picks up partners indiscriminately for casual sex. Rather, there is a natural regulation involved without a lot of unnecessary rules and laws. The result is that sex is treated in a wholesome manner, with courtesy, consideration, and politeness. Coarseness is unnecessary and unacceptable.

However, due to centuries of male domination, there remained a definite male prejudice in their views. For example, a married man can go into town to drink and be entertained by geishas. There may or may not be sex. The wife feels no competitive threat or jealousy. She will even help dress and groom him for the occasion.

Nudity in Japan was not the big deal it is in western countries. It was seen as natural and normal. Men and women bathe together in public hot springs and spas. Restrooms were not separated for men and women; for that matter, there weren't even any partitions or doors for the toilets.

Most American clergy would probably find these practices offensive and sinful. My experience was that the clergy is wrong—totally wrong. I imagine that with the Japanese' unfortunate desire to imitate the western world, many of these sensible customs will quickly evolve to become more like ours. Rather sad!

Burney and Mencher had plenty of money and easily entered into affairs with Japanese girls. Burney began a relationship with one of the waitresses, Fumiko, at the Officer's Club. He rented a small house in the village, outside of the base, for them to shack up in. This upset Fumiko's parents. Not because she was having sex before marriage, but because they knew Burney would eventually return to the States and she would be unable to get any Japanese man to marry her. Japanese men believed that once a Japanese girl lived with an American man, she would be too spoiled for Japanese married life. To solve this problem, the parents set up a room in their own home for their daughter and Burney to have their affair. This would effectively hide Fumiko's indiscretion from the eyes of the local town eligibles.

Mencher hooked up with a girl whom I never met. The arrangement with both girls was sex for gifts (and maybe a little money). As far as I know, there wasn't any dating, as such. I was tempted, at times, to do something similar; however, Bebe and I had resumed our relationship. We were writing regularly and I began to realize I was a one-woman guy. Not from any religious motive; it just seemed easier. Besides, juggling more than one relationship at a time was a bit too duplicitous for my comfort.

19. Passport Picture—ca. 1950

20. Teaching radar in Japan—ca. 1951

_____ENGAGEMENT ENVIRON

✦

MAKING THE COMMITMENT—1951

Bebe wanted to come to Japan, and I was lonesome; the idea sounded appealing to me. Bebe's mother, still in her advisory role, suggested that Bebe should become engaged first. This seemed to make things morally acceptable to her. I had no reluctance to the idea, so I headed to the PX (Post Exchange), where I bought the best ring I could afford—a whopping 1/4 carat. I sent it off, and in exchange Bebe showed up in Yokohama a few weeks later, in December 1951. She had taken a job with Civil Service. The government was desperate to fill over-seas jobs, so she was allowed to select from a list of locations. She chose Far East Air Materiel Command (FEAMCOM), which was located at Tachikawa, roughly twenty miles east of Tokyo and only about ten miles from Johnson Air Force Base, where I was stationed.

TACHIKAWA OR BUST

I went to the port in Yokohama to meet Bebe. She looked good, but a bit tired from her 11-day trip. We took the electric train to Tokyo. Almost all trains in Japan were electric. At the Tokyo station, we were hurrying down some steps to catch the train to Tachikawa. Bebe tripped. We had been holding hands, so I hung on to her, but she still fell, scuffing up a knee and putting a big run in her hose. This put her a little out of sorts, but she held up pretty well.

We got to the platform in time to get on an outbound train—the wrong one. In the last few months I had been to Tokyo a half-dozen times and never had a problem catching the right train back, even though they were annotated in Japa-nese characters. This time, after zipping along for over an hour, I realized that something was wrong. It never had taken this long before. To make matters worse, it was dark, and I couldn't recognize anything. After locating someone who could speak a little English, I learned we were on the wrong train. At the next stop we got off and caught a train back to Tokyo. Bebe was definitely becoming a little wilted.

In Tokyo, I made sure we were on the right platform and double-checked the color of the train. You're right! I managed to make the same goof again. Two hours later, we were back in Tokyo again. Bebe was a frazzle. She must have thought she had traveled 5000 miles just to be with an idiot. Finally I got it right, and an hour after that we were in Tachikawa.

They billeted Bebe in an old wooden barracks, along with the other women who had come over on her ship. Bebe had become friends with one of the girls on the ship and they were assigned as roommates. Some weeks later, during the night, the fire alarm sounded. The girls grabbed what belongings they could and ran outside. The fire department wasn't able to control the fire, and the building burned down. They found the body of her friend in her bed. She had been smoking and had apparently caused the fire.

GETTING WHEELS

Civil Service allowed overseas employees to ship a car to their duty station. Bebe had taken her car—the one I had sold her—to the port at San Pedro to take advantage of this benefit. When it arrived, we went to Yokohama to pick it up. It cost the government as much to ship the car as it was worth, about $500. Nevertheless, we had wheels now. We shared the car by an arrangement whereby each of us would have it every other week.

JAPANESE CUISINE—1952

While working at the Fuller Paint Company laboratory, I met Earl "Judge" Calvert. Everyone called him "Judge." I don't know why. He was the analytical chemist. All the others were formulation chemists. We became good friends because of our common interest in mineralogy.

Judge taught me several useful techniques for identifying minerals, such as how to do borax bead testing using a blowpipe. In return, I showed him how to use a homemade spectroscope to detect certain elements in mineral specimens.

He had an avocation of buying, selling, and trading minerals worldwide. He lived on a half-acre lot, the entire back yard of which was covered with barrels and piles of assorted minerals. This side business had grown to the point where he was one of the largest such dealers in the country. I was able to embellish my collection significantly with samples he sent me from his massive collection.

While in Japan, I corresponded with Judge occasionally, and one day I received a letter in which he mentioned a Japanese mineral dealer with whom he had done business for a couple of years. He asked if I would be willing to visit the dealer, who lived in Tokyo, and inquire about the availability of some choice stibnite crystals (antimony sulfide) that came from the Japanese island of Shikoku. Apparently this Japanese variety was among the finest available in the world.

I replied that I would be happy to talk to the dealer on his behalf. In a few weeks I received another letter from Judge. He had contacted the Japanese dealer and set up a date for us to meet. He also explained that the Japanese man owned a restaurant in Tokyo and had invited Bebe and me to be his guests, at which time we could discuss minerals.

On the agreed date, Bebe and I drove into Tokyo and parked, then we hailed a cab. We didn't want to attempt to find the restaurant, since addresses in Japan were impossible for Americans to comprehend. Their addresses were assigned as buildings were built, thus the numbers jumped around all over the place. We gave the cab driver the address, and off he sped. However, he didn't know where the restaurant was. So first he found the street, and then began a random hunt for the address. This consisted of stopping the cab and going into a building to ask if anyone knew where the address was located. Then we would zoom off in pursuit of that clue, which would invariably be wrong. This was repeated five or six times until we chanced upon the restaurant. With a beaming smile of accomplishment, the cabby accepted our agreed-upon fee. Cabs had no meters to track time or distance.

We entered the restaurant and the owner immediately greeted us. I have long since forgotten his name. He was short, thin, and probably about fifty years old. He led us to a private room (as seemed to be the case with all the Japanese restaurants we saw) where there was a beautifully lacquered, low table with cushions placed around it to squat on. Immediately, young ladies in colorful kimonos began serving us. Things started with the traditional small carafes of hot sake.

We began our discussion about the availability of the stibnite crystals. He informed me the mines on Shikoku Island were considerably depleted. The only nice specimens were now in the hands of dealers and collectors. He was sorry to say he did not have any left, but he would continue to inquire around to see if he could locate anyone who did. That concluded the business portion of the meeting.

It was obvious by now that the owner and his girls were fascinated by Bebe. They simply hadn't seen a blonde person before. Their first impression probably was that she was an old person whose hair had turned white, but up close they could see she was in her early twenties. The Japanese are much too polite to stare, but you could catch them, now and then, sneaking peeks.

Soon we were being served our meal. The owner probably knew that Americans didn't eat raw fish, squid, or eels, so he chose to serve us sukiyaki—duck skin sukiyaki! This was a step up from the ordinary thin strips of beef normally used. I would have rather remained on the bottom rung with beef. In Japan, pieces of sukiyaki (whatever kind) are picked up with chopsticks, dipped into a bowl of beaten raw egg, and then popped into your mouth. I was becoming apprehensive that I might not be able to keep my gag reflexes under control. Bebe, on the other hand, was far more experimental with her eating habits. She dove in with relish, while I was toying with my chopsticks as a stall. Not being able to put off the inevitable, I finally popped a piece—slimy with raw egg—into my mouth. I couldn't bring myself to chew the damned thing, finally settling to swallow it whole. I lied, with a smile and an approving nod, but the owner was more interested in Bebe. After that, I felt I could make it through the meal without gagging, but then came the soup.

The owner had decided to provide us with a real treat—fish-eye soup. This was a thin broth with dozens of fish-eyes floating around, many of them looking right up at you. I thought *Oh god, how can I possibly get through this? Is this man trying to get even with us for winning the war?* Bebe was eating her soup like a pro. As queasy as I was, I fought to avoid offending this nice fellow who was doing his best to be hospitable, so I took a spoonful of the floating spheres. It didn't taste too bad. Then I noticed the owner and Bebe were chewing theirs. *Oh, what the hell,* I thought, *I'll give it a try.* So my tongue moved several of the small spheres between my molars. I bit down, expecting some minor crunching, but no—these miniature balls shot out from between my teeth and ricocheted around in my mouth. With a quick shot of sake I washed the mouthful down. With a *lot of sake* I managed to finish my soup.

With much bowing and many "domo arrigatos" (thank you very much), we left and hailed a cab to take us to our car. At least we knew exactly where it was parked.

THE SADIST STRIKES AGAIN—1952

Burney never did buy a car, since his love-nest was within walking distance, but Mencher soon decided he wanted one. He had never owned a car before and had very little driving experience, but he wanted to travel around the country, so he bought an old Ford coupe.

In no time, Burney had a prank to play on him. Burney approached me to make a smoke bomb we could install in Mencher's car. It would go off when Mencher turned on the ignition, frightening our hi-strung friend into panic. Oh, it would be ever so funny.

Always eager to show off my explosives expertise, I agreed. On my next trip into Tokyo, I found a chemical supply company and bought a pound of ingredient "X" (my all-time favorite oxidizer) and some charcoal. Meanwhile, Burney rounded up a piece of tile pipe to contain the bomb, the idea being to direct the flames downward and away from the car.

The next Saturday, while Mencher was out of town in his new wheels, Burney and I constructed the bomb. I guessed at the proper mixture to make a lot of smoke and not cause an explosion. When I began to fold about half of the batch in heavy paper, Burney stopped me and said, "That's not enough. Put it all in." I objected mildly, but went ahead and put the whole batch in the folded paper packet, and then inserted a homemade electric fuse. At the school, parking was provided for those who had cars on the old aircraft taxi apron between the runway and the hangars. The front of our two hangars facing the runway had been enclosed with windows to provide natural lighting inside. What better observation place for watching the "fun."

Monday morning, while Mencher was teaching his class, Burney and I installed the bomb under his car. During the day, word spread, and by quitting time the other instructors and their classes had lined up behind the sill of the windows to watch. I was nervous about the double load of powder Burney had talked me into using, so I took a fire extinguisher from one of the classrooms and carried it to my observation position. Eventually, Mencher walked to his car, got in, and started up the engine. PSHOOSH! A big flame shot out from under the car, followed by a cloud of white smoke that totally enveloped the car. A second later, Mencher came flying out of the cloud, yelling, "FIRE, FIRE!" As the smoke rose, I could see small flames flickering under the car (old grease on the engine and frame was burning). I grabbed the extinguisher, ran to the car, and to the cheers of the crowd heroically put out the flames.

Burney, his sadistic need fulfilled, was laughing maniacally. Mencher was visibly shaken. Already, I regretted my participation. I led him over to the instructor's lounge, got him a cup of coffee and sat down with him to confess to our "joke." He never saw any humor in the prank, yet it didn't cause a fracture in our "odd-triple" relationship.

PROMOTION BY ATTRITION

One of the characteristics of overseas jobs was the constant turnover of personnel. Old friends and associates would leave and new people arrive. This attrition led to frequent opportunities for advancement. In a few months my senior instructor left and I automatically became senior instructor of the class over some new students. I had turned out to be a very good instructor—it was my bag. In about a year, Hartman got promoted to Director of the Tokyo office. He selected me to replace himself as supervisor at the school.

In this capacity I also became "house-mother" of the two buildings containing our quarters. Although it carried a little prestige, it was a real nuisance job. Any complaints the Air Force brass had about the civilians living on base was passed on to me for resolution. A typical example: The base commander's wife was offended by the open collars worn by the military and Rep's during the summer, because it allowed their T-shirts to show. The commander had solved this by issuing a base regulation for his military personnel to either wear a tie or otherwise prevent the offending underwear from showing.

Well, it's hot and humid in Japan during the summer. No one was willing to wear a tie. Some stopped wearing a T-shirt. This was in the days before antiperspirants and deodorants. The T-shirt had served the practical purpose of absorbing perspiration, and it could be changed every day, thus prolonging the wearing period of a uniform shirt to about a week.

When I attempted to pass along this new base regulation to my Reps, I was greeted with hoots and howls. I had a mini-rebellion on my hands. After cooling down some, we agreed to try to avoid a conflict with the CO (commanding officer). We would keep the offending underwear out-of-sight by folding down the front of the neck and holding it in place with a paper clip or staple. One innovative Rep persuaded his Japanese girlfriend to cut a "V" in the neck and re-hem it. That seemed to have caught on, since by the time I returned to the States you could find T-shirts with "V" necks in department stores.

THE PANCAKE MAN—1952

John Hedlund gathered pocketfuls of pancakes every morning at breakfast, but never ate them. No one knew what he did with them. However, I was soon to find out. In my new capacity as housemother, I had occasion to discuss some matter or other with him. Now Hedlund was certifiably "odd," and that was put-ting it mildly. He lived in a room at the far end of the building—by him-self—since *nobody* was willing to room with him. I walked down the long hall, stopped at his door, and knocked.

After some seconds of rustling sounds, the door opened just wide enough for me to see an eye staring out at me. "What do you want?" he challenged. I explained my business with him and he opened the door a little more—now just enough to recognize his face. His nose was hanging over the chain of his security lock. After a long silence he asked, "Do you want to come in?"

I responded with, "Sure. It will make it easier to talk." He unlatched the chain and slowly opened the door, just enough for me to squeeze through.

Cautiously, I entered, glancing about the room curiously, as if entering King Tut's tomb for the first time. Hedlund's eyes were locked onto me, eagerly observing my response to anything in the room. Well, he got one. Up on one wall I saw a large black escutcheon with a thick tree branch protruding from it. In life, the branch had supported many twigs and leaves. Now, it was very dead and macabre, and was painted black as well. It had an aura of evil, reminding one of those twisted, gnarled branches in haunted forests—the kind that reach out to snare terrified children who are fleeing some menace.

And there, on the end of each snaggy twig, was hanging a *pancake*. All in all, doz-ens of them. Hedlund, apparently encouraged by my fascination, finally was compelled to inquire, "Do you like it?"

In situations where I am on the spot, I can become quite a convincing liar. I answered, "Why, yes John, it's very—uh—original." I called him "John" to appear more sincere. Desperately in need of validation, and convinced he had received it (from the housemother yet), he ventured, "Oh, then let me show you something else."

As I stood there, trying to imagine what else there could be, he grabbed the handle of one of two footlockers stored under his cot. With a grunt, he pulled it out into the center of the room, got out a key and carefully unlocked it. He slowly raised the lid, as if opening pirate treasure, and there they were—hundreds of pancakes, hundreds of *moldy* pancakes—all carefully arranged in stacks (like doubloons?)

It took all the disingenuousness I could muster, but I said, "Wow, that is something!" John, beaming with pride, closed and locked the chest. Then he asked if I would like to see more. By then I had noticed a second cot in the room. Under it were two more footlockers, making four in all. I declined as tactfully as I could, lying that I needed to get going. Whatever matter led me there never got addressed.

STRICTLY BUSINESS—1953

During the winter of 1952–53, the Air Force decided it would be beneficial if our school were to get feedback from alumni in the field. It would require the civvy supervisor, Bill Lovejoy, and I (now the Tech supervisor) to take a trip into the field to gather this information. Lovejoy was about 35 and married. He and his wife lived in on-base housing. Lovejoy had been the civvy supervisor for several years, and he had been on a couple of these field trips before. He assured me they were great fun and seemed quite keyed up about the idea.

We were told the Air Force would fly us down to the southern island of Kyushu. Asaki Air Force Base was located there. A lot of airmen from there had attended our courses. In a theater of operation, when the military says they will provide air transportation it means you go to a military air base and attempt to hitch a ride to your destination. Usually that entails sitting around the flight operations center, waiting until a flight plan appears on the schedule for a plane going your way. In this case, the Air Force had asked for the information we were to gather, so they selected a flight for us from their restricted list of flight plans.

The chosen flight was a C-119 cargo plane. It was an odd-looking craft, with the cargo bay centered between two thin body sections that supported a wide elevator-rudder assembly behind the cargo bay. The cargo bay opened like a hatchback car, making for easy loading and for airdrops. This two-engine propeller-driven design had a terrible accident record; in fact, it was known as "The Flying Coffin."

To make matters more interesting, it was a bitterly cold January day. Many flights were reporting ice buildup on their wings. The risks were considered so high that we were required to wear parachutes. With some apprehension, Lovejoy and I climbed into the craft. Soon the Air Force pilot and his navigator came aboard. The pilot paused just long enough to give us some instructions before he entered the cockpit. He pointed to a red light above the cockpit door and said, "If we get into trouble, I'll open up the rear hatch, light this light, and sound an alarm. You jump out, count to ten, and pull your ripcord. When we come through this door, I don't want to see either of you here. Got it?" We nodded nervously.

The plane had no seats, just a metal bench on each side with depressions for your rear end. In a few minutes we were on our way. Things began smoothly enough, but as we headed south the weather worsened. It became bumpy. We had flown into thick clouds. I was reviewing what the pilot had said and thought, *It's below zero outside. If we have to jump, we'll just freeze on the way down.* Then, a horrible racket interrupted my thoughts. It sounded like someone was beating on the side of the plane with a sledgehammer. I just *knew* the plane was disintegrating and we were goners. In Sunday school, they always told me that atheists, when facing death, convert to believers. Not in my case. The issue didn't even enter my mind. What did enter my mind was the cynical "Flying Coffin" dub. I glued my eyes to the red light over the cockpit door. It never came on. Just the same, I was convinced the pilot and navigator would burst through the door at any second.

Lovejoy was scared too. However, instead of being obsessed with the red light, he was looking out the window. Of course he couldn't see more than a few yards, but it was enough for him to observe that ice was being flung off the props against the side of the plane. That explanation was less terrifying than that the plane was disintegrating, but only somewhat. The racket went on for about 20 minutes and then stopped as suddenly as it had begun.

It was dark when we landed at Asaki Air Force Base. We were met by a couple of lieutenants who seemed quite friendly. They piled our luggage in the back of a jeep and set off for the chow hall. After eating, one said, "It's early; let us take you to our private club." Lovejoy was beaming. I didn't know what they meant by "private club," but agreed. Back in the jeep, we drove past the guard gate and into the small village just outside the base. We stopped in front of what appeared to be a small Japanese hotel. When we entered, we were greeted by a papasan—an older Japanese man. He took us to a large room with a sawdust-burning heater at one end. The Japanese had very few fuel resources at the time. Chairs were lined up around the edge of the room. Sitting on them were about a dozen pretty, young Japanese girls.

The lieutenants proudly explained that this was a private officer's club for members stationed at the AFB. The members each paid a certain amount per month, and with the money, they leased this hotel. It operated exclusively for them. The papasan ran the place. The girls lived there, and each had her own room. They even had a full-time doctor to make sure the girls were kept free of diseases. A record player and a stack of dance music were near the heater.

The way it worked was straightforward. Members (and their guests, such as us) could come, dance with the girls, select one, and spend the night with her. Then I understood why Lovejoy was all smiles. He had heard about this place before. Even though he was married and his wife was in Japan, this form of recreation caused him no guilt. On the other hand, I wasn't prepared—either tactically or emotionally—for this. I had developed a strong need to present myself to the world as a good person—my old dichotomy. Worse yet, I had no experience with casual, overt sex; I was a still a child.

When they fired up the record player, everyone got up to dance—well, of course except me. The lieutenants and Lovejoy descended on me to join in. It was to no avail. I just couldn't let go. Now and then one of the girls would come over and try to seduce me. They thought I was just a little shy. Of course it was much worse than that. It was a neurotic self-image problem. The evening passed with me just sitting there like a jerk, and eventually it was bedtime.

One-by-one the officers (eight or ten of them) began to select their girls and head upstairs. Seeing that I was totally hopeless, the papasan came over and told me that I could spend the night in one of the girl's rooms. She could double up with one of the other girls. This mollified me, as I knew I needed to sleep *somewhere*, so he picked out a girl and I followed her up to her room. She laid out a pad on the floor and covered it with a silk-lined quilt. There was no heat upstairs and it was freezing. After making sure I didn't want her to stay, she left. I undressed to my underwear and slid under the quilt. The silk felt like a sheet of ice for a few seconds, then warmed to my body temperature. It was surprisingly comfy, and I slept like a baby.

The next day we interviewed the alumni from our training classes, took notes for our report, and by noon were back at Flight Ops, waiting for a plane to Tachikawa. The weather was nice and the flight uneventful. Later, I figured out that the jaunt was probably just a typical Korean War boondoggle, probably arranged by Lovejoy with our squadron commander. I doubt if anyone ever read our reports.

MUD & MOUNTAINS—1953

Every few weeks Bebe and I would drive somewhere to see parts of the countryside that were new to us. On one occasion we decided to try to drive to a large statue located on the top of a mountain. We thought it would be photogenic and hoped we could take some good pictures.

It was a nice day when we started out, but as we drove northward toward the mountains it began to cloud up. Soon it was raining Japanese style, a soft, continuous, drizzle. These rains are marvelous for the crops, but hamper getting around because they last for days. The Japanese live with the condition by carrying parasols with them everywhere during the rainy season. These are the picturesque ones you see in travelogues, made of bamboo and oiled paper.

Before the war, most Japanese roads were paved with asphalt. However, during the war most of the country roads had been stripped to provide asphalt for building aircraft runways in occupied Pacific islands. During our Japanese tour, these roads were still unpaved and rather like our country roads before the turn of the century. When it was dry, they were full of ruts and potholes; when rainy, they were a morass of mud.

Driving these roads was a challenge. In dry weather, a technique that one acquired had you steer along a favorable-looking rut, then when a better-looking one appeared, you made a quick jump into it. When you became proficient, you could travel along at 20 to 25 MPH, but in wet weather it was just a matter of maintaining control of your car to avoid sliding off into a ditch. Most roads had drainage ditches along the sides. Under these conditions, it was wise to stay under 15 MPH.

As we drove along, the steady, soaking rain changed the road from ruts to mud. Eventually we arrived at the base of the mountain. There was a narrow one-lane, dirt (now mud) road winding up the side. We couldn't see more than a couple of hundred yards for the rain, but we had come all this way, so up we started.

Japan is a small country, probably about the size of California, but it had a population of around 80 million people. As a result, every possible square foot of it was cultivated and inhabited by farmers living in small wooden, thatched-roofed houses. As we started up the mountain, we could see these little farmhouses. Their paper windows glowed dimly through the rain. They were scattered over the mountainside, but strangely, none were near the road.

The road was made for oxen-pulled carts, not cars. It was treacherous when muddy. In the steeper places, we found ourselves sliding backwards, but with persistence we managed to keep going. Then, at a curve, the road sloped a little and the car began to slide sideways. I did everything I could to steer toward the center of the road, but it was like being on a well-greased ramp. Off the road we slid. Both left wheels ended up in the ditch between the road and the mountain.

I began to stew about our predicament. Our only hope, I figured, was to get out in the rain and mud and *try* to install some emergency chains on the rear wheels. As I was thinking out this strategy there was a tap, tap, tap on Bebe's window. We looked up to see an old Japanese farmer. Bebe rolled down her window enough to hear what he was saying. It was all gibberish to us, except I did think he said, "Dijobi, Dijobi, OK." I had picked up a couple of Japanese words by then, and I thought he was saying, "It's all right, it's all right." There was no mistaking the "OK." It may have been the only English he knew. While this was going on, about ten or twelve more men and boys showed up.

Now, reflect on the situation for a moment. Here were two Americans stranded on a mountainside—Americans who were their hated enemy only a few years before; Americans who had dropped two atomic bombs on their cities; Americans who all but burned and leveled Tokyo, their capital; Americans who had likely killed some members of their families. Why on earth should they give a rat's ass about our predicament? In fact, wouldn't this be a good chance to get back a little?

But no, the group surrounded us—standing calf-deep in mud, lifted up the car, and put us back on the road. If ever I learned a lesson in human kindness, it was at that moment. They were all smiles. They knew that they had done a nice thing. We yelled, "Arrigato, Arrigato" to them, which we hoped meant "Thank you." Then they disappeared, as fast as they had appeared.

We went on to the top of the mountain, got some pictures, then drove—mostly slipping and sliding down the mountain road—and returned home.

FUJISAN (MOUNT FUJI)—1953

For centuries, Fujisan (the "san" is a suffix of respect in Japanese) or Mount Fuji has been the pride of the Japanese people. They traditionally believe it to be the sacred dwelling place of divine spirits and consider it an object of great beauty and idealistic perfection. Thousands, probably millions, of paintings and photos have been made of it, and essentially it has become a national icon. The mountain is 12,388 feet high—among the highest volcanoes in the world—located about 70 miles southeast of Tokyo.

Sometime in recent history, a minor eruption occurred on one side, causing a disconcerting blemish. To the Japanese, especially the artists, this loss of perfection and symmetry was untenable. However, it wasn't within anyone's power to repair. The best they could do was to ignore it, so none of the recent paintings or other art depictions of their famous mountain ever show this offensive disfigurement. The eruption occurred about two-thirds of the way up the mountain causing a protuberance that ended abruptly in a cliff several hundred feet high.

One of the fantasies many Americans had during their tour in Japan was to climb Mount Fuji. This was no walk in the park. It was an arduous undertaking. A glance at any picture of it shows it becomes steeper and steeper, the higher you go. Physics dictates that at the same time, the air becomes thinner and thinner. Very few ever actually attempted it, and of those who did, precious few made it to the top. Nevertheless, several of Bebe's girl friends had talked themselves into attempting the climb. Bebe got caught up in their enthusiasm and wanted to join the adventure. She had always considered herself of durable stock and was somewhat athletic. She felt sure she could make it. After all, she had heard that every year even a few older Japanese made the climb as a pilgrimage.

Since Bebe's Civil Service Contract would end in December, this was to be our last year in Japan. Also, since the mountain was only open to climbers in the summer months and it was now the end of July, Bebe knew this would be her only opportunity, so she expressed her wish for us to go along. Having only climbed mountains that were a third as high and knowing how exhausting that was, I said, "I don't think so." However, she didn't want to go without me, and since she seemed so intent on going, I finally stipulated the condition that if we went she would stick it out until we reached the top—no turning back. She accepted, and so I agreed.

A date was selected in August, the last month the mountain was open for the year. Four girls and two fellows were in the original group, plus Bebe and me; altogether eight of us. The girls made the plans. The guys just tagged along. We were advised that to get in a full day of climbing we should arrive at the base of the mountain about 3:00 a.m. Good grief! That meant getting up around midnight. In the middle of the night we piled into two cars and set off. A couple of hours later, we arrived at the mountain's base in a parking area and the road ended. From here on, there was only a mountain trail.

Over the years, the Japanese had established ten stations up the side of the mountain where you could stop and rest. The first station was a mile or two further on up the trail. Horses were available to get to Station One for those who could afford it. It wasn't considered cheating, just a practical way to get to the start of the climb, which "officially" began at Station One. In fact, in recent times the road has been extended up to Station Five, meaning now you only have to climb the top half of the mountain.

We each mounted a horse, which was led by a guide, and started into the dark. The blackness was only relieved by Japanese paper lanterns; each guide carried one on a pole. The weather was balmy—just ideal. The sky was jet-black and pierced by thousands of stars. It was extremely pleasant and very enchanting. Almost too soon we arrive at Station One.

Each station appeared to be operated by one or two Japanese families. I don't remember any that did not have some small children running about. No doubt some sort of franchise arrangement was involved. All the stations were just wooden shacks, some a little bigger than the rest. At any of them, you could get a bowl of steamed rice with a piece of fish, and green tea or a bottled soda drink. Most Americans were afraid to drink Japanese water, and many didn't care for green tea, so they settled for the bottled soft drinks. These were made in Japan and tasted pretty awful. Orange soda was the most palatable, and that is what most of us chose. Some of the bigger stations had sleeping space for those wishing to spend the night.

At Station One we each bought a walking stick for the climb. These were hexagonal wooden sticks, about five feet long. At every station on the way up you could have your stick branded with a unique brand that contained the station number. This provided proof you had climbed at least that high. The first brand was placed near the bottom of the stick, the others in sequence above.

At dawn, after having our sticks branded, we started out. Being typical Americans, none of us was in great shape, but we were young and that counts for a lot when endurance is required. At first it was deceptively easy. The temperature was still mild, and although summertime humidity in Japan is bad, we had enough breezes to be comfortable. Along the way we noticed some other climbers. A few were GI's in their khakis, fewer still were civvies like ourselves, most were Japanese of various ages making pilgrimages. Also, a number of Japanese teenage boys were carrying heavy packs of supplies up to the various stations. It was amazing to see them whiz by us, carrying probably 70 to 80 pound loads. We were told they could make two or three trips per day.

It was a long trek to Station Two. By the time we got there the sun was well up and it was getting uncomfortably warm. Off came our sweaters and jackets. We tied them around our waists. We bought a round of orange sodas and drank the unsavory, but hopefully sterile, stuff. The station had a pit fire, as did all the stations, over which they boiled rice and fish. More important to us, the pit fire was where they kept their station brands hot. We each got our walking sticks branded.

Then we were off again. The temperature was rising and the trail becoming steeper. It was beginning to get tiring. After a bit, some relief came. The sky became overcast as cloud cover drifted in. It caused no noticeable drop in temperature, but at least it shielded us from the blazing sun. We kept trudging up the mountain, from station to station, gathering our coveted brands. By twilight we had made it to Station Five.

This station had accommodations for spending the night. Well, "accommoda-tions" is a bit of a stretch. They had built a shelf along one wall that was about five and a half feet deep; okay for Japanese, but too short for American men whose feet hung over the edge. If you wanted to stay the night, you climbed onto the shelf and lined up side-to-side like sardines, head against the wall, feet at the edge of the shelf. Once arranged along the shelf, they provided one blanket for every three people—no pads or pillows. Since there were eight of us, we would have to share one of the blankets with a stranger. A lot of arguing ensued over this. Finally, the papasan agreed to let us have three blankets for just our group. Still, there was a problem. This was the 1950's, and most Americans still had sex-ual taboos. None of the girls was willing to sleep next to a guy. Finally, it was agreed that since Bebe and I were engaged, we could lie next to each other, pro-viding a male-female buffer for the string of bodies. The two fellows would be next to me, with the girls lined up on Bebe's side. We all were exhausted and slept well on our perch.

The next day, stiff from climbing and sleeping on boards, we crawled down from our loft. We ate rice and fruit, drank some tea, and then resumed our trek. Fortu-nately, it was still overcast. Our stiffened legs slowly flexed back to usefulness; however, every step was becoming more difficult. The slope mercilessly contin-ued to steepen, and the thinning air was beginning to take its toll as well. There were more and more calls for rest stops. The huffing and puffing became inces-sant. Finally, reaching Station Six, we held a council meeting. All the girls and one of the guys wanted to turn back. I reminded Bebe of her agreement. Not wanting to be thought of as a welsher, she agreed to keep going. One of the other girls changed her mind, saying if Bebe could go on, she could too, so it was decided that four of us would continue. The other four would turn back.

We waved goodbye as we split up. Bebe, two others and I continued our grueling ascent. By noon we had reached Station Seven. Here, in broken English, we were given a message that the others from our group were going to wait for us at Sta-tion Five (where they had the sleeping accommodations). We learned that the stations had a communication system. It consisted of bark-like yells up and down the mountain between stations. We all had heard these funny sounds as we were climbing, but had no idea what they were. We returned a message that we were fine, and then continued our climb. After some refreshments and a short rest, we were on our way again.

As we climbed toward Station Eight, we began entering the clouds that had been protecting us from the sun. It was like being in a dense fog, and it did seem a little cooler. After a while, we emerged from the clouds into dazzling sunlight. I hadn't brought sunglasses or a hat—two big mistakes. I still had enough hair in those days to protect my scalp, but with no hat my forehead began to burn. All I could do to protect my eyes was squint. As we approached Station Eight, we were rewarded by a beautiful sight. The afternoon sun was casting an immense shadow profile of the upper mountain onto the cloud layer below. We simply had to stop and marvel at it.

At Station Eight we noticed that we were being treated unusually well. Although the station keepers couldn't speak English well enough to express their feelings, you could see admiration in their eyes. To them, climbing this mountain was a test of religious devotion and resolve, but understanding that we didn't share their traditional beliefs, they seemed to interpret our dogged endeavor as an acknowledgment of their culture and people. For us, it certainly hadn't started out as such. However, by now our grueling efforts and obsessive focus were beginning to take on a spiritual quality. The mountain "telegraph" informed us that our friends were continuing to wait for us at Station Five. As we got our brands, we began to feel a little superior to our wimpy friends below. Now it was getting dark and we decided to spend the night there. This time we slept on the floor on a tatami, a Japanese mat woven from reeds. It was considerably better than sleeping on a shelf with your feet hanging over the edge.

The next morning we were fed boiled rice that was actually beginning to taste good, dried meat, and of course tea. We set off again, knowing we had to make it to the top today or turn around. The steepness of the mountain had increased to the extent that the trail had become a series of switchbacks. Of course this meant one had to trudge much farther. Each switchback resulted in a gain of only 30-40 feet in elevation. Worse yet, the surface had deteriorated into nothing but cinders and ash. For every step forward, you tended to slip a half step back. It was a long grueling grind, but eventually we reached Station Nine.

This station was only a small shack with few amenities, but it did have some orange soda, and most importantly a fire to keep their brand hot. It was nearly 10:00 o'clock and we wanted to get back down the mountain before dark. So after getting branded and resting a bit, we set out to make a sprint (who in hell ever came up with that use for the word?) for the top. At this elevation it had become quite chilly, so back on went the sweaters and jackets. Now the steepness had increased such that each switchback only gained about 10 to 15 feet of elevation. Because of the increased hazard, a cable had been strung between steel stakes that were set along the trail. It provided something to hold on to and helped you pull yourself along.

With so little atmosphere to attenuate it, the sun became intense. Since climbing above the clouds, my reddened forehead had advanced beyond ordinary sunburn. Now the skin had split like an overly ripe apricot and serum was running down onto my face. All I could do was to mop it with my handkerchief. The climbing was "killing" us, but we couldn't turn back now. Then, mercifully, at a little after noon we reached the top, where a Shinto torii (a gate-like shrine) is installed. There were no victory yells or raised arms to display egotistic symbolism as has since become so obscenely popular. Instead, we simply celebrated our accomplishment with congratulatory handshakes. However, inside everyone felt a rush of pride and achievement.

We dragged our spent carcasses across the mountain's rim—maybe a hundred yards—and peered down into its gaping maw. Surprisingly, one side of the crater was covered in snow. This was an area in the shadow of the rim where the sun never reached. After taking some pictures, we hobbled to Station Ten to get our all-important brands. After branding our sticks, they rubbed in a red pigment. This was intended to be absolute (non-fakeable) proof you had made it all the way to the top. In addition, they tied a pink pennant and some small bells to the top of each staff. When descending the mountain, these provided an easily recognizable indication of your accomplishment. After drinking some orange soda and taking a short rest, we started back down.

Now a wondrous thing began to occur. Whenever we approached Japanese climbers (young or old), these climbers would hear our bells jingling and see our pennants snapping, and as we passed by they would turn and bow to us—not as wartime victors, but far more significantly, as their cultural *equals*. How could anyone imagine a more rewarding acknowledgment of a hard-won goal?

We were anxious to make good time in order to get off the mountain before dark. One fellow in our group decided it would be faster and easier to just hike straight down the slope, skipping the switchbacks, so he started out and soon was moving ahead of us, as we took the slower, safer switchbacks down. Soon I noticed that he was taking enormous strides (twelve to fifteen feet with each step). Gravity had taken over; he was out of control! He couldn't stop and he was headed for the cliff below the eruption.

We knew, and so did he, that going over the edge would mean the end, so while hurtling down the slope, he made a fateful decision. He would hold his staff by the ends with his two outstretched arms and allow himself to fall face-forward on the cinders and ash, hoping he would skid to a stop. We were stunned when we saw him perform this maneuver; well, actually I thought he had tripped and fallen. He slid and slid. It didn't look like he would ever stop, but stop he did. We all scrambled down the trail, using the switchbacks out of fear for our own necks. There he was, sitting up and dusting himself off. He was okay, except his forearms were a bloody mess. Other climbers saw the mishap and came to offer help. We helped him down to Station Eight. There, they cleaned his wounds and provided some strips of cloth to bind them.

We continued our descent down the slopes until we reached our irresolute comrades at Station Five. They had been lounging around, eating, playing Japanese board games, and keeping track of us by means of the mountain telegraph. We rejoined them and continued down the mountain. We were now learning that a different set of muscles was involved in descending than those used for climbing. Our legs were aching in new and different places. *Finally*, in late afternoon we were back at the cars.

Our climbing sticks were too long to fit in our trunk, so I let them hang out, just tying them in with some twine. On the way home, the sticks worked loose and landed on the highway. I stopped and went back to gather them up. Somehow, one of the two with pennants and bells which we had received at Station Ten had broken in half. We had no conclusive way to tell which was which, but Bebe firmly assured me the one that was still intact was hers.

21. Climbing Mt. Fuji—ca. 1953
Beatrice (Bebe) and Mickey are in the foreground of group picture.

22. At the top of Mt. Fuji—ca. 1953

HOOKED ON HIFI—1953

During my last year in Japan, both Burney and I became interested in the latest technological rage back in the U.S.—HiFi. Advances in circuit design, vinyl records, lightweight pick-ups with diamond needles, and quality speakers all led to a startling improvement in sound recording and reproduction. Wow! This was a new and fascinating obsession for us.

The retail manufacturing industry hadn't caught up yet, so you couldn't just go out and buy a factory-built unit. It was rather as in early ham radio days; you'd just have to build it yourself if you wanted one. How-to-build books on the subject were available, and I immediately sent off for a couple of them, which I read obsessively and virtually memorized. Using the information provided in these sources, I set out to design two components. The first was a power amplifier. Big power back then was about 20 to 25 Watts. Nowadays, everyone wants 100 to 250 Watts. I can't imagine why, since 5 Watts of sound can blow you out of the room. It's like wanting a 400 HP car, I think.

Of course the designs were based on vacuum tubes; the word "transistor" had not yet come into being. I understood vacuum tubes, and eagerly set out to design the "perfect" power amp. Burney just watched and kibitzed. He was no circuit designer. Well neither was I, but I knew enough to learn. However, he did plan to build one for himself, using whatever design I created.

REARRY FINE JAPANESE TERRESCOPE—1953

During our stay in Japan, I had become aware that the country's optical industry was exceptionally fine. During the war, much of it had become a cottage industry, providing optical instruments for the military. Thousands of small lenses used in eyepieces were made in homes by children and old people sitting on the floor. They were provided with glass blanks, grinding tools and compounds, and a master gauge. After the lenses were coarse and fine ground to match the gauge, they were sent to an optical factory for polishing. Larger objective lenses and mirrors were made entirely at factories.

Traditionally, the Germans made the world's finest optics; Americans were in second place. However, the Japanese saw an opportunity in this field. It was a labor-intensive industry not requiring much raw material. Manufacturers attempting to recover from the devastating war years found this an ideal situation. Already, Canon and Nikon were making credible copies of German cameras (Leica and Contax).

To make superb optics, it was very important to have adequate testing and quality control. The Japanese, having inexpensive labor, could afford to spend the time necessary to test to higher standards. They achieved their goal in a few years and became the world's most popular producer of optical products.

Even as a boy, I was attracted to telescopes and microscopes because of my interest in astronomy, minerals, and to a lesser extent, biology. My first microscope was a cheap toy that I got from some kid on a trade. Later in high school, when I had a little more money, I bought a very old brass German-made microscope in a hockshop. It was not cheap, and it required a lot of cleaning and servicing to make it operate properly. After I got out of the service, I yearned badly for a telescope. I built my own small refractor, with the help of a man who owned a machine shop.

Walking along the Ginza, Tokyo's main drag, one day I spotted an optical store. Their window displayed a variety of microscopes. These were mostly student models for schools. I grabbed Bebe's arm and pulled her into the store with me. Fortunately, the salesman spoke good English and was very knowledgeable about Japanese optical products. I soon learned they could also obtain professional research microscopes. To show me what was available, he brought out an old, probably pre-war, catalog. It contained some fine looking instruments. They were dirt cheap at 360 yen per dollar. Before we left, I knew I had to buy one.

Bebe had the idea of becoming a nurse when we returned home. I doubted she would actually pursue that career, but I knew she was smart enough, a good student, and could make it if she wanted to. In any case, I selfishly used this goal to rationalize the purchase of a nice microscope. Bebe went along, as she did with almost anything. In this regard, she was probably the most agreeable person I ever knew. So it was up to me to pick out a model, which I did with relish. We bought a Magna brand binocular research model with a 4-objective lens turret, sub-stage illuminator, and filar micrometer. It only cost about 100,000 yen (under $300.00). In the states, it would have cost about $1400.00.

With that acquisition nailed down, I greedily began longing for a telescope, too. This time I appealed to Bebe with the argument that it would be great when we had kids. It could do so much to augment their public school education with advanced learning. Of course, advanced learning to me meant science. No problem; we could get that, too, if I wanted. In the purchasing area, things weren't entirely lopsided. We bought a nice string of Mikimoto pearls, a mink stole, a set of Noritake china, some cloisonné vases, and jade jewelry for Bebe.

Japan had one top-quality telescope maker: Goto Optical Co. They made all the fine astronomical telescopes for Far East observatories and universities. Each telescope was built to order. This meant I would need to come up with the specifications I wanted, and they would custom build it. That would not be difficult, since I had a good idea of what I wanted. It would be a 100mm (4 inch) refractor, mounted on an equatorial mount, with a clock drive and it would have a tripod. The salesman arranged an appointment with Goto Optical for me to go to the plant and discuss the details with them.

It was September, and on the appointed day the weather was beautiful. I stopped by the Ginza store to pick up the salesman. He would act as an interpreter. I have since forgotten where the company was located, but the drive took a little over an hour. When we arrived, we were ushered into a typical Japanese room with walls made of thin wooden frames covered with rice paper. A typical short lacquered table, surrounded with cushions, was in the center of the room. Three men appeared immediately. One was an old man, well into his sixties. The other two appeared to be in their 30's. The salesman introduced everyone. The old man was Mr. Goto himself, and the other two were his chief designers (one optical and one mechanical). After the traditional bowing, we were all seated and were served sake.

I handed my sheet of specifications to the salesman, who in turn handed it to Mr. Goto. He looked it over—I think mostly out of curiosity—then handed it on to his engineers. A lot of chatter ensued, that of course I couldn't understand. The salesman passed on a few technical questions about my specifications, which I answered. After the translation, the Japanese replied with the usual Japanese "Ah so, ah so," indicating they understood. Finally, the salesman said, "Yes, they make you a rearry fine terrescope. You be very proud." I was sure I would be. I was very proud and honored just to be in the presence of the finest telescope makers in the Far East.

The final problem was that we were leaving in December; that only left them three months maximum to build it. One of the frustrating characteristics of the

Japanese was their need to be agreeable, even if that meant being dishonest. I had run into that problem several times in the past. When you asked a merchant how long it would take to obtain or make something for you, he would come up with the answer he thought you wanted to hear. It was good etiquette, but lousy business. Every Japanese consumer knew the game and would always mentally double or triple such an estimate accordingly. I knew I had to make it clear—*really* clear—that I was leaving the country and must be given an honest date. I expressed this to the salesman in very firm terms, which he attempted to convey. Deep furrows formed on the Goto team's brows. This was *not* the Japanese way. A lot of gibbering, coupled with furtive glances at me, indicated this was more difficult for them to deal with than were my specifications. It was no doubt the first time they had ever dealt with an American—such strange people, these Americans. Finally, the salesman turned to me and said, "Terrescope be ready first week December."

I said, "OK." Every language understands OK. I wasn't sure of the proper Japanese etiquette for asking how much it would cost, so I turned to the salesman and asked, "Is it proper to ask for a price at this time?"

After some more chatter, I was informed it would cost 180,000 yen (exactly $500.00). That was about a third of the cost of an inferior American production-made telescope. Of course I agreed. We all stood up and the bowing ceremony began. It continued as the salesman and I backed and bowed our way out of the building.

In late October we went back to the optical store on the Ginza to check on the progress of things and to pick up the microscope we had ordered. The microscope was a beauty. After paying for it, the salesman told me that Mr. Goto had contacted him to invite me back to the company to view the final testing of the objective lens for the telescope. He explained this honor was not usually extended. I eagerly accepted, and a date was set for the following week.

When we arrived, again there was all the bowing and serving of sake, but this time things didn't seem so formal. The Japanese, like most Asians, seem rather enigmatic. However, this time I could see distinct signs of pleasure to see me—even tiny smiles at times. After the sake, they led me into the factory. What a shock! It wasn't the immaculate white-room kind of environment one would expect for an optical factory. The floor was dirt. Probably, the original plant had been bombed out during the war and this was some sort of temporary facility.

However, I noticed that where dust-free conditions were necessary, they had provided enclosures draped with fabric that had been coated with oil to catch the dust. Throughout the building, school-aged girls were walking about with sprinkling cans, sprinkling the dirt floor with water to keep the dust down. It was all so primitive, yet eminently practical—so typical of the Japanese.

I was led to a fabric-covered enclosure. They pulled back the flap and invited us inside. They had the final optics testing equipment there. On a table, covered with velvet, lay the two elements for my objective lens (a convex element of crown glass and a concave one of flint glass). On the table, in a beautifully made box, were the master glass gages against which my lens elements would be tested. There were four of them, one for each surface. These masters are meticulously made with great difficulty. Their entire surfaces must be accurate to a few millionths of an inch. The chief optical engineer turned on an overhead monochromatic light, took out one of the master gages and carefully laid it on the table. Then, he placed one of my elements on top. Dark and light bands form naturally across the lens surface from one side to the other. They are caused by interference of the monochromatic light as it bounces back and forth between the two surfaces. These patterns of bands make it possible to detect differences, measured in millionths of an inch, between the curve of the master gage and of the tested lens.

In America, and apparently in Germany, a practical compromise between perfection and labor expenditure had been established for fine lenses. If the lines are reasonably parallel and do not contain too much curvature, the lens is accurate to within about 1/4 wavelength of light (around 1/200,000 of an inch)—good enough. But the Japanese knew that only if they did better would they be able to enter into the world market to which they so desperately aspired.

That was when I became privy to their self-imposed standards. When they completed the test set-up, I was asked to look at the interference lines. My God! They were not only perfectly parallel, they were straight lines with no detectable curvature. When the optical engineer saw my amazement, he brought out a tiny bow made of a sliver of bamboo on which was strung a silk thread. The bow held the thread taut—absolutely straight. He held the simple contraption over the lens, moving the thread from line to line, proving that every one was perfectly straight. He beamed an unmistakable smile of pride. I unknowingly was witnessing the basis of the Japanese optical revolution: *real* quality.

When we returned to the "sitting" room, I expressed my appreciation for the tour and told them how impressed I was with their quality control. Then I proposed an arrangement, whereby when I returned to the states I could import their products. Again, a lot of chatter in Japanese, but finally I saw Mr. Goto nod to the others. He agreed. One of the engineers got some old, pre-war price sheets and gave them to the salesman. Of course they were all printed in Japanese, so he scribbled English translations of the descriptions and prices on them.

This was an unbelievable opportunity. Unfortunately, I am no entrepreneur. I was thinking only of my own ability to buy from them in the future. They had never exported to the West, and they were giving me this privilege. Had I been more visionary, I could have had exclusive rights to this first-rate source just when the space program was in its infancy and a high demand for telescopes was beginning to appear. After I got back to the U.S., I did import two 8" parabolic mirrors and their diagonals. I built a Newtonian reflector with one set and sold the other at a good profit, which covered the cost of them both. But that's as far as I took it. I missed out on a golden opportunity.

As promised, the telescope was ready in December. I eagerly took it back to the base to try it out before packing it for shipment. My first target was Jupiter. It was a stunning sight, even better than I had seen through the 10 inch Zeiss (German made) refractor at Griffith Observatory in Los Angeles. I knew I had a real treasure.

PREPARING OUR LEAVE—1953

Bebe had come to Japan on a two-year contract. It would be completed in December 1953. Although we could have stayed longer, we were both eager to return home to see our families and friends. Also, Bebe's parents were planning a nice wedding for us in January, on the assumption we would be back by the end of the year.

By this time, the U.S. had ended the occupation and returned Japan to its new democratically formed government. Traditionally, the Japanese had a two-class system: the very rich and the very poor. This resulted in some odd economic situations for Americans. The government had essentially frozen imports in order to prevent a drain of Japanese assets out of the country. However, the thousands of Americans in Japan were exempt from these laws and had been allowed to import anything they wanted, duty free. This showed up mostly as purchases of cars and cameras. To prevent greedy Americans from profiteering, it was required that they own such products six months before being allowed to sell them on the Japanese market.

Since the Japanese had not yet developed their consumer products industries (as they later did in spades), almost any foreign-made product was in high demand—a demand generated by the very rich upper class. It was common practice for GI's to purchase a nice German-made camera at the PX and head for the Ginza, the main street in Tokyo. Inevitably, a Japanese person would approach them with, "Hey, Joe. You want sell camera? I give you seventy five thousand yen. Yes?" That would usually be about twice what the GI had paid for it. This was the Tokyo black market. It was a market that would buy anything you had to sell: cameras, pens, articles of clothing, etc. If you were in a car, people would run alongside, attempting to get you to sell them your car. Being a black market, all deals were in cash (yen) on the spot.

During the summer we had bought a new car—a 1953 Plymouth that had been shipped over from the states. We needed to sell it before we left. A provision in the Japanese law allowed those with orders (military authorization to return to the states) to sell their car, even if it were owned less than six months, but there was a catch. In Japan, the U.S. military printed and used its own form of money. It was called script. Everything from $20.00 bills down to nickels was in the form of paper bills and looked very much like Monopoly money. It was illegal for either Americans or Japanese to possess regular U.S. money. Also, Japanese could not legally possess script. Americans could convert script to yen at banks and other legal sources, but conversion in the other direction was illegal.

This meant we could sell the car to a Japanese car dealer, but we would be paid in yen. Then, we would need to find some way to convert that yen into script, which could then be legally converted to U.S. dollars upon leaving the country. Since converting yen into script was illegal, the practice emerged that when you were about to leave, your friends and associates would buy your yen with their script, which you then would convert to U.S. dollars at the time of departure. To minimize the amount we would need to sell that way, we planned to order a new car (for delivery in the U.S.) from the dealer to whom we would sell our car. We were allowed to transfer $1000 out of the country in that manner. Once we arrived in San Francisco, we cancelled the order and bought a used car.

On our last weekend in Japan, a nippy December day, we drove in to Tokyo with the title to our old car in hand. Arriving at the dealership, we were ushered into a salesman's cubical. Since the amount he offered was about one and a half million yen ($4200), we didn't haggle over the price. We had paid only $2000 for the car, plus $500 to have it shipped over.

After the deal was struck and the papers signed, the man disappeared for a moment and then returned with this large box, containing over a million yen in thousand-yen notes. One thousand yen was the largest denomination Japanese note. Even so, it was only worth about $2.80. The box contained over 1000 such notes. We came unprepared. Where would we put them all? First, Bebe stuffed all she could in her purse. I began stuffing wads of them into my pants pockets and then into my jacket pockets. We were both wearing overcoats, so we stuffed more into those pockets. Now, out of pockets, the salesman located a paper sack and put the remainder in it. We walked out, looking like bank robbers with money hanging out of every pocket. Of course we no longer had a car, so we had to travel back to my base on the train. We weren't worried about being mugged. We had learned that Japan was a very civilized place.

We spent the balance of the week packing and peddling yen for script. It was surprising how fast that went. In two days we had converted all of it, mostly with the other instructors. On the next to last day, an Air Force truck showed up to take our boxed possessions for shipping. Incidentally, another benefit that personnel received when returning from overseas duty was that nothing had to pass through U.S. Customs. For those who had bought jewelry and art objects (silver, ivory, jade, etc.), this was a real savings.

On Bebe's final day, I accompanied her to Yokohama to catch her ship home. We kissed and waved good-bye. Once she was on deck, we threw handfuls of serpentine at each other. Eventually her ship pulled away and disappeared over the horizon. I was flying back and had to wait a few days for my flight. It left on Christmas Day. The flight back was a repeat, in reverse, of the flight over. One oddity occurred when we passed over the International Date Line. This moved us to a day earlier, providing a second Christmas.

REFLECTIONS

On leaving Japan, I was a much-changed person from when I arrived. Oh, I was just as neurotic as ever, but my understanding of a number of social issues had been broadened. For example, I had seen with my own eyes how much our government had lied to us when during the war they drummed endlessly about the horrible nature of the Japanese. We were told they were sneaky, ruthless, godless, and had no respect for human life. Caricatures depicted them as slant-eyed, buck-toothed, and mal-sighted. As slow as I am on the uptake, it only took a couple of days in this new land for me to see what a crock I had been fed.

Within a year I realized that this society was, in many ways, more civilized than my own. The Japanese were more polite and considerate, and much less aggressive than we were. I had seen thousands of them gathered in Hibia Park, Tokyo, celebrating the beauty of spring on one of their festive days. They sat in small circular groups on woven mats, drinking sake and singing. Drinking was followed by rather uninhibited merriment. A few overdid it and passed out. I watched for hours, taking pictures, and not once did I see any anger or fighting develop. Imagine several thousand Americans packed together and drinking heavily.

Their children are well-mannered and unspoiled. They attend school six days a week all year round. When they are outside at play, it is common to see little girls with babies tied on their backs. What an improvement over just confining them to a crib or playpen. Japanese respect and honor their elderly. They seek their council and wisdom.

Their streets were far safer than ours are. Women had no fear of walking alone along dimly lit, or even dark streets. Rape was virtually unknown. However, petty theft was common, as might be expected in a devastated country. You certainly wouldn't want to leave your camera on a park bench and walk away. Serious crime was very low until the introduction of gang operations by the western world in later years. Family violence was unheard of. Probably the most serious crimes were assassination attempts on political figures.

BACK HOME IN CALIFORNIA

It was late evening as the plane traversed its last few miles over the Pacific. I could see the whole coastline lit up like stars as we approached. A large lump formed in my throat. I don't believe it was due to any yearning to be back home. Rather, I think it was just because it was a beautiful sight. We landed at Travis Air Force Base. Since it was a day and a half before Bebe's ship was due to dock, I went into San Francisco and got a hotel room for us.

I killed the next day just walking around Frisco. At lunch time I went into a cafeteria. When I got to the cashier, he rang up the bill. It was 89 cents. I put a fifty-cent piece on the counter and waited for my change. I hadn't used U.S. money in two years and thought it was a silver dollar. The cashier looked at me and waited, while I looked at him, waiting for my change. Finally, he said, "Your lunch was eighty-nine cents, sir."

I replied, "Yes, I know."

Then he picked up the coin and held it in front of my face, saying, "This is only fifty cents!" I had to read the face of the coin to be convinced. Sheepishly, I dug out another half-dollar.

The next day, Bebe's ship was scheduled to arrive. I took a cab to the port and waited. Eventually I spotted something on the horizon. As the vessel got closer, I recognized it as hers. I thought *How amazing…seeing her off in Japan, and then being there to greet her on her arrival. More kisses and hugs. Then off to the hotel…*or so I thought.

Bebe told me that she and some of the people she met on the ship were going to stay at the Mark, the fanciest hotel in Frisco. They had planned a party on "The Top of the Mark," a world famous nightspot located on the hotel's roof. This shocked me quite a bit. We had dated for three years and we had been engaged for two more. During all that time, I had not become aware of Bebe's need for fun and partying. My neurosis had apparently suppressed such desires in me. In fact, I recall the confusion I felt when I would observe others dancing and appearing to be having a good time. I simply couldn't understand how such behavior could be considered fun.

In looking back, I think Bebe surely recognized this shortcoming in me, and had she been a little more self-confident and assertive, she might have broken off our relationship at that time, but her family was looking forward to the marriage. Bebe was their first daughter and they were planning a lavish (for their means) wedding in a few weeks. She simply couldn't disappoint them. The next day we caught a train to Los Angeles—and marriage.

____DOMESTIC EMBARK

◆

Wedding Preparations—1954
The Ceremony
The Honeymoon
On to College—1954
The Rocket Racket—1954
Domestic Life
Burney's Blunder
Audrey Arrives—1955
Importune Importer
Inadequate Income
Clouds on the Horizon
Barbara Blows In—1956
Home Sweet Home
Cyril

WEDDING PREPARATIONS—1954

The weeks before the wedding are a blur in my memory. I was living at my mom's house during that period. Bebe, of course, lived at home. However, we got together most evenings and on weekends. One of the first things we did was to buy a car: a 1953 Chevy Bellaire. It wasn't new, but we liked its looks. Now we both could drive around to visit old friends, updating our relationships.

Bebe's mom had given up on converting me to Catholicism, at least for the time being, but pointed out that to have a proper Catholic wedding I would need to take "instructions" from the priest. Since I had no objection, I agreed. A schedule of appointments was arranged with Father O'Malley, the parish priest in Bell Gardens, where Bebe's family lived. During three years of dating, prior to our going to Japan, I had read piles of Catholic literature presented to me by various family members. Therefore, I already had a substantial knowledge of Catholic catechism. Many of the arguments presented to me were unsophisticated. Probably, these were originally formulated to convert people from other religions, or to persuade those who had never given religion much thought. In my case, I had rather firm atheistic views that presented many paradoxes with Catholic teachings. I was told by the family that Father O'Malley could answer any questions I might have. However, poor old Father O'Malley was only trained in Catholic catechism and was not prepared for philosophical questions. When stumped, always his standard answer was "That's a mystery, my son; that's one of God's mysteries." Perhaps he was remembering the First Communion photo decapitations I had performed on him a few years earlier and was just getting even.

After that ritualistic farce, the family was now assured that I was suitable for marrying into their church. For my part, I saw no conflict. I regarded the issue of religion to be one for Bebe and me to sort out. I had discussed religion with Bebe, and I was convinced it was not very important to her. In fact, she didn't attend church the whole two years we were in Japan.

Bebe had bought enough silk brocade in Japan to make her wedding gown and dresses for her four bridesmaids. The material for Bebe's was white; each of the bridesmaids was a different pastel color. Bebe's mom made her gown, and each of the bridesmaids made their own.

Since I took movies of everything in those days, I asked Bebe's parents if they knew anyone who could take pictures of the ceremony using my movie camera.

Bebe's dad came up with Joe Cronin, his boss at Grinnell, a fire-sprinkler installation company. The Cronins were friends who frequently visited the Warings. My camera was a semi-professional Bolex H-16. Its operation was not exactly self-evident. I had met Joe several times in the past and thought with a little instruction he could probably do fine. One Sunday, when the Cronins were visiting, I got it out to explain its operation to Joe. Neurosis again! All I could get out of him was, "Yeah, yeah. I can run it." His ego wouldn't let him accept instructions. I gave up, but hoped he was right and could manage.

THE CEREMONY

On January 24, 1954, we were married. Bebe looked great and the wedding was very nice, except that it rained. The church was new, and the parking lot had not yet been paved. It became a muddy morass. More than one car got stuck, and men in their best duds had to slosh around in the mud to push them out.

Joe Cronin took a roll of movies of the ceremony, using my camera. I had little doubt we would get a fine record of the event. Wrong! He took pictures inside the church with the lens aperture set for daylight brightness. When the film came back, all you could make out were the flames on the candles. I learned Catholics use a lot of candles. Joe's ego was much too big ever to apologize for his goof.

We received a ton of gifts. The linens alone lasted all through our marriage and beyond. We probably could have reimbursed Bebe's dad for the wedding if we had held a garage sale to sell all the duplicate kitchen appliances.

THE HONEYMOON

Did we go to Niagara Falls or the Grand Canyon? No, we went to Las Vegas. I don't know why; we just did. We enjoyed the nightclub shows. Neither of us were gamblers, so we skipped that. We took a boat ride on Lake Mead, a man-made lake formed by backed up water behind Boulder Dam. We had already had a two-year honeymoon in Japan.

ON TO COLLEGE—1954

With the wedding out of the way, Bebe and I headed for UCLA to register for the spring semester, but we were too late. Registrations were filled. They suggested we apply at Los Angeles City College. That was an extension of the UCLA system. We did—took our entrance exams and were accepted.

Next, we hunted around that part of town for a place to live. We ended up in an over-the-garage apartment. It had been divided into two residences to maximize income. We slept on a rollaway bed in the living room, sharing the bath with a bachelor who lived in the bedroom down the hall. Nonetheless, for going to school it was fine. It was inexpensive, and that was important since we had no income. We were living on our savings from Japan (about $8000).

I don't remember the subjects Bebe took, except that she was in my German class. In addition to German, which I never passed, I took physics, advanced algebra, and English. I planned to get a degree in physics. Bebe had lost interest in her previous plans to become a nurse and just wanted to have a college education.

During the semester, my old back injury (from high school days) flared up. It was so bad that at times in class I couldn't concentrate on the lectures. Finally I went to an orthopedist. He fitted me with a steel brace that I had to wear day and night. I wore that miserable thing for a year and a half. However, eventually my back got better—probably in spite of the brace.

The most significant occurrence during that period was that Bebe got pregnant with Audrey. I had no idea how it happened. Well, of course, I knew how, I just didn't know *how*. Bebe had no explanation. That meant that at the very least we would have to postpone returning to college in the fall.

THE ROCKET RACKET—1954

I began looking for a job after we finished the semester. This was at the beginning of the cold war with Russia, and new military rockets and missiles were being developed and produced. I accepted a job as a technician with Firestone Tire & Rubber Company, who had a large contract from the Army to build Corporal missiles (an artillery missile with about an 80-mile range). It may seem odd that a rubber company was building missiles. I believe Firestone had made a lot of money during the war and was looking for diversification into the hi-tech arena. General Tire & Rubber Company was also doing a similar thing.

As a technician, I would test electronic equipment on the missile. It paid less than I had made at Philco. However, I viewed this as only a temporary job to maintain some cash flow in the short term. The company was located in Southgate, just a few miles from Bebe's family in Bell Gardens. That worked out fine, since Bebe wanted to be near her mom when the baby came. We leased a house near the plant for one year from a man and his wife who were teachers. They were going to tour Europe on sabbatical for a year.

I loved the job. I learned a lot about missile technology, especially guidance and control electronics. Transistors had not yet been developed, so all the electronics were designed using vacuum tubes. They were nearly the weakest component used in missiles. The vibration of the rocket engines would often cause them to short out and fail. Because of this, we had to subject every electronic flight package to a shake and vibration test. Inevitably, the test would be cut short as various vacuum tubes in the equipment failed. We just kept replacing tubes until we could get the unit through its test regimen.

Firestone had an award program for innovative ideas. If you had a good idea, or if you had developed an improvement, they would pay a cash bonus. I saw this as a gold mine. In no time I had developed an improved way to test the missiles accelerometers and received a couple of hundred dollars. The most sophisticated improvement I developed was related to the tuning of the missile's antenna system. My idea involved plotting the antenna's characteristics on a Smith chart. The locus formed a circle. Then, I would select the spot on the locus nearest to the chart origin as the point to tune the antenna. It was a big improvement, and I received five hundred dollars—more than a month's salary!

DOMESTIC LIFE

At home, I set up the Hi-Fi I had built in Japan. Having only listened to the radio and record players, it sounded good to me. The main problem was hum. That was the result of another vacuum tube shortcoming, so I redesigned the filament heater circuits (the main source of the hum) to provide DC instead of AC. That made a huge difference and I was proud of my modification.

I felt contented in this new domestic life. I was building a record collection and beginning to appreciate classical music. Things were going well with my new in-laws, and we visited them almost every weekend. Bebe's dad and I hit it off well. We both enjoyed some of the same hobbies, particularly ham radio and photography. However, I don't think that period seemed all that good to Bebe. She didn't seem to get much satisfaction out of her role as a housewife. She saw housework as menial—especially ironing. Her mother, the consummate homemaker, spotted this, and would invite Bebe to bring our wash over and she would do the wash for her. I think Bebe paid her sisters to do the ironing. Once or twice a week when I got home from work, I would find a note that she had gone to her mom's place. Then, I would drive over and we would be invited to stay for dinner—another payoff for Bebe. Although I saw this as minor shirking on her part, it didn't bother me all that much. I still remember this period as a pleasant one.

BURNEY'S BLUNDER

One day I got a letter from Burney, my sadist roommate in Japan. He was in a military jail in Tokyo. The Base Commander had ordered him arrested for attempted murder and placed him in solitary confinement while the Adjutant-General built a case against him. (We were subject to military law while in Japan.)

Burney was a gun enthusiast—a fine hobby for a sadist. According to his account, he had several friends in his room (my old room), and he was passing around some of the guns he had collected. One of the guns was a .357 Magnum revolver, the most powerful handgun in the world at the time. Burney's account goes that unbeknownst to him, one of the guys loaded the gun; no reason, just to see what it looked like with bullets in it, I guess. The gun was passed around and finally was returned to Burney—loaded. Burney, never one for caution or safety, raised the gun to "dry-fire" it over the head of his roommate, Ernie Zahn. Just as he pulled the trigger, Zahn stood up and caught the bullet in his upper right arm. Being a .357 Magnum, it almost tore his arm off.

Eventually, the Base Commander got a court marshal hearing convened. Although he charged Burney with attempted murder, the Board saw it as an accident, albeit stupid. They decided against a prison sentence and just kicked him out of the Far East. He was given 48 hours to pack up and leave.

Burney no longer had a home in the U.S. He needed an address to which he could send his belongings. He had several things to ship: expensive cameras, a microscope, some medical devices, Hi-Fi equipment, and a gun collection. Furthermore, he needed a place to stay until he established a new residence (in Texas). Well, how could a "good guy" refuse an old roommate buddy? "Sure, come on; we'll make room for you," I replied.

Soon afterwards, Burney showed up at the door. Our house had two bedrooms, so setting up a bed for him was easy enough. At first, Bebe didn't express any objection to the arrangement. However, after a few weeks of having him under foot, it began to annoy her. Certainly it interfered with going to her Mom's much of the time. Additionally, she was expected to fix dinner every night, *and* Burney was a hostile person, always playing jokes and pranks. Bebe deplored that behavior. After about a month she'd had her fill. She told me I had to get rid of him. So, as tactfully as I knew how, I asked him to move on, which he did. It was the last we ever saw or heard from him.

AUDREY ARRIVES—1955

Audrey Theresa was born February 11, 1955, at Saint Francis hospital in Lynwood, which is next to Southgate. She had the McCoy coloring: brown eyes and thick, black hair that reached down to her shoulders. The nurses and nuns made a huge fuss over her, especially her long hair, and hauled her all over the hospital, showing her off. I thought she was quite handsome.

At home, Audrey became the focus of everything. I think she provided Bebe with a sense of accomplishment she couldn't get from homemaking. In any case, she seemed well-suited to motherhood. That was evident in the home movies we made, but there was the siren call of Bell Gardens. Bebe's sisters all wanted to play with this new baby-toy. The older ones would argue over who would get to feed her, change her, and bathe her. With all this attention, Audrey surely was not a neglected child. However, I'll have to admit that one of my serious shortcomings is that I don't know how to deal with totally emotional beings such as infants and toddlers. I do much better when they get to be four or five years old. As a result, I probably didn't give her as much attention as a good father would have.

IMPORTUNE IMPORTER

I seem to have little intuition and no ability to foresee the future. Yet in a way I believe I did see that rockets were going to allow man to reach into space. This glimmer, coupled with my already existing interest in astronomy, resulted in a renewed interest in my agreement with Goto Optical to import their products. By coincidence, at work I met another technician, Lee Trecker, who had an avocation business at his home in Torrence, California, building piers for telescopes. (He invented the tubular-column pier with three legs connected to the bottom that every telescope manufacturer uses today.)

Lee was using rejected tubing from the Corporal Missile Program as a supply source for his piers. On the Corporal missile, compressed nitrogen was used to force propellants into the rocket engine; later missiles used turbo pumps. The front half of the missile contained a cluster of six-inch diameter aluminum tubes in which the pressurized nitrogen was stored during flight. Because of the high stress involved, the tubes were individually pressure-tested. Some would crack; some would even explode. Firestone gave the rejects to Lee. From them he sawed out good sections, which were long enough to build his piers.

At that time, Cave Optical was the best telescope manufacturer in the West. A fellow named Parks had developed and was manufacturing white fiberglass tubes that many telescope makers now use as the main tube to house the mirror. Parks' primary customer was Cave Optical, and at that time, like Lee, Cave was still operating out of his garage. Parks was also located in Torrence, not far from Lee's place.

Cave Optical was located in Long Beach, and they specialized in Newtonian reflectors. They liked Lee's innovative piers and incorporated them into their product. Lee had a nice sideline building the piers for them. However, he had ambitions of producing his own telescopes, which he planned to sell by mail order. Cave didn't want to support such competition and so wouldn't agree to make mirrors for him.

I told Lee of the arrangement I had with Goto Optical and how precise their optical products were. Immediately, he suggested we go into business together. He would build the piers and mounts, I would import the optics, and we would design our main tubes (obtained from Parks) to house the mirrors from Goto Optical.

Lee and I agreed to set up a business to build reflector telescopes. Lee already had some shop machinery: a metal lathe, drill press, power hacksaw, etc. We figured we'd need a milling machine, too, so I agreed to buy one, especially since I had a design in mind for a telescope camera that would take six images on 2-1/4 x 3-1/4 cut-film. That would absolutely require a vertical mill. I bought a used Benchmaster mill. It would do just fine. Leon Barris (my sister's husband) supplied most of the tooling for it.

I contacted Goto and ordered two eight-inch, f-8 (64-inch focal length) Pyrex mirrors, and a diagonal for each, at about $50 per set. While we waited for the optics, Lee fabricated an equatorial mount and one of his piers to support it. Still, we were going to need a finder scope for the telescope. I had recently stumbled upon an optical company that had been building 7X50 binoculars for the Navy during the war. Their contract was canceled and I bought all their binocular optics for the price of scrap optical glass. Hundreds of these lenses were in various stages of manufacture and inspection. About a third were coated, edged, and inspected. Another third were uncoated, but usable, and the rest were just so much glass. We designed a nice finder for the telescopes using these lenses.

In a couple of months the optics from Japan arrived. Lee had the first telescope ready for installation. We installed it, and after collimating the optics we took it outside for a test. It was a clear night for Los Angeles, and we looked at some nebula and Mars. Mars was at its nearest approach and appeared almost as big in the eyepiece as the full moon was to the naked eye. I was impressed with the images, especially since I had previously looked only through a homemade 8-inch reflector. Lee thought it was as good as Cave's scopes—maybe better.

The following evening we set up the scope in Lee's garage, with a sheet draped behind it, and I took a few photos of it for the ad we planned to run in Sky & Telescope magazine. To prevent shadows, I took a one-minute time exposure during which Lee kept moving the light about to illuminate the scope from every angle. Surprisingly, it turned out quite professional-looking.

INADEQUATE INCOME

Bebe became pregnant *again*, and *again* she had no explanation. I wasn't upset, but I began to realize that raising a family was going to cost more than I had expected. We weren't doing without anything important, but we were just breaking even with my salary. In the back of my mind I still fantasized about getting a degree in physics, so I wanted, if possible, to avoid dipping into our savings. The end of our lease was coming up, which meant finding another place to live, so in an attempt to solve both problems, I began to scan the want ads.

I had not been able to find a suitable house to rent, and we eventually had to move because the lease was up. Mom's apartment was empty at the time, so we moved into it. It was just a place to sleep. Bebe would take Audrey to her mother's house every day and spend the day there. I kept looking through the want ads and stumbled upon one by Convair (later General Dynamics) in San Diego. The Air Force had awarded them a contract to build an intercontinental ballistic missile (ICBM). It was called the Atlas. And of all things, they needed technical instructors. How fortuitous!

I went for an interview. With my two years experience teaching electronics for the Air Force and my one-year testing Corporal missile electronics, they were very interested. They offered me $500.00 per month; I held out for $550.00 and got it. That was more than a 20 percent increase over my Firestone salary. Bebe was agreeable to moving to San Diego. She always went along cheerfully with any moves my jobs required. In fact, I believe she viewed such changes as enjoyable adventures.

Of course this ended the business venture with Lee. I traded him one of the mirrors and surplus optics for one of his piers and mounts. He was disappointed that I had disrupted the new business by moving out of Los Angeles; however, he managed to persuade Cave to sell optics to him by saying he might otherwise import them from Japan at half the price. After I took the job in San Diego, I never saw Lee again. For many years he sold his telescopes under the name Treckerscope. Then his ads disappeared from Sky & Telescope magazine. Parks also went into the business of building complete telescopes. I see his ads yet in various telescope magazines; as I write this, it has been 45 years.

CLOUDS ON THE HORIZON

Our marriage began to have trouble after we moved to San Diego. I cannot moralize about that, since I don't believe such concerns are a matter of blame, and my views about human nature would not allow such presumptions in any case.

Once in San Diego, we found a small, inexpensive over-the-garage apartment in Point Loma. I was still trying to hold onto our nest egg in case the opportunity to return to school ever came about. However, with Bebe being pregnant with Barbara, I was rapidly concluding that wasn't in the cards.

I began my new job as an electronics instructor. My assignment was to teach classes on a tracking system Convair had developed called AZUSA. I can't imagine where they came up with that name, although there *is* a small town in southern California by that name. It was a very sophisticated system, using a ground-based transmitter with an array of antennas and an on-board electronics package called a transponder. It could track the missile to within a few yards. If the missile went off track, it would provide the Range Safety Officer with primary position data so he could decide whether or not to destroy the missile. Convair hoped it would eventually evolve into a ground-based missile guidance system.

It was a fascinating system, full of clever new concepts and technology. I enjoyed working with it. Things at home were not going all that swimmingly. Bebe suffered a lot of "morning sickness" from her pregnancy. Besides, she was cooped up all day in the apartment. A pattern developed such that when I arrived home in the evening she would be very quiet and uncommunicative. Of course, I couldn't help noticing, and would probe around for what was bothering her. I was beginning to learn that when Bebe was miserable, as she surely was, withdrawal was her way of telling me. Her only escape from these unpleasant days was on weekends when we would drive up to see her family. There, she would transform into her usual self.

BARBARA BLOWS IN—1956

The next major event occurred when Barbara was born, February 12, 1956, at San Diego Mercy Hospital, *one* year and *one* day after Audrey's birth. Bebe's mom attended the event, as I think she did for all her grandkids. Barbara was totally different from Audrey. She had the Waring's coloring: blue eyes, and what little hair she had was blonde. We felt fortunate; two bright, healthy kids with all their fingers and toes.

One day when I returned from work, things seemed worse than normal. I had very little understanding of emotional matters, and was still of the belief that husbands went to work and earned a living while wives were happy as homemakers.

After a difficult dialog trying to get to the bottom of the matter, Bebe finally said she believed she would be a lot happier if we had our own home. That made sense to me. After all, the apartment and the neighborhood were both rather drab, and being close to the coast, it was damp and often foggy.

HOME SWEET HOME

We spent the next several weekends house hunting. San Diego was a beautiful place. The skies were azure blue, the temperature mild, and the city just the right size (about 100,000 people). Furthermore, you could choose your climate. Within about twenty miles you could select from a beachy, humid, salt-air environment such as Point Loma, to an arid, near-desert atmosphere inland such as La Mesa or El Cajone, or anything in between. We had enough of the coast, so we looked further inland.

We discovered a new subdivision located in the low hills of La Mesa, fell in love with the area and selected a two-bedroom, bath-and-a-half, on a corner lot. The price was $14,900. By now I knew full-time college was out of the picture and any further education would require night school. We made the down payment of around $750 from our savings. Being a veteran, I got a VA loan with only 3.5% interest.

The place came with a refrigerator and stove, and we bought furniture for the rest of the house. We both loved our new home. This was a new subdivision, and all the neighbors were just moving in. We made friends with several of them. The man across the street worked at Convair, so he and I formed a carpool. That allowed Bebe to use our car half of the time.

The house next door remained unsold for several months, but eventually a Mormon family from Utah moved in. They had seven or eight little kids. The husband was a math professor in Salt Lake, and had taken a position with Convair at a much higher salary than the university paid. He seemed to be a rather self-centered person. His wife took care of all the kids with no help from him. Even with that large family, he set aside one of the three bedrooms as his study. When he came home in the evening, he'd lock himself in it to read and do his research. His wife just had to cope. I guess she had no choice. Bebe thought she was crazy to put up with such an arrangement, but felt sorry for her, and they became good neighbor-friends.

Audrey and Barbara were developing into fine kids. They were both healthy and bright, and seemed happy, if a bit too shy. No problem; in those days shyness was considered an asset for girls. Audrey had begun crawling, and Bebe wanted her to be able to crawl around outside. We didn't have a fenced yard, so I built a small enclosure with posts and chicken wire. Bad idea! She just sat out there and ate dirt and spiders. Barbara was developing into a very active kid. She all but wore out her swing and horsey. She seemed to need to be constantly moving. Perhaps that was an early sign of her later athleticism.

To augment our income, I obtained accreditation from the State of California as a vocational teacher (electronics, of course). I taught a 3-hour class twice a week, which paid $2.00 per hour. That added a little over $50.00 per month to our income. With the extra money we bought an electric organ for Bebe. It was a Hammond; very popular in music bars in those days. She took to it like a chicken goes after a June bug.

The marriage went along well during this period. On many weekends we were able to provide Bebe with a break from housework and the kids by driving up to visit her family in Los Angeles. I was happy with my work, my home-life, my kids, and my in-laws. I have fond memories of those days.

CYRIL

At work I became acquainted with a strange fellow named Cyril Smythe. He had an enormous need to compensate for feelings of inadequacy. His neurotic response was an attempt to be significantly unique. He surrounded himself with unusual, novel, and sometimes even bizarre things. For example, he lived on the side of a hill in El Cajone in a small barn that he had converted into a sort of house. It had running water, but no sewer; stuff just ran down into a gully.

He was married to a pretty, but extremely dependent young woman. They had a little boy who had never had a haircut. Ringlets cascaded down to the middle of his back and he looked, for all the world, like a cute little girl. Their "bedroom" had wall-to-wall mattressing. Foam rubber had just come out and he thought that was clever—and naughty. The boy played in an outside pen that had been built for goats. Cyril laughed heartily whenever he related that. The only expenditures he allowed his wife now and then were little cutesy decals. She had hundreds of them pasted all over their "kitchen."

Cyril controlled the money and spent most of it on his neurotic need to achieve distinctiveness. He owned expensive stereos, cameras, and polarized projection equipment that only a professional could have justified. He spent hours displaying this equipment and projecting his stereoscopic photographs on special-made screens, hoping to wow you. His wife would sit there, glowing with admiration.

Another garish item was his shop. He had bought a streetcar from the city of San Diego. He had positioned it on the side of his hill. It provided a startling view from the road below, just as he planned. In it were tons of expensive machines and tools used to support his unusual and bizarre hobbies.

Cyril's real pride and joy was his car. It was *homemade*. It had only three wheels—two in back and one in front. He had bought it from some inventor who thought it would make him rich, but no one was interested in it—well, except for Cyril. On a couple of occasions when I didn't have a ride, he took me to work in it. What a thrill! The engine was in the back and you felt like you were in the front seat of a roller coaster. You could see the street fly by, right under your nose. The poor stability was frightening. Once you got up to about 40 MPH it began jumping around like a grasshopper. It was all Cyril could do to keep it on the road. At 50 MPH, I was begging for my life. Of course everyone on the highway stared. Cyril was in his element.

23. Opening Wedding Presents—ca. 1954

24. Ray, Bebe and Children—ca. 1962

PART IV

STORIES OF THE SPACE PROGRAM YEARS

THE ATLANTIC MISSILE RANGE, Lure of the Cape—1957–1962

✦

Where to Live?
Atlas Away—1957
Near Disaster—1957
Inter-missile Diversions
Project Score
Miscellaneous Atlas Launches
The LO2 Tanking Incident—1958
Project Mercury—1959
Big Joe
Other Mercury Activity
Friendship 7—1962

WHERE TO LIVE?

While I was teaching at Convair, the company was building their first Atlas launch complexes at Cape Canaveral, and they were in the mode of staffing up crews to man them. They planned to build four—Launch Complexes 11 through 14—and build them in reverse order to their numbering, beginning with Launch Complex 14.

Florida was not considered a desirable place to live in those days, except perhaps for Miami. The Cape area was primitive...hot and humid, located adjacent to the Banana River which stank badly from rotting vegetation, and it had no decent water—only smelly sulfur-water wells. None of the homes had air conditioning. The area was infested with mosquitoes, cockroaches, enormous spiders (of which I was terrified), and snakes of many varieties—which were mostly very big or very long, sometimes both. I was told that in bygone days people tolerated a particularly large ugly spider because they killed the cockroaches. The wild animals actually included black panthers. I saw one crossing the highway not far from the center of Cocoa Beach.

The only decent shopping was sixty miles away, in Orlando. Cocoa and Rockledge, on the immediate mainland, had a few stores and even a small movie theater. We soon learned that appliance stores in the area carried very little stock. Instead, they depended on customers to pick items from their catalogs. These required a minimum of six weeks for delivery. Rockledge had the only hospital in the area. Its main business was delivering babies and handling emergencies. Anyone needing an operation went to Orlando. Telephones were all "party-line," which you shared with one to three other homes. TV reception was terrible. Only two TV stations were available: one in Orlando, the other in Daytona. You got more static than picture from either channel because both were so far away.

Not surprisingly, Convair wasn't having much success in finding people willing to transfer there. In desperation, the Air Force provided an incentive bonus of $225.00 per month to entice people to go. Well, that did it for me. It amounted to exactly a fifty percent increase in my salary. Bebe and I discussed the matter, and true to her adventuresome spirit, she was all for making the move.

I immediately applied for a transfer to the Launch Operations Division and began making plans for the reassignment. The company offered a preliminary trip to allow employees to find living arrangements before sending for their families. I arrived in Cocoa Beach in January, 1957. In those days if you were going to work at the Cape, there were only three little towns nearby: Cocoa Beach, to the south; Cocoa/Rockledge, on the mainland to the southwest; and Titusville on the mainland to the north. Most employees settled in Cocoa Beach.

Prior to all the missile activity, Cocoa Beach was a quiet little sportsman's surf-fishing village. It had one grocery store, one gas station, a couple of restaurants, a barbershop, and a hole-in-the-wall post office. Streets in town were unpaved, except for the main north-south coastal highway (A1A) and a short stretch of the main cross street. All other streets were sand; Florida is just one enormous sand-bar.

I bought a cheap car (translate: old) as my first task after arriving in Orlando, and then headed for the coast. The novelty of the scenery was captivating—enormous cumulus clouds, which were never seen in Southern California, and palm trees growing wild everywhere. Convair had contracted nearly half of the rooms at the newly built Starlight motel on the beach as temporary accommodations, and I was among its first occupants. The plaster was not yet dry. I stayed there for several weeks, then moved into a three-bedroom house that Jack Moline—a Convair employee and a compulsive entrepreneur—had set up as a rooming house. It was cheaper than the motel.

I rented a small duplex on one of the sand roads called Orlando Avenue and sent for Bebe and the kids. Poor Bebe. She got stuck with all the packing and moving and had to arrange for someone to lease our house. She found a dependable couple, and soon she and the kids, with our furnishings, were on their way.

Construction practices in Florida, at least in that part of the state, were very different than I was used to. In California, houses were built on foundations above the ground. Most were frame construction with stucco outside and plastered walls inside. The floors were usually hardwood, except for linoleum in the kitchen and tile in the bathroom. The windows were either sash or sliding. Heating and cooking were done with natural gas that was cheap, clean, and piped-in. Almost all residential areas had a sewer system.

In Florida, most houses were built of concrete block on a slab foundation that was finished with a layer of terrazzo. Windows were jalousie, to allow maximum breeze to flow through since the houses had no air conditioning. These places were *not* comfortable. It was always humid in the summer, and the air was suffocating when there was no breeze. In the winter, the cold penetrated the un-insu-lated cement blocks. Then it was like living in an igloo. Heating furnaces burned oil and required regular refills of a storage tank. There was no sewage system; every house had a septic tank. The ground water table was high in the area, and during the rainy season the septic tanks would frequently back up. Several local companies did a brisk business emptying overflowing septic tanks. Thinking back, I'm surprised Bebe didn't complain about the big step down from our nice new, comfortable home in La Mesa. If she was disappointed, she never let on.

While living in the duplex, we became acquainted with the Wydicks, who lived next door. Bebe and Cathy became good friends. They didn't have any kids, but soon Cathy became pregnant. According to Bebe's account, she thought it would be neat if they both went through a pregnancy together. So, as had been the case in the past, Bebe allowed herself to get pregnant without mentioning it to me. Once again, I felt rather left out, but I reasoned that if it made her happy, I would have no problem with another baby.

However, one problem I did have was tending Barb at night. Often she would wake up in the middle of the night and start fussing. Somehow, Bebe could sleep through it. I absolutely could not. Like any baby, she would go to sleep if we put her in bed with us, but we didn't think that was a suitable solution. Giving her a drink of water or juice would solve the problem for a while, but then she would begin fussing again. If we tried to ignore her, hoping she would eventually fall asleep, she would pull herself up by the bars in her crib and start shaking the lift gate to make a racket. All this shaking would eventually cause the latch to release, the gate would slide down, and Barb would tumble out onto the terrazzo, then serious crying would begin.

One night the racket started up. Bea was sleeping through it, as usual. While lying there, my mind took a diabolical twist. I began to consider spiking some orange juice for her. I calculated the ratio of her weight to mine; figured how much booze it took to give me a buzz; and divided the amount by the ratio. Then I maniacally made my way to the kitchen, where I prepared the concoc-tion—orange juice and vodka. With a twisted smile I carried it to the bedroom. Barb, like a good Irishman, chugged it down. I snuck back to bed and never heard another peep all night.

After several months of living in the miserable duplex, we decided to look for a more comfortable house. Many Convair employees were buying houses in a subdivision that Convair was subsidizing. The place was in Cocoa Beach on the Banana River and was called Convair Cove. I never considered living in Florida as a permanent thing, so decided to continue renting. After all, we were still making payments on one house in San Diego. However, the Wydicks did buy one of these and put in a swimming pool.

We found a small older frame house on Orlando Ave. It was only a block or so from the old duplex; however, it was insulated and much more comfortable. The floors were wood and it had awning windows. This was a big improvement over the jalousie windows in the duplex that leaked air like a sieve. In the winter it was snugly warm. During the summer it did a good job of keeping out the heat. Bebe liked the location because it was only a block and a half from the beach.

Cocoa Beach didn't have much to recommend it, but it did have a beautiful beach. The water was warm, rather like bath water. Of course the kids loved it. Bebe and the kids spent many pleasant days playing on the sand and in the surf. You could watch the pelicans fishing. They would skim across the water, spot a fish, rise into the air, and then dive headlong into the water. It seemed they never missed getting their fish.

Craig was born November 7, 1958 at Wuestoff Hospital in Rockledge (just south of Cocoa). Bebe's mom flew from Los Angeles to help with the new baby. Craig appeared to be a healthy baby, and I was happy to have a boy since our other two children were girls.

My mother planned a trip to visit us in Florida, and Bebe's sister Frances arranged to come with her. They came by Greyhound bus, my Mom's standard mode of travel. After visiting a month or so, Mom went to Wisconsin to visit her family. Frances stayed in Florida and got a job with Convair in the Logistics Department.

Then Bebe's brother John graduated from high school. He thought Florida sounded more exciting than the west coast, so he also decided to make the trip. He had a Volkswagen and drove cross-country almost non-stop. He got a job with Convair as a technician, working in my complex. That was convenient, since I could ride to work with him and Bebe could have our car.

John was an innovative guy. He became fascinated with rockets, and we decided to build some model rockets and launch them. In those days you couldn't go to a model shop and buy rocket kits. The only supplies available were a few small booklets on how to build the rocket motors. A solid rocket motor uses one piece of propellant called a "grain," and I knew of one company that sold tools for forming grains inside a heavy-walled cardboard tube.

I thought I knew enough about gunpowder and explosives to make the solid propellant, so John and I embarked on this endeavor. I would design and build the electrical launch control system. John would design and build the launcher. We would both build the rockets. The Atlas missile used a hold-down and release system. This intrigued John, and he wanted to incorporate one in his launcher.

Our first missile had two stages. The first stage was a cluster of four rockets; the second was a single rocket. We designed and built our own electric igniters. John wanted his hold-down and release system to release only if all four first stage engines were firing (similar to the Atlas). He planned to implement this by stretching a piece of small solder below where the flame from each rocket would exhaust. The heat would melt the solder, and when all four links melted, a relay would de-activate and cause the hold-down mechanism to release. Yeah, right!

On the big day of the launch we found an abandoned area next to the Banana River and set up our stuff. John's launcher was impressive—painted red and white to keep aircraft from running into it. It was about four feet high. We ran a multi-wire cable about 100 feet from the launch area to the control panel I had built. The control panel had arming-safing switches, a firing switch, lights, and even a countdown clock. We had even written a countdown procedure.

Stepping through the countdown like pros, John installed the solder links in the base of the launcher, installed the igniters in the booster engines, lowered the rocket down the tower to the firing platform, and then connected the igniters to the electrical firing circuits. After jogging back to the control panel where I was waiting, we continued the count until we got to the point for arming the igniters. After getting an "Arm" light, I pressed the "Fire" button. A roar and a big flash of light emanated from the launcher. Automatically, our heads turned upwards—these things travel fast—but there was no streak skyward. The four engines were burning furiously at the base of the tower; the hold-down hadn't released. After several seconds, the four boosters were expended. At that point the second stage ignited. With no hold-down mechanism to hold it back, it shot skyward, leaving its first stage behind.

We raced to the launch tower to see what had happened. After removing the first stage cluster, we could see that three of the four solder links had melted through, but the fourth link had a slight bow in it, allowing the jet flame to melt it only half way. Well, it wasn't what we planned, but it was fun and exciting. All in all, a bit childish for two grownups, I suppose. It was just our fantasy—a bit like old men playing with their model trains while wearing engineer's caps and red bandanas.

ATLAS AWAY—1957

Although all missile launches were secret, the launch schedule always managed to leak out. On launch day, many of the wives and kids would make a day of it at the beach. The press always got the word as well. People with binoculars would keep track of the countdown progress. The main cue was LO2 (liquid oxygen). When it was pumped aboard, it would cause frost to form and the upper half of the vehicle would turn white. A vent valve on the top of the missile released excess oxygen gas as it "boiled" off. This valve cycled open and closed to maintain proper tank pressurization, providing telltale wisps of vapor. Then, when they were ready to launch, the valve was closed. Everyone watched for this final disappearance of the vapor and would stand up to watch the show ("Go or blow," as we used to joke).

The Atlas was entirely different from any other missile ever built. It was a balloon made of thin stainless steel. The maximum thickness was only 40/1000 of an inch. It had no other structure or bracing to provide strength and maintain its shape. It had to be kept pressurized at all times or it would just collapse upon itself (like any balloon) into a heap of twisted sheet metal. For routine handling and testing, the tanks were pressurized to 30 pounds per square inch, but for flight the pressure was doubled to 60 pounds. At this flight pressure you could have taken a heavy ax and hit the tank as hard as possible and the ax would have just bounced off. It was an incredibly innovative idea to cut the missile's weight to an absolute minimum, thus providing greater range and payload.

Another unique Atlas innovation was the stage-and-a-half concept. All other long-range missiles depended upon staging (individual missiles stacked one above the other) to achieve altitude and distance objectives. Normally, missiles had two—but sometimes three—stages. The big disadvantage was that rocket engines were very difficult to start and get running properly. The second (and third) stages had to ignite in flight, where there was no second chance; many, many failed. However, the Atlas had two large booster engines (150,000 pounds thrust, each) and one sustainer engine (60,000 pounds thrust). All three were ignited on the ground where, if a problem developed they could be shut down, fixed and another attempt made. After two minutes of flight, enough fuel would have been burned so the heavy booster engines could be jettisoned, and the sustainer engine would be able to continue accelerating the missile alone.

The Germans, who had developed the V2, used graphite vanes in the rocket jet to provide thrust vector control. After the war, they came to this country and led the Army's missile effort in Huntsville, Alabama. They always employed this method. However, the German team was not involved on the Atlas because it was an Air Force project. The Atlas designers decided upon a new vector control concept. They would *gimbal* the engines. This would generate greater vector thrust, needed for larger missiles, than graphite vanes could provide. However, gimbaling did have one shortcoming: it could not provide roll control—only pitch and yaw. In the Atlas, this was solved by the use of two booster engines that could be gimbaled individually to provide the necessary differential roll vector. Fine, but after the two boosters were jettisoned and the missile was running on its sustainer engine, there would be no roll stabilization. This was solved by adding a small (1000 pound thrust) engine on each side of the missile body. These were called "vernier engines." As far as I know, Atlas is the only missile to have ever employed them.

Those days were fascinating. Everything was very, very secret. We were in a deadly race with the Soviet Union to develop long-range missiles with which to deliver nuclear warheads. Reliability was low. Probably half the missiles failed in some way. On June 11, 1957, our first Atlas (4-A) rose off the pad beautifully. When it got a few thousand feet up, something went wrong and one of the booster engines shut down. The missile tumbled end-over-end out of control. Since it was directly over the Cape, the Range Safety officer sent a destruct command. What a sight! An enormous blast of yellow flame threw thousands of shards of stainless steel (the missile's skin) everywhere. Some were several feet across, others only a few inches. We who were watching from the next pad over gazed in fascination at the shower of glittering pieces floating above us. Then, crash! One of the big pieces landed on the road between the blockhouse and the launch pad. That was too damned close. Those pieces were like razors and we realized we could be killed. Everyone dove for cover under cars in the parking lot.

Soon, crashing and clanking was occurring everywhere. It was several minutes before all the little pieces reached the ground.

From a bystander's point of view, that missile appeared to be a failure. However, in fact, it was considered a 90 percent success. Many of the new engineering concepts had proven to be valid. The launcher hold-down and release system worked perfectly. Fuel and LO2 turbines and tank pressurization worked as designed. The engines performed flawlessly (until the failure), but the most important validation was the ultra-light weight balloon tanks. Many missile engineers of the day believed a missile could not be constructed from a metal skin only 40/1000 of an inch thick. They reasoned that it would simply tear apart under the stresses and vibrations of flight.

Although I was not part of the launch team on that first Atlas from Pad 14, I was for the second shot. It was to be fired from the same Pad. I was assigned as the RF (radio frequency) engineer. My job was to check out the Azusa, Dovap, and the Range Safety Command systems; and then to man these system consoles from the blockhouse during countdown and launch. The Azusa and Dovap were tracking systems, and the Command System was a receiver coded to respond to commands from the Range Safety Officer. If the missile went off course, he would first send a command to shut down the engines, followed two seconds later by a command to destroy it.

The Atlas didn't have much ordnance capability on it. The main one was the Destruct System—the only one on the "A" series. It consisted of two small packages, each containing 1.25 pounds of C-4 Harrisite explosive. One was mounted on each side of the missile at the location where a bulkhead separated the LO2 tank above from the fuel tank below. When set off, it would rupture this bulkhead, allowing the two liquids to mix and explode. Since the Destruct System was controlled by "my" Range Safety Command System, I was assigned to be the Ordnance Engineer as well. Fine. I liked explosives.

Later, on the "B" series, jettison-able booster engines were added. This required a group of explosive bolts that held the booster engines to the main body. After about two minutes into the flight, the booster engines were shut down, the bolts blown, and the boosters jettisoned. On later "C" and "D" series, explosive bolts were used to hold the payload on the nose of the vehicle until re-entry was to begin, then the bolts were blown, allowing the re-entry vehicle (which eventually would contain the warhead) to separate from the missile body. To ensure ade-

quate separation, a final Ordnance System, consisting of two small solid propellant rockets (one on each side of the missile) were employed. They were mounted
to thrust upward to slow the missile, allowing it to back away from the re-entry
vehicle. These were called Retrorockets.

After three months of testing the components of the next Atlas (6-A) in the
hanger, it was finally taken to Pad 14 and erected for final checkout. On September 25, 1957, it also rose majestically into the air. Then, in an apparent duplica-
tion of the first flight, it began to tumble out of control. Again, the Range Safety
Officer pressed the destruct button and blew it to pieces. The only redeeming
thing for me was that my Range Safety Command System and Destruct package
had worked perfectly. No one rushed to pat me on the back for that.

What on earth had caused both missiles to fail in an apparently identical manner?
It turned out that the problem was with the missile's skirt. In the aft section, the
engines were surrounded by a honeycomb aluminum structure referred to as the
skirt. Its purpose was to protect the engines from flying debris, kicked up while
the engines were firing near the ground. However, the engineers in San Diego
finally realized that as the missile gained velocity upward, the skirt created a vacuum that drew hot exhaust gases up into the engine compartment. These hot
gases burned and charred critical engine control wiring, leading to the failures.
The fix was easy—just shorten the skirt. The mini-skirt ended such problems.

By now the second launch pad, Complex 13, was activated. Our launch crew was
assigned to it. The crew on Complex 14 and our crew alternated, firing the series
"A" Atlases—eight in all. Series "A" consisted of only short-range tests (about
500 miles), designed to verify the various systems. These did not include separation of the booster engines; that was planned for series "B."

NEAR DISASTER—1957

Back at the Cape, we were still having mixed feelings about the first two missiles
having to be destroyed after rising only a couple of thousand feet when it was
reported that photo analysis of both missile destructions showed that in each
case, only one of the two Destruct packages had exploded. Immediately, the
Range Safety people (who did not work for Convair) were all over us, particularly
focusing on me and Bill Brown, who was the RF & Ordnance engineer on Missile 4-A. They got Air Force authority to look through all of our procedures for

installing and testing the Destruct System, all of the inspector's records involved, Bill's notebooks and my notebooks, and they had interviews with anyone who could possibly shed light on the events. No procedural discrepancies were uncovered. Both Bill and I had witnessed personally the installation of the Destruct packages and the electrical checks performed on them. We were the ones who had switched the "Arm/Safe" switch to "Arm" in the blockhouse at T -2 minutes, and then verified that the indicator lights for both Destruct packages had switched to the "ARMED" position.

There certainly appeared to be a systemic problem, especially since the photos indicated the same Destruct packages (#2) failed on each flight. The San Diego engineers, convinced that the Destruct packages had armed properly, were concentrating their search into the firing circuits between the Range Safety Command unit and the Destruct packages. I couldn't imagine that being the problem, as these circuits had been checked dozens of times during the course of missile testing and launch preparation. Nothing had changed, except that during these tests a dummy Destruct package (one with no explosive in it) had been used.

It seemed to me that somehow the #2 Destruct packages might have been commanded to return to the "Safe" mode. But if that happened, I surely should have noticed the lights on the Blockhouse Control panel change from "Armed" (red) to "Safed" (green). Then I remembered a problem our launch control electrical engineers had experienced some weeks before with one of the umbilical connectors. Umbilical connectors are large, carrying over 100 circuits each. These provide connections between the missile and the ground launch control circuits prior to launch. Physically, the connectors are attached to the missile by a ball and detent mechanism that is released by an electrical command at lift-off, allowing the umbilicals to fall free.

The problem the electrical engineers had experienced was that one of the umbilicals had hung up during a test, and so had not disconnected completely. They concluded the reason for the hang-up was that the cable connected to it was very heavy and stiff, producing a binding force on the ball and detent mechanism. The problem was remedied by rerouting and supporting all umbilical cables to minimize such binding.

To me, a real clue for our problem was that when the partially ejected umbilical connector malfunction occurred, *some* of the circuits remained connected, due to the connector being cocked. *Wow!* I thought, *Maybe the umbilical pins were not all disconnecting at the same time, even during a normal disconnect.* I obtained electrical diagrams of the pin assignments for the Umbilical, through which the Destruct packages were controlled. Sure enough, the "Arm" and "Safe" commands were assigned to higher numbered pins, while the "talk-back" signals (those signals that indicated the actual position of the "Arm/Safe" mechanism) had been assigned to lower numbered pins. The lower numbered pins were above the ball and detent mechanism, which was located in the center of the connector, and the higher numbered pins, below. These talkback circuits were used not only to light the "Armed" and "Safed" indicator lights in the Blockhouse, but also to terminate the "Arm" or "Safe" command from the Blockhouse to the Destruct package.

I realized the talkback circuits were designed to terminate the "Arm/Safe" commands after the Destruct package had moved to the commanded position. However, it was never intended that the talkback circuits could ever operate the Destruct package's "Arm/Safe" mechanism. But if the Umbilical ejected at a cocked angle, the circuit logic would be altered momentarily, such that when the "Armed" talkback voltage disconnected it would allow the "Arm" relay to de-energize. This would cause a "Safe" command to be sent through the *still-connected* Umbilical "Arm/Safe" command pins to the Destruct package before the Umbilical completely disconnected.

As I pointed out before, engineers hate to have an outsider point out a problem in their design, but there could be no denying this circuit was the cause of the two Destruct packages not detonating. I called the San Diego design group with my analysis. Unenthusiastically, they said they would look into the matter. In less than 2 weeks we received EO's (Engineering Orders) from the San Diego design group to modify these circuits. The Range Safety Officer and his gang were relieved the problem had been resolved; they didn't want missiles buzzing around overhead that they couldn't destroy when they had a mind to.

By now the second launch pad, Complex 12, was activated, and our launch crew was assigned to it. Our first Missile was 10-A. It was to be the third Atlas launch, but it experienced an abnormal number of problems during checkout. As a result, Missile 12-A, being readied by Zane's crew on Complex 14, was launched first on December 17, 1958. We followed with 10-A on January 10, 1958. Both were successful.

INTER-MISSILE DIVERSIONS

The "A" series tests lasted from the summer of 1957 to the summer of 1958. During this period the crews had slack time between missile arrivals. They played cards frequently. Some played football on the grassy expanses of the complex. Others caught up on their reading. On one such occasion, my new junior RF engineer, Carl Combs, and I began making paper airplanes with a bent paper clip in the nose on which to hook a rubber band for launching. We continued improving the design and soon had these flying from one end of the small parking lot to the other. Another engineer, Bill Daley, became fascinated with our efforts. Now, Bill was known as "cheap." He carried his loose change in one of those little leather snap purses. He never gambled with playing cards, but Carl and I managed to taunt him into a bet. We said we would bet him 50 cents that we could launch one of our paper planes over the top of the launch tower. The tower was 125 feet high. Greed lit up in Bill's eyes; however, he wanted some ground rules. The rules were that the plane could be made only of paper; the hook could be made of metal, but just enough to support a stretched rubber band; the launcher must be made of rubber, and could be any size. The bet was on!

Carl and I folded a dart-like plane from a sheet of 11 x 14 inch paper and attached a heavy-duty paper clip, bent to form a hook, then, for the launcher we got a box of rubber bands from supply and daisy-chained them together until it was about four feet long. We were ready. By now, most of the crew had heard about the bet and followed us down to the launch pad to watch. Carl was a skinny guy, about six foot two. He would hold the rubber bands high between his outstretched hands. I would hold the plane, pulling it down and back to the ground. After taking careful aim, I released the plane. It soared skyward—white against the bright blue sky. It was going to be close. Bill's face became sullen, as he could see it might make it. It disappeared over the top of the gantry. Did it land on top, or go over? The crowd ran around to the other side, and there it was on the ground. It had made it, but just barely. There was a roar from the bystanders. Bill came over and ceremoniously unsnapping his leather purse, handed Carl and me each a quarter, then, with head drooping, he shuffled back to the Ready Room to nurse his financial loss.

PROJECT SCORE—1958

The U.S. was behind Russia in developing large missiles. Sputnik had demonstrated the U.S.S.R.'s capability, which proved to be an embarrassment to the U.S. The government wanted something to regain national prestige. Unbeknownst to any of the crew (even the Test Conductor, Curt Johnston), the Air Force and San Diego management had been approached by the government to fire Missile 10-B into orbit under the code name "Project Score." Only an essential few were told about it, and it remained an unbelievably well-kept secret. President Eisenhower gave his go-ahead for Project Score, on the condition that if it failed the world would not know about it. For cover, the shot was alleged to be an attempt to achieve a record-breaking flight to a target 7000 miles down-range.

The home operation in San Diego sent a crew of technicians to install some special instrumentation. This was not a particularly unusual practice, since the Atlas was reaching altitudes that could provide needed research. To avoid interference with normal operations, these efforts were often assigned to third shift. However, in this case, many mysterious things began to occur. For example, one day while making some last minute checks on my RF (radio frequency) systems, I noted a gold-plated box mounted in one of the missile's equipment pods. It had several coaxial cables connected to it. I traced the cables to antennas that were not a normal part of the missile. In my mind I wondered, *Why gold-plated? Nothing else in the vehicle is. Why does it need antennas? What is it for?*

Another suspicious thing was that the missile had been shipped from San Diego without the usual blunt nose cone and the re-entry separation system (explosive bolts for detaching the payload, and the small retro-rockets). Since these items were in my area of responsibility, I asked Curt Johnston what was going on. He claimed he didn't know. (He actually didn't; he was not in on the secret.) He checked with Travis Malloy, the Chief Test Conductor, who was one of only three Convair employees at the Cape who knew about the true mission. Malloy, not wanting suspicions to build, agreed with Johnston that the mission needed a regular nose cone and a re-entry vehicle separation system. This was a lie, of course. He then gave Johnston orders to proceed with installation of these items—total subterfuge.

Since these were my sub-systems, I got the job of designing and installing the components: explosive bolts, retro-rockets, a control box, and necessary wiring. It was all for show to convince the Complex 11 launch crew that this was a standard full-range shot. Believing the Air Force had changed its mind about the mission, I proceeded to design, install, and test a re-entry separation system.

On the morning of the launch, December 18, 1958, I went to the launch tower to make my routine physical checks of the missile's equipment pods. They were all sealed up! Normally they were sealed after the system engineers completed their final inspections. Now I was suspicious. Apparently, the technicians that had been brought in from San Diego to install the gold plated equipment, antennas, etc. had made more changes during the night and sealed their work from view. Immediately, I headed for the shop that was located in the base of the launch pad. I asked the technicians, "Who sealed the pods?" No one knew. All they knew was the San Diego technicians had worked the third shift; it must have been them. One of the techs whispered to me to follow him. He led me to some stacks of boxes. Hidden behind the stack was the Azusa transponder I had previously installed to track the missile. The transponder had been removed from the equipment pod on the missile and hidden prior to sealing the pods for flight.

I raced back up to the missile. Sure enough, the retro-rockets had been removed. I climbed the last flight of stairs to look at the re-entry vehicle. The standard blunt warhead had been replaced by a long pointed cone (like an inverted ice cream cone). Hell, even someone as naive and easily duped as I could now see this baby was destined to go into orbit. Things were getting exciting.

In those days, any attempt to put an Atlas into orbit would require stripping it of all unessential equipment and hardware to minimize weight. But how could they ever launch the missile without an Azusa? Azusa was the primary, absolute-must-have system for Range Safety tracking. The Range Safety Officer would never let them launch without one. Right? Wrong! Later, during the countdown when the Azusa System was to be given its final check, the Azusa ground station reported they couldn't get a signal from the missile. After some frantic rechecking, they announced over the net, "No Azusa response from Atlas 10-B at Pad 11." My engineer, Jim Harrington, was operating the RF Systems console in the Blockhouse. He reported the "failure" to the Test Conductor, Curt Johnston, who promptly contacted the Range Safety Officer. Everyone on the net was stunned when the Range Safety officer said "We'll go without Azusa. Radar will be the primary tracking system." He was in on the ruse, too.

Normally, on a full-range shot such as this was supposed to be, the tanks would contain slightly more propellants than required to reach the target. During flight, the ground-based guidance system would track the vehicle, constantly calculating the impact point based upon its current velocity. When the proper velocity was attained, a signal would be sent to the missile to shut down its sustainer engine. This signal was known as Mark V. However, to achieve orbit it would be necessary to burn every drop of fuel available. For this shot, the tanks would be loaded with all the propellants they could hold, and there would be no Mark V signal sent.

Since President Eisenhower had made it clear that if the missile didn't attain orbit (or otherwise failed), it was not to appear as another embarrassing "space failure"—just a routine ICBM test shot. Therefore, one additional deception had to be implemented. Another of my engineers, Jim Starkey, was given the assignment, without explanation of course, to sit in the basement of the Blockhouse during the countdown. He was given a small cable with a switch attached to the end. At exactly the time during the flight when a Mark V signal would be expected, he was to press the switch. The cable had been jury-rigged to one of the blockhouse consoles to light the Mark V indicator. When illuminated, the console operator would announce "Mark V" over the net, completing the illusion of a normal flight.

Everything went like clockwork. The entire missile (less the booster engines, of course), weighing 8750 pounds, went into orbit. It was a marvelous accomplishment. The vehicle could easily be seen from the ground at night as it passed overhead. The crowning achievement occurred when a radio command was sent to the vehicle to begin a broadcast of a prerecorded tape carried in the gold-plated box I had spotted. It was a message from President Eisenhower:

"This is the President of the United States speaking. Through the marvels of scientific advance, my voice is coming to you from a satellite circling in outer space. My message is a simple one. Through this unique means, I convey to you and to all mankind, America's wish for peace on earth and good will toward men everywhere."

It was the Christmas season, and the transmissions became known as Eisenhower's Christmas Message. Project Score had been a total success; it made Sputnik appear puny. After almost 500 revolutions around the earth, Atlas 10-B plunged into the Pacific Ocean on January 21, 1959.

One of my engineer friends, Jim Brown, thought the occasion deserved a memento. This was during the early days, when space souvenir pins, photos and documents had not yet come into being. Jim convinced me that he and I should design a "frameable" document to commemorate the occasion. We went to a print shop in Cocoa and eventually emerged with a suitable design. All the launch crew, the 18 engineers who were responsible for testing and launching the missile, signed it and we had copies printed for the entire launch team. In the years following, NASA picked up on the idea and began printing similar documents to honor their various space achievements. But ours was the first!

THE LO2 TANKING INCIDENT—1958

Every Atlas missile was subjected to a static firing to prove out the propulsion system, and to validate its many systems prior to launch. A static firing was conducted exactly like a launch, except that the hold-down and release mechanism was not released. The engines were shut down after having been fired for a specific number of seconds. The recorded data was then closely examined to verify proper engine performance before the missile was committed to launch.

At each launch complex, RP-1 fuel (refined kerosene) was stored in a large tank on the east side of the launcher. Liquid oxygen (LO2) was stored as far as possible from the fuel on the west side of the launcher in a large Dewar tank. A Dewar is a dual-walled vessel with a vacuum in the space between the walls. It's exactly like a thermos bottle, except it's made of steel instead of glass. These tanks were about the size of railroad tank cars. It required several loads from tanker trucks to fill them. A concrete and earthen barrier was located between the LO2 storage tank and the launcher. This barrier seemed to me to be totally unnecessary, since liquid oxygen cannot explode unless mixed with some kind of fuel. The engineers who designed these things weren't stupid, but they certainly didn't have the intimate knowledge of explosives as I had acquired from having built bombs as a kid.

One day at Complex 11, the LO2 storage tank was being filled by a series of tanker trucks. One had parked next to the storage tank and the driver was in the process of transferring his load into the storage tank's interface plumbing. Although this was a somewhat hazardous procedure, the rules only required unauthorized personnel to remain 100 feet away, and of course no smoking. I happened to be in the technician's shop, located under a concrete ramp that led up to the launcher, and the earthen barrier prevented me from seeing the filling operation. I heard someone yell, "Fire in the LOX area." (At that time, they were still using the obsolete expression "LOX" instead of "LO2" for liquid oxygen). The truck driver didn't have enough presence of mind to shut off his pump or close the valve. When he saw smoke, he just panicked and ran for his life up the road to the blockhouse. I have never seen grown men so terrorized. Technicians and engineers were running in all directions like a disorganized stampede.

The perimeter of each launch complex was marked by a single-lane road and a chain-link fence that formed a circle around the complex. This circle had a radius of about 300 yards from the launcher in the center and it included the block-house. Well, most of these crazed men were running east (away from the LO2 storage tank). When the technicians and engineers got to the fence, some of them attempted to climb over. It was topped with three strands of barbed wire. A few made it, but cut themselves doing so. The rest dug under the fence in several places, which made more sense because Florida is just sand. Most kept going till they got to the beach. Then they walked over to the adjoining launch complex, Complex 12, and eventually crossed a field separating the two complexes, ending up at the Complex 11 blockhouse. Here, they and those from the nearby Ready Room took refuge to wait for what they thought would be the inevitable blast.

Not a soul was left in the launch area except me. Smoke was beginning to rise above the earthen barrier, but I couldn't see the source. Knowing the risk was minimal and wanting to get a better view, I made my way to the launcher. There I climbed the ladder to the level of the transfer table upon which the service tower sat. The transfer table was a heavy steel structure used to carry the service tower back to a storage area when the missile was ready to be launched. I reasoned that even if I were wrong and some sort of an explosion occurred, I could just duck under this massive structure. From there I could see the truck, but not the LO2 Dewar tank. The truck had caught fire, probably when the pump motor over-heated. By now the truck's engine was burning. Apparently, the driver was new at his job, as LO2 was spilling out of the transfer hose connection that was improperly secured. Over the next half hour or so some small explosions occurred as gasoline from the engine spilled on to the ground and mixed with the LO2. The spillage of LO2 fueled the fire, and soon the whole front of the truck was ablaze. Now everything that was combustible was exploding like so many homemade bombs. Even the front tires, as they melted from the heat, mixed with the LO2 and made fair-sized bangs.

Back at Blockhouse 11, the frightened occupants were taking turns watching the show through four periscopes. Some actually believed the LO2 tank could blow up like a small atom bomb. Then one of the observers spotted me. Immediately, they decided that I was stranded and that I had to be rescued. The launch pad safety representative was "volunteered" for the job. He had a small truck, fitted with flashing red lights. They opened the blockhouse door (the big steel vault type) just enough to let him out. He dashed to his truck and soon was on the perimeter road, with red light flashing and siren blaring. I watched him circle the complex, totally ignorant of what he was doing. Then he approached the launcher from the east and frantically waved at me to come down to the truck. I'm a bit slow, but I finally figured out that he was rescuing me, so I climbed down and let him take me around the perimeter road to the blockhouse. Here they had opened the vault door a crack so we could slip in, and then shut it securely behind us. People rushed up to ask me if I had been terrified. They thought I was crazy when I said I wasn't—that I was just enjoying the show. The rest were making a hero of the pad safety representative for risking his life to save me.

The fire did get worse; it certainly got a lot hotter. The outside steel wall of the Dewar got so hot that the vacuum caused it to collapse inward, leaving a large depression. Later inspection determined it was still functional, so the tank was never replaced, thus it provided a permanent marker of the near disaster (ha!) that day.

PROJECT MERCURY

The Russians had been testing their Vostok capsule, beginning with its first unmanned launch in April 1961. It was apparent to U.S. planners that the Vostok was being developed to put a man into space. The U.S. was attempting to beat the Russians to this goal with its own manned program: Project Mercury.

Both countries wanted desperately to seize this prize for nationalistic propaganda. The Russians intended the Vostok program to establish the viability of their booster and space capsule using dogs and instrumentation. All their tests were to be orbital. The U.S. approach was more conservative. It was to send animals and men into sub-orbital flights and follow those with launches into full orbit. The sub-orbital flights would use Mercury capsules atop Army Redstone missiles. The full orbit flights were to use the same type Mercury capsules boosted by Air Force Atlas missiles.

The Air Force decided that Mercury-Atlas, as well as other "Space" shots, would be launched from Complex 14. Our crew was selected to perform these launches, so we were moved from Complex 11 to Complex 14.

BIG JOE—1959

An early concern in the Mercury program was to prove the feasibility of an ablation type heat shield. A safe mission absolutely depended on such a shield protecting the capsule from burning up, due to the atmospheric friction of re-entry, therefore one of the early development tests was to demonstrate this capability. The test was called "Big Joe."

Big Joe consisted of a Mercury boilerplate capsule (stripped down version) on top of an Atlas booster. The Atlas guidance program was modified to fly a normal apogee, then to nose over and accelerate the capsule to a velocity equal to re-entry from orbit. The Re-entry System was then to separate the capsule from the Atlas, after which it would orient itself for its re-entry plunge.

Big Joe was launched September 9, 1959. The flight was going perfectly, then a voice came over the net, saying "We have no indication of booster separation." Good grief! Booster separation was one of *my* systems. A chill ran up my spine; however, I could do nothing but wait until after the flight when we could look at the telemetry records.

In a normal Atlas flight, the booster engines are shut down after about two minutes of flight, then the latching bolts that hold the booster engine assembly to the missile are unlatched by ordnance; finally, the missile accelerates away from the booster assembly (in effect jettisoning it). For the remaining three minutes, the sustainer and vernier engines provide thrust that continues to accelerate the missile.

A few hours later, when the telemetry records became available, several people, including myself, went over the data with a fine-toothed comb. The booster cut-off signal had been commanded, and the booster engines had shut down. A command had been sent to the booster separation system, but separation had not occurred. That's all the telemetry could tell us. It looked bad for me.

The next day a team of investigators descended on Complex 14, and particularly on me. They wanted to see all our procedures and the inspection records for installing the booster latch ordnance and for connecting the circuits. After reviewing these documents, they interviewed everyone involved: the responsible engineer (me), the technicians who performed the hook-ups, and the inspectors who witnessed each step. They found no discrepancies, which didn't make them happy, as they were there to ferret out whoever screwed up.

Then word came from the Project Office that NASA considered the flight as a total success. It seemed that the weight of the attached booster engines fooled the guidance system into causing the missile to travel in a higher arc than programmed. As a result, the capsule re-entered at a greater velocity than expected. The capsule's heat shield had survived 10,000 degrees Fahrenheit—considerably more than planned. NASA was jubilant. Now the pressure was off. However, the question of what happened still remained, so on the next several launches we added a number of telemetry measurements to attempt to pinpoint the problem, should it recur. It never did.

Nevertheless, I was still embarrassed by the whole episode. I spent hours mulling over the schematics and wiring diagrams of the separation circuits. Finally, a possibility occurred to me that could explain the failure. Each of the ordnance-operated latches had a positive and a negative terminal that was connected to an igniter inside. All ten of the latches were located around the circumference of the missile and were wired in parallel. The designers in San Diego had attempted to provide redundancy to the system by completing the circuit in a full circle, such that if a connection were somehow broken or missing, current to fire the ordnance beyond the break would come around the circle from the other direction. However, if a technician cross-wired any of the connections during installation, this hook-up would result in a short circuit and *none* of the ordnance would fire.

That had to be it, I reasoned. If the full-circle redundancy feature had not been employed, cross-wiring a connection would not have mattered. As a result, it had not been considered as something to prevent. I knew the design group in San Diego would never be willing to give up the redundancy feature. That left me with only the option to change the installation procedure to ensure that cross wiring wouldn't occur. I proposed that each positive-voltage wire's segments involved be marked with Glyptal, a reddish colored varnish used by inspectors, to identify the positive wires. The idea was adopted at all the launch pads.

However, when the designers recognized that we had discovered the cause of the separation failure, they elected to redesign the electrical harness such that it would no longer be possible to cross-wire the connections. Of the hundreds of Atlases flown over the years, the booster separation system never failed again.

OTHER MERCURY ACTIVITY

Concurrently, other unmanned test flights were being conducted at Wallops Station, Virginia (to verify the escape, landing and recovery systems) and at the Atlantic Missile Range (AMR) from the Army's Redstone Complex, and at our Complex 14.

One of these unmanned tests was Mercury 2, launched on January 31, 1961, atop a Redstone Missile. It contained a chimpanzee, Ham. The next flight was to be manned by Alan Shepard. However, Mercury 2 flew higher than expected and its heat shield was lost after splashdown. NASA, being very conservative, elected to fly another unmanned test, Mercury 2A, to verify that all problems were corrected. It was launched on March 24, 1961.

Then the worst possible news for the U.S. was heard. The Russians announced they had successfully put a man, Yuri Gagarin, into a single earth orbit on April 12, 1961, and had recovered him safely.

The irony was, had it not been for NASA's conservativeness, the U.S. could have put Alan Shepard into space, even if just a sub-orbit, in March, and beaten the Russians with a man in space.

Shepard finally flew in Freedom 7 ("7" for the seven astronauts) on May 5, 1961, followed by Gus Grissom in Liberty Bell 7 on July 21, 1961. Both were sub-orbital flights using Redstone boosters. Grissom's Liberty Bell 7 capsule sank because of the hatch blowing open. Grissom swore in later investigations that he had not operated the hatch-blowing switch.

The U.S.S.R. launched a second manned capsule, Vostok 2, on August 6, 1961. It orbited the earth 17 times. The passenger, Gherman Titov, was recovered safely. The Russians had established a commanding lead in space. A step forward for the U.S. was made when our crew launched Mercury 5 containing a chimpanzee, Enos, into orbit November 29, 1961. The flight was planned to be three orbits, but control problems caused the flight to be shortened to two orbits.

FRIENDSHIP 7—1962

[Caution—Name drop ahead]

Finally, we had Mercury/Atlas 5 ready atop an Atlas missile designed to put a man into orbit. The astronaut would be John Glenn, who chose the name "Friendship 7" for his capsule. NASA, still nervous about manned launches, decided the Atlas launch crew might take matters more seriously if we got personally acquainted with the astronauts, so on several occasions, the astronauts were brought to our Ready Room (engineering office) for casual get-togethers. Here, we were allowed to ask questions about themselves and their Mercury capsule. In turn, they would ask us questions about the Atlas systems and about testing procedures. At the end of the sessions, NASA provided some 8 x 10 prints of space subjects, which we could have autographed by the astronauts.

At the first meeting, Alan Sheppard sat for a while, fidgeted, and paid little attention to what was going on. He was obviously bored. After a bit he got up, and without comment, just walked out. He never returned to any of the later meetings. On one occasion I asked John Glenn why the Mercury capsule was painted black. He thought for a few seconds and finally answered, "Damned if I know." Scott Carpenter (the backup astronaut for Glenn) offered the theory that it would absorb and radiate heat better than a shiny surface could.

I liked Scott Carpenter the best. When asked to autograph a picture, he would inquire about the person to whom it was to be given and would add some original words above his signature. I gave most of these pictures to members of the family.

I don't know whether the astronauts gained confidence in the launch crew or whether any of the launch crew became more conscientious about their work because of these meetings. As for me, I was sobered by seeing and talking to the guys who were actually going to sit atop that enormous "bomb." If it were to blow up, it would have been about 100,000 times more powerful than the biggest bomb I had ever built as a kid.

Pre-launch preparations and systems checkouts had proceeded smoothly. Now the day of launch was here. It was February 20, 1962. I went to the pad to personally observe the installation of the Destruct packages. I had seen it all before, but something was eerie about watching the technician remove the green "dummy" Destruct packages used for testing and replacing them with the bright red packages containing live detonators and explosive. After that installation, I carefully watched the electrical hookup of the ten ordnance devices that would cause the booster engine assembly to jettison. Finally, I climbed up several decks in the service tower to witness installation of the two retro-rockets and the separation system connections.

As I walked back to the blockhouse, I had a mild anxiety attack—that "elevator falling" feeling in the pit of your stomach. That had never happened to me on any of the previous launches; this was different. In the blockhouse I took my station at the RF (radio frequency) console. This console contained the switches to arm and safe the Destruct package. It also contained indicator lights for verifying that the range safety commands (sent by radio link) were received and decoded properly. In flight these would be sent by the range safety officer if the vehicle went off course (as happened on the first two Atlas flights). The console also contained four voltmeters with which to monitor the telemetry batteries. The telemetry system ran off independent batteries, so it would continue to operate in the event of missile power loss.

The missile had already been loaded with fuel. This was not considered hazardous, since it was just refined kerosene. Next, the NASA van carrying John Glenn drove to the bottom of the launch pad where there was an elevator. After ascending to the top deck, he was helped into the cramped capsule and hooked up. After closing and sealing the hatch, the NASA and McDonnell Aircraft technicians cleared the pad.

The service tower was moved from around the missile back to a parking area. Everyone was cleared from the pad. By now we (the launch crew) were all inside the blockhouse. The enormous bank-vault-like doors were closed and bolted, sealing us in. Next, LO2 tanking was begun. This was a very hazardous operation. The top half of the missile became white with frost from the sub-zero temperature of the cryogenic LO2.

After tanking was complete, last minute operations were performed by countdown, such as switching the missile to internal power, verifying flight pressurization, topping off the boiled-away LO2, and making final checks of telemetry. The count ticked down to T -2 minutes. Here I switched the Destruct packages to "ARM." The two indicators for "Safed" extinguished and the two red "Armed" lights lit. Not hearing an explosion, I relaxed a bit. In the remaining two minutes

I had no further operations except to monitor the voltmeters. They looked fine. I peeked across the room to the Astronaut Medical console. It had a display of Glenn's pulse. I thought his was quite low, so I compared it with mine. His was 100 to 105; mine was over 120. He was sitting on top of a couple hundred thousand pounds of high explosive. I was 800 feet away from the vehicle and protected by a ten-foot thick shell of reinforced concrete. I concluded we had one cool cat out there.

Then, over the net came the voice of the Test Conductor, Tom O'Malley. "T-18 seconds and counting, vernier engines start." At that moment, he pressed a button on his console, and everything from that point on became controlled automatically. The two vernier engines ignited, but we couldn't hear them from inside the blockhouse. Then, after about 10 seconds, the sustainer and the two booster engines fired up. We could hear them! The missile was being held down to the launcher by the 5000-PSI pneumatic hold-down and release mechanism.

During this last ten seconds, the senior propulsion engineer scanned his instruments for any indication of engine mal-operation. If he observed low thrust or rough combustion he would yell, "Engine shutdown" on the net. The Test Conductor would respond by hitting a large red button on his console, shutting down all the engines. The Test Conductor also had an "Abort" button. If the Atlas caught fire, began loosing pressurization, or otherwise became unstable, he could press it and the Mercury capsule would have been pulled free of the Atlas by its launch escape rocket to an altitude sufficient to allow its parachute to deploy.

Everything went perfectly, and at T-0 the umbilical cables fell free and the hold-down and release system rotated back its giant heads, releasing the missile from the launcher. Slowly, Mercury-Atlas 6 lifted into the air, and over the net came the words "May the Wee Ones be wich ya, John." It was Tom O'Malley, with his notorious Irish brogue.

The launch and boost into orbit were successful, as were the three revolutions in orbit. However, while John and his ground controllers were preparing for re-entry, a panel light in the capsule indicated one of the heat shield attachments was loose. This was a serious matter! If the heat shield came off during re-entry, certainly the capsule would burn up. After some hasty consideration, the ground controllers decided not to jettison the capsule's retro-rockets after they had fired, as was planned. The retro-rocket package was located under the heat shield and held in place by three straps. Normally, after firing, these straps and the retro-rockets are jettisoned. In this emergency, they would be retained, hoping they could hold the heat shield in place, at least until the retro hardware burned up. However, a significant risk was that the retro-rockets might damage the heat shield as the rockets burned and melted away.

There seemed to be no other options, so John was notified of the decision. When the time came for re-entry, John maneuvered the capsule into the proper orientation (heat shield facing forward), and the retro-rockets were fired. As instructed, John did not jettison them. As the capsule entered the atmosphere, the temperature increased until the retro-rocket package burned off. John could see the glowing pieces of metal fly past his window. The heat shield wasn't damaged, re-entry was successful, and John and the capsule were recovered successfully. Later investigation revealed that the heat shield was not actually unlatched. The problem was just a faulty indicator circuit.

The flight was headline news at the time. America had finally put a man into orbit and successfully returned him to earth. At that time, it was the high point of my career. However, the jubilation was very much dampened by the fact that the Russians had soundly beaten us in this endeavor. My attention now turned to the speech President Kennedy made back in May 1961, in which he committed the U.S. to send a man to the moon in this decade. Now that seemed like a real challenge. I wanted to be a part of it. The project was called Apollo.

North American Aviation in Downey, California had received the contract from NASA to build the Apollo spacecraft. This was only a stone's throw from Bell Gardens, where Bebe's parents lived, so I had no difficulty selling her on my changing jobs and returning to California. I contacted North American, who made an offer that I accepted. In short order we were packed up and on our way back to the West Coast.

_____STALKING THE MOON

✦

Back in California
North American Aviation
The Apollo Spacecraft
Every Silver Lining Has a Cloud—1962–65
Marital Metamorphosis
Flip Side
The Schism
Merritt Island Launch Area (MILA)
My Job
Locking Horns—1964
Moving on
The Accident
A Wounded Animal
Rolling Over
A Sighting
The Saturn-5/Apollo Spaceship

BACK IN CALIFORNIA

[1]In 1962 I left the Convair Company and began working for North American Aviation, who had just won a contract to support the NASA Apollo Program. North American was based in Downey, so we temporarily moved back to California. We bought a new 1962 Chevy—nothing fancy, just wheels—and then began looking for a place to rent. That wasn't easy. Everything near the Downey plant was unavailable or too expensive. We kept looking eastward to find something affordable, and finally came across a nice house in Buena Park near Knott's Berry Farm. It was about a 14-mile drive to work, but an easy drive on the freeways.

Our furniture arrived almost immediately, and we settled in. We entered Audrey and Barbara into school, but Craig, being only four, stayed home. The Warings were glad to see us, even though we had left three of their kids in Florida. Those three had married and they were firmly planted there. My mom was still living in our old house in Montebello Park. I'm sure she was glad to have us back in Los Angeles. Florida is a long way off when you travel by bus, as she did. Also, I believe she was happy that I would be nearby to help her keep the old house in repair. Shirley's husband, Leon, had been stuck with this thankless task until they moved to Banning.

When we first returned to California, Bebe and I had hoped we could be transferred back to the Cocoa Beach area as we had done before with Convair. This was always in the back of my mind, and I was still hoping the opportunity would arise. Eventually, I managed to negotiate a transfer to the Launch Operations group. It would be moving people to Florida later in the year.

However, as matters between us worsened, I began entertaining thoughts of a separation, or even a divorce. The time for the transfer was less than six months off. I decided I had to make a decision soon. I felt very anxious, and my thought processes were circular and confused. I knew I was too miserable to stay in the marriage as it was, and I didn't know any way to repair it. In addition, I anguished about the kids being adversely affected by a divorce.

---

1.   There appears to be a question whether the year was 1960 or 1962. The chapter titled "A Chronology of Whereabouts and Travels" indicates that it was 1960.

One day at work, while doing research in the company library, I happened across some monthly journals of *The American Psychiatric Association*. In one of them I found an article that discussed divorce and its psychological consequences. I labored through the article, which contained a lot of terms I wasn't familiar with, but I was able to understand their conclusion regarding the effect of divorce on children. It stated that most children are not emotionally scarred by amicable separations and divorces. This being particularly true when neither parent attempts to set the children against the other parent and the children are allowed regular visits with the absent parent. But most importantly, it said great harm might be done to children who are trapped in a dysfunctional family devoid of love and filled with hostility.

This resolved the most important of my concerns: how the children would be affected. I knew breaking up the marriage and leaving the kids would cause me a lot of emotional distress, but I reasoned I could cope and eventually recover. I decided divorce was the only real solution. The next step was to discuss the matter with Bebe. Much to my surprise, she was amenable to the idea. Apparently, she had been entertaining similar thoughts. Her main demand was that she keep the kids. I readily agreed, because I knew she was a good mother and could do a much better job than I could do.

NORTH AMERICAN AVIATION

I had decided to leave the Convair Company and take a position with North American Aviation, who had just won a contract to support the NASA Apollo Program. This necessitated our temporarily moving back to California since North American was based in Downey. They had initiated a large expansion effort to support the new contract, and things were chaotic. Dozens of new people were being hired every day. Spaces between buildings were being filled with portable offices. I was located in one of them, and I was assigned to the Ground Operations Support System Group. This group would eventually be assigned to various tracking stations around the world. This wasn't exactly what I had planned on, but because of the organizational confusion, I decided to stay put for the time being, although I was eager to get back to the excitement of launching manned space flights in Florida.

I became totally immersed in my work. At that time, the Apollo spacecraft was just a set of specifications. There were no blueprints yet, let alone hardware. I was soon sought after by several of the design groups because of my experience at Cape Canaveral. They knew nothing about Cape operations, especially regarding Range regulations and procedures. I was the only new employee, so far, who had actually worked at the Cape. A couple of North American old-timers had worked on the Hound Dog and Navaho programs in Florida, but they seemed to be hidden in the woodwork.

My experience on the Mercury Program was especially valuable, since it was the first manned spaceflight program. On several occasions I was invited to give talks to groups of designers and managers on how the Cape's Range Safety, Pad Safety, and Vehicle Launch Escape systems were implemented. I'm a nervous and reluctant public speaker, but my experience in Japan as an instructor was helpful.

I became accepted as a de facto expert on matters pertaining to Cape operations, and soon found myself being asked to review designs for various Avionics (onboard electronics) and their checkout equipment. A desperate need for this firsthand kind of information existed in the early days of the Apollo Program. Eventually, the design groups developed official channels through NASA for such information. Nevertheless, I believe my efforts helped get the electronic design ball rolling, probably several months sooner than otherwise would have been expected.

It was during this period of time, 1962–'63, that Bebe and I were divorced and that I moved from California back to Florida to work on the Apollo Program.

THE APOLLO SPACECRAFT

It was an absolutely fabulous vision—men traveling to the moon and back—and to enter into a race with the Soviet Union to accomplish such a feat first made it all the more exciting. The pride of the country, as well as its military prowess, was at stake. Wow! I was eager to participate.

The original concept for the spacecraft was a single vehicle that would be boosted by an enormous rocket to the moon. There it would settle into a lunar orbit, descend to the moon's surface and land. When ready to return to earth, it would fire its engines to achieve trans-earth flight, where it would enter earth orbit. The manned capsule would make a fiery descent back to earth for an ocean recovery as the Mercury and Gemini capsules had done.

The heavy thrust engines on the spacecraft were planned to be solid propellant, because designers still were uneasy about starting liquid engines in flight. Since solid propellant engines can't be throttled or turned off and on, it was planned that they be fired in clusters to produce just the amount of acceleration needed for various phases of the mission.

This method of achieving such a mission had a poor probability of success. Eventually, the advocates for liquid propulsion prevailed. Additionally, since having the entire spacecraft descend to the moon's surface would require a much larger booster rocket, a radical refinement was approved in which a smaller vehicle, the Lunar Excursion Module (LEM), would descend to the surface, while the main spacecraft (Apollo) remained in lunar orbit.

Now it was settled and the design phase began. The Apollo spacecraft would carry three men. It would have a Service Module attached which contained a liquid propellant engine for trans-lunar and trans-earth flight. A second spacecraft, the LEM, would allow two men to descend to the moon, while the third man baby-sat the Apollo "mother-ship." After lunar exploration was complete, the LEM (which was supplied with its own liquid fueled engine) would lift off from the moon's surface, then rendezvous and dock with the Apollo. The LEM would then be jettisoned. Next, the Service Module engine would be fired to provide trans-earth trajectory. On approaching the earth, the Service Module engine would be fired again to slow the craft into earth orbit. Once that was achieved, the Service Module engine would be fired for a final time to slow the craft down for re-entry into the earth's atmosphere. The Service Module would then be jettisoned and the Apollo capsule would hopefully make a controlled re-entry to be recovered at sea.

EVERY SILVER LINING HAS A CLOUD—1962– 65

I have struggled with whether to go into Bebe's and my marital troubles in this book. But since these problems culminated in a divorce, which certainly had an important effect on our lives, as well as our children and families, I feel they should be included. I hope to present the matter in a balanced manner, but such occurrences always involve strong emotions, so this will likely contain some of my biases. I hope that when Bebe writes her autobiography, she will include her perspectives on the matter.

I no longer believe that marital discord, separation, and divorce are necessarily a matter of one party or the other being wronged. Although this may be true in some cases, I am convinced that it wasn't in ours. Unfortunately, religion and the prevailing social mores and laws assumed that at least one of the parties must have done something morally or legally wrong. For that reason, it required one party to sue the other for divorce.

Our marriage had trouble during the time we lived in San Diego. However, after we moved to Florida in 1957, our situation improved (at least from my perspective), to the extent that I felt things had worked themselves out and the marriage was doing well. Actually, I remember this time (1957–62) as the best years of our marriage, and I have many fond memories of that period.

MARITAL METAMORPHOSIS

Upon our return to California in 1960, everything seemed OK at first. We lived in a nice house and the girls were in school much of the day. Craig, born in Florida on November 9, 1958, was long out of diapers and wasn't a big burden, and Bebe's parent's lived only 20 minutes away. I was in a carpool, so that provided Bebe with wheels on most days. She visited her mom frequently. Some of her younger sisters—Pam, Georgie, and Rita—were still living at home and they helped her take care of the kids. Another sister, Catherine Bell (Cassy), had married a fellow named Eddie Brock. They lived nearby in Garden Grove, so this provided another family member she could visit.

On many weekends we visited Bebe's parents. Her dad, "Chick," and I were good friends. Bebe's mom, Helen, was involved in church, family and shopping, but she seemed to like me and we got along fine. Whenever our family decided to spend the day visiting her parents, I would stop by the liquor store and buy a fifth of Ancient Age, Chick's favorite, and some Seven-up. We would all get a buzz and have an excellent time. Bebe's mom always urged me to drink enough to "loosen my tongue." I have no idea what secrets she thought I kept, but she seemed to believe liquor could pry them from me.

Several of Bebe's mom's relatives (the Ryan side of the family) lived in the Los Angeles area. I remember four of Bebe's aunts and their families. Also, Bebe's maternal grandfather had married twice. His second wife, now a widow, and her two kids, Bill and Patricia, lived just down the street from Bebe's parents. Even though Pat was Bebe's aunt, she was the same age as Bebe, and they had attended school together. On any given Sunday, one or more of these families might drop by the Waring house to visit.

The Waring house was small, probably 700-800 square feet. Chick had built it himself in the early 30's. They were a Catholic family, and soon it was overflowing with kids: nine in all. The picture I am trying to paint is that this home was teeming with life. On weekends, usually at least one other family was visiting the old homestead. Often Bebe and I with our kids, and sometimes one of the other families as well, were visiting there. I can't imagine where everybody sat. I enjoyed these cramped get-togethers, and felt accepted by everyone.

FLIP SIDE

[2]While living in Downey and working for North American, my job involved taking frequent business trips, sometimes to Houston, where NASA was headquartered, but mostly to the Cape. In the early days, while I was assigned to the Ground Operation Support System, I frequently traveled with my lead engineer, Charlie Ackerman. He was an outgoing, friendly guy, married, and had four kids. Often Bebe and I would give him a ride to the airport so his wife could have their car while he was away. On one of these rides, he mentioned to Bebe that North American had a bowling league and was looking for people to form some teams. I thought it might be a good idea for her to join, as it could provide some socializing outside of the family. She decided to sign up.

Surprisingly however, instead of this weekly night-out reducing the disharmony in our home-life, it seemed to be having an opposite effect. It was about this time that I begin to notice a coolness developing between us. It seemed like *deja vu* of when we were living in San Diego and Bea would become moody and uncom-

---

2.   The chapter titled "A chronology of Whereabouts and Travels" indicates this period of time was 1960, but the story titled "Back in California" indicates this period was 1962.

municative. When we visited her parents she seemed all right, but at home things were quiet and tense.

Noting that we had gotten along well during the two years we were in Japan and the four years in Florida, it seemed to me our problems might somehow be connected with living in California. I wondered if being near her family had any bearing on the matter. However, since her family seemed to like me and we always enjoyed visiting them, I disregarded that thought.

I considered that Bebe was not fond of homemaking, but since she seemed to do well during the years in Florida, I concluded that was not the problem. Having virtually no understanding of psychological matters, I was thoroughly confused. This was especially so since I pictured myself as being a good husband and father. I judged myself using the social mores of the time: I went to work every day, made a decent salary, didn't hang out at bars or run with a crowd, didn't abuse her, didn't chase other women…Oh, I was *so* good. I think our families saw me much that way, as well.

Nevertheless, our relationship continued to deteriorate. Soon our love life dwindled to near nothing. Even as naive as I was, I finally sensed her rejections were directed against me personally, not just homemaking. One significant sign, indicating a rejection of me, was that she took up smoking. I interpreted that as a personal rebuff, since she knew how much it would offend me. My self-esteem began to crumble. I had always thought Bebe saw me as an intelligent, desirable partner. Now her behavior convinced me this was no longer true.

I simply wasn't capable of understanding or adjusting to the changes in her. The whole thing was an enigmatic nightmare to me. In an act of exasperation, I swapped the girls twin beds with our double bed. That was my way of expressing anger at her rejections. Bebe showed little response, other than appearing somewhat relieved by the change. Other symptoms began to appear. The ironing just piled up. Often I found myself having to ask her to iron a shirt for work. She would comply, but her expression revealed she felt put upon. Coming home from work became an anxious time for me. I began to feel that I should just "open the door and throw in my hat" as the saying goes. Sometimes she would greet me with, "You take over the kids. I've had them all day." Most evenings were unpleasant, with conversation being minimal. Thank goodness for TV!

Occasionally I would ask her what she thought was wrong. Her responses seemed specious, revealing nothing from which I could form a conclusion. In retrospect, I think she had decided that I, not homemaking, was her real problem, and she probably felt that it would be fruitless to confront me with her criticisms. Since I viewed myself as nearly faultless, she was very likely right. Assuredly, this resulted in her feeling trapped, resentful, and angry with me.

These feelings of rejection caused intense anxieties that I had never before experienced. I tried not to expose my distress to the family, and not to let it affect my work. In time, however, things became so unpleasant (at least for me) that I suggested we see a marriage counselor. Surprisingly, Bebe agreed. I now think she believed a counselor might be able to communicate the validity of her thoughts and feelings that she felt unable to express. We began going to a psychologist once a week. Right off, he said we needed to have separate sessions. I believe he had quickly concluded that Bebe wouldn't open up in front of me, so we each had an hour session while the other sat in the waiting room. He only charged $10.00 an hour, so it didn't break us.

After a few months of consultations, the therapist informed me we both had problems and mine were somewhat more serious than Bebe's. He went on to explain that I was neurotic. That was the first time I had been told that. I had always known I was a little different, maybe even a bit eccentric, but neurotic? Good grief! They put neurotics in institutions, don't they? This nearly floored me. I thought he was full of shit. After all, I was a nearly perfect husband.

He went on to explain that neurotic people tend to marry for the wrong reasons. I have no idea what he told Bebe, but later events seemed to indicate he told her much the same thing. In any case, he offered no suggestions for any therapeutic treatment, nor did he provide a referral. With no remedy being proposed, we stopped the sessions. I was left with the distinct feeling that little or nothing could be done to improve things, rather like being told that our marriage had an incurable illness.

THE SCHISM

Since Bebe and I both wanted to exit the relationship without bitterness, we decided to proceed as amicably as possible. We agreed that in order to save money we would retain one lawyer to handle the case. Also, we agreed that since the law required one party sue the other, I would sue her for the divorce. Fortunately, the laws had evolved to recognize that some marriages couldn't work, even if neither partner had "wronged" the other, so I was able to use "irreconcilable differences" as the basis of the suit.

After setting up an appointment with an attorney, we went together to his office to be instructed on such matters. Bebe made it clear she wanted to get a job and would use her family as baby-sitters. Based upon that, the attorney suggested I pay alimony for one year to allow her time to find suitable employment. In addition, I would pay child support until each child was eighteen. He came up with amounts, based upon a formula that considered my salary and the number of children. Bebe and I agreed upon the amounts and the division of our properties. She was to keep the car, most of the furniture, appliances, and the bank account—that didn't have much in it. I was to keep a bed, my clothes, cameras, other hobby stuff, and the second trust deed to the house we had sold in San Diego. The deed wasn't of much value, because the owners were never able to make their payments. The attorney set his fee—$300.00—which I was to pay. I didn't have the cash, so I sold my sound movie projector. It just covered the amount.

Next we told our families. I wasn't present when Bebe told her parents, so I don't know how they took it. Later, on occasion, they would ask me for an explanation of what happened. I think they believed I was unhappy with Bebe and wanted the divorce. I never knew what Bebe had said to them. In any case, I just told them I was convinced that Bebe didn't love me any more. I knew "being chronically miserable" would not seem a good enough reason from their viewpoint. My mom was upset by the news, to some extent for concerns about Bebe, the kids, and me, but I believe that largely it was because she was mortified. There had never been a divorce in her family—not even of my cousins. This was a significant stigma for her. For over a year, she never told anyone—not her family, or even her friends. But eventually, after I had moved to Florida, leaving Bebe and the kids in California, she was no longer able to hide the fact.

Finally, in December 1963, our case came up to be heard. The court was in Santa Ana (south of Los Angeles). Since the divorce was to be uncontested, Bebe didn't appear. But needing a witness, I took my mom. After the lawyer presented the case, the judge asked me some stupid, but I suppose legally necessary, questions. Finally, he granted the divorce, pending the California required interlocutory period of one year. That meant the divorce would not be final until a year later. I was granted the final judgment on January 11, 1965. Legally, the marriage had lasted almost exactly eleven years.

A month or two after the court appearance in December 1963, I flew to Florida, bought a used Volkswagen, and rented a small one-bedroom duplex in Satellite Beach. It was a fair distance to work each day, but living inexpensively was my main concern. Bebe got stuck with all the problems of packing and shipping my stuff to Florida. She stayed in the Buena Park house for a while, but soon moved to a second story apartment. No doubt this was a cost saving move.

Eventually Bebe found a secretarial job at, of all places, North American. But even odder, it was in my home department. She used to joke that she always knew about my salary and raises. On occasion, I would be sent on trips to the North American home plant in Downey. I couldn't help but run into her there; and in one case I was assigned a desk only a few feet from hers. But, it was all friendly. There was little doubt that we were both happier for the divorce.

While on these trips to the Downey plant, I always stayed at the same motel. It had a small pool, and I would bring the kids over on weekends to splash around. The kids seemed to be getting used to a part-time dad and appeared happy enough. Occasionally, Bebe would even invite me to her place for dinner—like old friends, which we were.

Back in Florida, I soon found that living in Satellite Beach made too long a drive to and from work. I found an apartment much closer to the base on Merritt Island. Merritt Island is separated from the mainland by the Indian River and from the beaches by the Banana River. Both "rivers" are actually salt-water inlets. They rise and fall with the ocean tides. The apartment was a nice two-bedroom place in a complex with lawns, trees, swimming pool, and a clubhouse. I converted one bedroom into a shop. This was a real luxury for me, since it was air-conditioned.

Bea and I had agreed that each year I could have one of the kids come spend the summer with me. [3]Eventually, the first summer arrived and I sent a ticket for Audrey to fly out. She was about ten at the time. During the week, while I was working, she stayed with her aunt Fran, who lived in Eau Gallie (now a part of Melbourne). On weekends I would pick her up and try to come up with some-

---

3.   It was actually Craig who went to Florida that first year. This is based on the mem-
      ories of Craig, Audrey, and Barbara, and confirmed with dated photographs.

thing she would find interesting to do. One week I took some time off and we toured the state. She seemed to enjoy that a lot, especially trying out the pools at each motel along the way. She wouldn't stand for us staying anywhere that didn't have a pool. At the end of summer, she flew back home to resume school.

25. Audrey and Ray in Florida—ca. 1965

26. Barbara and Ray in the Carribean—ca. 1966

27. Craig and Ray on Train—ca. 1964

28. Firestone Award—ca. 1954
Mickey developed a better method of tuning the missile's antenna
system. It was a big improvement and he received five hundred
dollars—more than a month's salary!

TECHNOLOGY UTILIZATION

Award Certificate

PRESENTED TO:

RAY E. MCCOY

THIS _6th_ DAY OF ___December___ 19 _77_

IN RECOGNITION OF YOUR CONSCIENTIOUS CONTRIBUTION TO THE TECHNOLOGY UTILIZATION PROGRAM FOR THE FOLLOWING INNOVATION

SID 20134 Electrical Ground Monitor and Alarm

Rockwell International
Space Division

29. Rockwell Award—ca. 1977

30. Shuttle Avionics Integrated Laboratory Group—ca. 1986

The SAIL Group which Mickey supervised at Johnson Space Center
Mickey (Ray) is standing at the top rightmost position.

Merritt Island Launch Area (MILA)

The old area called Cape Canaveral (renamed Cape Kennedy after the president's assassination) was soon covered with missile launch complexes. NASA found it necessary to build its new launch pads (39A, 39B, & 39C) farther north along the coast. About 2-1/2 miles inland, on Merritt Island, they constructed the Vertical Assembly Building (VAB), where the Apollo vehicles and their Saturn boosters would be stacked. From there, an entire vehicle would be transported on an enormous tractor crawler to one of the coastal launch pads. The NASA Industrial Complex was located about three miles due south of the VAB. Since most of these new facilities were located on Merritt Island, the facilities area was named Merritt Island Launch Area (MILA). Later, politics would cause it to be renamed John F. Kennedy Space Center (KSC).

In the old days, control of a missile prior to launch was accomplished via thousands of wires laid in cables between the launch pad and a blockhouse located about a thousand feet away. However, by now digital technology had advanced, making it possible to send commands and to monitor measurements through coaxial cables from miles away.

The Saturn booster rockets were controlled from the Launch Control Center (LCC), located adjacent to the VAB. However, the control and monitoring of the Apollo spacecraft (Command Module & Service Module) when it was on a launch pad was from one of several computerized rooms located in the Manned Spacecraft Operations (MSO) building. The MSO building was located in the NASA Industrial Complex mentioned above, and required a coaxial cable run of over five miles to the launch pad. Most of my work during the Apollo years was based in the MSO building.

My Job

Earlier experience on the Atlas program had qualified me in the areas of Radio Frequency (RF) Command and Tracking Systems, Telemetry, Power Distribution, and Ordnance. A large number of specialties were required of each person in the Atlas launch crew, since each crew consisted of only 18 engineers. NASA used far more engineers and duplicated every contractor engineer with one of their own. Altogether, there were hundreds. Each subsystem (for example, Power

Distribution) had a Rockwell supervisor and about 15 engineers. Some engineers specialized in testing, some in configuration modifications and repairs, others in planning and scheduling. Generally, several of the more senior engineers were assigned the tasks of writing and editing test and countdown procedures, and manning the control console during test and countdown operations.

Some of my old specialties, such as RF Systems and Ordnance, mainly applied to boosters, so I ended up in Power Distribution. During a mission, the Apollo used fuel cells for primary power. Batteries were used for re-entry and emergency power. The fuel cells operated from hydrogen and oxygen, and these were stored as cryogenic super-fluids. Since this was a specialization unto itself, it was handled by a separate Fuel Cell Systems group.

Rockwell Corporation and North American Aviation merged during this time. The aerospace division was called North American Rockwell. After a couple of years, it was changed again to Rockwell International (aka Rockwell.)

LOCKING HORNS—1964

When the engineers first arrived in Florida (from Rockwell in California), construction of NASA's facilities on Merritt Island was in process. The Air Force provided Rockwell with temporary office space in trailers located on the Cape side of the Banana River. It was near the hangar area where the Atlas and other Air Force missiles were tested before being moved to their launch pads. I was assigned the task of setting up a battery laboratory in one of the nearby hangars.

Our first Apollo spacecraft was being prepared in Downey. The first few vehicles were boilerplates. A boilerplate spacecraft has the same physical shape, but little or none of the sophisticated equipment or functions of a true spacecraft. Their main purpose was to provide flight dynamic data for validating aerodynamic designs. Soon the first boilerplate arrived, and in a nearby hangar we began running a series of tests on it. Cables ran all over the floor to temporarily installed control consoles. It was still the old technology of control and monitoring through copper wires.

Few sub-systems were provided in these early boilerplate vehicles. Even so, a moderate amount of power was required to run them, so batteries were used. The Apollo boilerplates contained two main batteries. These were of a new technology, using electrodes composed of silver oxide and zinc. A solution of potassium hydroxide was used as the electrolyte. Although their power-to-weight ratio was high (desirable for spacecraft use), their shelf-life time period left something to be desired. As a result, they were shipped dry. The electrolyte was added and the battery charged shortly before use. This filling and charging operation was performed in the battery lab whenever a set of batteries was needed to support a test or launch.

The new battery technology had been developed under NASA contract by Eagle-Pitcher, a high tech battery company. NASA had an electrical laboratory located in Houston, where their electrical engineers validated these new developments for use in space. There, the principal NASA engineer was a fellow named Bob Munford. Bob had conducted a series of experiments to determine the optimum amount of electrolyte to be added when preparing the batteries for use. One of Bob's concerns was to ensure that the batteries did not contain any excess electrolyte. He feared that if they did, the cells might self-discharge through the excess liquid when the battery was inverted or subjected to zero gravity. Since a battery containing 20 cells was extremely expensive (thousands of dollars), he made his determinations using single cells, assuming his test results would apply to complete batteries.

The day of our first boilerplate Integrated Test (all systems running together) arrived and the two technicians assigned to me prepared a set of new batteries in our lab. This consisted of injecting a measured amount of electrolyte into each cell, then charging the batteries according to a specified regimen. After the set was installed in the spacecraft, the Integrated Test was started. We were only about 2/3 of the way through the test when one of the main batteries failed. In a matter of minutes, the other failed as well.

Although I had watched the techs measure and inject the electrolyte and was sure they had done it properly, management jumped to the conclusion that we had screwed up. The test was scrubbed, and we had an unpleasant debriefing. I was directed to straighten out the techs and/or the lab procedure. This being the only set of batteries we had, we needed to recharge them for the next test.

That night we recharged both batteries and the next morning another attempt to run the Integrated Test was initiated. Again, the batteries failed! Furthermore, one of them had become excessively hot. I was no expert on these batteries, but I knew you couldn't ignore a hot battery. I rushed it to the lab and had it disassembled. Several of the cells were almost too hot to handle, but once we had removed them from the metal battery case they cooled off and appeared to be undamaged.

Management began to panic. They demanded that I consult with our Rockwell battery engineers in Downey. That was rather a waste of time, since Rockwell's engineering department battery group was just a bureaucratic monitoring operation. Occasionally, these engineers would tour Eagle-Pitcher's facility. Their main purpose was to receive Eagle-Pitcher's progress reports, which they converted into weekly statuses for their own department heads. They had virtually no hands-on experience. Just the same, the department flew one of these experts down to "straighten us out." Fortunately, he brought along a battery to replace the one that had overheated.

Of course my NASA engineering counterpart, Bill Patterson, had contacted his people in Houston. He was told by Bob Munford that we must be doing *something* wrong and simply insisted we take extra care to prepare the new battery properly. With *everybody* watching, we activated and charged the new battery. On the following day we tried again to run the Integrated Test. Guess what? Both batteries failed again.

By now I'd had enough. It was like being the conductor of a train that derailed. No matter what the cause, the conductor was always blamed. I decided to perform some experiments with the batteries to see if I could learn what was happening to them. First, I got the senior lab technician to obtain some test equipment from the shop's electrical crib. I planned to monitor the internal resistance of the cells during discharge. I had already learned that our battery "experts" in Downey had no experience with, or even knowledge of this parameter, whereas I considered it to be absolutely essential information.

I had a good supply of individual cells on which to perform my tests (from the battery that had overheated). However, as I was preparing to connect the test equipment, I realized I had two problems: first, a cell's direct current (DC) output voltage (about 1.2 volts) would interfere with a conventional resistance measurement, and secondly, the internal resistance of the cell would be extremely low (only a matter of milliohms), so any measurement would be seriously compromised by the resistance in the test leads of the measurement setup.

I began to think I was licked. After mulling hard about the first problem, I decided instead of using DC, which is normally used to make resistance measurements, we might be able to use alternating current (AC). Using AC would effectively ignore the cell's bothersome DC voltage component. For the AC source, I brought an audio signal generator and a hi-fi amplifier from home.

The second problem (measuring such low ohmic values) gave me real pause. My solution was "brilliant"; although unknown to me, it had been discovered over a hundred years before. I reasoned that if we could inject the excitation current into the cell through one circuit, and measure the resulting AC voltage developed across the cell's terminals through a separate circuit, the resistance of the test wiring wouldn't affect our measurements. Well, of course it worked just fine, as scientists had established a hundred years earlier. It was a rather obscure technique known as "4-wire resistance determination." In ignorant bliss, I was very busy patting myself on the back.

We began a series of measurements of the cell's internal resistance and soon verified that the resistance increased during discharge, as I might expect. However, as the resistance increased, more and more power was being dissipated within the cell. Eventually, a point was reached where the cell began to heat and its output voltage decreased; it was failing! This occurred after the cell was only partially discharged. The problem surely was due to excessively high internal resistance.

My suspicions quickly turned to the amount of electrolyte in the cells. Hastily, we took some cells and added a few percent more of electrolyte to them. After recharging the cells, we repeated the discharge test and found that the internal resistance remained low throughout the discharge (a good sign), and there was minimal heating.

Based upon these findings, I took one of the old batteries (used in two previous Integrated Tests) and had the technicians add 5 percent more electrolyte to each cell. This battery was then included in the set sent to the spacecraft for another try. Toward the end of the Integrated Test, one of the two main batteries (the new one) began to lose voltage. I told the test engineer to switch the loads from the failing battery to the other bus (the older battery I had "doctored"). The test was successfully completed, to a chorus of cheers.

Launch day was rapidly approaching. The boilerplate was to be boosted into orbit by a Saturn I (S-I) rocket from Complex 34. The S-I consisted of a cluster of eight Redstone missiles, producing a total thrust of 1.3 million pounds. This booster was not powerful enough to send a spacecraft to the Moon. It was being used to launch the boilerplates and early spacecrafts into earth orbits while the much bigger Saturn II (S-II) booster was being developed. The S-II would consist of three stages, the first producing 7.5 million pounds of thrust.

Over the years, during development of the Mercury and Gemini missiles, NASA had established the practice of holding a pre-launch meeting to review and resolve issues pertaining to the upcoming launch. Ranking NASA officials conducted these meetings, and everyone having significant managerial responsibilities for the launch was present. At the time of this meeting, the "battery flap" had not been settled, and so was on the agenda. I was directed to attend, in case there were any questions about battery preparations. I had heard that Bob Munford from NASA's Houston Electrical Department would make a presentation on the spacecraft's batteries.

On the morning of the pre-launch meeting, I showed up. The meeting room was very large. There was an elevated platform with tables in front for the NASA dignitaries. Another table was set at an angle next to the elevated stand for prominent technical people; Munford was seated there. The remainder of the room was filled with chairs, grouped for seating the various operations participants: NASA (launch operations), Marshall Space Center (booster), and Rockwell (spacecraft). I found a chair in the Rockwell section.

The meeting got under way and over an hour was spent discussing S-I booster issues. The S-I was the main concern, as this was its first flight. The boilerplate spacecraft had few systems aboard. It had none that was the same as those to be used in later Apollo spacecrafts. However, it did contain a prototype electrical system that would power the other equipment that was aboard. There were no fuel cells; everything would be powered by batteries.

Eventually, the issue of battery reliability came up. Bob Munford was asked to give his presentation. It was quite complete, with charts and view-graphs. At the conclusion, he asked if there were any questions. Bob Gore, one of the Rockwell Test Conductors, asked him about the battery failures we had experienced. Munford showed some uneasiness, but assured the group that he had performed hundreds of tests that demonstrated the batteries were reliable. He said he believed the problems Gore was referring to probably resulted from lack of experience in the new battery lab.

Then Gore responded with, "Ray McCoy, who is in charge of our battery lab, had run some tests which indicated that the cells were running 'dry' and that the only battery to have successfully operated through an entire Integrated Test had extra electrolyte added." The NASA dignitaries began to whisper among themselves. A very noticeable murmur emanated from the audience, then they called Bob Munford to the platform. After a short discussion, the chief NASA official announced that the batteries for the flight would be prepared according to the existing NASA specifications.

[CAUTION: Name-drop ahead]

Then Scott Crossfield stood up. Crossfield was a veteran test pilot of the X-15 rocket aircraft program at Edwards Air Force. He was the first person to fly the X-15, and the first to fly over twice the speed of sound. He and his co-worker, Chuck Yeager, were made honorees of the National Aviation Hall of Fame and had been presented many other aviation and space awards. After completing his career as a test pilot, Rockwell had placed him in charge of their Apollo operations at the space center. When Scott spoke, everyone listened. He was easily the most widely known and respected person there.

Addressing the Board, Crossfield recommended, "Before you make your final decision regarding battery preparations, I would like to hear what Ray McCoy has done with these batteries in our battery lab." The NASA elite readily agreed. Instantly, the hairs stood up on the back of my neck. My God! I hadn't prepared anything. No charts, no view-graphs—no nothing. All I had were some test sheets with the results of the internal resistance experiments.

Normally, I abhor public speaking, because I get too nervous. But—and this is a big but—if I know my subject and feel confident about it, I can manage. I stood up, test sheet papers in hand, and proceeded to describe my experiments, using AC and my (I still thought it was my idea) 4-wire method of measuring internal resistance. Then I followed with some data that indicated that with only the Houston specified amount of electrolyte the internal resistance during loading could increase to an unacceptable level causing overheating and the output voltage to drop. I pointed out that Bob Munford's experiments in Houston used single cells. Therefore, if one of his single cells began to generate heat from inadequate electrolyte, it could easily conduct the heat away to the surrounding air, whereas in a battery which had to be used on the spacecraft, the heat generated by the 20 cells was trapped and would accumulate until the rising temperature resulted in many cells beginning to fail. Finally, I concluded by disclosing that I had added five percent electrolyte to all the cells in one of the batteries used in the final Integrated Test.

Test Conductor Gore interrupted. He reminded the group, *again*, that the only battery that had survived the duration of the Integrated Test was the one that Ray had "doctored."

Bob Munford was beginning to look frazzled. The *coup de grace* for him came when Crossfield added, "I recommend that for this flight, we adopt Ray's findings for battery preparation." Another whispered conference ensued on the platform, but it was short. Respect for Crossfield had caused them to reconsider their decision. Finally they announced, "The batteries will be prepared according to Ray McCoy's recommendations." Man, what a rush!

MOVING ON

As I remember, eight or ten boilerplate flights had originally been scheduled. However, things were going along rather smoothly and NASA elected to cut out most of the later ones to advance the schedule. I believe they ended up flying only three. Schedule pressure was great, because President Kennedy had committed us to "…landing a man on the moon and return him safely to earth by the end of the decade…" in his earlier 1961 speech, and we were a *long* way from doing that.

The first nearly complete Apollo arrived. It was to be put into earth orbit, but it would be unmanned. Instead, it would contain a "canned man," a rudimentary subsystem that would perform *some* of the functions of a crew. Its flight was successful, so the next flight was to be manned. This first manned spacecraft was designated Apollo 1. The booster vehicle was another Saturn S-I. Again, it would be launched from Pad 34.

THE ACCIDENT

On the evening of January 27, 1967, I was attending a basketball game at Cocoa Beach High School. That same night, Apollo 1 was at Launch Pad 34, atop its Saturn booster. The astronaut crew, second shift engineers, and technicians were running a final simulated launch countdown and flight test in preparation for the actual flight scheduled a week later. It was a full dress rehearsal. The crew was suited up, the crew compartment hatch was sealed, and the atmosphere in the spacecraft was replaced with 100% oxygen, as for an actual flight.

Back at the high school gym, I was sitting in the bleachers when someone ran into the gym and yelled, "There's been an accident at the Cape!" Most people who lived in Cocoa Beach in those days were in some way connected with Cape operations. The game stopped, and a few people with portable radios turned them on to get details. On a radio near me, I learned that it was a spacecraft fire at Pad 34. That was *my* vehicle! I sped to the Cape.

When I arrived, emergency vehicles had surrounded the pad. I soon learned that all three astronauts had been killed in a crew compartment fire. Security was cordoning off the area, so I headed for the blockhouse. I found a great deal of confusion, much like an anthill on which you poured hot water. However, as with an anthill, organization began to become apparent surprisingly quickly.

First, they sorted people into groups. The booster engineers and technicians were off to one side (this was a spacecraft fire and they likely were not involved). The Apollo people were gathered in another area. By this time, Rockwell engineers who had been manning consoles in the Manned Spacecraft Operations (MSO) building some five miles away were showing up. Within an hour they had set up interview rooms with tape recorders and they began debriefing everyone, one at a time.

Even though I hadn't been on the Cape at the time of the accident, I was still interviewed, since I was the supervisor in charge of the spacecraft's electrical system. One of my lead engineers had been at the control console in the MSO building when the fire broke out. He was debriefed extensively. I never saw any of the engineers or technicians who were on the launch tower when the fire broke out. They were busy removing the hatch and helping to retrieve the bodies.

A Wounded Animal

Up to this point, NASA had an enviable string of good fortune. They had never lost a human life during the Mercury or Gemini programs. This was actually incredible, considering that missiles were still very unreliable. I think their secret lay in the fact that they were willing to commit large resources in manpower to every phase of their programs. Most military rocket and missile programs had been conducted with a minimum of personnel to keep down costs; that's how they won contracts. NASA, on the other hand, had plenty of money from Congress, and elected to use it to pay their contractors to hire many more engineers, technicians, and inspectors than were commonly used on military contracts. Furthermore, NASA hired its own engineers and inspectors to double check everything done by the contractors. All in all, their manned space programs employed tens of thousands of people, compared to the hundreds typically employed by the military.

Now, NASA had a major disaster on their hands. Their near-perfect record had been shattered. Criticism began to flow from every quarter: the public, the media, and worst of all, Congress. NASA immediately put the program on hold and ordered an investigation. These were rational moves, but the investigation seemed to me to be highly biased to assure any blame would be levied on the contractors.

Before I continue describing the investigation, I should describe the managerial hierarchy in place at the time. Prior to the fire, I was an engineering supervisor in charge of the Apollo electrical systems (except for fuel cells). I had about 15 engineers in my group, two of which were lead engineers, each responsible for their own sub-group. One sub-group had the responsibility of writing and conducting spacecraft test procedures and countdowns and troubleshooting problems (anomalies) which arose. The other sub-group was responsible for implementing the engineering modifications that were issued by the electrical design group in Downey, California, and for repairing any damage incurred on the spacecraft during its checkout at the space center.

The day following the fire, NASA ordered security (Cape security was performed, under Air Force contract, by Pan American Airways.) to confiscate all engineering and inspection records. These consisted of dozens of file cabinets containing drawings, procedures, test data, etc. They were all moved into two large rooms in the MSO building, where they were guarded 24 hours a day by armed guards. The rationale, of course, was to "protect" this material from tampering by any culpable contractor personnel. A board was set up, headed by NASA managers and directors, to establish courses of investigation and to review the results obtained by them.

One of the first assignments from the board was a step-by-step review of test procedures that were being used at the time of the fire, test procedures that had been performed in the weeks prior to the fire, and all modifications and repairs (including associated inspections) performed while the spacecraft was at the Cape. These reviews were conducted by Rockwell Test Engineers and their NASA engineering counterparts.

In the meanwhile, an extremely detailed analysis of all commands, responses, and instrumentation traffic over the digital links between the control room (in the MSO building) and the spacecraft on the launch pad was initiated. Hundreds of thousands of commands, responses, and measurement data had to be examined. This effort was so daunting that computer programs had to be written to perform much of the task.

NASA needed to get answers quickly. The investigation was given top priority and was conducted around the clock.

The NASA investigation board decided they wanted every wire in the spacecraft to be "rung out." This meant every wire had to be tested for continuity from one end to the other for shorts to any other wire in its cable, and for shorts to ground. Since the spacecraft had thousands of wires, this would be a long arduous task. My boss convinced NASA that this should be done on third shift to free the spacecraft for other inspections during the day, and that it should be performed by someone totally familiar with the spacecraft's electrical system. He volunteered Ray McCoy. They agreed wholeheartedly—much better than having an ordinary technician bumbling around inside the crew compartment.

So I found myself on third shift, ohmmeter in hand. When I got to the top of the launch tower, there was an armed guard and one of the astronauts. I stripped down to my underwear and donned a "bunny suit." This was standard procedure to prevent spacecraft contamination. It was hard to imagine how I could contaminate this burned-out, charred mess. These suits were spotless white when I went into the spacecraft and black as a coal miner when I came out.

As I obtained a reading on each wire, I yelled it out the hatch to an inspector, who then recorded it. The astronaut witnessed every reading and watched me like a hawk to make sure I didn't try to alter any evidence. I spent two and a half months at this.

On several nights, FAA fire experts came by. They illuminated the interior of the crew compartment with various wavelength of ultra-violet light and photographed the resulting fluorescence. This made it possible to see the propagation of the flames from the deposits of various plastics and other organic materials. It was evident that the fire had started in the lower left front side, near the foot of the left couch.

Other analyses also substantiated that the fire had started in this area. There were exposed electrical harnesses there as well as 1/4" and 3/8" stainless steel lines. The lines were part of the Environmental Control System (ECS). They carried a mixture of water and glycol (similar to the anti-freeze mixture used in automobiles) to provide cooling to the crew compartment. Water/glycol mixtures are not ordinarily combustible, but in a 100 percent oxygen atmosphere, they burn furiously!

During seemingly endless third-shifts, I was slowly plodding through the measurement of the thousands of charred wires and cables. It was essentially a colossal waste of time. Virtually every measurement indicated a shorted circuit; no useful data was obtained. However, in the meanwhile, the analysis of telemetry data was beginning to paint a picture.

The astronauts suits had been instrumented to not only monitor their heart rate, blood pressure, breathing, etc., but also to monitor their body motions. Immediately prior to the fire breaking out, a sharp body movement was recorded. Simultaneously, a spike of current appeared on a main electrical bus. Then dozens of instrumentation sensors recorded surging temperatures, pressures, body movements, etc., followed by loss of signals from most telemetry channels.

The outputs from the astronaut's microphones were on tape and were replayed to see what could be determined from their communications. The recorded outputs were mostly unintelligible. I listened over and over and decided that I heard one astronaut yelling at the top of his lungs to "Pull up, pull up!" Most others who listened to the tape said they couldn't make out much of anything. However, two or three thought I might be right. What I heard made sense, since the hatch was behind the head of the astronaut who was in the center couch. It was his job to open it in an emergency. The hatch was out of reach for either of the other two astronauts.

Further support for what I heard came later in an engineering group presentation to NASA, explaining the details of the hatch mechanism and its operation. Part of the procedure to open the hatch required "pulling up" on one of its handles. Later, when redesigns for future Apollo spacecraft were being established, the designs adopted a simplified hatch mechanism that did not require the "pulling up" operation.

Since evidence had indicated that the fire was started by an electric spark from a shorted circuit, I was *very* determined to understand exactly what caused the short. After all, the electrical system *was* in the arena of my responsibility. Therefore, every morning after I finished my third shift duties, I would stop by my office in the MSO building to see how the investigation was progressing. I was provided with several printouts of key measurements that had been recorded immediately before and during the fire.

From these I concluded that one of the astronauts had probably pushed a small bundle of wires with his left foot, against the edge of an aluminum frame that was part of the ECS System, and that this had crushed the insulation on a wire carrying 28-volt DC power, causing a short to ground and a large spark. In a 100 percent oxygen atmosphere, nearly everything is combustible: wire insulation, plastics, cloth, and even thin sections of most metals. At least one water/glycol line near the fire's source ruptured, feeding the flames like a blowtorch. In a matter of seconds, the whole interior was a raging inferno. The high temperatures that were reached caused some of the aluminum equipment frames partially to melt. The astronauts were killed immediately.

The crew had been cooped up in the spacecraft all day, and there had been several delays. I believe, in an attempt to get into a more comfortable position on his couch, one of the astronauts used his left foot to push against the equipment bay, and possibly, being frustrated, he may have pushed against the frame quite hard, crushing the wire.

ROLLING OVER

Back in Washington, during the months the fire investigation was going on, NASA was wringing their collective hands, frantically trying to figure out how to survive this disaster. There was a real risk that Congress might decide to withdraw its funding, killing any hopes for a manned moon program. Additionally, if the public lost enthusiasm or confidence, this would further jeopardize the support in Congress.

Soon newspapers and technical publications were reporting investigation findings as NASA released them. There was no attempt to cover up the cause of the fire (i.e. a short circuit that started a fire in an oxygen rich atmosphere). Articles soon appeared criticizing Rockwell's engineering decisions to use a 100 percent oxygen atmosphere, exposed wire harnesses, a complicated hatch design, etc.

It should not go without mention, however, that NASA reviewed *every* design developed by Rockwell. These were not rubberstamp reviews. They were formal affairs in which the Rockwell designers would travel to Houston and appear before a Design Review Board. The board consisted of NASA engineers and managers who would ask questions and listen to answers until they were satisfied with the design. If they weren't satisfied, they would direct changes to be made. Furthermore, they had a small army of inspectors who monitored everything the Rockwell inspectors did.

Concurrently, NASA was informing Rockwell corporate executives that the only way NASA could avoid canceling Rockwell's contract (worth billions) was if Rockwell accepted the blame; and then, to show Congress that sufficient corrective action had taken place, Rockwell would replace all of their top management at the Space Center. Since Rockwell had no choice, they agreed.

A massive purge followed. Everyone in a managerial position above supervisor was axed, with the only exception being one of the key directors that even NASA recognized to be too valuable to let go. All the rest were either fired or reassigned elsewhere in the company.

A SIGHTING

One night, about a month prior to the accident, I had been out on a date and was walking my friend from the car to her door. Back then, because of my interest in astronomy and the novelty of maybe spotting a satellite, I had developed the habit of looking up and scanning the sky whenever I was outside at night.

It was about midnight on this occasion, in mid-December—a crisp, clear night. The first thing I spotted was the constellation Orion, almost directly overhead. I directed my friend's attention to the group of stars that made up the constellation, then continued to show off a bit by telling her that Orion was a mythical hunter and pointed out the stars that made up his shoulders, belt, and sword. I was about to move on to his dog, Sirius, when I spotted a group of lights coming from the west and traveling due east across the sky.

There must have been about a dozen of them, but I couldn't take a count, since they kept weaving in and out among themselves. The lights appeared as red glows, much like a cigarette would from some distance away in the dark. At the time, I joked that they looked like a flock of ducks with lit cigars stuck in their butts. The group was bunched into an oblong cluster stretched along the direction they were moving. They could easily have fit in the area covered by a full moon.

That late at night, Cocoa Beach had rolled up its sidewalks. It was totally quiet, except for an occasional car moving along A1A (the coastal road about a block away). The glowing objects made absolutely no sound that we could perceive. Except for their weaving motions, they just glided at a constant speed out over the Atlantic, and in less than a minute were out of sight.

That occurrence was my one and only UFO sighting. Lucky for me, I had a witness. I never reported the event, fearing I might have my secret clearance revoked. In those days, the government was unbelievably paranoid about the "Communist threat." It was not uncommon for them to pull someone's clearance for reasons even sillier than claiming to have seen a UFO.

THE SATURN 5/APOLLO SPACESHIP

After months of investigating the accident, things slowly returned to normal. Back at the Downey plant, Rockwell finished the construction of spacecraft Apollo 4. The jump from Apollo 1 to Apollo 4 probably resulted from NASA's decision to not fly any more Saturn 1 boosters, but instead to go directly to the new, much more powerful, Saturn 5. The Saturn 5 consisted of three stages. The first stage, S-I (not to be confused with the old Saturn 1), was fitted with five F-1 engines, each developing 1.5 million pounds, and thus providing a total thrust of 7.5 million pounds at liftoff. The second stage, S-II, had five J-2 engines, each with a thrust of 200 thousand pounds, for a total of a million pounds, and a third stage called S-IV; by this time it was decided that the S-III stage was not needed.

On top of the S-IV sat the Adapter Module that provided the housing for the Lunar Excursion Module (LEM), the only vehicle that would actually land on the moon. Situated above it was the Apollo Service Module (SM), containing an engine to provide trans-lunar propulsion each way, and the three Fuel Cells and their Cryogenic System to generate electrical power. The Command Module (CM) sat on top of the SM. The CM was the living quarters for the three astronauts on the trip to Moon orbit and back to Earth. Finally, above the CM was perched the Launch Escape System (LES). This was simply a large solid propellant rocket that could be fired to pull the CM free from the rest of the stack (in the event of an impending disaster while on the launch pad or during the first few thousand feet of flight). Once beyond this point, the LES was jettisoned.

Note: This is the last narrative that Ray was able to write prior to his death on May 31, 2001. He had planned the next chapter to be about the moon landing. Ray was an active participant throughout the Apollo and Skylab Programs. Before his death, he created a chronology of Atlas and Apollo launches, which is included in the addendum of this book.

A great deal of additional information is available at www.nasa.gov on the Internet or by contacting the NASA Public Affairs Office.

31. Ray and Thelma McCoy—ca. 1986
At home in Pasadena, Texas

32. Ray at home in Pasadena, TX—ca. 1987

33. Ray and his cat at home in Pasadena, Texas—ca. 2000

Ray had a game going with the cat such that he would pet its head and when he would stop, the cat would touch him as if asking him to resume petting. He would then resume and after a while would stop again, and the cat would respond with "the touch" again. This cyclic interplay occurred many evenings, and was a great source of enjoyment to Ray.

34. Ray, Craig and his wife, Vana—ca. 1992

35. Craig, his son Brendon, and Ray—ca. 1996

36. Ray and Thelma—ca 1984
Picture was taken shortly before their wedding
in Bay Area Park, Clearlake, Texas

37. Ray, Thelma and her son John Haigerty—ca. 1992
John lived in the Clearlake area of Houston, about fifteen miles from Ray
and Thelma's home. This picture was taken at Ray and Thelma's home in
Pasadena, Texas.

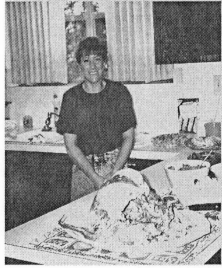

38. Thanksgiving Time—ca. 1999
Ray with stepson, John Haigerty, John's wife Teresa, and daughter,
Heather Chance

39. Ray at his 75th birthday celebration—ca. 2001

40. Attendees at Ray's 75th birthday celebration—ca. 2001
Attendees were: Audrey, Craig, Barbara,
Thelma, Ray, his sister, Shirley, and her husband, Leon Barris
This picture was taken a couple of weeks before Ray died at the end of
May.

PART V
ADDENDUM

ATLAS LAUNCH CHRONOLOGY

Launch Date	Missile Type	Description	Result Comment	My Test Conductor
06/11/57	4-A	1st "A" flt.	destroyed	Harrison
09/25/57	6-A	2nd "A" flt.	destroyed	Jeremiah
12/17/57	12-A	3rd "A" flt.	success	Zanes
01/10/57	10-A	4th "A" flt.	success	Shotwell
1958	-A	5th "A" flt.	failed	
1958	-A	6th "A" flt.	failed	
04/05/58	-A	7th "A" flt.	600 mi.	
1958	-A	8th "A" flt.	success	
07/19/58	3-B	1st "B" flt.	failed gyro	
08/02/58	4-B	2nd "B" flt.	success	Zanes
08/28/58	5-B	3rd "B" flt.	success	
09/14/58	-B		success	
09/18/58	-B		failed	
1958	-B		failed	
11/28/58	12-B	1st operational flight – 6325 miles		
12/18/58	10-B	Project "Score"	success	Johnston
12/23/58	-C	1st "C" flt.	success	Moline
1959			failed	
1959			failed	
1959			failed	
1959			failed	
06/04/59	5-D			
09/09/59	-D	Big Joe	no booster separation	Johnston
10/04/59			full range	
10/29/59		Pictures from 300 mile altitude		
11/26/59		Atlas/Able 4 Lunar Probe	payload failed @ 45 sec.	Johnston
12/18/59		2nd operational flight - 6325 miles		

Atlas Launch Chronology 1957 - 1959

41. Atlas Launch Chronology

Launch Date	Missile Type	Description	Result Comment	My Test Conductor
01/06/60		2nd full-range	6325 mi.	
02/04/60	42-D			
02/26/60	-D	Atlas/Agena: Midas-1	staging failed	Johnston
03/24/60		1st inertial guidance		
05/20/60		Long range shot	9040 mi.	
05/24/60	-D	Atlas/Agena: Midas-2	success	Johnston
07/1960	-D	Unmanned Mercury	failed @ 65 secs.	Johnston
08/09/60				
08/12/60	-D	Radiation experiment	5000 mi.	Johnston
09/19/60		Long range shot	9000 mi.	
09/25/60	-D	Atlas/Able 3 Lunar orbit	fail upper stage	Johnston
11/1960	-D	Data capsule test	5000 mi. recovered	
09/29/60	-D	M/A-2: Monkey "Enos"	success	Johnston
12/15/60	-D	Atlas/Able cislunar	failed @ 70 secs.	Johnston
12/1960	-D	Mark 3 nose cone	VAFB, 4384 mi.	

Atlas Launch Chronology - 1960

Launch Date	Missile Type	Description	Result Comment	My Test Conductor
02/19/61	-D	M/A Sub-orbit		Johnston
04/25/61	-D	M/A-3		Johnston
1961	-D	M/A		Johnston
07/29/61	-D	Atlas/Agena-B		Johnston
07/31/61	137-D			
08/22/61	-D	Atlas/Agena: Ranger 1		
09/13/61	-D	M/A-4: 1 orbit unmanned	success	
10/21/61	-D	Midas-4, AF satellite (?)		
11/29/61	-D	Mercury-5, Monkey, "Enos"	2 orbits, recovered	Johnston
01/26/62	-D	Ranger-3: Moon	missed target	
02/20/62	-D	Mercury-6: Glenn	3 orbits, success	O'Malley

Atlas Launch Chronology – 1961 - 1962

APOLLO LAUNCH CHRONOLOGY

Launch Date	Designation	Description	Comment
01/21/1967	Apollo 01 S-1	Final test before 1st manned flight	Fire in Command Module at pad 34; all 3 crewman killed.
11/09/1967	Apollo 04 S-5	Unmanned reentry "skip" test	Successful
04/04/1968	Apollo 06 S-5	1st manned Apollo flight (earth orbit)	Some booster problems (SC OK)
10/11/1968	Apollo 07 S-5	Unmanned 10 day earth orbit	Successful
12/21/1968	Apollo 08 S-5	1st manned to Moon (10 orbits)	Successful
03/03/1969	Apollo 09 S-5	LEM docking tests in moon orbit	Successful
05/18/1969	Apollo 10 S-5	LEM descent 10 mi. from Moon	Successful
07/16/1969	Apollo 11 S-5	1st Moon landing	Successful
11/14/1969	Apollo 12 S-5	Landed at Surveyor 3 site	Successful
04/11/1970	Apollo 13 S-5	Planned for 3rd landing	aborted flight; used LEM as lifeboat
01/31/1971	Apollo 14 S-5	Space hikes on Lunar surface	Successful
07/26/1971	Apollo 15 S-5	Extra-vehicular activity (EVA)	Successful
04/16/1972	Apollo 16 S-5	Several EVA's	Successful
12/07/1972	Apollo 17 S-5	Search for volcanism	Old volcanic rocks found; last Apollo Moon Mission.

Apollo Launch Chronology

42. Apollo Launch Chronology

_____DESCENDENT LINEAGE—CHARLEMAGNE TO LEWIS McCOY

(**Bold** indicates lineage path)

Charlemagne Emperor of Holy Roman Empire (b. 742 Ingolheim—d. 813/4 Prussia)	Hildegard of Vinzgau Empress of Prussia (b. 758 Prussia—d. 783 Austrasia)
Louis I Emperor of the West (b. 778 France d. 840 Hesse)	Ermengarde Empress of the West (b. 778 Belgium—d. 818)
Lothaire I King of Italy (b. 795 Germany)	Hermengarde Queen of Italy (b. 800 France)
Giselbert Count of Moselle (b. 830 Austria)	**Ermengarde Burgundy** (b. 832 France)
Regnier I Duke of Lorraine (b. 860 France—d. 916)	Alberade Duchess of Lorraine (b. ~865 France)
Giselbert Duke of Lorraine (b. 890 France—d. 939 Prussia)	Gerberge Queen of France (b. 913 Prussia—d. 984 France)
Renaud de Roucy (b. 931 France—d. >992)	Alberade de Lorraine (b. 930 France—d. 972/3)
Gilbert de Roucy (b. 956—d. ~985 France)	?
Ebles I Count of Reims (b. ~994 France)	Beatrice Countess of Hainault (b. ~998 Duchy of Lower)
Hildonin IV—Count of Montdidier (b. ~1021 France)	**Alice de Roucy** (b. ~1014 France—d. 1063)
Falko "Canon" de Grandson (b. 1050 Switzerland)	**Adelheid de Roucy** (b. 1050 Switzerland)
Ebal I de Grandson (b. 1087 Switzerland)	Adelheid (b. 1091 Switzerland)
Barthelemy Sire de Grandson (b. ~1110 Switzerland—d. 1158 Jerusalem)	?
Ebal III Sire de Grandson (b. 1133 Switzerland—d. >1177)	Jordane (b. ~1134)
Ebal IV Sire de Grandson (b. ~1154 Switzerland—d. 1234/5)	Beatrix de Geneva (b. 1154 Switzerland—d. 1235)

Peirre I Sire de Grandson
(b. 1190 Switzerland—d. 1257)

William de Grandison
(b. ~1255 England—d. 1335)

John Patshull
(b. ~1274 England)

Robert de Tudenham
(b. ~1295 England—d. 1361)

John de Tudenham
(b. 1346 England—d. 1392 England)

Robert Tudenham
(b. ~1372 England—d. 1417)

Edmund Bedingfield, Sir
(b. ~1400 England—d. 1451 England)

Thomas Bedingfield
(b. ~1428 England—d. 1453 England)

Edmond Bedingfield
(b. ~1450 England—d. 1496 England)

Christopher Browne
(b. 1450 England)

Chrisopher Browne
(b. ~1482 England—d. 1538 England)

Thomas Browne
(b. 1533 England—d. 1590 England)

Abraham Browne
(b. 1585 England—d. 1650 Massachusetts)

John Lewis
(b. 1603 England—d. 1657 Massachusetts)

Isaac Lewis
(b. 1657 Massachusetts—d. 1691 Massachusetts)

Agnes Neuchatel
(b. ~1194)

Sybil Tregoz
(b. 1271 England—d. 1334)

Mabilia de Grandison
(b. ~1294[?] England)

Cathering Patshull
(b. ~1300 England—d. >1383)

Margaret de Weyland
(b. ~1350 England—d. <1416 England)

Margaret de Herling
(b. ~1350 England—d. <1416 England)

Margaret Tedenham
(b. 1404 England—d. 1474/5 England)

Anne de Waldegrave
(b. ~1429 England—1453 England)

Margaret Scott
(b. ~1453 England—1513/14 England)

Agnes Bedingfield
(b. ~1485 England—d. ? England)

Katherine Browne (sibling)
(b. ?)   .

Joan Sayer
(b. 1552 England—d. >1610 England)

Lydia Hodges
(b. 1580 England—d. ? Massachusetts)

Mary Browne
(b. 1629 Massachusetts—d. 1657 Massachusetts)

Mary Davis
(b. 1661/2 Massachusetts—d. 1731 Massachusetts)

Isacc Lewis
  (b. 1683 Massachusetts—d. 1763 Massachusetts)

Nathan Lewis
  (b. 1721 Massachusetts—d. 1804 Massachusetts)

Benjamin C. Lewis
  (b. 1762 Massachusetts—d. 1854 Ohio)

Matthew B. Lewis
  (b. 1809 New York—d. 1883 Nebraska)

Elisha Jay Lewis
  (b. 1845 Michigan—d. 1931 California)

William Garside Lewis
  (b. 1868 Iowa—d. 1955 Wisconsin)

Ray Ernest McCoy, Sr.
  (b. 1894 Ohio—d. 1946 California)

Ray Ernest McCoy, Jr. [Mickey]
  (b. 1926 California)
Shirley Edna McCoy
  (b. 1934 California)

Hannah Hallet
  (b. 1687 Massachusetts—d. <1746 Massachusetts)

Mary Newhall
  (b. 1722/3 Massachusetts—d. 1794 Massachusetts)

Eunice Mosher
  (b. 1773 Massachusetts—d. 1862 Wisconsin)

Roxalana L. Munger
  (b. 1909 Massachusetts—d. 1877 California)

Elizabeth Hannah Garside
  (b. 1842 Ohio—d. 1868 Iowa)

Emma Jane Brookens
  (b. 1868 Wisconsin—d. 1931 Wisconsin)

Lenys Emma Lewis
  (b. 1900 Wisconsin—d. 1986 California)

43. Genealogical Data

Note: This represents only the *direct* lineage from Charlemagne to our family. There are, of course, hundreds of correlative ancestors. Not surprisingly, many of them are also of European nobility; particularly prior to the year 1400.

Most of this material is courtesy of Erin Donalson. She is a great-great-granddaughter of William G. Lewis, which makes her a first cousin, twice removed, to Shirley and me.

Ray (Mickey) McCoy

AFTERWORD

Ray's children and I have heard the anecdotes and stories detailed in this book several times over the years. As Ray typed these stories for the book, he stored them in several files on his personal computer. Compiling them into a collection from these various files has been a therapeutic and a very enjoyable experience for me.

Ray had a remarkable memory for detail. Not many people can remember when they were two years old, but he could. His earliest memory was of an afternoon when he was two. It was a summer day and a rain shower had just passed through. He remembered lying on the sidewalk in front of their house, dressed in a little sun suit, enjoying the feel of the warm concrete and the scent as the rain water evaporated.

Until the very end of Ray's life, his ability to recall details of his experiences was clear and strong. He enjoyed relating these to me again as he typed his anecdotes. While he worked on this project, a period that extended over the last two years of his life, one theme stood out remarkably clear to me. He was satisfied with his life. He felt it had been successful, and that he had enjoyed it immensely along the way. The concluding sentence of his preface sums it up very well. In his own words, "To all my family and descendants, I sincerely hope your life will be as interesting and satisfying for you as mine has been for me."

Ray lived seventy-five years, from May 29, 1926 to May 31, 2001.

0-595-30744-2

Printed in the United States
41675LVS00003B/62